The First Modern Jew

The First Modern Jew

Spinoza and the History of an Image

Daniel B. Schwartz

PRINCETON UNIVERSITY PRESS

PRINCETON AND OXFORD

Published by Princeton University Press, 41 William Street,
Princeton, New Jersey 08540
In the United Kingdom: Princeton University Press, 6 Oxford Street,
Woodstock, Oxfordshire OX20 1TW

press.princeton.edu

ISBN 978-0-691-14291-3

Library of Congress Control Number: 2011942572

British Library Cataloging-in-Publication Data is available

This book has been published with the generous assistance of the
Foundation for Jewish Culture and its Sidney and Hadassah Musher
Subvention Grant for First Book in Jewish Studies

This book has been composed in Janson Text

Printed on acid-free paper. ∞

Printed in the United States of America

1 3 5 7 9 10 8 6 4 2

To Alisa

Contents

Illustrations

Preface and Acknowledgments

On a blustery October morning five years ago, I went to the YIVO Institute for Jewish Research in lower Manhattan to speak at a most unusual semiseptcentennial. Headlining the YIVO schedule for that day was an event entitled: "From Heretic to Hero: A Symposium on the Impact of Baruch Spinoza on the 350th Anniversary of His Excommunication, 1656–2006." The list of speakers read like a "who's who" of recent Spinoza scholarship, with names like Steven Nadler, author of *Spinoza: A Life*, the definitive biography of Spinoza in English; Steven B. Smith, a leading authority on Spinoza's political thought; and above all Jonathan I. Israel, author of two magisterial works on Spinoza and the European Enlightenment. Household names for me, but not, I figured, for those outside the academy, even for the stereotypical New York Jewish culture-bearers. I did not know what size audience to expect, but an auditorium that seated 250 filled to three-quarter capacity seemed optimistic.

I guessed wrong. By the time I arrived the event had already sold out. This came as a surprise not only to me. One journalist, blogging about the conference in the *New York Observer*, wrote: "I almost didn't get in. The conference was sold out, there were scores of people waiting for an extra ticket on 16th St. I of course played the press card, but happily for all of us, Yivo lowered the screen in its main hall, allowing the overflow to watch the event on simulcast."[1] Whether they sat in the auditorium or the hall just outside, well over three hundred New Yorkers chose to spend their Sunday afternoon listening to six hours of lectures on a seventeenth-century philosopher whom few in the audience, frankly, were likely to have read.

The spillover crowd for this YIVO symposium in 2006 was simply one example of a surge of interest in Spinoza since the turn of the millennium that transcends the academy and cuts across nations, disciplines, and genres. We find evidence of this fascination in the audience for Israel's *Radical Enlightenment: Philosophy and the Making of Modernity* (2001), which has been called "one of the most important books on Spinoza in the past hundred years" and—notwithstanding its forbidding length—"certainly among the most popular."[2] We find it in the fact that a weekly news magazine like *Le Point*—a kind of French equivalent to *Time* and *Newsweek*—would choose to run a cover story on Spinoza in the summer of 2007, labeling the Amsterdam heretic "the man who revolutionized philosophy."[3] And we find it in the enthusiastic response to David Ives's 2008 play *New Jerusalem: The Interrogation of Baruch Spinoza*, whose "box-office success" was referred to by one of the most recent repertory theaters to perform it as "one of the more staggering surprises of the summer."[4]

I, too, am fascinated by Spinoza. But I am also fascinated by the fascination with him, by the extremity of feeling this early modern philosopher, dead more than three hundred years, continues to evoke. Moreover, the Jewish fascination—because it reverberates through practically every major Jewish ideological response to modernity and is so closely bound up with the struggle to define what it means to be a modern, "secular" Jew—has a fascination all its own, and it is the subject of this book.

In the pages that follow, we will come across several testimonies by modern Jewish writers that recount their initial discovery of Spinoza as a transcendent, even revelatory experience. My road to Spinoza, I confess, began with much less fanfare, while I was a graduate student in Jewish history at Columbia University. Asked by one of my advisors, Yosef H. Yerushalmi, about my plans for a dissertation topic, I spoke vaguely about my interest in historical consciousness and modern Jewish identity; he recommended a study of the Jewish reception of Spinoza. From his crowded bookshelves he pulled down what would prove my first and most essential reference work: Adolph Oko's *Spinoza Bibliography*, with its over six hundred pages of entries of "Spinozana." Steering me to this subject, while at the same time withdrawing to enable me to write this work as I saw fit, would be reason enough for thanks. I am also grateful to Professor Yerushalmi for his meticulous comments on early drafts of individual chapters, for his rich and stimulating pedagogy in Jewish history, and for the confidence he expressed in my work and me at key moments over the years. I am deeply saddened that he died before this book was complete, though also appreciative that I was fortunate enough to be one of the last of a long line of trained scholars in Jewish history to benefit from his vast erudition and thoughtful tutelage. May his memory be for a blessing.

I am equally indebted to Michael Stanislawski, a master teacher of modern Jewish intellectual and cultural history and my other mentor throughout graduate school. There are only so many "highlights" in graduate school, yet certainly our independent study of one of his many areas of expertise, the East European Haskalah, where I first encountered various thinkers who figure prominently in this book, ranks among them. Moreover, the deftness with which he weaves together literary and historical analysis in his writing has served as a model and inspiration for my own work. Finally, I am thankful to Professor Stanislawski for his expert direction of this project in its dissertation stage, for reading drafts so rapidly and incisively, and for providing repeated encouragement along the way.

Many other teachers, colleagues, and friends have played an important role in the evolution of this book from conception to completion; here I can single out only a few for mention. Sam Moyn contributed greatly to this study as an early backer and penetrating critic; I especially appreciated his apt remarks on my treatment of the German Jewish reception of Spinoza. Similarly, Jeremy Dauber gave charitably of his time to discuss initial drafts on Spinoza's East European Jewish reappropriation. Steven Nadler brought his unsurpassed knowledge of Spinoza's biography to bear on my early chapters; I thank him as well. Others engaged in the study of Spinoza's reception at some level—including Allan Nadler, Jonathan Skolnik, and Adam Sutcliffe—generously welcomed me into the club, inviting me to speak at conferences, acting as respondents for my papers, and just simply giving me the benefit of their conversation. I thank Adam Shear for his astute comments on individual conference papers as well as on my original dissertation. David Biale's work on historical heretics and modern Jewish identity was an early inspiration for this study, and I am grateful to have benefited from his close reading of my work as it has evolved from dissertation to book. Jim Loeffler, Noam Pianko, Deena Aranoff, and Rebecca Kobrin were invaluable as readers, interlocutors, and friends at different points in this process. Alan Stadtmauer served, yet again, as a pivotal sounding board in the gestation of my ideas. And Lauren Wein, with her keen editor's eye and insider's knowledge of the world of publishing, offered crucial counsel at many anxious moments.

Since arriving at George Washington University, I have learned enormously from my colleagues in the history department and Judaic studies program. I am especially grateful to Max Ticktin, who read Yiddish poetry on Spinoza with me one semester every Friday morning and made thoughtful comments on an early draft of my chapter on I. B. Singer; to Andrew Zimmerman, who was kind enough to read my book manuscript when it was close to finished and to help me see how its argument appeared to a general reader; and to Tyler Anbinder, Robert Eisen, Jenna Weissman Joselit, Bill Becker, Marcy Norton, Chris Klemek, and Yaron Peleg for their mentoring and advice. It was also serendipitous that I joined the George Washington faculty at around the time Brad Sabin Hill became the head librarian of the Kiev Judaica collection. I have profited greatly from his knowledge of Hebrew and Yiddish Spinozana, not to mention from his friendship.

In the fall of 2009 I was fortunate to participate in a research group on the topic of "Secularism and Its Discontents: Rethinking an Organizing Principle of Modern Jewish Life" at the Center for Advanced Jewish Studies (CAJS) at the University of Pennsylvania in Philadelphia. The months spent as the Louis and Bessie Stein fellow in residence at the CAJS and on leave from teaching were a boon to this project. They allowed me the time to write an additional chapter, for one, but, even more important, were the Wednesday-afternoon presentations, and the spirited question-and-answer sessions that followed, which helped immensely to sharpen and deepen my framing of the key questions in the book. Special thanks to David Ruderman, for offering me the fellowship, and to David Myers and Andrea Schatz, for not only conceptualizing the topic of our research group, but for their probing questions and helpful comments on my own work.

Beyond CAJS, I would like to acknowledge the Memorial Foundation for Jewish Culture, the Center for Jewish History, and the Lane Cooper Fellowship for their financial support while this work was in its dissertation stage; the Columbian College of Arts and Sciences at George Washington University and the Gudelsky Foundation for similar support during the process of revising the dissertation into a book; and the Foundation of Jewish Culture for their support in both phases, first in the form of a dissertation fellowship and, toward the end, through a generous subvention grant. Thanks also go to the directors and staff of the archives and libraries I consulted, which are listed in the bibliography.

Princeton University Press has published many important books by or on Spinoza over the years, and so I am extremely gratified that my book will appear under their imprint. My editor Fred Appel has been a strong advocate of this project from the beginning. I thank him for soliciting a book proposal from me before the manuscript was yet complete, and for his patience and encouragement ever since. Many thanks as well to his assistant Diana Goovaerts for her help in keeping the project moving along, to Brigitte Pelner for steering the book through the production process, and to Marsha Kunin for her scrupulous and thoughtful copyediting.

David Singer, a terrific scholar of Jewish intellectual history who also happens to be my father-in-law, has been a wonderful guide throughout this process. His role has spanned from preliminary sleuthing, to reading everything from my first stab at a draft of a dissertation chapter, to the final draft of this book's epilogue. As for my mother-in-law, Judy, her matchless combination of calm, empathy, and intelligence makes her one of the best people I know to talk to. Both have my deepest admiration. To my parents,

Steven and Helen, who have remained unstinting in their belief in me and the path I have chosen through its peaks and valleys, and who have blessed me in ways too numerous to mention, I am exceedingly grateful. My siblings as well as sisters- and brothers-in-law have likewise been a considerable source of support.

Finally, I want to thank my wife Alisa, to whom my debt is inestimable. This book has been long in the making. It was conceived when we were still practically newlyweds, and the course of its development has been interrupted by times of both delirious joy and devastating sorrow. Throughout, she has made sacrifices to enable me to follow my chosen career and finish this book; throughout, she has remained a pillar of love, strength, and support—the best of wives, the best of mothers, and the best of friends. From the bottom of my heart, this book is dedicated to her. As for our two darling children, Max and Sophie, their arrival may have delayed the completion of this work somewhat, but they have made life itself immeasurably sweeter.

D.B.S.

Note on Translations and Romanization

All quotations from Spinoza's *Ethics* and Letters 1–29 are taken from *The Collected Works of Spinoza*, trans. Edward Curley, vol. 1 (Princeton, 1985), which is almost universally regarded as the standard-bearer among English translations. Since the second volume of Curley's edition of Spinoza has yet to appear, for citations from the *Tractatus Theologico-Politicus* and from the rest of the letters, I have relied on Samuel Shirley's translation, which is included in his recently published *Complete Works*, ed. Michael L. Morgan (Indianapolis, 2002).

For the romanization of Hebrew and Yiddish in the text, I have generally followed the Library of Congress standards, with the exception of certain personal or place names where a particular spelling has become widely accepted (e.g. Baruch instead of Barukh Spinoza, Aaron Zeitlin instead of Arn Tsaytln).

Introduction

Spinoza's Jewish Modernities

I.

Ask a Jew a question, the old joke goes, and he will answer you with another question. However trite, this saying seems particularly apt to the problem of defining Jewishness in the modern world, which has come to be identified with a question as terse as it is dizzyingly complex: "Who is a Jew?" While boundary questions have accompanied Jews throughout their millennial history of exile and dispersion, modernity has seen a dramatic increase in both their number and intensity. In premodern times, the near universal authority of Jewish sacred law (or Halakhah), combined with the near universal pattern of Jewish self-government, made for near universal consensus on the religious, ethnic, and corporate determinants of Jewish identity. Being Jewish meant that one was either matrilineally a Jew by birth or a convert to Judaism in accordance with Halakhah; it also meant that one belonged to the autonomous Jewish community, membership in which was compulsory for all Jews. The challenge to traditional rabbinic norms that began with the Enlightenment's critique of religion eroded the halakhic parameters of Jewishness; the leveling of the ghetto walls as a result of Emancipation did the same for the physical barriers; and, for all the new boundaries that have been erected in the past three hundred years (in the case of the State of Israel, actual political and territorial boundaries), the situation that prevails today is one of definitional anarchy, where not only *who* or *what* is Jewish, but to an even greater extent the criteria for exemplary Jewishness, are bitterly contested. The crack in what was once more or less united in Jewish life—religion and ethnicity—has resulted in infinite permutations of Jewish identity where one or the other is primary, and at the extremes, to the prospect (if rarely the plausibility) of Judaism without Jewishness and Jewishness without Judaism. All the above have conspired to make "Who is a Jew?" a conundrum for which, indeed, there is no simple answer. We might even say that the hallmark of modern Jewish identity *is* its resistance to—and, at the same time, obsession with—definition. It is shadowed by a question mark that constantly looms.

Like battles over national identity in the modern state, which tend to be fiercest along the frontier, clashes over the nature and limits of Jewishness have frequently taken the shape of controversies over the status—and stature—of marginal Jews past and present. There is, by now, a virtual cottage industry of academic and popular literature asserting the Jewishness of "cosmopolitan" intellectuals of Jewish origin, in particular those who innovated in dramatic, even revolutionary ways. These allegations are often sophisticated arguments, grounded in thorough empirical research and sensitive to the complexities of identity. Yet their discursive origins stand at a long distance from the ivory tower of scholarship. They start, typically, as efforts to lodge a uniquely Jewish claim to a Heine, Einstein, or Freud, motivated in part by a desire for standard-bearers of an agnostic and even atheistic Jewish identity. And even in their more sober, scholarly form these arguments often betray, wittingly or unwittingly, their authors' deep spiritual kinship with their subject.

The Jewish rehabilitation of historical heretics and apostates with a vexed relationship to Judaism has become so much a part of contemporary discourse that it is difficult to imagine secular Jewish culture without it. Yet this tendency has a beginning as well as a template in modern Jewish history. The *Ur*-reclamation in the litany of such Jewish reclamations is that of the Amsterdam philosopher, arch-heretic, biblical critic, and legendary conflater of God and Nature, Baruch (or Benedictus) Spinoza (1632–1677)—"the first great culture-hero of modern secular Jews," and still the most oft-mentioned candidate for the title of first modern secular Jew.[1]

II.

Spinoza, famously, was a lifelong bachelor who left no offspring. Yet, if not a biological father, he has few equals when it comes to claims of intellectual fatherhood. A bird's-eye-view of his reception in Western thought reveals a running perception of Spinoza as a "founding father" of modernity, or perhaps we should say modernities, given the diverse and often contradictory schools of thought from the seventeenth century onward laid at his doorstep. Liberals and communitarians, absolute idealists and historical materialists, humanists and antihumanists, atheists, pantheists, and even panentheists have claimed Spinoza as a precursor. In the past two decades alone,

Spinoza has been credited with fathering, or at least foreshadowing liberal democracy, radical Enlightenment, the turn toward immanence in contemporary thought and culture, neo-Marxist theory and politics, even recent trends in brain science.[2] A recurring hero in master narratives of secularization, he has also figured prominently in movements, from Romanticism to "deep ecology," that have sought to resacralize the natural world.[3] One would be hard-pressed to identify more than a handful of developments in modern thought that have not been traced, at one point or another, to the seventeenth-century freethinker.

The Jewish reception of Spinoza presents a similar panoply of paternity claims. Excommunicated by the Sephardic Jews of Amsterdam in 1656 for his "horrible heresies" and "monstrous deeds," Spinoza defected from Judaism, rejecting its traditional beliefs, practices, and teachings—but without ever converting to another religion. For this reason he is often seen as an originator in yet another sense—namely, as the first modern, secular Jew.

Yet Spinoza's Jewish modernity has been construed no less diversely than his philosophical modernity *tout court*, or, for that matter, than the label "modern, secular Jew" itself. Over time, partisans of Jewish liberalism, nationalism, socialism, and various cross-pollinations of these and other isms have held up Baruch or Benedictus as a harbinger. He has figured as the quintessential "non-Jewish Jew" and as Judaism's best ambassador for the monotheistic idea, as a prototype of assimilation and a prophet of political Zionism, as a consummate rationalist and a closet Kabbalist, as a "reforming Jew" and a radical secularist. The mutability of his image has been such that in the course of his reception he has been linked to personalities who span the gamut of modern Jewish cultural icons—from other exemplars of secular heresy like Heine, Marx, and Freud; to such medieval luminaries as Maimonides and Ibn Ezra; to the other famous seventeenth-century Amsterdam heretic Uriel Acosta (or da Costa); to the towering figure of both the German and Jewish Enlightenment, Moses Mendelssohn; and to messiahs like Jesus and Shabbetai Zvi. To quote one leading Jewish cultural historian, Spinoza has served as a "palimpsest for a variety of constructions of modern Jewish identity."[4]

This book is a study of the rehabilitation of Spinoza in Jewish culture. More specifically, it is about the appropriation of Spinoza by a range of modern Jewish thinkers in order to validate—and in some cases critically interrogate—their own identities and ideologies. Spanning from Spinoza's excommunication in 1656 to the effort of certain Zionists three centuries later to reverse the ban, and from the beginnings of the cult of the Amsterdam outcast among nineteenth-century Jewish intellectuals to the emergence of this very cult as a literary and cultural topos in its own right, it explains how and why a notorious insurgent came to be seen as a turning point between the medieval and the modern in Jewish history and a patron saint of secular Jewishness. In short, this is a history of the heretic turned hero. Yet it is more than merely a postmortem for Spinoza in modern Judaism. More generally, it is about how Jews from the Enlightenment to the present, by remembering and reclaiming Spinoza, have wrestled, in the absence of compulsory models, with what it means to be a modern, secular Jew. Indeed, the Jewish reception of Spinoza is nothing less than a prism for viewing the intellectual history of European Jews from the seventeenth to the twentieth century.

But would Spinoza, in fact, accept responsibility for fathering any of the multiple Jewish modernities ascribed to him? Would he acknowledge paternity?

III.

Here we must make a crucial if often neglected distinction between the original intent of a particular thinker and how he or she is received. One path to understanding Spinoza's Jewish legacy—indeed, the road most taken to date—is trying to ascertain, on the basis of his own texts and whatever are deemed the most pertinent biographical, historical, and philosophical contexts, his own views on the nature and future of Jewishness. Since this is a matter heavily reliant on interpretation, opinions—not surprisingly—differ: over whether he should be considered the first secular Jew or an originator of Jewish secularism, over what construction of secular Jewishness, if any, he would be most likely to underwrite—indeed, over whether he should be considered a Jewish thinker in an affirmative sense at all. This dissension notwithstanding, those who proceed on this path seek Spinoza's meaning for Jewish modernity in what they hold Spinoza himself—the Spinoza of history—actually meant.[5]

This book approaches the topic of Spinoza's meaning for Jewish modernity from the vantage of his reception.[6] It is a study, in other words, of the Spinoza of memory, not of history. In method it bears similarity to a form of historical inquiry dubbed by Egyptologist Jan Assmann "mnemohistory," which "unlike history proper is concerned not with the past as such, but only with the past as it is remembered."[7] I do not argue in this book that Spinoza was the first modern Jew, nor do I go so far as to claim that his rupture with Amsterdam Jewry marked the inception of the modern period in Jewish history or of modernity *in toto*. In fact, I am rather skeptical of such arguments, both as a general rule—periodizations that focus on a single individual tend to lie in a nebulous no-man's-land between history and mythology—but also because in the case of Spinoza, this is a purely anachronistic construction, one that did not have, because it could not have had, any meaning for Spinoza himself.

Yet, whatever the truth or falsity of the view of Spinoza as "founding father" of the modern Jew, it is incontestable that he came to be regarded as such: by generations of freethinking Jews of various stripes, but also by a host of Jewish thinkers deeply wary of secularism and modernity, who despite recoiling from much of what they found in Spinoza—his far-reaching assault on the *raison d'etre* of Judaism in the *Tractatus Theologico-Politicus* [*Theological-Political Treatise*], his uncompromising rejection of the reality of the supernatural—could not shake the feeling of trailing in his wake. The enduring effects of this image suggest that any effort to cleanse Spinoza of his Jewish appropriations—necessary though this may be in the quest for the historical Spinoza—cannot serve as the final word on Spinoza's Jewish legacy. If our aim is to chart the concrete reverberations of Spinoza's heresy in Jewish culture—to discover Spinoza's meaning for Jewish modernity in the history of his meanings—a preconceived notion of the "real" Spinoza may be more a hindrance than a help to understanding, since it risks preventing us from appreciating the impact of the appropriation of Spinoza by modern thinkers, whatever the justification.[8] As Moshe Idel has written with regard to the study of Judaism, "the history of misunderstandings is as important as theories of understanding."[9] Just as no scholar of religion would argue that a certain religion is only what its sacred works mean in context, so no student of a certain secularism—here Jewish secularism—should make such a claim vis-à-vis its classic figures and texts. One could write a magisterial study of the French Revolution, isolating its numerous causes both short- and long-term, adducing all the relevant contexts, giving as accurate a picture of the Revolution in its historical moment as would appear feasible—and still a surplus would remain. For the "history" of the Revolution includes how it has been remembered, even misremembered. It includes how the Revolution came to figure as the ultimate myth of modernity, a model for later revolutionaries to reenact and for their opponents to resist.[10] On a different scale, the same holds for the appropriation of Spinoza by Jews. However wide of the mark, such usage is a valuable window into the afterlife of Spinoza in modern Jewish consciousness, an afterlife that must be distinguished from the historical Spinoza, but which nevertheless forms part of the "history" of this arch-heretic and philosopher in the broadest sense.

Such appropriations of Spinoza are also, just as crucially, a window into how Jews have constituted a sense of their own modernity and the place of

"the secular" therein. For all the ink that has been spilled over the years—
and especially, it seems, in recent years—on the concept of the secular, the
process of secularization, and the ideology of secularism, the literature on
the subject still remains essentially divided between two "master narratives"
with remarkable staying power. To one side lie those who portray the rise of
a secular, this-worldly orientation as a repudiation of a religious past, a rupture in the course of historical time between a "premodern" age grounded
in divine authority, belief in the supernatural, and a general reliance on
the tried and true and an authentically "modern" era committed to human
autonomy, natural reason, and innovation.[11] To the other side lie those who
stress the theological origins and dimensions of modernity and the premodern roots of secularism.[12] Yet for all the seeming incompatibility of these
secularization stories—one of conscious rebellion *against* religion, the other
of development from *within* it—they intersect in fascinating ways in Jewish
appropriations of Spinoza.

On one hand, the modernity-as-rupture story has figured prominently
in perceptions of Jewish history—and Spinoza has been arguably its preeminent symbol. His excommunication from Sephardic Amsterdam has served
as a kind of primal scene of Jewish modernity, act one in the advent of the
emancipated Jew. Unlike the eighteenth-century German Jewish philosopher Moses Mendelssohn, the other most oft-mentioned candidate for the
title of "first modern Jew," who became a model of Jewish-liberal symbiosis
and of the reconciliation of Judaism and Enlightenment, his seventeenth-
century predecessor would appear to epitomize not symbiosis, but separation; not reconciliation, but refusal. Spinoza *rejected* whatever concessions
would have been necessary to remain in the Jewish community, opting instead for an uncompromising commitment to secular, cosmopolitan reason
and the "freedom to philosophize." He *rejected* the premise that the Bible,
in its entirety, was the word of God, a move that led him famously to spurn
the Maimonidean tack of reading scripture allegorically, all so as to shore
up its authority and to maintain fidelity to revelation. He *rejected* faith in a
personal, providential, and above all transcendent God, endorsing instead
a theology of pure immanence that denied the reality of the supernatural.
All told, his name and legacy seem synonymous with a flat no to tradition,
without equivocation.

Whether this equation of Spinoza's modernity with rupture holds up historically is debatable. Scholars from Manuel Joël in the nineteenth century
to Harry Wolfson in the twentieth to Steven Nadler today have pointed
to a medieval Jewish template for much of Spinoza's thought, arguing that
his articulation of the new emerged out of a deep and critical engagement
with earlier traditions of biblical interpretation and religious philosophy.[13]

Others, like Jonathan Israel, have questioned the degree of this indebtedness.[14] Whatever the proper interpretation of Spinoza, the history of his rehabilitation in modern Jewish culture—of his conversion into an icon for iconoclasts—reveals a thoroughly entangled relationship between the old and the new, the traditional and the modern, indeed the sacred and the secular in the evolution of Jewish secularism. It may have been a perception of rupture from tradition, of a radical break with the past and embrace of the new, that conditioned and fueled the modern Jewish reappropriation of Spinoza; but Spinoza—even as a figure of rupture—came to provide many aspiring secular Jewish intellectuals with a touchstone and origin, with a feeling of being part of an immanent tradition of Jewish heresy, at times even with a surrogate father to replace the biological fathers and biblical Father of fathers they had rejected. On one hand, reclaiming Spinoza was a way of both secularizing Jewishness—by redrawing the boundaries of Jewish culture not only to accommodate but to venerate an implacable opponent of rabbinic Judaism—and of "Judaizing" secularity—by defining values such as "the freedom to philosophize," the questioning of authority, the embrace of reason, science, and even universalism itself as distinctively "Jewish." Yet in this very secularization of Jewishness and Judaizing of secularity via Spinoza we find, time and again, a striking persistence of sacral metaphors and motifs. The appropriators of Spinoza have invariably drawn on frames, scripts, and schemas with a long pedigree in the Jewish religious imagination, be it by depicting the Amsterdam heretic as a messiah of modernity or a "new guide to the perplexed," recounting the first brush with his philosophical writings in the language of biblical prophecy, or even invoking the rabbinic formula to declare the ban null and void. The conferring on Spinoza of the label "first modern Jew" based in part on his rejection of the contemporizing biblical interpretation characteristic of rabbinic midrash has, from the beginning, been entwined with his own contemporization to speak to later dilemmas of Jewish identity; while the very construction of Spinoza as the "first secular Jew" has been saturated throughout with religious rhetoric.

Yet for all these paradoxes, if there is one aspiration that comes through repeatedly in the Jewish recovery of Spinoza, it is the hope of finding intellectual lineages of modernity and our "secular age" that are, to some degree, Jewish, or at least not solely Christian. The notion of a new secular outlook gestating while an insular Jewish minority, still subservient to rabbinic law and communal coercion, remained obstinately indifferent to the winds of change about it, stuck in its "self-imposed immaturity," would become a pillar of Enlightenment antisemitism. As we will see in chapter 1, the excommunication of Spinoza would be seized on as fodder by many *philosophes* persuaded of a chasm between Judaism and Enlightenment.[15] (Of course,

his having emerged from the Jewish community would be seized on by critics of his philosophy as proof of the religiously subversive ideas indigenous
to Judaism.) Even today, though usually free of the malign intent of the
radical enlighteners, many accounts of the origins of secularism—including
ones written by scholars of Jewish history and thought—skip over the Jewish experience. As Ben Halpern wrote more than two decades ago, in an
entry on "Secularism" for an anthology of essays on Jewish thought, "the
history of Jewish secularism (unlike secularism in Occidental Christendom,
which is a native growth maturing over the whole extent of European history) is the application to Jewish matters of standards carried over from the
outside."[16] The history of the Jewish reclamation of Spinoza is, to a considerable extent, a rejoinder to this statement. From Berthold Auerbach, the
nineteenth-century German Jewish author whose pioneering reception of
Spinoza is the subject of chapter 3, to the American Jewish writer Rebecca
Goldstein today, laying claim to Spinoza has been tantamount to laying
claim to a Jewish role in the shaping of the modern and the formation of
the secular.

IV.

As a study of the resonance that Spinoza has had for secular Jewish intellectuals, this book can be considered an inquiry into his "Jewish reception." But
what exactly is meant by this phrase? Beyond the problem of parameters—
the difficulty of determining how broadly or narrowly to circumscribe Spinoza's Jewish reception—there is also the question of just how *singular* it
truly is. Spinoza, after all, has been claimed not only as a harbinger of Jewish
secularism but of secularism, period. A prototype for sundry constructions
of modern Jewish identity, he has also been credited with anticipating everything from militantly atheistic to "God-intoxicated" pantheistic forms
of free thought, from democratic liberalism to Marxist materialism to the
fashionable "bio-politics" of today's radical critics of neoliberalism. By what
right, then, do we treat the Jewish appropriation of Spinoza as anything
more than a variation on a theme? For some, the very fact that Spinoza
became an icon among Christian authors first might seem reason enough
to chalk up the Jewish rehabilitation of Spinoza to the old Yiddish saying, *Vi
es kristelt zikh, azoy yidelt zikh*. As it goes among Christians, so among Jews.

The challenge to the uniqueness of the Jewish encounter with Spinoza
has grown even more pointed with the new interpretation of the Enlightenment and the origins of "philosophical modernity" proposed by the historian

Jonathan Israel over the last decade. Starting with his *Radical Enlightenment* (2001), Israel has assiduously argued that the Enlightenment, wherever it took root, divided into two warring factions: a one-substance "Radical Enlightenment" that reduced God and nature as well as mind and body to the same thing and jettisoned tradition, refusing to paper over its rupture with the past, and a two-substance "Moderate Enlightenment" that sought to promote greater rationality in increments but was reflexively accommodating of traditional religious belief, scriptural authority, and the status quo.[17] Spinoza, per Israel, was central to both: He was "the intellectual backbone" of the Radical Enlightenment on the one hand, both source and symbol of its metaphysical and political secularism, and on the other, the ultimate bête noire of mainstream moderates, who opposed him as strenuously and obsessively as their more militant foes celebrated him. These two intellectual camps and the controversies between them, moreover, were remarkably cosmopolitan, contradicting, according to Israel, what was, for a time, the conventional wisdom that the "Enlightenment" was, in fact, a panoply of smaller "Enlightenments," divided by region, nationality, culture, denomination, and discourse. Though Israel has yet to target it expressly, there is little doubt that, on the basis of this global approach, the idea of a distinctively Jewish reception of Spinoza—like the ideas of a distinctively Jewish Enlightenment, Jewish secularism, and Jewish modernity—would meet with skepticism.

Whatever the merits of Israel's thesis regarding Spinoza's colossal impact on modern Western thought in general, it certainly resonates with his impact on Jewish culture. As we will see in chapter 4, attitudes toward the Amsterdam philosopher *did* catalyze a division of the nineteenth-century Haskalah into "radical" and "moderate" camps. Overall, however, I contend that Israel's pan-European model goes too far in effacing the peculiarities of Spinoza's Jewish reception, in large measure because of the preoccupation of the latter with the theme of *identity*, with the question of whether Spinoza was, in fact, a "Jewish thinker," or "one of us." All the thinkers to be dealt with in this book acknowledged, indirectly or overtly, that Spinoza had a more loaded significance for them given their common Jewish origins. Some pursued, others resisted, still others dithered over a domesticating of Spinoza's image within modern Judaism; yet they all believed that Spinoza had a special charge and relevance for them as Jews and "intellectuals." To whitewash this specificity—to treat their receptions of Spinoza as a mere copy, or even a variant of a broader cultural phenomenon—would simply be a bad approach to the study of history. At the same time, in forming their impressions of Spinoza, these thinkers were not only in dialogue with earlier or contemporary Jewish reactions to the Amsterdam heretic. They were

also absorbing, building on, tweaking, revising, and sometimes outright repudiating non-Jewish framings of Spinoza's "Jewishness" and "modernity."
Jews were shaped by—but they also in turn shaped—the shifting cultural
memory of Spinoza; contra that Yiddish saying, there is no question here of
one-sided influence and imitation. More so than with any archetypal "Jewish" figure with the exception of Moses and Jesus, the battle for control
over Spinoza's image has occurred not simply within Judaism, but within
an intellectual field occupied by both Jews and non-Jews. It is thus a central
contention of this work that the individuality of a "Jewish reception" of Spinoza must be sought *within*, and not radically apart from, a reception where
Jewish and non-Jewish voices have long been intertwined.

V.

The writing of history, as decades of postmodern criticism have made plain,
is not a purely inductive process.[18] Any historical narrative, however scru-
pulously loyal to the sources, is inevitably a result of innumerable conscious
and unconscious decisions on the part of the author about what to select
from an often overwhelming amount of evidence and how to structure the
presentation of whatever is selected. Reception histories must be especially
selective. No doubt, a "metahistorical" analysis of this historiographic genre
would reveal a remarkably similar form and flow. Practically every reception study can be stripped down to a sequence of variations in the understanding of its subject, since if the memory of a historical person, object,
or event merits tracing to begin with, it is likely to be diverse and protean,
as otherwise it would not make for a very interesting or illuminating history. Yet any subject worthy of a reception history will also likely have a
bounty of representations to choose from, ensuring that no one narrative is
like another. The story of Spinoza's Jewish reception can be told in myriad
ways. What follows is a brief discussion of my methodology, or how *I* have
opted to tell this story—and why I believe this angle is both essential and
illuminating.

To start, this is a cultural history of Spinoza's Jewish reception. Readings, including translations of Spinoza's works will certainly figure in our
analysis, though this is emphatically *not* a history of the reception of a particular text or set of texts; and while modern Jewish philosophers of note
can be found in both prominent roles and cameos, this is not a history of the
Jewish philosophical response to Spinoza per se. My focus is rather on the
place of Spinoza in the Jewish literary and cultural imagination. Spinoza's

reception by later Jewish philosophers constitutes only a slice—and by no means the largest slice—of a broader cultural phenomenon in which artists, novelists, dramatists, rabbis, publicists, historians, and even politicians have played a profound, even formative role. In trying to recover the Spinoza image in Jewish culture, I rely on a rich variety of sources, including not only philosophical treatises, but also things like historical novels, newspaper articles, anniversary tributes and Festschriften, visual representations, autobiographies, diaries, and correspondence. I also devote special attention to the "how" as much as the "what" in this study of cultural recuperation, considering the role played by schemas and metaphors (Spinoza as the "new" Maimonides), the rhetorical pairings of Spinoza with other historical icons, even by the sacred echoes of the Hebrew language itself in the creation of "the Jewish Spinoza."[19]

The story I tell stretches from seventeenth-century Amsterdam to eighteenth-century Germany to nineteenth-century Central and Eastern Europe to twentieth-century Israel, Europe, and America, before concluding in an epilogue that considers the current vogue in appropriations of Spinoza. After an opening chapter that analyzes the "prehistory" of the Jewish rehabilitation of Spinoza, exploring how his Jewish origins figured in fashioning him into a cultural symbol among non-Jews first, I trace his shifting image across a spectrum of modern Jewish movements and milieus, from the Berlin Haskalah to early religious Reform and Wissenschaft des Judentums (the Science of Judaism) in Germany to the East European Haskalah, Zionism, and Yiddish culture. Yet the table of contents, structured around individual receptions of Spinoza and the reception of these receptions, compensates for this broad chronological, territorial, and ideological sweep. Five thinkers stand at the center of my narrative. Chapter 2 probes the pioneering if only partial vindication of Spinoza by the Enlightenment philosopher Moses Mendelssohn (1729–1786), the first Jewish thinker, I contend, for whom Spinoza served, both positively and negatively, as a point of reference—in his own eyes, and certainly in the eyes of others. Staying in Germany but skipping ahead fifty years, chapter 3 finds the roots of the heroic and prototypical image of Spinoza in the historical fiction of the young Berthold Auerbach (1812–1882), using his engagement with the Amsterdam heretic in the 1830s as a lens for exploring tensions in early Reform Judaism between organic and revolutionary visions of religious change. Chapter 4 traces the migration of Spinoza's Jewish reception eastward into the Hebrew Enlightenment of Central and Eastern Europe, concentrating on the writings of the Galician-born *maskil* (or Jewish enlightener) Salomon Rubin (1823–1910), the most zealous champion of Spinoza in nineteenth-century Hebrew letters and the first to translate the *Ethics* into Hebrew. Chapter 5

looks at twentieth-century Zionist appropriation of Spinoza as both a precursor and posthumous beneficiary of secular Jewish nationalism, devoting
special attention to periodic efforts, first in Mandate Palestine and later in
the State of Israel, to close the book on ostracism of Spinoza by formally
revoking the excommunication—a campaign initiated by the protagonist
of the chapter, the Russian Zionist scholar and Hebrew literary critic Yosef
Klausner (1874–1958). The sixth and final chapter explores how the Yiddish
writer and Nobel laureate Isaac Bashevis Singer (1904–1991) struggled to
come to terms with modern Jewish identity not by engaging with Spinoza
directly, but by dealing in fiction with various Jewish understandings of, and
reactions to, Spinoza as secular hero.

My decision to study Spinoza's Jewish reception in rival Jewish movements through the prism of individual encounters with Spinoza is not simply an aesthetic choice but relates to a central contention of the work. If
the first and most obvious source of the diversity of the Jewish reception of
Spinoza was the fact that he elicited a welter of ideological and discursive
fashionings, there was another way in which this ambiguity was manifest
not just between, but within the many permutations of his image—even
within those treatments that most resembled an embrace. When we zero in
on concrete "uses" of Spinoza, we find that his invocation as a precursor was
rarely a matter of making him a stand-in for a flattened, already worked-out
image of the "modern Jew": Spinoza the liberal Jew, Spinoza the maskil,
Spinoza the Zionist. More often than not, it was part of the construction
of an identity, with all the attendant ambiguities of this process, and not
its finished product. What appears from afar an uncomplicated gesture of
ideological appropriation (or expropriation, as the case may be) may reveal up close a dense undergrowth of questions and tensions. This becomes
clearer the more intently we interrogate the lives of those who sought to
reclaim Spinoza.

In *Freud's Moses* (1993), his penetrating study of the Jewish identity of the
founder of psychoanalysis, Yosef H. Yerushalmi aptly observes that "to be a
Jew without God is, after all, historically problematic and not self-evident,
and the blandly generic term *secular Jew* gives no indication of the richly nuanced variety of the species."[20] Broadening this category of the "Jew without
God" to include one who has given up faith in the personal, commanding
deity of biblical revelation, without necessarily repudiating the existence of
God altogether—that is, someone like Spinoza—we can better understand
the resonance of the Amsterdam heretic within Jewish culture. What gets
obscured in the debate over whether Spinoza was the first modern or secular Jew is not simply the anachronistic nature of this perception or even of
the very debate itself. We also lose sight of the driving force behind this

reputation, the connection between the "historically problematic and not self-evident" nature of secular Jewish identity and the need to find a historical beginning and script for it and thereby firm it up. If the continued obsession with Spinoza in Jewish culture, as we enter the second decade of the twenty-first century, is any indication, what it means to be a modern, secular Jew remains as elusive—and the genealogical imperative that feeds on this elusiveness as powerful—as ever.

FIGURE 1.1. Anonymous, Portrait of Spinoza, ca. 1665. Herzog August Bibliothek Wolfenbüttel.

CHAPTER 1

Ex-Jew, Eternal Jew

Early Representations of the Jewish Spinoza

I.

The year 1670 had hardly begun before the first Latin edition of the *Theological-Political Treatise* appeared anonymously and under false imprint in the Dutch Republic.[1] And this brief for the "freedom to philosophize" had hardly begun to circulate before word spread of what one objector memorably dubbed the *"liber pestilentissimus"* (or most pestilent book).[2] Here was a book that denied biblical prophecy was a source of truth, rejected miracles, read scripture as a human document, limited the role of religion to guaranteeing social obedience while relegating the pursuit of truth to philosophy, and argued for stripping religious communities of the right to coercive authority separate from the sovereign power. In short, here was a book that sought to displace once and for all organized religion as a bedrock of state and society.

It took all of four months for the first published reaction to appear—a tractlet by the Leipzig philosopher Jakob Thomasius, best known as Leibniz's teacher—blasting the "author afraid of the light" for purporting to support greater liberty in philosophy alone when in fact he sought anarchy in religion as well.[3] Thomasius was genuinely ignorant of the man behind the *Treatise*; in this he seems to have been more the exception than the rule. "It is said that the author is a Jew by the name of Spinosa, who long ago was expelled from the synagogue on account of his monstrous opinions": so wrote the German professor of rhetoric J. G. Graevius to the twenty-five-year-old Leibniz in the spring of 1671.[4] Leibniz made sure to echo these sentiments in a letter to the Jansenist Antoine Arnauld later that fall, even while simultaneously dashing off his first missive to the man he fawningly addressed as "Mr. Spinosa, celebrated doctor and profound philosopher."[5]

This was only the beginning of a raucous reaction against Spinoza throughout the West. Amazingly, Western Europe continued to be beset

by war, the early modern Dutch Republic grew ever more religiously frag-
mented, yet in regard to the philosophy of Spinoza a remarkable ecumen-
ism prevailed: He was vituperatively attacked on all sides. The barrage only
intensified with the appearance in late 1677 of Spinoza's *Opera posthuma*
[Posthumous Works], which contained the *Ethics*. Here the "hidden teaching" on which the "theological-political" critique of organized religion
rested—the conflation of God and Nature—was made utterly manifest.
Calvinist theologians of the Dutch Reformed Church instantly tried to
have his work suppressed, branding the *Treatise* and later the *Opera posthuma*
"as horrible and blasphemous as anything the world has ever seen."[6] The
states of Holland banned both works; the papacy added them to the Index
of Forbidden Books.[7] All told, by the end of the seventeenth century, state
governments and churches throughout Europe had proscribed Spinoza's
philosophy either officially or de facto. Meanwhile, Cartesians largely dis-
owned him, fearful lest their efforts to wall off the new rationalist and mechanical science from fundamental dogmas of Christian faith be damaged
by association with the unfettered "freedom to philosophize" sought by
Spinoza.[8] Protestant sects that on balance were more liberal than Reformed
Calvinism or Catholicism, including the Remonstrants, Mennonites, and
Quakers, even the staunchly nonconformist Dutch Collegiants with whom
Spinoza is believed to have affiliated, at least for a time—all these groups
were in the main repelled by Spinoza's monism and determinism and were
well-represented in the torrent of anti-Spinoza literature. No one could
safely acknowledge any sympathy for Spinoza's ideas and maintain a reputation as a "respectable" thinker.

The criticism of Spinoza's thought went along with gibes against his
name and character. Most famously, the Kiel theologian Christian Kortholt substituted "Maledictus" (the accursed one) for "Benedictus," a swap
that became a favorite of Spinoza's many adversaries for the first century
of his reception.[9] The more common target of puns was the philosopher's
surname *Espinosa*, which means "thorn" in Spanish.[10] Spinoza was also labeled an "exotic animal," a "frivolous bird," even a sodomizer—the latter
by a Dutch Collegiant no less.[11] The worst came in 1702 in an anonymous
thrashing of Spinoza that ended on this vivid note: "These are the horrid
teachings, the repulsive errors, that this impudent Jewish philosopher (to
put it nicely) has *shit* into the world."[12] But the two words that were probably used to describe him most frequently could be found in the caption to
a popular engraving of Spinoza from around 1700: *Benedictus de Spinoza,*
Judaeus et Atheista.[13] Benedictus de Spinoza, Jew and atheist.

Amid this spate of polemics and vulgarities, the Jews of Holland and
Western Europe largely kept to the sidelines. They held their fire despite

the singling out of Judaism for especially withering treatment in the *Treatise*. Spinoza's charges cut right to the heart of postbiblical Judaism. By interpreting the biblical concept of election as a doctrine referring solely to political and material prosperity, Spinoza dismissed one of the cornerstones of Judaism—the idea that even in exile, the Jews remained the "chosen people" of God. On similar grounds, he denied the identification of the Halakhah as a "divine law" and insisted that the practices instituted by Moses (the so-called ceremonial law) had a mere political significance and retained validity only so long as the ancient Jewish commonwealth stood. Spinoza also portrayed Moses in a less flattering light than Jesus, used the Hebrew Bible rather than the New Testament as the basis for his biblical criticism, and on several occasions referred to the Jews as Pharisees in a manner that seemed designed to capitalize on the negative Christian connotations of the label. Yet none of this elicited a reaction. For the period between 1656 and 1755, the year that Mendelssohn's *Philosophical Dialogues* appeared, there is but a single work by a Jewish author that is a rejoinder to Spinoza's philosophy, the *Certamen philosophicum* (1684) of the Portuguese converso turned Sephardic apologist Isaac (Balthazar) Orobio de Castro (1617–1687).[14] And even this treatise was written solely at the behest of a Dutch Collegiant troubled by Spinoza's geometrical proofs in the *Ethics* for a metaphysical monism and determinism.[15] It dealt only obliquely with Spinoza and not at all with the devastating criticism of Judaism in the *Treatise*.

The standard explanation of this general silence vis-à-vis Spinoza is that the Jews had years before issued their definitive statement on the matter. On July 27, 1656, the Sephardic community of Amsterdam, known as the Kahal Kados Talmud Torah, issued this writ of excommunication against the twenty-three-year-old Spinoza:

> The Senhores of the Mahamad make it known that they have long since been cognizant of the wrong opinions and behavior of Baruch d'Espinoza, and tried various means and promises to dissuade him from his evil ways. But as they effected no improvement, obtaining on the contrary more information every day of the horrible heresies which he practised and taught, and of the monstrous actions which he performed, and as they had many trustworthy witnesses who in the presence of the same Espinoza reported and testified against him and convicted him; and after all this had been investigated in the presence of the rabbis, they decided with the consent of these that the same Espinoza should be excommunicated and separated from the people of Israel, as they now excommunicate him with the following ban:
>
> After the judgment of the Angels, and with that of the Saints, we excommunicate, expel and curse and damn Baruch d'Espinoza with the consent of God,

Blessed be He, and with the consent of this holy congregation [Kahal Kados] in front of the holy Scrolls with the 613 precepts which are written therein, with the anathema with which Joshua banned Jericho, with the curse with which Elisha cursed the youths, and with all the curses which are written in the Law. Cursed be he by day, and cursed be he by night; cursed be he when he lies down and cursed be he when he rises up; cursed be he when he goes out, and cursed be he when he comes in. The Lord will not pardon him; the anger and wrath of the Lord will rage against this man, and bring him all the curses which are written in the Book of the Law, and the Lord will destroy his name from under the Heavens, and the Lord will separate him to injury from all the tribes of Israel with all the curses of the firmament, which are written in the Book of the Law. But you who cleave to the Lord your God are blessed.

We order that nobody should communicate with him orally or in writing, or show him any favor, or stay with him under the same roof, or come within four ells of him, or read anything composed or written by him.[16]

Six weeks after its proclamation, a Portuguese copy of the ban, or *herem*, was officially entered into the community's Book of Ordinances, whence it did not resurface for two hundred years.[17] What were the "horrible heresies" and "monstrous actions" referred to in the preamble to the writ of expulsion? What were, for that matter, the "various means and promises to dissuade him from his evil ways" that the community had tried? The Mahamad—that is, the lay leaders of the Sephardic congregation—were not forthcoming with such details. Nothing is said about which taboos in particular he had violated. Nor do we have any detailed testimony about the causes and circumstances of the ban from a Jew who was witness to the events firsthand. It is certainly plausible that Spinoza was propagating ideas in the mid-1650s similar to what he published in the *Treatise* and *Ethics* years later (in which case his excommunication would be no mystery whatsoever), but there is no unimpeachable proof to support this presumption.[18] Scholars have thus been forced to rely on hints and allusions, circumstantial evidence and collateral sources in venturing hypotheses about why Spinoza was excommunicated. From the new theories that continue to be added to the myriad already suggested, it seems fair to wonder whether a measure of consensus will ever be reached on this question.[19]

One thing is clear: The community evidently viewed Spinoza as a very wicked and dangerous heretic, since they slapped him with a ban of exceptional harshness. In sound and fury as well as in scope, his writ of expulsion exceeds all but one of the more than one hundred listed in the community's Book of Ordinances.[20] Clearly, this was no ordinary herem. Beyond forbidding all personal contact with the heretic, the board of governors also outlawed reading "anything composed or written by him." This meant that even a rebuttal of the *Treatise* or the *Opera posthuma* would presume some form of reading of the texts themselves and thus constitute a violation of the terms of the herem, putting the polemicist himself at risk of communal censure. The lack of extant published responses to Spinoza by Jews for the first hundred years of his reception (barring the one indirect polemic by Orobio) would thus seem to testify to the success of the 1656 prohibition in squelching any and all engagement with the Amsterdam heretic.

The more we learn about early modern Amsterdam and the Western Sephardic Diaspora, the more problematic this picture of scrupulous obedience of the herem becomes. We know that as early as 1658, only two years after the ban, Spinoza, along with another recently excommunicated heretic—the former converso Dr. Juan de Prado—dined on several occasions at the Amsterdam residence of a convalescing Spanish caballero, where they were regularly joined by two seemingly untroubled members of the Sephardic community, "good" Jews who refused the pork offered them.[21] We also know, from both external sources and internal Jewish polemics, that by the first half of the eighteenth century, freethinking, antirabbinic, and deistic tendencies were increasingly rife among a rarefied clique of upper-crust and cosmopolitan Western Sephardim and a smaller number of Ashkenazim living in port cities like Amsterdam, Hamburg, and London.[22] It stands to reason that many of these irreligious Jews would have read Spinoza or at least absorbed his ideas secondhand. No less likely is it that their opponents within the Jewish community—defenders, like Orobio, of miracles, divine providence, and the binding authority of both Written and Oral Torah—were compelled to develop working knowledge of the deistic and pantheistic heresies they were countering. The notion that "[t]he Jews, even the ones who did know Latin, would not read the *TTP* [the *Tractatus theologico-politicus*], since it was written by an outcast" overrates the deterrance of the herem and, in a broader sense, the ability of Jewish communal authorities throughout the eighteenth-century Western Sephardic world to enforce their decrees.[23]

These qualifications aside, it remains a fact that Jewish voices were almost entirely absent in the discourse about Spinoza until the middle of the eighteenth century. They may have read him, but they did not—at least to our knowledge—write about him. This is true of both the majority who detested Spinoza (and would be expected to submit more readily to the terms of the ban) and the radical fringe receptive to his biblical criticism and one-substance doctrine. Of the various freethinking tracts affirming Spinoza and his philosophy that were written in this period and that have trickled down to us, we are aware of not one from the hand of a Jew.

The fashioning of Spinoza into a symbol was thus initially left to non-Jews. In what follows, I discuss the relevance of Spinoza's Jewishness to this early mythmaking. The shapers of Spinoza's early image typically assigned his Jewishness a significant role, albeit not a positive one. Two basic plotlines à propos this particularity developed in the late seventeenth and first half of the eighteenth century. One emphasized contrast, the other continuity. The first of the two frames—we might call it the "ex-Jew" (*ex judaeo*) frame—originated in the pioneering biographies of Spinoza and made Spinoza's *excommunication* and estrangement from Judaism seminal aspects of his image. The second—we might, for lack of a better phrase, call it the "eternal Jew" frame—vouched for the ineffaceable nature of Spinoza's religious past, claiming his philosophy to be no more than a dressed-up version of Jewish *esoteric* lore. The imaging of Spinoza's Jewishness tended to oscillate between these poles. When, later on, Jews began to take a new look at the seventeenth-century heretic, they joined this already existing discourse. In rethinking Spinoza's Jewishness, they were also rethinking representations of this identity they had inherited.

II.

Data about the life of the philosopher are strewn across the spectrum of early Spinoza and anti-Spinoza literature, yet three figures were especially important in the formation of his myth: Jean-Maximilien Lucas (1647–1697), Pierre Bayle (1647–1707), and Johannes Colerus (1647–1707). Lucas was the author of what is considered to be the "oldest biography of Spinoza," written not long after his death in 1677. He was also the only one of the three who was unequivocal in his admiration of the philosopher. As both a Huguenot and a freethinker, Lucas had two marks against him in the France of Louis XIV, so, like many in his situation, he had immigrated to Holland in the early 1670s, where it seems he became a member of Spinoza's circle. He wrote *La vie de M. Benoit de Spinosa* as a tribute to an "illustrious friend" and "Great Man" he considered a beacon to lovers of reason everywhere. "This is what I counsel to steadfast souls," Lucas concluded, "to follow [Spinoza's] maxims and his lights in such a way as to have them always before their eyes to serve as a rule for their actions."[24] In the words of Paul Vernière, the author of a classic study of the French reception of Spinoza through the Revolution, "[w]ith the devoted biographer Lucas, a legend is born."[25] Spinoza's beginnings were pivotal to this legend. Though his Jewish pedigree had drawn notice since the moment he gained a public reputation, little was actually known about his upbringing and eventual falling-out with the Portuguese Jews of Amsterdam. What stood out was simply that Spinoza had left the Jewish community; the road to this break was foggy.

Lucas was the first to expand on this skeletal frame. He transformed the *ex judaeo* status of the philosopher from a biographical eccentricity into a watershed of mythic proportions. His narrative divides roughly into two halves, with the excommunication right in the middle. "BARUCH DE SPINOSA," it begins, was born to a poor Portuguese Jewish family—a family so poor that they could not afford to stake him to a career in business and thus had him study "Hebrew literature" instead.[26] This field, "the whole of Jewish science," per Lucas, was unable to satisfy a mind as brilliant as his for long. Through Spinoza's own critical reading of the Bible followed by the Talmud he realized the futility of searching for "Truth" in either. Nevertheless, he kept quiet, not wanting to cause a scandal. Great things were expected of him: The original chief rabbi of the Talmud Torah congregation of Amsterdam, Hakham Saul Morteira (or Mortera) (1596–1660), "a celebrity among the Jews, and the least ignorant of all the Rabbis of his time," saw Spinoza as his prize student. He took Spinoza's reserve as a mark of humility, marveling that "a young man of such penetration could be so modest." By walling himself off, Spinoza was able for a while to avoid rousing too much suspicion.

Then, one day, two of Spinoza's contemporaries approached him "professing to be his most intimate friends" and mentioned to him their own skepticism of rabbinic teachings. In this way they managed to coax out of him his true thoughts. Spinoza claimed that the Bible describes God in corporeal terms, that it makes no mention of immortality of the soul, and that it characterizes angels as subjective visions rather than real beings. Almost immediately, he regretted saying anything. He broke off the conversation, avoided their attempts to renew it, and eventually cut them off entirely. Once they realized he meant to snub them for good, the two friends determined to take revenge. They started by whispering against him in the community that "the people deceived themselves in believing that this young man might become one of the pillars of the Synagogue; that it seemed more likely that he would be its destroyer, as he had nothing but hatred and contempt for the Law of Moses."[27] When the two presented this charge before the "Judges of the Synagogue," the latter were at first so irate that "they thought of condemning him [Spinoza] without hearing him first." Spinoza, calm as always, "went cheerfully to the Synagogue" after receiving their summons.

Morteira, "having heard of the peril in which his disciple was placed," dashed toward the synagogue and joined the judges. He pled with Spinoza to repent of the views ascribed him; the latter held firm. He threatened, as chief of the synagogue, to expel the accused instantly if he did not show remorse; Spinoza replied cheekily "that he knew the gravity of his threats, and that, in return for the trouble which he had taken to teach him the Hebrew language, he was quite willing to show him how to excommunicate."[28] The rabbi predictably exploded with rage at this retort. He adjourned the trial and "vowed not to come there again except with the thunderbolt in his hand." Still, he allowed some time to pass, believing Spinoza would flinch once he realized the severity of the punishment he faced. But Spinoza didn't waver. On the contrary, hearing that a date had been appointed for his expulsion, he responded: "All the better; they do not force me to do anything that I would not have done of my own accord if I did not dread scandal."[29]

Unwilling to settle for merely banning from the synagogue someone who seemed altogether unmoved by such a punishment, the Jews, led by Morteira, pressed the Amsterdam magistrates to evict Spinoza from the city. The magistrates, though unconvinced by the evidence against the defendant, reluctantly acceded to the Jewish community's petition and condemned Spinoza to temporary exile. Spinoza thus left his native city for the Dutch village of Rijnsburg. Once there, he dedicated himself entirely to the search for truth, setting out on the path that would lead to the *Treatise* and the *Ethics*. He never had anything to do with Jews or Judaism again.

Here and there in the narrative, one can make out echoes of events that probably have a basis in fact. Some kind of confrontation between Spinoza and Morteira is hinted at in an internal history of the Talmud Torah congregation written by Daniel Levi (né Miguel) de Barrios, a onetime Andalusian Marrano who became the most celebrated poet and chronicler of the Portuguese community of Amsterdam.[30] We know that the relapse of De Prado, a former converso and deist in the Amsterdam community who appears to have been connected with Spinoza around the time the latter was excommunicated, and may even have been the cause of his heretical turn, was detected in part by using his students as spies.[31] Finally, there is no reason to suppose that the divorce between Spinoza and Sephardic Amsterdam was anything but entirely mutual. Still, the flat-out falsehoods in this account are many. From the alleged poverty of Spinoza's youth to the notion that Morteira, as "chief of the synagogue," had the power to impose the "thunderbolt," from the claim that the Jews convinced the city magistrates to expel Spinoza from Amsterdam, to the depiction of the Jewish excommunicators as foaming at the mouth, this is a highly slanted version of Spinoza's origins, written to show Jews and Judaism in the ugliest light possible. "But what I esteem most in him," Lucas wrote, "is that, although he was born and bred in the midst of a gross people who are the source of superstition," he had emancipated himself entirely "of those silly and ridiculous opinions which the Jews have of God."[32] Lucas's biography of Spinoza plays up the Jewish past of the philosopher, but only as a benighted foil to the rationality, cosmopolitanism, and tolerance that Spinoza, by his heroic repudiation of Judaism, is meant to embody. It is an early illustration of a stream within the radical Enlightenment that opposed Judaism not, like earlier Christian theological anti-Judaism, for rejecting the messiahship and divinity of Jesus, but as the ultimate "source of superstition."

Lucas's iconization of Spinoza went unprinted for four decades after its composition, circulating only in various manuscripts that belonged to the burgeoning corpus of "clandestine literature" associated with the radical Enlightenment. In 1719 two editions of the biography were published in Amsterdam—one in tandem with the *Traité des trois imposteurs* [Treatise of the Three Impostors], a work that became perhaps the most notorious antireligious tract of the eighteenth century.[33] But these imprints were rapidly suppressed, so few copies are extant. The only other edition that appeared over the rest of the century shared the same fate.[34] Outside, then, of a small number of texts whose existence was known to a select few, Lucas's account survived only piecemeal—through interpolations made to other biographies of Spinoza, which would not be traced back to their originator until much later.[35] Familiarity with his profile of the philosopher in its entirety was undoubtedly slight.

The framing of the life of Spinoza in the early Enlightenment thus largely fell to two other foreign-born residents of the Netherlands, Bayle and Colerus. From 1681 until his death in 1706, Bayle lived as an exile in Rotterdam, teaching philosophy and history to fellow Huguenot refugees at the École Illustre while writing the works that made him the leading skeptical philosopher of the late seventeenth century. Of the many persons he assayed in his landmark of Enlightenment literature, the *Dictionaire historique et critique*, the one who merited the longest treatment was Spinoza, the focus of an entry that combined biographical précis with philosophical censure. Because of the popularity of the book of which it was a part, this article did more to influence the eighteenth-century image of Spinoza than any other work.[36] Colerus, or Johann Köhler, hailed from Düsseldorf. In 1693, after serving as the pastor to the Lutheran community of Amsterdam for fourteen years, he moved to The Hague to accept a parallel position. There, he happened to take lodgings in the house where Spinoza had boarded initially after settling in the city—his final place of residence—some twenty-three years earlier. Just behind this house stood that of the painter Henryk van der Spyck and his family. Members of the Lutheran congregation, they had rented to Spinoza the room in which he lived until his death in 1677. Ex-

actly what role these coincidences played in encouraging Colerus to write
a biography of Spinoza is unclear. In any event, he made extensive use of
the reminiscences of Spinoza's former landlord and his parishioner Van der
Spyck in putting together his narrative. In 1705 his *Korte, dog waarachtige
Levens-Beschryving van Benedictus de Spinosa* [Short, but True Biography of
Benedictus de Spinosa] appeared in print, followed a year later by English
and French translations of the Dutch original.[37] This was by far the longest
and most informative of the early accounts of Spinoza, and in the end also
the most authoritative.

Unlike Lucas, Bayle and Colerus were at most grudging admirers of
Spinoza. They concurred entirely with the general view of his philosophy
as absurd and depraved, Bayle calling his doctrine of the unity of substance
"the most monstrous hypothesis that could be imagined,"[38] Colerus referring to his strict determinism as "the most pernicious atheism that was ever
seen in the world."[39] For Bayle the motives for opposing Spinoza were first
and foremost philosophical. As a skeptic he objected to the presumption of
the infallibility of reason that lay at the core of Spinoza's system. Reason
alone could not serve as the final word on what to believe, for the claims
of the heart—"the proofs of feeling, the instincts of conscience, the weight
of education, and the like"—held equal, if not stronger right to authority.[40]
This starting point, Bayle believed, would neutralize Spinoza's geometric
demonstrations even if their logic were impeccable, though, in fact, they
were so full of "perplexities" and "impenetrable demonstrations" that "no
balanced mind"—a mind, that is, not given over entirely to metaphysical
speculation—"could ever be unaware of them."[41] Colerus's antagonism to
Spinoza had a more theological provenance. He was, after all, an orthodox
Lutheran, who could not be anything but outraged by Spinoza's assault on
the fundamental mysteries of Christian faith. Indeed, the early editions of
his biography were bound together with a sermon he had given from the
pulpit in 1704, defending, contra Spinoza and Spinozists, the literal truth of
Jesus's resurrection.

Yet for all their hostility to Spinoza the philosopher, neither Bayle nor
Colerus could find much fault with how he comported himself. The acquaintances of the philosopher whom they interviewed all had generally
nice things to say. Spinoza was "sociable, affable, honest, obliging, and of
a well-ordered morality."[42] While thrifty and abstemious, he took breaks
from his meditations and lens grinding on occasion to smoke a pipe or to
chat amiably with his landlords.[43] Despite belonging to no confession, he
would urge the children of his proprietors to "go often to Church and . . .
be obedient and dutiful to their Parents," and inquire of the family when

they returned about the pastor's sermon. To the question posed to him one day by his landlady of whether she could be saved through her religion, he answered that "[y]our religion is a good one, you need not look for another, nor doubt that you may be saved in it, provided, whilst you apply your self to Piety, you live at the same time a peaceable and quiet Life." He was a man who mostly kept to himself without being antisocial, a master of his passions without being severe. Simply put, he was a mensch.

Bayle and Colerus, then, while certainly less kind to Spinoza than the philosophe Lucas, were similarly taken by many of his personal qualities. Their biographies contributed greatly to enshrining such attributes as mildness, objectivity, prudence, self-sufficiency, and gravitas in his public image. And while less thematically integral to the story they told than it was to Lucas's narrative, the Jewish origin of the philosopher still figured prominently in their depictions. The gist of the portrayal of this origin was more or less the same in Bayle and Colerus as it was in their predecessor; the accent in all three fell on rupture. "A Jew by birth, and afterwards a deserter from Judaism, and lastly an atheist": Thus Bayle opened his article on Spinoza in the *Dictionaire*. Colerus echoed this notion of a neat break, pioneering what we might call the "Baruch/Benedict distinction" in the Spinoza literature. "*Spinosa*," he began, "that Philosopher, whose name makes so great noise in the World, was originally a *Jew*. His parents, a little while after his birth, named him *Baruch*. But having afterwards forsaken *Judaism*, he changed his Name, and call'd himself *Benedict* in his Writings."[44] Here, for the first time, the passage from "Jew" to "ex-Jew" in Spinoza's case was equated with his *renaming*. Like a convert, "Baruch" was reborn as "Benedict."

Neither Bayle nor Colerus detected any source within Jewish thought or society for the system of Spinoza; in the chain of causes each put forward, the stimulus came solely from without. Bayle presented Spinoza as "the first to reduce atheism to a system" by marrying Cartesian method to ancient Far Eastern monism.[45] Colerus traced his intellectual development back to the Flemish nonbeliever Franciscus van den Enden, who tutored Spinoza in Latin and laid the ground for his discovery of Descartes.[46] This omission was not per se a slap at Judaism. Bayle and Colerus, after all, had deep contempt for Spinoza's philosophy. It was not *that* they severed the mature thinker from his Jewish education, but *how* they did it that conveyed a pejorative image of Judaism. Whatever stigma they imputed to Spinozan "rationalism," their words betrayed no less an aversion to Jewish "irrationalism." Bayle stated flatly that "since he [Spinoza] had a mathematical mind and wanted to find a reason for everything he soon realized that rabbinical doctrine was not for him."[47] His Lutheran counterpart made this repulsion even stronger: Embracing the rationalism of Descartes, Spinoza ipso facto turned his back on rabbinic Judaism, a religion "without the least appearance of Reason."[48]

The construction of Judaism as the counterpoint to reason, order, and good sense found its ultimate symbol in the excommunication. We have already seen how Lucas seized on this episode, constructing an account that centered on a dramatic face-off between Spinoza and Morteira, the young prodigy's greatest champion turned his most vehement foe. Lucas wrote omnisciently, never revealing his sources for this version of events, and the pathos so evidently striven for in his crafting of the story raises serious doubts about its veracity. In contrast Bayle and Colerus both presented themselves as sleuths in search of testimony. Bayle devoted little space to the excommunication in his *Dictionaire*, stating simply that he had "looked into the circumstances of it without having been able to dig them out." We can safely assume that he looked hard, not only because he thrilled to such detective work, but because of his general preoccupation with the theme of religious coercion and the autonomy of individual conscience, even to the point of gross error.

This fascination was evident in his *Dictionaire* entry on Uriel da Costa (1585–1640), who, next to Spinoza, was the other legendary heretic in seventeenth-century Sephardic Amsterdam. In his autobiography, *Exemplar humanae vitae* [A Specimen of Human Life], written shortly before his suicide in 1640, Da Costa, a Portuguese "New Christian" who had fled to Amsterdam in his late twenties with the aim of returning to the faith of his fathers, recounted his peripatetic journey from Christianity to Judaism, to openly expressed doubts regarding rabbinic Judaism and in particular the Oral Torah, to total skepticism of revealed religion.[49] The Sephardic community of Amsterdam twice placed Da Costa under herem for his heterodoxy, yet both times the heretic grew despondent after living like a recluse for several years and, though his views had not changed, sought reinstatement. On the second occasion, the Mahamad made readmission contingent on his acquiescence to a public humiliation. The only source for this episode is Da Costa, and there are some today who hold that his account of it in the *Exemplar* is a fabrication written and inserted into the text by a later Christian editor.[50] What his autobiography describes, nevertheless, is a ceremony in which Uriel, after recanting his heresy before the entire congregation, was stripped to his waist, bound to one of the columns of the synagogue, whipped thirty-nine times, forced to lie prostrate by the threshold to the sanctuary, and finally trampled on by all the members of the community as they exited. Utterly mortified, Da Costa—after writing a personal history about his trials—ended up shooting himself to death in 1640, not long after the revocation of his herem. Bayle included in his *Dictionaire* a slightly cropped version of Da Costa's autobiography annotated by his own commentary, and the abridged account found there of a Jewish anathematization ("this small specimen of *Jewish* ceremonies") was undoubtedly in the mold of what the French skeptic had hoped to find in the case of Spinoza as well.

Colerus, who was familiar with Bayle's writings on Spinoza, was even more persistent in his quest for evidence about the excommunication. Pumping the Van der Spycks of The Hague for gossip about their most notorious tenant bore many dividends, but they had little to offer about this episode in Spinoza's life. From acquaintances of Spinoza, the clergyman learned that he had spoken of the Jews' having formally expelled him in his absence and of his having severed "all Friendship and Correspondence with them" from that moment on.[51] But what exactly had been the nature of this ceremony? Who had officiated over the ban, and what was the formulary that had been used against Spinoza? Colerus thought that he had struck gold in the testimony of some Jews from Amsterdam, who claimed that the "Chacham Abuab," "a *Rabbin* of great Reputation amongst 'em," had been the one to pronounce the sentence. The reference was to Hakham Isaac Aboab da Fonseca (1605–1693), who in 1656 had been one of the chief rabbis of the Sephardic Talmud Torah congregation of Amsterdam. Colerus tracked down the rabbi's sons in the hope they might furnish him with a copy of the writ of excommunication, but they dodged his request.

The Lutheran preacher would not let the matter lie. Stymied in his attempt to obtain a traditional writ of excommunication from the Jews, Colerus had better luck with a Christian Hebraist named Surrenhusius, who was a professor of Hebrew at the Athenaeum Illustre, the prototype of the University of Amsterdam. Surrenhusius provided the author with a Latin translation of a generic formula, taken from a medieval work of Jewish ritual and civil law. Colerus translated the document into Dutch and printed it in full. Compared to the actual text of the herem, it was close to four times as long and more fulminating by far.[52] At no point did Colerus categorically assert that this was the anathema used in Spinoza's case. But that appears to be how it was read. "His long conjectural description of Spinoza's excommunication," writes Richard Popkin, "was accepted as fact in the popular literature."[53]

To sum up, though Spinoza's early biographers were unable to obtain reliable information about the excommunication, they were nonetheless instrumental in making this episode both a pivotal moment in his personal history and a prime example of the backwardness of Judaism and religious power. Particularly in eighteenth-century France, in large measure because of Bayle's influence, Spinoza and Da Costa came to loom over the discourse surrounding the legitimacy of Jewish communal authority. When the revolutionary Abbé Henri Grégoire (1750–1831) wrote his prize-winning essay in support of Jewish "regeneration" in 1787, he advocated Jewish individual rights while calling for the abolition of the organized Jewish community. "If this right, however, be left them, confined to objects merely of a religious nature," Grégoire added, "it must have no relation with those of a political society, and must never brand a citizen with infamy, *as the synagogue of Amsterdam branded Uriel Acosta.*"[54]

Yet however prominently the excommunication came to figure in the image of Spinoza and his "precursor," it was not inevitable that this emphasis would emerge. Jarig Jelles (c. 1619/20–1683), a Dutch Mennonite who was the editor of Spinoza's posthumous works and one of his oldest and closest friends, glossed over it completely in his preface to the *Opera posthuma*. Meanwhile, around the time that Bayle and Colerus were polishing off their profiles of the Amsterdam heretic, another story line about Spinoza was taking shape. This one made little fuss about the excommunication, focusing instead on what this much-hyped rupture was allegedly concealing—an underground channel between Spinozism and Judaism.

III.

In 1699 Johann Georg Wachter (1673–1757), a German deist and philologist, published *Der Spinozismus im Jüdenthumb* [Spinozism in Judaism].[55] Writing in German instead of Latin, the better to ensure a wide readership in his native language, Wachter ventured a brash new theory for the intellectual origins of Spinoza's *Deus sive Natura*. To this point, still only twenty-two years after the original publication of the *Ethics*, efforts to construct a pedigree for what appeared to contemporary readers a baffling mix of God-talk and atheism had largely centered on Cartesianism. In 1697 Bayle added to this matrix the influence of Eastern religion (in particular Confucian theology), suggesting that the renegade Jew had translated an ancient and exotic conception of unified substance—a conception traditionally concealed from the masses—into the "systematic" idiom and "totally new method" of Cartesian rationalism. Now Wachter, in a tome of over three hundred pages, argued that the search for Spinoza's sources should return to the world from which he came. The identification of God with the world was of kabbalistic, hence Jewish origin. Spinozism was not a break from Judaism, but its truest expression.

Wachter claimed to have made this discovery through conversations with Moses Germanus, a late seventeenth-century German proselyte to Judaism who had settled in Amsterdam. Germanus, né Johann Peter Spaeth, had flitted between various Christian denominations before finally undergoing circumcision and joining the Portuguese community of Amsterdam, whereupon he became a noted polemicist against Christianity and heresy. While in Amsterdam between 1698 and 1699, Wachter entered into a debate with his fellow German over Judaism and the Kabbalah; *Der Spinozismus im Jüdenthumb* was his account of the controversy. Wachter blamed Germanus's embrace of Judaism on his encounter with Kabbalah years earlier while assisting Christian Knorr von Rosenroth, a Christian Hebraist and theosophist steeped in Jewish mysticism, in the editing of the *Kabbalah denudata* [Kabbalah Unmasked, 1677–84].[56] This multivolume anthology—a work of great import in the history of Christian Kabbalah—consisted of translations into Latin of a variety of Hebrew and Aramaic kabbalistic texts. Whatever knowledge of Kabbalah Wachter owned came primarily from this compendium. The thirteenth-century Zohar was the most significant mystical opus excerpted therein, yet it was the abridgement of a work by the Sephardic Jew Abraham Cohen Herrera that absorbed—and alarmed—Wachter the most.

A son of former Marranos, Herrera had grown up in Florence and Venice, before moving to Amsterdam shortly after a Portuguese community emerged there in the early seventeenth century. Through his teacher Israel Sarug, an eminent kabbalist, Herrera had imbibed a modified form of Lurianism, the stream of Jewish mystical thought attributed to the Safed spiritualist Isaac Luria, which was then crystallizing in the Ottoman East. In accord with the philosophically inflected tradition of Italian Kabbalah, Herrera proceeded to give the Lurianic myth a strongly Neoplatonic flavor in his magnum opus, the Spanish *Puerta del Cielo*.[57] Translated into Hebrew by Amsterdam rabbi Isaac Aboab de Fonseca in 1655, just a year prior to Spinoza's excommunication, Herrera's book would enter the limelight of European letters through Rosenroth's condensed Latin version of 1678.

Wachter's sensationally titled *Der Spinozismus im Jüdenthumb* did much to advance Herrera's (not to mention Spinoza's) recognition. The Lutheran author based his argument for the pantheistic character of the Kabbalah on Herrera's presentation of Lurianic cosmogony. Before creation, according to Lurianism, there was only the one and infinite God, or En-Sof (Infinite). To bring the world into being, God had first to *limit* his own unbounded plenitude, in the face of which no finite creation could prevail. The Lurianists imaged this restriction of the divine nature as a process of *contraction*, in Hebrew *tsimtsum*, wherein God essentially made room for that which taken alone was not God. But did this act of self-limitation engender a genuine cleavage between God and the world? Or was the cosmos simply a *determination* of the universal divine power, so that in fact even after creation there remained but a single all-embracing reality—the one and infinite En-Sof? This was the interpretation favored by Herrera. In proposing that nature existed *within* God—a doctrine that scholars of religion today call *panentheism* and distinguish from pantheism proper, the view that God and the world are synonymous—Herrera had several texts within classical Jewish literature on which he could draw.[58] The line between strict theism and panentheism was never one the fashioners or transmitters of rabbinic Judaism felt compelled to fix clearly; nor was it ever a spur to sectarian division. Provided one affirmed a transcendent God who was the creator and master of the universe—which Herrera and Lurianism most certainly did—the loose criteria for acceptable monotheistic belief were apparently satisfied.

Wachter, however, seized on Herrera's words to argue that the Kabbalah obliterated the distinction between God and the universe and thus deified the material world entirely. This divinizing of everything (*daß alle Wesen Gott seye*), even the basest sort of matter, was the core doctrine of the Kabbalah, which Wachter simply equated with the philosophy of Judaism proper. Why, then, did the Jews not expressly promulgate this doctrine? Because, Wachter alleged, they recoiled from its consequences for religious tradition and decorum.[59] But Spinoza had no such hesitancy. While rejecting the entire mythological lexicon of Jewish theosophy, he made the *Grundlehre* of the Kabbalah—the idea "that outside the intellect in the world (*logos*) there is nothing but the one divine substance"—into the cornerstone of his own system. "We owe a great debt of gratitude to Spinoza," Wachter thus concluded, "since he was willing to communicate his error so frankly."[60]

The only explicit reference to the Kabbalah in Spinoza's writings is found in the ninth chapter of the *Treatise*. After criticizing those who impute covert divine inspiration to the words and even the letters of scripture, Spinoza finally names his target, claiming: "I have also read, and am acquainted with, a number of Cabbalistic triflers whose madness passes the bounds of my understanding."[61] Clearly, no common ground between Spinoza and the Kabbalah existed on the subject of hermeneutics. His metaphysical system was a different story. Wachter pointed to other passages from Spinoza's oeuvre that appeared to identify a source within Jewish tradition for his identification of God and Nature. In the seventy-third of Spinoza's epistles, the philosopher explained that "[a]ll things, I say, are in God and move in God," adding that "I affirm this together with Paul and perhaps together with all ancient philosophers . . . and I would even venture to say, together with all the ancient Hebrews, as far as may be conjectured from certain traditions, though these have suffered much corruption."[62]

Spinoza would once again mention the "ancient Hebrews" in the second book of the *Ethics*. This allusion comes in the scholium to what is arguably the most well-known proposition in the entire work—proposition 2:7, which condenses Spinoza's philosophy of identity into a statement of splendid concision: "The order and connection of ideas is the same as the order and connection of things." On this idea, that "a mode of extension and the idea of that mode are one and the same thing, though expressed in two ways," Spinoza commented: "Some of the Hebrews seem to have seen this, as if through a cloud, when they maintained that God, God's intellect, and the things understood by him are one and the same."[63] Wachter framed his attempt to expose and refute Spinoza's "deification of the world" in the third and final chapter of his book with references to these two excerpts, which, he claimed, drove home "the consensus between the Jewish *synagoga* and her faithful child Spinoza."[64]

Whether this image of Spinoza has any merit is a question that has engaged thinkers throughout the reception of the Amsterdam philosopher. Generally free of Wachter's malign intent and slapdash approach, scholars continue to debate the possibility of a kabbalistic root to certain of Spinoza's ideas.[65] The truthfulness of the "Neoplatonic Kabbalist" Spinoza, however, lies beyond the scope of this study. The concern here is with the afterlife of Wachter's thesis. In 1707, eight years after the publication of *Spinozismus im Jüdenthumb*, the French Huguenot Jacques Basnage echoed the earlier interpretation in his multivolume *Histoire des Juifs*, the first history of the Jews written after Josephus.[66] Without mentioning Wachter's book, which he may not have read, Basnage asserted that Spinoza's monism derived from kabbalistic principles, explaining that the philosopher had suppressed this influence because he "was so extremely jealous of the Immortality of his Name, that he designed to pass for an Original, and an Inventer of his Opinions."[67] Like Wachter, Basnage went on to argue that Spinoza had "undermined the Foundation of the *Jewish* Religion" largely by pursuing the logic of kabbalistic teachings beyond where the kabbalists themselves were willing to venture. Leibniz, in never-edited notes for a refutation of Spinoza, proved receptive to Wachter's conflation of the Kabbalah with the system of his chief philosophical adversary.[68] Right through the "pantheism controversy" between Mendelssohn and F. H. Jacobi in the 1780s, the Spinoza-Kabbalah nexus remained a topic of discussion. In the opinion of the leading expert on Wachter, "*Spinozismus im Jüdenthumb* became one of the most influential books to be written about Spinoza in the first hundred years after the appearance of the *Opera posthuma*."[69]

Why did the image of Spinoza as a cryptokabbalist prove so contagious in the eighteenth century? Undoubtedly, its appeal had much to do with making Judaism responsible for Spinoza. For a freethinking critic of the Bible like Wachter, or a rationalist metaphysician like Leibniz, putting the blame for Spinoza on a "foreign" element like the Kabbalah may have unconsciously served as a means of bleaching their own intellectual resumes. Still, this explanation is only partly valid. The Kabbalah, after all, called forth diverse responses from medieval and early modern Christians. Some, like the editors of the *Kabbalah denudata*, were convinced that it contained a pristine theosophy whose discovery could purify Christianity, persuade the Jews to convert, and accelerate the coming of the millennium; others denounced the Kabbalah as "a completely irrational and contradictory curd."[70] Ambivalence was characteristic not only of the collective reaction but even of individual impressions over the span of a lifetime, Wachter being a striking if somewhat extreme illustration of this pattern. Seven years after publishing *Spinozismus im Jüdenthumb*, he issued a much shorter book entitled *Elucidarius cabalisticus* (1706).[71] Written in Latin instead of German, the new tract maintained the basic thesis of the original work—that the dominant impulse in Spinozism came from the Kabbalah—while retracting his earlier condemnation of both. Instead, he now came to the defense of Spinoza's pantheistic theology and the kabbalistic En-Sof, insisting that both were in accord with natural religion and pure philosophy.

For our purposes, what is most important is the narrative frame that Wachter's thesis helped establish. Spinoza was not only a Jew by origin; he was an exponent of a distinctive if esoteric Jewish teaching, his excommunication and geometrical idiom notwithstanding.[72] Though initially meant as a stigma, this view of Spinoza would later be appropriated by East European maskilim eager to reclaim Spinoza for Jewish thought and identity. Their efforts at rehabilitating the Amsterdam heretic would be preceded by the more cautious advances of a German Jewish enlightener, who regarded Spinoza, and the attempt to "Judaize" him, with a mix of sympathy and suspicion. Let us turn to Mendelssohn.

*FIGURE. 2.1. Johann Christoph Frisch, Portrait of Moses Mendelssohn, 1786. Bildarchiv Preussischer Kulturbesitz/Art Resource, NY.

CHAPTER 2

Refining Spinoza

Moses Mendelssohn's Response to the Amsterdam Heretic

I.

Moses Mendelssohn is a watershed figure in both the German and the Jewish reception of Spinoza; he is also a deeply elusive one. In the history of the image of Spinoza, he looms large for several reasons. The first is his pioneering role in softening Spinoza's heretical reputation in German thought and thus aiding his integration into the canon of modern Western philosophy. He opted for this role at the beginning of his career; toward the closing stages, he played it more by compulsion. Whatever the impetus, his two major engagements with Spinoza—in the anonymously published *Philosophische Gespräche* [Philosophical Dialogues] of 1755 and the "pantheism controversy" of thirty years later—broached the possibility of a reconciliation between Spinozism and theism. Yet this was only one aspect of Mendelssohn's legacy vis-à-vis the Amsterdam heretic. Near the end of his life, in *Jerusalem* (1783), Mendelssohn defended Judaism by effectively rebutting Spinoza. Soon thereafter, in his feud with the German antirationalist thinker Friedrich H. Jacobi (1743-1819), he endangered his health and, it is thought, hastened his death, all in order to keep the stain of Spinozism from clinging to the name of his late friend Lessing. Indeed, Mendelssohn furnished ammunition for friends and foes of Spinoza alike. His legacy was one of both reclamation and resistance.

Arguably, Mendelssohn was the first Jewish thinker to regard Spinoza as a Virgil-like mentor in his intellectual development. This claim is ventured cautiously, because Mendelssohn left no record of how he became acquainted with the life and work of Spinoza. In the narrative of Mendelssohn's philosophical origins eventually propounded by his maskilic admirers, it was not Spinoza but another Sephardic thinker who emerged as his guide. In 1742, when the adolescent Moses, the son of Mendel the scribe, turned thirteen, a new edition of Maimonides' *Moreh nevukhim* [Guide for the Perplexed] was printed for the first time in nearly two hundred years, by a Jewish publisher in the Prussian town of Jessnitz, not far from Mendelssohn's hometown of Dessau.[1] Mendelssohn's perusal of this classic of medieval Jewish philosophy became a pivotal moment in his later legend. In a story first told by Mendelssohn's maskilic biographer and repeated in print many times thereafter, the philosopher was said to have attributed his well-known humpback to all the time spent hunched over the *Guide* in his youth, engrossed in study.[2] Without placing as much weight on rumors of this kind, Alexander Altmann, the doyen of twentieth-century Mendelssohn studies, continued to ascribe seminal significance to the German Jew's engagement with Maimonides, claiming that "[t]he vistas opened to Mendelssohn through his study of the *Guide* were of incalculable value in his early intellectual development."[3]

It is unlikely that Mendelssohn's first exposure to Spinoza was as shaping a factor in his maturation as his discovery of Maimonides. Nor is it surprising that the eighteenth-century Jew would have been reticent about his degree of indebtedness to a notorious atheist and heretic. Yet it is hard to imagine the opening chapters of his *Philosophical Dialogues* without some formative encounter with Spinoza. Through Neophil, who, in the first two dialogues, steadily wins over his initially skeptical interlocutor Philopon, Mendelssohn made his literary debut in German by going further than any moderate enlightener before him in applauding Spinoza. Not only did he praise the *moral* standing of Spinoza—a step that even staunch foes like Bayle and Colerus had taken, albeit without the zeal that Mendelssohn would demonstrate. He also sought to credit Spinoza as a *metaphysician*, specifically by casting the Amsterdam philosopher's monistic concept of being—which Bayle had derided as "the most monstrous hypothesis that could be imagined"—as a necessary, if erroneous precursor to the philosophy of Leibniz. This was not an altogether new thesis. German Pietist theologians like Joachim Lange and Johann Franz Budde, faith-philosophers who deplored the attempt to constrain God via the rules of logic, had already blasted the rationalism of Leibniz and Christian Wolff as Spinozist to the core.[4] What was audacious in Mendelssohn's *Dialogues* was the inflection of this claim. Here a nexus of the two thinkers was proposed not to smear Leibniz, but to redeem Spinoza. That another major aim of the work was to defend Leibnizian metaphysics against its increasingly ascendant detractors in the German philosophical establishment made this appropriation even more striking.[5]

The crux of Mendelssohn's argument was that Spinoza, not Leibniz, had originated the concept of "preestablished harmony." As articulated by Leibniz, preestablished harmony was a solution to the mind-body problem, which had gained new urgency in the seventeenth century as a result of Cartesian dualism. Descartes' identification of mind and matter as distinct "substances"—the first defined by the "attribute" (or essential trait) of "thought," the latter by that of "extension"—raised the problem of their interaction. How could a physical sensation provide "sufficient reason" for a change in mental state, and vice versa, if body and soul were metaphysically independent of each other, each expressing itself via its own immanent chain of causes? In a nutshell, Leibniz came up with the preestablished harmony as a way out of this dilemma. He eliminated the problem of interaction by positing a world of noninteracting monads, whose coordination had been "preestablished" by God prior to creation. In other words, if I stubbed my toe, it was not this physical event itself that directly *caused* me to feel pain; rather, the collision triggered some bodily change that was the necessary corollary to the mental state of pain. The coincidence of these independent sensations was determined in advance, without the need for any continuous intervention to keep mind and body in sync, as occasionalist thinkers like Malebranche argued. The preestablished harmony was thus Leibniz's way of maintaining a metaphysical pluralism while remaining loyal to the logical definition of substance.

Before Leibniz, however, Spinoza had ventured his own resolution of the difficulties that Descartes had left dangling. For Spinoza, only a being subject to *no* limits, conceptual or ontological, could be considered a substance. Given this strict definition, only one such being could and did exist: God-or-Nature. Mind and body were two of the infinite *attributes* of this ultimate reality, expressions of its essence in thought and spatial extension respectively. As attributes, each was fully self-contained and autonomous in its own sphere; thoughts were caused solely by other thoughts, things by other things. The only limit of thought was that it was not extension, and vice versa. By rejecting the Cartesian premise of the metaphysical discontinuity between God, mind, and body—a premise that Leibniz would seek to save with his preestablished harmony—Spinoza eliminated the need to appeal to some external cause to explain their interaction. A physical entity and its mental representation were united by virtue of being "one and the same thing, explicated through different attributes." This identity was famously conveyed in Spinoza's proposition that "[t]he order and connection of ideas is the same as the order and connection of things." The reality articulated under the attribute of Thought as a chain of mental causes was necessarily the same as that conveyed under the attribute of Extension as a series of physical causes.

Thus, both Spinoza and Leibniz arrived at a metaphysics wherein body and soul are conjoined yet noninteractive. Mendelssohn saw this as proof

that Leibniz had borrowed heavily in developing arguably the most important element of his system—and without proper acknowledgment.
To Philopon's complaint—"Do you know that you have now put me in a
rather embarrassing situation regarding the uprightness of our Leibniz?"—
Neophil responds, "As inappropriate as this behavior would have been for
a philosopher like Leibniz, I nevertheless believe that he is to be excused
in this case," especially in light of the all too common human tendency to
"pass judgments on truths according to a certain genealogy."[6] Mendelssohn
in this exchange pardoned Leibniz for plagiarism while raising eyebrows
just enough to convey a certain measure of pique with "the greatest, but also
the most careful philosopher." For the twenty-five-year-old German Jew,
the time had come to show courage and integrity where Leibniz, however
prudently, did not. The first step was to disown the practice of slandering
or suppressing a point of view "according to a certain genealogy," an art-
fully ambiguous phrase on Mendelssohn's part that manages to evoke not
only Spinoza's heresy, but also his Jewish extraction. Removing this barrier
would make it possible to engage with Spinoza's thought sympathetically,
and to realize that embedded in its dense undergrowth of error and confusion there stood a constructive contribution to philosophy. This contribution could be isolated from the absurdity of the whole, as Leibniz already
did stealthily in the case of the preestablished harmony, and as Mendelssohn himself would proceed to do with his notion of a "refined pantheism"
(geläutertes Pantheismus), to which we will come shortly. In short, this is a
plea for a hermeneutic of charity and criticism combined, of appropriating
what is true or proximate to truth and discarding the rest. Most historians of
philosophy agree that Mendelssohn exaggerated the resemblance between
Spinoza and Leibniz in making the former the inventor of the preestablished harmony, but the accuracy of this argument need not concern us
here.[7] If anything, the fact that Mendelssohn may have minimized the gap
between the two philosophers speaks to how far he was willing to go in
redeeming Spinoza.

   This eulogy reaches its rhetorical crescendo toward the beginning of
the second of the four dialogues. The conversation between Neophil and
Philopon turns from the originality of Leibniz's preestablished harmony to
the reputation of metaphysics in a more general sense. Philopon opens by
expressing his astonishment and dismay that "this former queen of the sciences," which was "so much exalted by the Germans in the past . . . has sunk
so low in the present day." Neophil replies that the "source" of this "evil" is
plain enough: "our [i.e., the German] slavish imitation of a people"—namely,
the French—who prefer "stylishness of manners" and superficial wit to serious exploration of the "rigorous and fundamental matters" of metaphysics.

Such contempt, Neophil laments, has even taken root among "[h]onorable Germans."[8] The background to this scathing critique of French cultural hegemony, which sounds like something that might come from the pen of the later Herder or Fichte, was the waning influence of the rationalist metaphysics of Leibniz and Wolff in Berlin intellectual circles. In the middle of the century, a faction emerged in the Berlin Royal Academy that strongly opposed the Leibniz-Wolff school. Led by the French head of the Academy, Pierre Louis Moreau de Maupertuis, this group expressed a disdain for metaphysics that was reminiscent of Voltaire, the French philosophe whose hostility to the Leibnizian idea of "the best of all possible worlds" would soon be immortalized in *Candide* (1759). Their bias had support in high places. In 1750 the Prussian monarch Frederick II ("the Great"), an ardent admirer of French high culture and an amateur philosophe himself, brought Voltaire to Berlin. While the relationship between these two would ultimately go sour, forcing Voltaire to quit Berlin for good three years after his arrival, Frederick's contempt for speculative rationalism and preference for all things French would endure, posing a stern challenge to the once-commanding position of Leibniz and Wolff in German philosophy. No doubt Frederick was one of those "[h]onorable Germans" who derided metaphysics and whom Mendelssohn had in mind.

In the *Dialogues*, for the first time but not the last, Mendelssohn came to the rescue of the German tradition of metaphysics. Yet after stumping for the authentic German character of metaphysics, he shifts his ground in what immediately follows. To Philopon's question—"Will the Germans, then, never recognize their own worth?"—Neophil responds:

> Certainly! Leibniz, Wolff, and their various successors, to what a level of perfection and completeness they have brought philosophy! How proud Germany can be of them! Yet what does it help to claim more for oneself than is right? Let us always acknowledge that someone other than a German, I add further, someone other than a Christian, namely, Spinoza, has participated immensely in the work of bettering philosophy. Before the transition from the Cartesian to the Leibnizian philosophy could occur, it was necessary for someone to take the plunge into the monstrous abyss lying between them. This unhappy lot fell to Spinoza. How his fate is to be pitied! He was a sacrifice for the human intellect, but one that deserves to be decorated with flowers. Without him, philosophy would never have been able to extend its borders so far.[9]

Having encouraged Philopon, by virtue of his previous comment, to boast of a forte in philosophy native to a specific people, Neophil immediately qualifies himself, unsettling the association between "Germanness" and metaphysics he just established. With this reply to Philopon, Mendelssohn synthesizes the different threads of his rehabilitation of Spinoza into a new narrative. Against the blanket condemnation of Spinoza for having grown entangled in metaphysical speculation to the point of saying things that were completely absurd, Mendelssohn insists on placing Spinoza's errors in context. Yes, Spinoza had become lost in the "labyrinth of his meditations" and as a result said "much that agrees very little with his innocent way of his life." But his missteps were both necessary and in hindsight fecund. The intellectual difficulties raised by Cartesian dualism for the interaction of mind and body were so profound that someone had first to unite them as attributes of a single substance before Leibniz's preestablished harmony could recommend itself as an alternative. However offensive to notions of divine and human freedom, the monism of Spinoza had opened up a path in the void, serving as a bridge between Descartes and Leibniz. Viewed in context, his was not a philosophy that bespoke the arrogance of reason or diabolical inspiration, but rather self-effacing mediation to the point of martyrdom.

Mendelssohn thus took a theme already adduced in the first dialogue—Spinoza's innovation of crucial elements of the Leibniz-Wolffian philosophy—and endowed it with the dimensions of a tragic heroic myth, constructing a fresh tale about Spinoza. Yet the revisionist force of this new story line cuts much deeper than the image of Spinoza as a "sacrifice for the intellect." Mendelssohn could have vouched for Spinoza's import to the history of philosophy while turning a blind eye to his Jewishness. For a first-time Jewish author in German, like Mendelssohn, this would arguably have been the safer path. Instead, he deliberately inserted a reference to this identity, and in a way that tried to spin it deftly to his own advantage. "Let us always acknowledge that even someone other than a German, I add further, someone other than a Christian, namely, Spinoza, has participated immensely in the work of bettering philosophy." With this, he countered, even if unintentionally, the two paradigms for making sense of Spinoza's origins discussed earlier. For both the "*ex judaeo*" and the "cryptokabbalist" frames, the issue was essentially the same: namely, how Jewish was Spinoza's thought? Either Jewishness was synonymous with a past repudiated in the course of becoming a philosopher, or it was an inescapable heritage of mystical nonsense hardly concealed by the foreign idiom of the geometrical method. Mendelssohn sidestepped these terms entirely.[10] By identifying the Amsterdam thinker as "other than a Christian" rather than as a Jew outright, he shifted the problem from the nature of Spinoza's Jewish identity—which simply from the point of view of his own status in the Jewish community he had no interest in plumbing—to the image of metaphysical thought as essentially Christian, or at least non-Jewish in character. It is this restrictive definition that creates the preoccupation with Spinoza's heredity in the first place.

Spinoza's Jewishness serves to illustrate, then, the speciousness of demarcating philosophy on the basis of confessional ("other than Christian") and national ("other than German") differences. And yet, what cultural distinctiveness Spinoza's philosophy possesses in this account is largely a product of Mendelssohn's earlier contrast between two styles of philosophizing. With his metaphysical focus, Spinoza is evidently *closer* to the German intellectual tradition than to the French. At a time when Spinoza had become a principal inspiration for French materialists like D'Holbach and La Mettrie, Mendelssohn sought to wrest him away from the *Freygeister* and remake him in the image of the German religious Enlightenment, with its characteristic moderation and harmonistic approach to reason and religion.[11] Still, he would not erase his difference, the fact that Spinoza was both "other than a German" and "other than a Christian."

II.

In the *Philosophical Dialogues*, Mendelssohn expressed his displeasure with the cold shoulder that Spinoza had received in philosophy, arguing that he deserved not scorn and exclusion but to have been "decorated with flowers." What, though, about the rejection he had endured at the hands of the Jews themselves? From his own adherence to Jewish law and lifelong affiliation with the Jewish community, it was clear that Mendelssohn eschewed the model of Spinoza. He avoided, however, any acknowledgment of whether in his critique of Judaism—as in his metaphysics—Spinoza had made productive errors and merited better treatment. It was only in the last five years of his life that Mendelssohn would really address this question, and in an oblique fashion that shied, at least at first, from mentioning the arch-heretic by name.

In 1782 Mendelssohn reissued Menasseh ben Israel's *Vindiciae Judaeorum* [Vindication of the Jews (1656)] in German translation complete with his own preface. His decision to publish a new edition of this work came on the heels of several hopeful developments concerning Jewish political and cultural status in Central Europe. Three years earlier, the now-deceased Gotthold Ephraim Lessing had stirred German audiences with his portrait of a Jew as Enlightenment hero in *Nathan the Wise*. Subsequent to this, in 1781, the Prussian civil servant Christian Dohm wrote *Ueber die buergerliche*

Verbesserung der Juden [On the Civil Improvement of the Jews], a treatise advocating that the Jews of Alsace be granted rights almost entirely on a par with those of other subjects. This was followed in January, 1782, by Joseph II's Edict of Toleration, the first of a series of measures by the Habsburg emperor designed to lift traditional restrictions on the Jews of his dominion and so to make of them "useful subjects." Mendelssohn believed that a reedition of the seventeenth-century Dutch rabbi and humanist's rebuttal of clerical arguments against the readmission of Jews to British soil might benefit the proponents of Jewish civil equality in his own day.

In particular, he hoped that it would bolster the effect of Dohm's treatise, which he had urged the German scholar and bureaucrat to write in the first place. But his gesture of support was far from a blank check. Mendelssohn differed with Dohm on several points, one of them involving what powers would remain at the disposal of the Jewish community after the state had granted individual Jews civil rights. Dohm, in his essay, allowed for the continuation of Jewish juridical autonomy to a fairly substantial degree. Arguing that Jews should be permitted to "live and be judged" by their own traditional laws, if they so desired, he also underscored the right of the community to its chief weapon of enforcement. "The Jewish community, just as any other organized religious society," he wrote, "should have the right to excommunicate for a period of time or permanently, and in case of resistance the judgment of the rabbis should be supported by the authorities."[12] This would have no impact on the political status of the excommunicate, who could live without a church affiliation and prove "a very useful and respected citizen" notwithstanding. If confronted with the case of Spinoza, Dohm would in all likelihood have conceded the prerogative of the Sephardic community to expel him, especially since the Amsterdam philosopher was under no compulsion to join another religious denomination.

Mendelssohn, famously, demurred. He opposed church and synagogue discipline in all its incarnations, excommunication most of all. Firstly, coercion was radically antithetical to the spirit of religion, whose true mission was to educate, not to exclude. For Mendelssohn the main issue was not, as for Dohm, whether ecclesiastical power—Jewish self-government included—could be retained in a polity based on the civil rights of individuals, but its illegitimacy in any circumstance, since "expelling must be called irreligious." Implicit in this reaction to Dohm was the notion that the rabbinic ban on Spinoza was unjustified. Even if Spinoza had no interest in being a "tranquil spectator" in the synagogue, even if he was happy to be free of "meetings for worship" and "external religion," the Sephardic community, by expelling him, had employed a coercive measure incommensurate with religion and Judaism rightly understood.

Mendelssohn's political theory thus clearly militated against the herem on Spinoza. Did it go further than that in reclaiming him? This question would arise as a result of the controversy created by Mendelssohn's preface. A few months after the publication of this work, there appeared an anonymous letter to Mendelssohn, which attempted to drive a wedge between the German Jew's noncoercive understanding of religion and his Judaism. Entitled "The Search for Light and Right," the missive—believed today to have been written by August Friedrich Cranz (1732–1801), a German satirist—asserted that religious power was the "master-spring of the whole machinery" of Judaism and that a church founded on the ideals of openness, rationality, and respect for conscience propounded by Mendelssohn could be found only in Christianity. For the sake of intellectual honesty, Mendelssohn had to choose: either Judaism—that is, "the proper Jewish ecclesiastical system, together with all scriptural appointments, rabbinical interpretations thereof, and statutory laws thereon"—or his rousing vision of a religion of reason and freedom. To opt for the latter would mean that "[y]ou, good Mr. Mendelssohn, have renounced the religion of your forefathers. One step more, and you will become one of us."[13] In a postscript to this letter, David Ernst Mörschel, a military chaplain from Berlin, went a step further, suggesting that Mendelssohn's endorsement of a purely "rational devotion" was a betrayal not only of Judaism but "of revealed religion in general." Like the author of the anonymous pamphlet, he challenged Mendelssohn to come clean about his true sentiments.

Jerusalem was Mendelssohn's rejoinder. Released in April 1783 the book was both an expansion on earlier arguments concerning church-state relations and an apologia for Judaism before the court of the Enlightenment critique of religion. While debate continues over the radicalism and coherence of the philosophy of Judaism expressed in *Jerusalem*, what is clear is that Mendelssohn wished to show that the choice demanded of him by Mörschel and the unnamed "Searcher" was unnecessary.[14] Loyalty to Judaism was fully compatible with freedom of thought and voluntarism in religion, something that could not be said to the same degree about Christianity. Underlying this conviction was Mendelssohn's claim that what had been vouchsafed by God to the ancient Hebrews as part of the covenant between them was essentially a body of commandments—a "revealed legislation," as Mendelssohn put it, and not a "revealed religion." Ostensibly, by emphasizing the legalistic nature of Mosaic Torah, Mendelssohn had played right into the hands of Judaism's deistic detractors; in fact he aimed to show that it was precisely this characteristic that made Judaism consonant with natural religion. For Judaism did not espouse any irrational mysteries of faith; nor did it promulgate any religious verities that were exclusive to revelation. As for the "eternal truths about God and his government and providence" required for human felicity, these could certainly be found in Hebrew scripture yet were never alleged to be anything more than the universal axioms of natural religion, over which Judaism claimed no monopoly. What was peculiar to the Sinaitic epiphany was simply the "laws, precepts, commandments and rules of life" which had been ordained by God as the constitution of Judaism, along with the particular historical narratives that accounted for the basis of biblical legislation.

The view of the revelation to Moses as fundamentally legislative has long struck readers as a significant affinity between Mendelssohn and Spinoza.[15] In the *Treatise*, Spinoza claimed that what the Jewish people had received in revelation was not a special metaphysical knowledge—a bequest that would have been inconsistent with the noncognitive nature of prophecy—but a "ceremonial law" meant to serve as the foundation for the ancient Israelite polity. Similarly, Mendelssohn asserted in the second part of *Jerusalem* that "Judaism boasts of no *exclusive* revelation of eternal truths that are indispensable to salvation" and is best understood as a "revealed *legislation*" rather than "revealed *religion*." He resorted to the same phrase used by Spinoza to denote this unique dispensation—the "ceremonial law"—and, like Spinoza, he also underscored its originally (at least partly) political inflection. According to Mendelssohn, the Mosaic Law was initially the charter for a biblical commonwealth wherein state and religion were one and the same, and God alone was king. On this ground, Mendelssohn sought to counter those, like the anonymous "Searcher," who insisted that Hebrew scripture was the font of "ecclesiastical law" and Judaism the quintessential church. In fact the Bible recognized no separate sphere of religious authority. The notion that the power to excommunicate derived from a fundamentally Hebraic ethos was without merit. An argument that Spinoza had made to sever the links between the Dutch Reformed Church and the "Old Testament" prophets in his own day was converted by Mendelssohn into a vehicle for saving the Hebrew Bible from deistic assault.

Thus far did Mendelssohn allegedly follow Spinoza and no farther. Having taken two famous contentions of the *Treatise* as his point of departure, Mendelssohn finished in a radically different place. In contrast to Spinoza, Mendelssohn held that the "ceremonial law" was not exclusively political. From the outset, the regulations of the Torah also possessed religious depth and significance: "All laws refer to, or are based upon, eternal truths of reason, or remind us of them, and rouse us to ponder them. Hence, our rabbis rightly say: the laws and doctrines are related to each other, like body and soul."[16] The Mosaic commandments were designed to serve as mnemonics of the cardinal verities of natural religion, as performances of universal precepts about God and providence, and not merely as temporal measures of the ancient commonwealth. Mendelssohn's break with Spinoza over the *nature* of the revealed law corresponded to his divergence on the question of its *authority*. For Spinoza, the raison d'être of biblical legislation disappeared with the downfall of the Hebrew theocracy; for Mendelssohn, this collapse brought an end to the political character of the law, while leaving its spiritual dimension untouched. The Halakhah consequently retained its binding claim on the conduct of the individual Jew. It was for Mendelssohn—as it was emphatically not for Spinoza—a "divine law." Yet with the demise of territorial sovereignty went the loss of any constitutional right of coercion on the part of the law. Henceforth, whether or not to obey would be a matter of individual choice, with the religious leadership of Judaism in position only to persuade and not to punish its recalcitrants. This was to be the pièce de résistance in Mendelssohn's response to his critics, the most immediate explanation for why present-day Judaism was neither a symbol nor an executor of religious power. It was also the weakest link in his argument, ignoring how the ban had functioned as the cornerstone of Jewish communal autonomy in the Diaspora. Mendelssohn knew of this history, and even acknowledged it at the end of his preface to Menasseh ben Israel's *Vindiciae Judaeorum*. Yet he considered it aberrant, a deviation from what should have been, and presented postbiblical Judaism in *Jerusalem* in the light of his normative ideal.

Recently, some scholars have questioned whether Mendelssohn indeed wrote *Jerusalem* with Spinoza's *Treatise* in mind. Among other things, they have pointed to the fact that Mendelssohn mentions Spinoza only once in *Jerusalem*, and there with reference to his metaphysics only.[17] They have also harped on the unsubstantiated nature of the standard assumption that Mendelssohn had direct knowledge of the *Treatise*, while suggesting that any proximity in theme was at most a reflection of the broad dissemination of Spinozistic ideas (as opposed to Spinoza's own ideas) in the eighteenth-century Enlightenment, or even a mere accident.[18] These revisionists are right about one thing: The view that Mendelssohn was targeting Spinoza in *Jerusalem* has relied on proof of philosophical and literary resemblance as opposed to hard evidence of historical influence. Therefore, it has perhaps been averred with too much certainty in the past. Be that as it may, the similarity in Mendelssohn's tack vis-à-vis Spinoza's metaphysics in the *Philosophical Dialogues* and, in effect if not, incontrovertibly, in intent, with his critique of revelation in *Jerusalem* is striking. In both cases, Mendelssohn operated by selective appropriation. Whether in his theory of substance or his understanding of the Sinaitic revelation, there were sparks buried in Spinoza's otherwise scandalous philosophy worth rescuing. If carefully isolated from the errors that surrounded and sometimes followed from them in their original setting, these ideas could serve as take-off points for alternative solutions to the problems that nagged at Spinoza—answers that successfully avoided the dead-end road followed by the Amsterdam heretic. Spinoza could be reclaimed, because he had already been defused. Mendelssohn had begun his philosophical career as an advocate for this approach, and implicitly it remained his credo twenty-eight years later.

Jerusalem, as mentioned earlier, appeared in April 1783; Mendelssohn died less than three years later in early January 1786. In between, he became embroiled in a controversy with F. H. Jacobi, a German antirationalist thinker, over the philosophy of Spinoza and its place in the weltanschauung of Lessing. This *Pantheismusstreit*, or "pantheism controversy," as it became known, would demonstrate that Mendelssohn had been prescient in rehabilitating Spinoza years before, but not in the assumptions that had governed this gesture. If Mendelssohn thought that Spinoza's challenge had been resolved by thinkers like Leibniz, Wolff, and himself, and could thus be shown its rightful due in retrospect, the extraordinary statement attributed by Jacobi to Lessing—"[t]here is no other philosophy but the philosophy of Spinoza"—was proof that the radical pantheist remained explosive.

III.

The pantheism controversy began in the late summer of 1783 with Jacobi's assertion in a letter to Mendelssohn that Lessing, during a visit Jacobi had paid him at his home in Wolffenbüttel in June 1780, less than a year before his sudden death, had declared himself a Spinozist. For the next two years Jacobi and Mendelssohn carried on a private correspondence over the meaning of this revelation, with their mutual friend Elise Reimarus serving as a go-between for their missives. Then, in the fall of 1785, the debate suddenly went public. Earlier that July Mendelssohn had written Jacobi that he was about to publish a work that would hopefully "establish the *status controversiae* and thereby give the debate its proper introduction."[19] Not wanting to be preempted by Mendelssohn, especially as he feared being tarred as a Spinozist in the process, Jacobi rapidly collated the entirety of their epistolary exchange into a book surrounded by his own narrative about the controversy. As a result, Mendelssohn's *Morgenstuden* [Morning Hours] and Jacobi's *Über die Lehre des Spinoza, in Briefen an den Herrn Moses Mendelssohn* [Concerning the Doctrine of Spinoza in Letters to Herr Moses Mendelssohn] appeared at roughly the same time. The first, without alluding to the debate with Jacobi, sought to cushion the impact of any impending report of Lessing's Spinozism, though only in three chapters of a book otherwise devoted to a broad range of metaphysical problems. The second laid bare the background to this project in juicy detail, printing Mendelssohn's letters despite never having received permission to do so. Quickly, Mendelssohn fired back in a work entitled *An die Freunde Lessings* [To Lessing's Friends]. He finished the manuscript in late December and rushed to deliver it to the printer before the New Year. It is said that in his haste he left his home to walk to the publisher without a coat. Not in good health to begin with, he died on January 4, 1786. His polemic against Jacobi thus appeared posthumously. The death of his adversary notwithstanding, Jacobi answered the pamphlet with an angry rejoinder of his own, *Wider Mendelssohns Beschuldigen* [Against Mendelssohn's Accusations]. While this was the end of the conversation between Mendelssohn and Jacobi, the controversy expanded to include other leading voices in German thought, from Kant to Herder. Next to the publication of Kant's *Critique of Pure Reason* in 1781, the *Spinozastreit* was the most important event in German philosophy of the 1780s, and the sweeping revision in the attitude toward Spinoza and his pantheism that it spawned would take its place alongside Kantianism as one of the chief pillars of the emerging movement of German Idealism.[20] And it had all begun with a note from Jacobi to Mendelssohn in September 1783.

The disclosure that Lessing was a crypto-Spinozist was a blow to Mendelssohn on several levels. First, there was the simple fact that the news had come from Jacobi and not from his late friend himself. In his notorious tell-all, Jacobi let it be known that Lessing, even while confiding in him, had deliberately kept Mendelssohn in the dark about his conversion. Mendelssohn put his best face on this revelation at least as far as Lessing was concerned. In *To Lessing's Friends*, he opined that his friend had wished to spare him the pain of realizing how far apart in outlook the two had grown—a gesture of kindness that contrasted sharply with Jacobi's treachery.[21] Yet one wonders if Mendelssohn, in some corner of his mind, did not hold himself partly accountable for Lessing's Spinozist turn. It has long been thought that the *Philosophical Dialogues* of 1755 reflect actual conversations between Mendelssohn and Lessing on the former's "own plan to rehabilitate the much abused Spinoza."[22] The book—whose original publication Lessing, apparently, had seen to—came to light not long after the two thinkers had become fast friends in 1754. "To what extent Lessing had known Spinoza's thought prior to his friendship with Mendelssohn cannot be established with any degree of likelihood," Altmann concedes. "But it was undoubtedly Mendelssohn who introduced Lessing to a deeper understanding of philosophy in general and of Spinoza in particular."[23] Their early discussions made a strong mark on Lessing, evident in his writing soon after their acquaintance that "[h]is [Mendelssohn's] honesty and philosophical mind make me anticipate in him a second Spinoza, equal to the first in everything but his errors."[24] A quarter century later, Lessing had gone well beyond the qualified appreciation of Spinoza that Mendelssohn had proposed. From his allusion to Mendelssohn's likely surpassing of Spinoza in 1754, he had journeyed to the point of reportedly claiming that "[t]here is no other philosophy but the philosophy of Spinoza." Still, it was quite possibly Mendelssohn who had planted the seed of this enthusiasm.

Beyond the personal slight, and the fear of what association with the atheist par excellence of the Enlightenment might do to his friend's posthumous standing, Mendelssohn was discomfited by Jacobi's deeper agenda in divulging Lessing's Spinozism. Jacobi's attitude toward Spinoza was paradoxical: He opposed him strenuously, and yet agreed in essence with Lessing that he was the zenith of philosophy, at least of speculative reason. Years of wrestling with the *Ethics* had led Jacobi to conclude that Spinoza could not be overcome with his own rationalist weapons. For all its pretense to detachment and remaining above the fray, philosophy was ultimately consumed by an "uncontrolled addiction to explaining," a "need to reconcile things by means of clear conceptualizations, to the total disregard of all else."[25] This affect propelled philosophy toward greater and greater abstraction until it culminated in a system that was all-encompassing and self-sufficient, able to account for all particulars with a general, immanent, and inexorable causality—a system, in short, much like that of Spinoza. Thus the phrase that became Jacobi's rallying cry: "Consistent philosophy is Spinozist, hence pantheist, fatalist and atheist." Reason, in stretching itself to embrace everything, lost its moorings from what was most real according to Jacobi: the sheer givenness of *my* existence, the individual texture of *my* experience, the undeniable feeling of *my* freedom to choose. The more one traveled down the path of ratiocination, the closer one came to Spinoza's God—"the principle of *being* in all that exists, entirely without individuality, simply and plainly infinite"—and the farther one wandered from being itself. For the mind adrift on this path, the way back to being was not to try to match Spinoza proof for proof, but to suspend dogmatic reason and take what Jacobi called a *salto mortale*, a head-over-heels somersault into faith in a personal God. This is what he had urged Lessing to perform during his sojourn at Wolffenbüttel. Lessing had wryly demurred—"Even to do that would entail a leap I may no longer ask of my old legs and my muddled head"—but his willingness to stick with Spinoza was useful to Jacobi. Bringing this tidbit to Mendelssohn's attention was, for Jacobi, the first step in fatally crippling the compromise position of the religious Enlightenment. In a pattern by now familiar to Mendelssohn, a Christian scholar once again sought to confront him with a stark choice, this time between Spinozism and the *salto mortale*.

In both the final chapters of *Morning Hours* and his front-on riposte to Jacobi in *To Lessing's Friends*, Mendelssohn focused on framing the issue of Lessing's Spinozism in a way that would limit the damage to the reputation of his deceased comrade and vindicate his own resolute adherence to a middle-of-the-road path in metaphysics. His apologia for Lessing drew on an argument he had initially advanced in the *Philosophical Dialogues*. There, in addition to claiming that Spinoza was the founder of Leibniz's preestablished harmony, Mendelssohn had ventured that the philosophy of the *Ethics* could be interpreted so as to "exist with reason and religion":

> NEOPHIL . . . You know, the Leibnizians attribute to the world a twofold existence, as it were. It existed, to use their language, among possible worlds in the divine intellect prior to the divine decree. Because it is the best, God preferred it over all possible worlds and allowed it actually to exist outside him. Now Spinoza remained at that first stage of existence. He believed that a world never became actual outside God and all visible things were not subsisting for themselves, up to this hour, outside God, but instead were still and always to be found in the divine intellect alone. What, then, the Leibnizians maintained about the plan of the world as that plan existed in the divine mind *antecedenter ad decretum* ("before the decree") is what Spinoza believed it possible to maintain about the visible world.[26]

Here, then, was another way in which Spinoza's one-substance doctrine could be seen as only a single step removed from Leibniz's metaphysical pluralism. Spinoza and Leibniz, in this reading, were at one in asserting the existence of the world in the mind of God, only for Spinoza this was the actual, visible world, whereas for Leibniz it was only the best of all possible worlds prior to the divine decree of creation, which permitted the universe to exist outside God. Without endorsing this ideal monism, which he continued to regard as erroneous on several crucial points, Mendelssohn nevertheless saw in this reinterpretation a means of reconciling Spinoza's system with a broadly theistic outlook.

Thirty years later, in *Morning Hours*, Mendelssohn essentially dusted off this argument from his youth and recast it to fit the views of his late friend. After once again underscoring—emphatically—his rejection of any speculative metaphysics that did not maintain an irreducible gap between God and the universe, Mendelssohn struck a more apologetic tone in the last

two chapters of the work. Basing himself in part on ostensibly pantheistic fragments strewn throughout Lessing's oeuvre, Mendelssohn portrayed
their author as a specific kind of pantheist, one who rejected not so much
an "extra-mundane God" as an "extra-divine world." In other words, Lessing went no further than Leibniz's *antecedenter ad decretum*, holding that the
world exists necessarily and eternally *within* the mind of God. Mendelssohn
labeled this viewpoint not panentheism or acosmism, but a "refined pantheism" or "refined Spinozism." Having formulated Lessing's theology thus,
Mendelssohn concluded that "[i]f my friend [Lessing], that champion of a
refined Spinozism, concedes all this . . . then morality and religion are in no
danger; for, after all, this position is distinguished from our system only by
a degree of subtlety which has no practical consequence."[27] Mendelssohn
went so far as to suggest that Lessing had been "on his way to link pantheistic concepts even with positive religion," much as had been done by theistic
writers "with the Ancients' system of emanation . . . throughout the centuries." Like Neoplatonism, Spinozism could eventually be accommodated to
"orthodox doctrine."[28]

IV.

The religious divide between Mendelssohn and Jacobi shadowed their correspondence from the outset. In one of his letters to Jacobi, Mendelssohn
described the *salto mortale* as an "honourable retreat to the shelter of faith"
that was "entirely in keeping with the spirit of your religion which imposed
an obligation to suppress doubt by means of faith."[29] Jacobi happily assented
to this equation of faith-based religion and Christianity, replying to Mendelssohn that "[i]t is a different faith that is taught—and not demanded—by
the religion of the Christians. A faith which deals not with eternal truths but
with the finite contingent nature of the human being."[30]

References to the confessional background of the two contestants were
mostly held in check over the course of their private communication, but
with the publication of Jacobi's exposé, they moved to the center. Furious
at Jacobi's attempt to humiliate both him and Lessing, Mendelssohn wrote,
in *To Lessing's Friends*, what was perhaps his most personal and embittered
work in German. He cast Jacobi as but the latest Christian pietist to try to
"guide me to the bosom of faith" by converting him and, in the mold of the
second part of *Jerusalem*, struck an emphatically Jewish note throughout.

The amplifying of this element was evident in a new wrinkle in his defense, not only of Lessing, but of Spinoza himself:

Lessing, a follower of Spinoza? Good Lord! What have a person's speculative views to do with the person himself? Who would not be delighted to have had Spinoza as a friend, no matter how great his Spinozism? And who would refuse to give Spinoza's genius and excellent character their due?

As long as my friend still was not accused of being a secret blasphemer and a hypocrite to boot, the news of his being a Spinozist was a matter of complete indifference to me. I knew that there is also a refined Spinozism which rhymes very well with all that is practical in religion and morality. . . . I knew that, in the main, this refined Spinozism can be easily reconciled with Judaism, and that Spinoza, irrespective of his speculative doctrine, could have remained an *orthodox* Jew [italics mine] were it not that in other writings he had called genuine Judaism into question and in so doing stepped outside the *Law*. Obviously Spinoza's doctrine would come much closer to Judaism than does the orthodox doctrine of the Christians. If I was able indeed to love Lessing and be loved in return where he was still a strict follower of Athanasius (or was at least considered so by me), then why not all the more when he approximated Judaism, and where I saw in him an adherent of the Jew, *Baruch Spinoza*?[31]

What is *new* about this passage is less the substance itself, hints of which we have found in Mendelssohn's earlier work, than the provocative highlighting, even flaunting of Spinoza's Jewishness. In *Jerusalem* Mendelssohn had established Judaism as a "revealed legislation" as opposed to "revealed religion," with membership determined by observance of the Law and not by adherence to a particular creed. Now he applied this interpretation to Spinoza, portraying his pantheism as a matter of indifference from the point of view of Jewish self-definition, indeed going so far as to assert that the seventeenth-century arch-heretic "could have remained an orthodox Jew were it not that in other writings [i.e., the *Treatise*] he had called genuine Judaism into question and in so doing stepped outside the Law."[32] Furthermore, in *Morning Hours*, Mendelssohn had shown that "there is also a refined Spinozism which rhymes very well with all that is practical in religion and morality." Clearly, this meant for Mendelssohn any variety of natural religion, of which he had already claimed elsewhere in his work Judaism to be the most perfect, but now, in *To Lessing's Friends*, he spelled this out, noting that "in the main, this refined Spinozism can be easily reconciled with Judaism." Not only this, it was "much closer to Judaism" than to the "orthodox doctrine of the Christians." Lessing had therefore "approximated Judaism" by embracing a "refined pantheism" and becoming a disciple of the Amsterdam philosopher. Perhaps most strikingly, the latter appears no longer under the coy disguise of "someone other than a German" or "other than a Christian"; he is simply "the Jew, *Baruch Spinoza*."

This was as close as Mendelssohn ever came to an expressly Jewish reclamation of Spinoza. Yet his comments were distinguished by their pathos,
not by their prescription of a fundamentally new tack toward Spinoza. From
the start of his career to its finish, Mendelssohn maintained a consistent ambivalence vis-à-vis Spinoza; he wanted to salvage what was best in Spinoza's
philosophy and to inoculate religion and morality from what was worst.
He believed he had achieved this goal in the idea of a "refined Spinozism."
He could not have expected, let alone have wanted, that later generations
of Jews would take his statement that Spinoza "could have remained an orthodox Jew were it not that in other writings he had called genuine Judaism
into question" as an endorsement of his further rehabilitation—a development that only intensified as the number continued to escalate of those
who, like Spinoza, had "stepped outside the *Law*." But this, as we will see, is
exactly what happened.

*Figure. 3.1. Julius Hubner, Portrait of Berthold Auerbach, 1846. Deutsches Literaturarchiv Marbach.

CHAPTER 3

The First Modern Jew

Berthold Auerbach's *Spinoza* (1837) and the Beginnings of an Image

I.

In September 1829, German Jews celebrated the hundredth birthday of Moses Mendelssohn.[1] The Enlightenment luminary known in his day as the "Socrates of Berlin" had long been eclipsed in German philosophy, yet he was still very much alive in the cultural memory of the German Jewish *Bürgertum*. In Berlin, Dessau, Frankfurt am Main, Hamburg, Dresden, and Breslau, Jewish communities observed the jubilee with secular commemorations that included speeches, toasts, poems, and even chorales composed in honor of Mendelssohn. At the Berlin gathering, in the "tastefully furnished hall" where Mendelssohn's marble bust stood on display, illuminated and decked with flowers, the keynote address was delivered by Leopold Zunz (1794–1886), one of the founders of the recently inaugurated Wissenschaft des Judentums, the modern critical study of Judaism. Zunz referred to himself and all those assembled as "Mendelssohn's spiritual legacy," adding "we belong to him like the student to the teacher who shows him the correct path."[2] In celebrating "the eternal Moses Mendelssohn," Zunz and his comrades were in effect paying homage to the first modern Jew.[3]

Three years later was the anniversary of another historic Jew and philosopher. November 24, 1832, was the bicentenary of the birth of Baruch Spinoza. Not surprisingly, those Jewish communities that had paid homage to Mendelssohn in 1829 remained mute with respect to the seventeenth-century excommunicate. Yet the occasion did not pass entirely unnoticed. That fall, a sympathetic biographical sketch of Spinoza appeared in the reform-oriented German Jewish journal *Sulamith*.[4] Though modest compared to the Mendelssohn festivities of 1829, this eulogy was itself a milestone, being the first article, laudatory or otherwise, ever to be devoted to Spinoza in an identifiably Jewish publication. Its author was a Jewish university student named Ludwig Philippson (1811–1889)—the same Philippson who later would become perhaps the prime molder of nineteenth-century German Jewish public opinion as editor of the *Allgemeine Zeitung des Judentums*, the most influential and widely circulating Jewish newspaper of its era.[5]

Philippson was the sole Jew to pay written tribute to Spinoza in 1832. The rest of the 1830s and 1840s, however, witnessed continued signs of a reentry of Spinoza into Jewish consciousness. For some left-wing German Jews at this time—most of them members, like Philippson, of a rising generation of Jewish intellectuals born in the first two decades of the century, who had received (if not always completed) a university education that exposed them to the latest currents in German thought—Spinoza became the subject of growing interest and even identification. This attraction stemmed not only from his then fashionable pantheism, but from what was seen as his relevance to the origins of modern Jewish identity. Two individuals within this early group of Spinoza admirers remain familiar names today: the poet Heinrich Heine (1799–1856) and the pioneering German socialist later turned pioneering Jewish nationalist Moses Hess (1812–1875).[6] Yet the most concerted effort to convert Spinoza into a prototype of the modern Jew in this period was made by the author Berthold Auerbach.

Though little read today, Auerbach was one of the most popular and critically acclaimed German authors of the nineteenth century. A prolific writer of novels, essays, criticism, and short fiction, he was best known for the work that marked his breakthrough—his fabulously successful *Schwarzwälder Dorfgeschichten* [Black Forest Village Stories], a series of novellas, begun in 1843, that intimately recreated the disappearing peasant culture of his native Swabian region in the style of the emerging European realism. Blending nostalgia for the local peculiarities of provincial life with liberal optimism and commitment to progress, Auerbach's sentimental stories struck a chord with middle-class German readers, providing them with an idealized image of their national character. For a time, he enjoyed a degree of acceptance by non-Jewish Germans as "one of us" exceeding that of virtually any of his German Jewish forerunners and successors in the arts. Since he had "made it" without ever renouncing his Jewish identity, his German Jewish contemporaries celebrated him as one of *their* own as well.

Auerbach also earned notice during his lifetime as a great partisan of Spinoza. In 1841 he became the first to translate Spinoza's entire oeuvre (at least what was known of it at the time) into German, complete with an introductory biography.[7] But this was not the first fruit of his literary engagement with the Amsterdam philosopher. Four years earlier, in 1837, he made his fictional debut with *Spinoza, ein historischer Roman* [Spinoza, a

Historical Novel].⁸ This was the first attempt ever made to portray Spinoza as a fictional protagonist—a landmark in his cultural, if not philosophical reception. It was also a landmark in his Jewish reception. The early biographies by Lucas and Colerus had made the Jewish beginnings of Spinoza a prominent part of his myth, but they had depicted primarily the mature thinker *after* his break with Judaism.⁹ Auerbach focused on the previous years, devoting unprecedented attention to evoking, however fancifully, the Sephardic Amsterdam that had shaped and yielded the budding philosopher, and which he had eventually left behind. In Spinoza's rupture from Amsterdam Jewry, coupled with his refusal to convert to Christianity, Auerbach saw the dawn of a new age in the history of the Jews and humanity at large, an era that would end with the emancipation of all individuals from given identities and sectarian hatreds and the realization of the Enlightenment vision of a religion of reason. The latter hope is made explicit in an epilogue to the novel, in which the figure of Ahasverus, the Wandering Jew—the personification of Jewish exile in an old Christian legend—appears to the recently excommunicated Spinoza in a dream and declares him to be both his redeemer and the redeemer of all mankind, conferring upon him the status of secular messiah.¹⁰

The image of Spinoza as a pioneer on the road leading "out of the ghetto"—indeed, as what Leo Strauss would later call a "symbol of that emancipation which was to be more than emancipation but secular redemption"—might thus be said to have had its genesis in a work of historical fiction from 1837.¹¹ At a time when within German Jewish enlightened circles, it was Mendelssohn who was generally held up as the progenitor of the "modern Jew," Auerbach was one of the first to give priority in this pedigree to Spinoza. Yet despite the obviously foundational significance attributed to Spinoza in the novel, the form of the Jewish identity he is meant to exemplify is not entirely evident. In his earlier writings, Auerbach had allied himself with the nascent Reform movement within German Jewry.¹² There, he expressed confidence that a modernized Judaism, understood solely as a religious identity and not as an ethnic or national one, could continue to thrive and maintain its "mission" even under conditions of emancipation. This distinguished him from his fellow Spinoza enthusiasts Heine and Hess, both of whom, at least at this stage in their careers, were more zealous in their rejection of revealed religion and indeed enlisted Spinoza in support of this vision. Did Auerbach's invocation of Spinoza in his 1837 novel—an invocation that contained definite elements of personal identification—signify a deviation from his prior stance on the so-called Jewish Question, or were these positions, at least in his own mind, consistent? Could the seventeenth-century heretic be claimed as a forerunner of a liberal Judaism? Or did he exemplify a more "ruthless cosmopolitanism" at odds with the persistence of any degree of Jewish particularism?[13]

Questions of this nature were at the core of Auerbach's reception of Spinoza. I contend that his historical novel, when studied against the backdrop of his previous Jewish writings, evinces a very personal—but also very contemporary—tug-of-war between two different visions of Jewish modernity: one more reformist and accommodating of a religious framework for change, the other more uncompromisingly radical. In essence, Auerbach was the first not only to *present* Spinoza as the first modern Jew. He was also the first to *project* dilemmas of Jewish identity of a much later generation back onto him. Perhaps in this respect, more than any other, his use of the Amsterdam heretic would prove prophetic.

II.

"The subject interests me greatly," David Fränkel (1799–1865), the editor of *Sulamith*, wrote to his former pupil Philippson in the summer of 1832, responding warmly to the idea of including a short biographical sketch of Spinoza in the next edition of his periodical. "Fundamentally, Spinoza lived such that *today* he would be considered a *good Jew*, since, in spite of everything, he remained what he was. The opposite, it seems to me, is not proven; *thus he can be counted among the Jews.*" Fränkel concluded by noting that "the controversy between Mendelssohn and Jacobi must certainly be known to you and what the former—Mendelssohn—expressed regarding the Jew Spinoza."[14]

The allusion was to Mendelssohn's final work, *To Lessing's Friends* (1786), where the German Jewish philosopher had issued his most personal apology for Spinoza yet. To show how far he was willing to go in identifying with Spinoza—a gesture he hoped would sap Jacobi's revelation of Lessing's Spinozism of its ability to scandalize—Mendelssohn highlighted (one might even say magnified) the Jewishness they bore in common. He referred bluntly to "the Jew, *Baruch Spinoza*," and added that the Amsterdam heretic "could have remained an orthodox Jew were it not that in his other writings he had called genuine Judaism into question and in so doing stepped outside the *Law*."[15] Nearly five decades later, Fränkel, while linking himself to Mendelssohn's "coattails," went much further. Spinoza the Jew, even Spinoza the "fellow Jew," had become—perhaps for the first time— Spinoza the "good Jew." What made such a label thinkable (which is not to say accurate, or, for that matter, widespread) by 1832? In what follows, before turning to Auerbach, I focus on three fundamental developments in both German Jewish intellectual and cultural history and the German reception of Spinoza that facilitated the formation of this new framing in the years following Mendelssohn. These include the growing challenge to the authority of the Law within Judaism; the embrace of Spinoza as a religious thinker within German Romanticism; and the spate of German Jewish conversions to Christianity in the first three decades of the nineteenth century. Together, these trends appeared to open the door to a dismissal, or at the very least a reduction, of the main charges against Spinoza from the perspective of Judaism: namely, that he was an antinomian, an atheist, and an apostate.

The rethinking of the place of the Law in Judaism opened one door—the main door, really—to a Jewish reclamation of Spinoza. For premodern Judaism, Spinoza's utter rejection of the continued authority and religious value of the commandments (the "ceremonial law") constituted, arguably, his greatest heresy. Historically, to be a "good Jew" involved, at a minimum, submission to the yoke of the Written and Oral Torah, predicated on the belief that the Law was divine at its source, absolute in its scope, and—at least in theory—complete, eternal, and unchanging. Even Mendelssohn, for all his tinkering with Spinoza's metaphysics to show how it might be kept on the safe side of heresy, conceded that by "step[ping] outside the *Law*" Spinoza had "called genuine Judaism into question." Yet Mendelssohn's line in the sand was quickly washed over. Continuing a trend that had begun prior to the Haskalah, Jews throughout most of Western and parts of Central Europe in the nineteenth century steadily ceased to feel bound by the Halakhah, and abandoned whole areas of it, as they moved out of the ghetto and adopted a more secular lifestyle.[16] Especially in major cities, there existed sizable constituencies of Jews who were alienated from the Law, yet who nevertheless remained members of the official Jewish community. One can safely assume that most of the celebrants at the Mendelssohn festivities of 1829 were not strictly observant. Traditionalist rabbis and the emerging representatives of Jewish "orthodoxy" held these Jews to be as much sinners, heretics, renegades—in short, "bad Jews"—as the deliberate lawbreakers of earlier eras. By the 1830s, however, they faced a growing internal challenge from advocates of Jewish religious reform who argued that the process, and project, of emancipation—and the reality of mass Jewish defections—demanded new standards of virtue.

One way of interpreting the rising Reform movement is to see it as a bold attempt to alter the definition of the "good Jew" such that observance of the traditional Law was no longer a prerequisite. Or, to modify Mendelssohn's claim, Reform held that one *could*, conceivably, "step outside the

Law" *without* "calling genuine Judaism into question." Indeed, the more extreme Reform thinkers would eventually go a step further: One actually *had*
to "step outside the Law" to practice "genuine Judaism."[17] Yet in its radical
as well as moderate incarnations, German Jewish Reform would close ranks
around the conviction that the "essence of Judaism" lay elsewhere than in
the "four cubits" of the Law.

The rise over the first half of the nineteenth century of a Reform theology in Germany centered on antinomianism (or, at the very least, non-
nomianism) made a reappropriation of Spinoza for liberal Judaism conceiv-
able in two respects. At a minimum, it effectively lifted what previously
had been an insurmountable barrier to rapprochement. It also introduced
the possibility of perceiving Spinoza as a table-setter for the critique of the
Law, even if not a "reforming" Jew himself. This is how he appears in what
many consider the first work of Reform philosophy, Saul Ascher's *Leviathan* (1792).[18] One of the young Jewish Kantians to emerge in the 1780s
and 1790s, Ascher sought, in *Leviathan*, to counter his mentor's critique of
Judaism as a heteronomous system of externally legislated law that failed to
pass the Enlightenment test of a religion of reason. He did so by repudiating the strategy behind Mendelssohn's defense of Judaism before this same
bar. Mendelssohn, in *Jerusalem*, had argued that Judaism was essentially a
"revealed legislation" that commanded only actions, not beliefs, and thus
contained no dogmas or mysteries of faith that contradicted the "natural
religion" of the Enlightenment. Nine years later, Ascher reversed the hierarchy of law and belief in Judaism. What was elemental was faith, more
specifically certain principles (Ascher listed fourteen) that lay at the core of
Judaism; the role of the Halakhah throughout history was only to provide a
set of performative rituals that could anchor these principles in lived experience. "We fail to understand, however," he wrote, "that if our faith is strong
we do not need symbols and if we make a genuine effort to achieve earthly
happiness we can liberate ourselves from the law."[19] In this respect, Spinoza
also went astray by reducing Judaism to the "ceremonial law," mistaking the
merely temporal for the essential.[20] Yet his basic innovation—the historicizing and thus relativizing of Jewish law—could be seen as an anticipation of
Ascher's own project. Moreover, Ascher had no sympathy for the conventional view of Spinoza as a heretic in philosophy and an enemy of religion.
"Would that I should be worthy in my life," he wrote, "to see critical theology absolve Spinoza of heresy in the same manner that philosophy has
succeeded in purifying the name of this remarkable man from the epithet
of 'atheist.'"[21]

Here was an allusion to the second sweeping change that underlay the
Jewish reclamation of Spinoza. The very desire to repossess Spinoza evident

in Fränkel's letter ("thus he can be counted among the Jews") has to be understood as a response to his astonishing rehabilitation within German philosophy in the wake of the pantheism controversy. Through no intention of Mendelssohn and Jacobi, their open quarrel over Lessing's Spinozism only encouraged other admirers of the seventeenth-century thinker to step forth. "Apparently overnight," writes Frederick Beiser, a leading scholar of German Idealism, "Spinoza's reputation changed from a devil into a saint. The scapegoat of the intellectual establishment in the first three quarters of the eighteenth century became its hero in the last quarter."[22] Goethe and Herder were among the first and most famous to confess their Spinozism; other leading lights of the era, including Schleiermacher, Schlegel, Novalis, Schelling, Hölderlin, and the young Hegel, would eventually follow. The result was a Spinoza revival so epic in scale that it became a cornerstone of German Idealism and Romanticism and a watershed in the reception of the philosopher in general.

Of the many facets of this volte-face in Spinoza's image, two are most relevant here. To begin with, the perception of Spinoza as a prototypical modern thinker gained in authority. His one-substance doctrine was increasingly regarded as a defining juncture in the history of thought, a challenge to be confronted by friend and foe alike. "There is no other philosophy than the philosophy of Spinoza," Jacobi quoted Lessing as having confessed to him privately.[23] Hegel would ultimately take a dimmer view of Spinoza's metaphysics, yet he also identified the monism of the seventeenth-century Jew as a necessary starting point for philosophical speculation, stating, "You are either a Spinozist or not a philosopher at all."[24]

The other notable development was a new understanding of Spinoza's *Deus sive Natura*, his identification of God with infinite nature. Throughout the Enlightenment, this was generally held to be tantamount to atheism and materialism. Radical enlighteners, as Jonathan Israel has shown, often celebrated Spinoza for this very reason, heralding him as both a source and symbol of an uncompromising critique of religion rooted in a rejection of supernaturalism; the vast majority of moderates and conservatives opposed him vigorously on this same basis. The Romantics, on the other hand, appropriated Spinoza as an out-and-out *religious* thinker—a "God-intoxicated man," in the well-known words of the poet and fragmentist Novalis. They took his "God-or-Nature" concept to be an admission of pantheism (where God and the world are one) or even panentheism (where God fully permeates the world but is not exhausted by it), not atheism. Spinoza, in this reading, had sought not to dismantle a religious view of the universe but to divinize the latter down to its smallest particle. Freed of its dated "geometrical" mode of demonstration and transposed from a mechanistic to a vitalistic paradigm, Spinoza's monism appeared to the Romantics to unite a consistent naturalism with a belief in a cosmic and immanent God—and thus to bridge the widening chasm between religion and science. With its pinnacle in the intellectual love of God (*amor dei intellectualis*) described in the final book of the *Ethics*, the system of Spinoza seemed to offer a "viable middle path" between the equally unpalatable alternatives of orthodoxy and radical secularism.[25] Here was a rational, scientific, modern outlook that still had its moorings in a religious sensibility.

This interpretation of Spinoza's thought in a spiritual key was paralleled by a construction of his character as a model of perfect equilibrium. Indeed, even stern critics of his philosophy had often credited Spinoza for his temperance and probity. Now, however, Spinoza's life and thought began to appear more closely aligned. Goethe's attribution of an "all-composing calmness" to Spinoza bespoke the dominant early Romantic picture of the philosopher as a sublime figure, lifted above the "storm and stress" of the passions.[26] No longer was Spinoza enlisted mainly as an exemplar of radical revolt against scriptural and ecclesiastical authority. He was invoked instead as an emblem of *Ruhe* (calmness) and resignation, an exponent of a philosophy that resolved all dissonance in the "One and All" (*Hen kai pan*) of its pancosmic vision. The Romantic Spinoza, in short, was the very epitome of the German ideal of *Bildung*, the synthesis of reason and feeling into a whole, integrated self. He exemplified unity, from the individual personality to humanity to nature and the cosmos. He was, in short, so evidently *good*.

At no point, however, did this change of attitudes to Spinoza redound to the benefit of the image of Judaism in German letters. For those who were most fervent in their appreciation of the thinker, Spinoza was a "good Jew" to the extent that his philosophy bore traces of *conversion* to a Christian outlook, however unorthodox. "And so whereas others vituperate him as an atheist, I prefer to call him and cherish him as the greatest of theists [*theissimum*], indeed the greatest of Christians [*christianissimum*]": thus wrote Goethe in 1785, defending Spinoza in a letter to his chief prosecutor in the pantheism controversy, F. H. Jacobi.[27] Herder, in his *Gott: einige Gespräche* [God: Some Conversations] (1787) argued that embracing Spinoza's immanentist theology did not mean rejecting Christianity but rather recognizing that the doctrine of love (*agape*) in the Gospel of John pervaded everything from the works-based morality of the *Treatise* to the *amor dei intellectualis* of the *Ethics*.[28] And indeed, the *Treatise* at least exoterically *does* make a concerted effort to accommodate its universal religion to the teachings of Jesus and the apostles while reserving its harshest criticism for the particularist law and unwarranted superiority complex of the "Pharisees" past and present. Thus, it became possible to view Spinoza as a philosopher who would belong to a Christian genealogy of modernity.

For the growing number of nineteenth-century German Jews eager to acquire German high culture and almost religiously devoted to the value of Bildung, the bidding up of Spinoza's stock made a claim to his inheritance in principle attractive, and thus his quasi baptism in need of a rejoinder. Even those, like Fränkel himself and the vast majority of his generation of Jewish enlighteners, who remained leery of Spinoza's pantheism and biblical criticism could increasingly take pride—Jewish pride—in the perceived saintliness of his character and in his newly prototypical image in modern religion and philosophy.[29] Moreover, we know of at least one early-nineteenth-century German Jewish thinker beholden to Idealist thought who took the step of asserting the equivalence of Spinoza's monistic metaphysics with the "essence of Judaism." His name was Immanuel Wolf (Wohlwill), and he was one of the founders, in 1819, of the Berlin-based Verein für die Cultur und Wissenschaft der Juden (The Society for the Culture and Science of the Jews), the group credited with originating the movement for scientific study of Judaism (Wissenschaft des Judentums). In his essay "On the Concept of a Science of Judaism," which opened the first and only volume of the scholarly journal published by the short-lived Verein, Wolf identified the cardinal and distinguishing idea of Judaism as "the unlimited unity of the all." Chronicling the evolution of this concept, Wolf singled out "Benedict de Spinoza" for praise for his landmark role in translating the Jewish idea of the unity of God from a revealed truth originally "posited as a datum . . . at a time when man's mind was far from ready to grasp it in all its universality" into the language of "pure speculative thinking." He described Spinoza as "a man whose subtlety and profundity were centuries in advance of his time, whose highly significant influence on the more consistent and profound philosophies of the present day is unmistakable, who did indeed renounce the external rites of Judaism but who had understood all the more its inner spirit."[30]

Finally, and arguably at the most basic level, Fränkel's branding of Spinoza as a "good Jew" reflected the transformation, over time, of a negative into a potential positive. "[I]n spite of everything, he remained what he was": Spinoza, in other words, had not converted to Christianity. Antagonists and admirers alike had long seized on this fact to argue that Spinoza remained, in some sense, Jewish, though whether this formed a part of his self-identity after the ban is still a moot question. But for this non-apostasy (or, at least, nonconversion) to furnish evidence that Spinoza was not simply a Jew, but a "good Jew" required the rise of a new—and from the standpoint of a committed Jewish enlightener like Fränkel, profoundly worrisome—cultural tendency.

From 1770 to 1830, the Jews of Berlin—the city of Mendelssohn, the cradle of the Haskalah movement and the early struggle for emancipation—suffered what came to be known as a *Taufepidimie*, or "epidemic of baptisms."[31] However hyperbolic this label has come to seem in retrospect, the scale of the attrition over a sixty-year period—some sixteen hundred Berlin Jews overall, including one in seven Berlin Jews born after 1800—was without parallel in German Jewish history. Adding to the shock was the fact that the wealthy business elite—the supposed bedrock of the community—were, especially after 1800, heavily represented among the class of converts. "In fact," writes Steven Lowenstein, an expert on German Jewish history, "one could even say that becoming a Christian was a kind of fashion among certain prominent Berlin Jewish families of the period."[32] All who converted felt estranged from traditional Judaism; most were also left cold by the Haskalah's effort to create an "enlightened" alternative; few, however, were driven by genuine Christian piety and conviction. On balance, the decisive motivation was more social than religious, and testified above all to the stymieing of the efforts at emancipation. The patriarch of a Berlin Jewish family might seek finally to be rid of the stigma of Jewishness and to enjoy a status, legally and socially, commensurate with his affluence. The daughter might be compelled to convert in order to marry a non-Jewish suitor. The son might find that, without baptism, his path to an academic career, or to a professional position in the law, was blocked. Whatever the specific reasons case by case, by 1832 one could speak of a "who's who" of notable German Jews turned Christian. The roster included Rahel Varnhagen (1771–1833), née Levin, a Romantic poet and legendary *salonnière*; Ludwig Börne (1786–1837), né Lob Baruch, a left-wing political journalist, polemicist, and satirist; and Eduard Gans (1797–1836), a professor of law at the University of Berlin, who, before his conversion in 1825, had been Zunz's colleague in the early Wissenschaft des Judentums movement. There was, of course, Heine—like Gans, a former participant in the *Verein* as well as an 1825 convert—who famously referred to his baptism as an "entry ticket to European culture." Yet it was the family Mendelssohn that became most synonymous with the *Taufepidemie*. Of Mendelssohn's six children, four converted, all following their father's death in 1786. Of his grandchildren, only one went to his grave as a Jew.[33]

Against this backdrop, it is understandable that a lifelong reformer like Fränkel, distressed at the loss of many of the "best and the brightest" to Christianity over the previous three decades, might eye Spinoza's Jewishness in a newly favorable light. The market, after all, had not stood still.

"Spinoza lived such that *today* he would be considered a good Jew"—today, when his refusal to adopt the Christian faith set him apart from the legions of prominent and not-so-prominent German Jews who had done so since Mendelssohn's time.

These three shifts—the flagging attachment to Jewish law among urbanizing German Jews, the mitigation of Spinoza's insurgent image in German thought, and the rash of conversions to Christianity—formed a crucial context for Auerbach's reception of the Amsterdam philosopher. Together they seemed to point to the possibility of reclaiming Spinoza—the "God-intoxicated man" who had rejected the Halakhah but never converted to another religion—for Jewish identity without being considered ipso facto an atheist or an apostate. One could conceivably embrace Spinoza while still working for the reform, not the repudiation of Judaism. And Auerbach, as we will see, appeared especially keen early in his career to remain on the side of the reformers.

III.

Auerbach discovered Spinoza in the summer of 1830, while he was living on his own in Stuttgart, trying to gain admission to gymnasium. In many ways, it was love at first sight. Writing that summer to his cousin Jakob Auerbach, the eighteen-year-old Berthold (né Moses Baruch) remarked that he had recently "read some Spinoza" and learned that "he too was originally named Baruch and had latinized his name into Bendict." Out of reverence for the "great thinker," he decided to do likewise: "My name," he announced, "is now Moses Baruch Berthold Benedict Auerbach, and truthfully it's enough to have *one* distinguished name, and I should have so many?"[34]

The psychological distance Auerbach had to travel from his rural boyhood to the brink of entering a German gymnasium may explain the intensity of his attachment to the Amsterdam philosopher who, like him, had started out as Baruch.[35] Auerbach, the ninth of eleven children, spent his formative years in the Black Forest hamlet of Nordstetten, immersed in the traditional way of life of village Jews.[36] At age thirteen, immediately following his bar mitzvah, he left Nordstetten for an old-fashioned Talmudic yeshiva in the nearby town of Hechingen, where it was expected he would study to become a rabbi. But the school made a very negative impression on Auerbach: He felt alienated from the single-minded focus on Talmud along with the subject matter itself. After two years he left Hechingen for the more cosmopolitan setting of Karlsruhe, where he could continue his reading of Jewish texts in preparation for the rabbinate while auditing classes in the humanities at the local gymnasium.

His decision to shun the traditional milieu for the training of future rabbis and pursue an education combining traditional with secular learning proved far-sighted. In 1828 a new Jewry law in the southern German principality of Württemberg was issued that placed the rabbinate fully under the supervision of the civil bureaucracy, stipulating among other things that all future rabbinical candidates hold a university degree.[37] To qualify for university, one first had to receive a diploma from gymnasium. Thus, in 1830, at the advanced age of eighteen, Auerbach headed to the capital city of Stuttgart to try to gain admission to gymansium. That August, after having failed in his initial attempt, Auerbach passed the entry exam and was admitted.

During his two years at gymnasium, Auerbach grew steadily more radical in his religious views. According to his biographer Anton Bettelheim, reading Goethe's *Two Biblical Questions* as well as Spinoza's *Treatise* shook his belief in the unassailability of the Bible and revelation.[38] In a letter to his cousin, who was also planning on becoming a rabbi, Auerbach chided him—"a youth of my Jacob's talents"—for engrossing himself in the study of Talmud, the "Jewish Koran."[39] To his former teacher in Nordstetten, he confessed his ambivalence about pursuing the rabbinate.[40] Indeed, when he entered the University of Tübingen in the summer of 1832, it was as a law student. Yet in the winter semester Auerbach switched back to theology, perhaps as a result of the impression made on him by David F. Strauss, the rising star of the Tübingen faculty, recently arrived from Berlin, where he had been a student of the late Hegel. Strauss's *Life of Jesus* was still a few years away, yet his reputation for Hegelian unorthodoxy was already forming.[41] His lectures on Hegel and philosophy appear to have drawn Auerbach back to the ambition of becoming a Jewish reformer, inspiring him with the goal of achieving a theological synthesis of "pure Mosaism" with the dominant Hegelianism.[42]

If Auerbach was in fact back to his original plan of becoming a rabbi, he was soon to be disappointed. In the summer of 1833, while studying in Munich, he was arrested for membership in one of the nationalistic student fraternities at Tübingen, part of a crackdown following the failed Frankfurt putsch earlier that year.[43] Though only briefly detained, he was placed under investigation and shortly thereafter expelled from Tübingen. Eventually he was permitted to enroll at Heidelberg, though without the stipend he had enjoyed earlier. While living in Stuttgart in the fall of 1835, where he was preparing for the exams in theology that were a prerequisite for his rabbinical candidacy, Auerbach learned of a further price for the ongoing investigation of his case: He would not be allowed to sit for the exams, and as a result would not be able to be certified for the now state-sponsored rabbinate. The 1828 Württemberg *Erziehungsgesetz*—the same law that years before appeared to have vindicated his flight from the Hechingen yeshiva—now blocked the path to his chosen career. In early 1837 the criminal investigation finally came to an end. Auerbach was found guilty and given a mild sentence, a seven-week imprisonment in the Hohenasperg fortress outside Stuttgart.

By this time, Auerbach had begun accepting writing commissions as a source of much-needed income. In 1836 he issued the first work in his own name, a sixty-eight-page pamphlet against contemporary forms of antisemitism entitled *Das Judenthum und die neueste Literatur* [Judaism and Recent Literature]. The immediate background to this piece was the scandal that had been caused by Young Germany, a militantly secular and avant-garde literary faction that included the emigrés Börne and Heine and the novelist and playwright Karl Gutzkow (1811–1878). The frank discussion of sexuality and caustic treatment of organized religion in works such as Gutzkow's most notorious novel, *Wally, die Zweiflerin* [Wally, the Skeptic], were offensive to German liberals and conservatives alike.[44] Thanks to the Jewish origins of both Börne and Heine, the notion that Young Germany was a Jewish movement—epitomized in its dubbing by the famous critic Wolfgang Menzel as "Young Palestine"—quickly took root.[45] Like the Young German writers, Auerbach was also contemptuous of the often reactionary nature of late German Romanticism. Yet he was equally wary of the strident secularism and heretical image of the movement—a discomfort made even more acute by the anti-Jewish sentiments its appearance had provoked. He wrote *Das Judenthum* mainly to refute the suspected Jewishness of Young Germany, though the essay took the form of a much broader counterattack on the treatment of Jews and Judaism in German literature. As a statement of Auerbach's views on the "Jewish Question" written only a year prior to his *Spinoza* novel, it warrants discussion.

In *Das Judenthum*, Auerbach offers the first glimpse of a political and religious liberalism that would characterize much of his oeuvre. While embracing the ideals of universalism and humanity, he insists that progress toward these goals be evolutionary as opposed to revolutionary. On these grounds, Auerbach rebukes those radical secularists committed to a "war of extermination against everything prevailing in religion, the state, customs and morals."[46] He is especially biting in his criticism of Heine, whose sensualism—and apostasy—he deplored. Against Heine's vision of "a new religion," a "so-called pantheism" that will bring about a "rehabilitation of the flesh" utterly emancipated from the "spiritualism" of Judaism and

Christianity, Auerbach argues that progress can and should occur within the framework of the revealed religions.[47] This is the only course compatible with the historical process rightly understood: Since "[w]e cannot go back, we must go forward," Auerbach wrote. "[I]t is necessary to penetrate the old forms and wed the new spirit to the old, and thereby . . . bring about a . . . renaissance of the positive religions in keeping with the times.[48]

In taking this stance, Auerbach was signaling his support for a German liberal tradition that viewed the steady advance of reason and freedom not as an abandonment, but as a development of the legacy of the past, including its religious aspects.[49] Lessing's *Die Erziehung des Menschengeschlechts* [The Education of Humankind] of 1777, with its vision of human history as the progressive translation of revealed truths into truths of reason, was perhaps the most salient expression of this tendency. Indeed, Auerbach pays tribute in his essay to the "humanists" of the German Enlightenment—Lessing and Herder, Goethe and Schiller—contrasting their "practical liberalism" favorably to the haughtiness of the eighteenth-century Encyclopedists and, by implication, the French-influenced Young Germany. Unlike those Germans affected by *Gallomanie*, these were "real Germans" (*echt deutsche Männer*), who "sought equal recognition for the demands of reason and those of the religious spirit." Committed to advocating the cause of Enlightenment *among* the common citizenry rather than *against* them, they tempered their zeal with discretion, tailoring their appeal to the Christian beliefs and sensibilities of their target audience.[50] It was the gradualism of their approach to social and religious change, their commitment to shepherding the particular in the direction of the universal without disowning the former entirely, that appealed to Auerbach so strongly.

It appealed to him as both a German *and* a Jew, for if there was one point about which he deviated from virtually all German thinkers in this period it was over the ability of Judaism to adapt to modernity. Within German Idealism, it was more or less a consensus that while a reformed Christianity could serve as a basis, or at least a vehicle, for a modern religion of reason, Judaism could not provide such a foundation. As the religion of a single people, it was seen as intractably chauvinist and exclusive, and with its strict legal character, it seemed totally at odds with a modern ethos stressing human autonomy.[51] For Hegel and other German thinkers, Judaism was a fossilized relic of history, incapable of progress or development. While this did not rule out the granting of civil rights to Jews as individuals, most believed that Judaism itself could not survive the encounter with modernity.

Auerbach disagreed. Sketching in broad strokes the evolution of the Jewish spirit, he described Judaism as a religion whose nature and history vouched for its capacity for progress. In this he echoed an argument with

roots in the Verein of the early 1820s, which the rabbi and religious reformer
Abraham Geiger (1810–1874) had recently revived. An extraordinarily pre-
cocious scholar of history, philosophy, and theology, with a doctorate from
the University of Marburg and a rabbinic post in the small town of Wies-
baden, Geiger emerged on the scene in the mid-1830s as the lead voice in
the effort to harness Wissenschaft in the service of Reform and thereby
endow the movement with more clear-cut conceptual underpinnings.[52] His
ambition was clear—to evaluate Jewish religious literature with the same
philological and historical methods used by radical Christian theologians
like Strauss of Tübingen to study the New Testament. In this goal, however,
he was guided by the Idealist assumption that through a sympathetic understanding of sources in their specific contexts—a kind of reasoning almost
entirely foreign to traditional Judaism—one would ultimately penetrate to
the original and animating idea behind them.[53] He believed, moreover, that
a grasp of the *development* of this idea in history would enable one to distinguish the "essence of Judaism" from its litany of outward forms, the value
of which was only relative. The Halakhah, Geiger indicated, was one such
form. From this, it followed that the project of modernization should seek
theoretical orientation not within the normative framework of Jewish law,
but by connecting itself to the spiritual core at the heart of Judaism—a
connection that could only be forged by the scholar trained in Wissenschaft. Though undeniably radical in his rebellion against *halakhic* authority, Geiger nevertheless insisted that change occur not via a total rupture
with the past, but in continuity with the determining *Geist* of Jewish history.
"[S]alvation will be found," he wrote, in the lead essay to the first volume of
his journal, "not in a violent and ruthless break with tradition, but in careful
research into the deeper decisive factors in history."[54]

Soon, Auerbach would strike up a lifelong friendship with Geiger, yet
already here he showed himself to be impressed by the latter's Reform philosophy, with its emphasis on the tracing of a telos immanent to Judaism.[55]
Countering the myth that Judaism had essentially stood still after the loss of
its political sovereignty, Auerbach insisted that Judaism had demonstrated
itself throughout its history as a religion capable of adaptation and development. If this notion had frequently served to legitimate reform against its
internal opponents, here it was directed externally, testifying to the ability
of Judaism to adjust to the opportunities afforded by emancipation and integration. Auerbach offers no program for change, but this is incidental to
his concerns here. Whatever form change takes, he appears to be suggesting, it should occur not through radical leaps, but in fundamental continuity
with the vital core of Jewish history, for "only when we attach ourselves to
the inheritance of the past can it be advanced . . . according to nature."[56]

Echoing Geiger, he argues that the task of distinguishing the essential from the peripheral in Judaism belongs to Wissenschaft. He remains confident, however, that Judaism can endure such scrutiny, contending, "The unification of faith and knowledge is, to Judaism, no mere fleeting demand of the times, but an eternal law."[57] However it may evolve, "Judaism can and will satisfy all the higher needs of mankind for all time."[58]

How does this liberal religious vision, optimistic at least in so far as the encounter between Judaism and modernity is concerned, relate to the image of Spinoza in Auerbach's novel of only a year later? Could Spinoza be reconciled with the view that "Judaism can and will satisfy the higher needs of mankind for all time"?

IV.

After concluding a contract with a Stuttgart publisher during his six-week internment in the Hohenasperg fortress, Auerbach completed his two-part novel about Spinoza in about seven months, in what he confessed to his cousin was a fit of inspired writing. "Dear Jakob! What my Spinoza was to me, what he is to me! I cannot explain it, a sacred awe seized me, whenever I thought about him."[59] Though mesmerized by the aura of his philosopher-hero, Auerbach intended the book as more than simply a portrayal of the young Spinoza. Entitled *Spinoza, A Historical Novel*, it was set forth in the preface as the first of many "Jewish novels" that would comprise a series called The Ghetto.[60] These works would complement the historiographic project of Wissenschaft des Judentums, providing a historical-fictional equivalent to the task of preserving images of a traditional way of life before its inexorable decline. "Jewish life is decomposing more and more," he wrote, "with one fragment after another being sloughed off; thus it seems to me that the time has come to let poetry and history and both together capture its movement in images."[61] Echoing the historicist rationale of his Wissenschaft colleagues, Auerbach goes on to argue that his program for Jewish literature will transcend the mere derision of the eighteenth century toward the unenlightened past. Instead, it will grant even the most absurd of beliefs and superstitions "poetic justice," appreciating their conformity with the spirit of their former setting. The contempt for Enlightenment negativity is familiar from *Das Judenthum*. At the same time, there is a new note of melancholy and doubt over the future of Judaism that contrasts with the forward-looking optimism of the prior work. "Nostalgia grips us," he writes, "when we observe this past; we have lost its old inwardness and only bit by bit gained a new version."[62] What was argued with assurance in the previous book—namely, that even with emancipation, Judaism would remain a vital and essential component of the *Weltgeist*—stands here under the shadow of a question: With the inevitable disappearance of traditional society, whither Judaism?

In choosing Spinoza as the subject of the first novel of this series, Auerbach confessed that he had started with what should have been its final installment, since it was Spinoza who had initiated the demise of the ghetto.[63] Yet the idea had gripped him so that he could not resist it; moreover, he added, if Spinoza had launched the unraveling of the traditional community, this process was still far from complete.[64] Though identified as a historical novel in the title, the book can also be read as a nineteenth-century bildungsroman in its depiction of the development of the hero from youth to maturity. It is meant to span fourteen years in Spinoza's life: from 1647 [*sic*], when the fifteen-year old protagonist is first encountered at the burial of Uriel Acosta, the other classic seventeenth-century Jewish heretic, to 1661, when he departs from Amsterdam, symbolizing the final rupture from his place of origin and the beginning of his career as a philosopher.[65] A period that in the early biographies of Lucas, Bayle, and Colerus had received only a few pages here circumscribes the entire narrative. Nevertheless, these biographies—particularly that of the Lutheran preacher Colerus—are the main source for Auerbach's reconstruction, an indebtedness he acknowledges in the voluminous chapter notes appended to the end of the book.[66] As he does with Spinoza's philosophy, Auerbach lifts a great deal that is attributed to the post-1661 period in the early accounts, retrojecting this material into his fictionalized version of the hero's "years of apprenticeship."

The novel traces Spinoza's evolution from rabbinic prodigy to lonely dissenter. His development is presented as a progressive emancipation from all prior social and religious bonds: from folk belief and superstition, from belief in both rabbinic authority and biblical infallibility, from observance of the law, from family and community, and eventually even from his coterie of non-Jewish friends and mentors. The result is that Spinoza ends up radically alone and autonomous, a stranger to both the Jewish and non-Jewish societies of his era. This alienation is the most pronounced feature of Auerbach's Spinoza—a fate that is saved from tragedy by virtue of the hero's extraordinary equilibrium and the retroactive vindication granted him by posterity, which the author symbolizes by crowning him as the secular messiah of modernity in a dream scene at the end of the novel.

That the bildungsroman would have appealed to Auerbach as a medium for revisiting Spinoza is understandable. The organic notion of development associated with this genre stipulated, as Goethe put it in his *Wilhelm*

Meisters Lehrjahre, that "all that we encounter leaves traces, everything con-
tributes imperceptibly to our formation."[67] Applied to Spinoza, this principle suggested an avenue for considering the significance of his Jewish
background to his philosophy that would resist two previously adduced alternatives in the history of his reception, both advanced by non-Jews starting in the seventeenth and eighteenth century. One frame—what we called
in chapter 1 the "ex-Jew" frame—was typical of the early biographies of
Spinoza; it cast Spinoza's Jewish inheritance as an antithesis to his rationalism, meaningful only in terms of bringing the latter into bold relief. The
other, "eternal Jew" frame identified Spinoza's Jewish birthright as the essential if implicit content of his thought, presenting Spinozism as a veiled
form of Kabbalah or Jewish mysticism. Auerbach, in line with the idea of
Bildung, proposed an option between these two extremes—that of perceiving Spinoza's Jewish origins as a shaping influence in the making of the
philosopher, while at the same time as only a preliminary stage in a path
that ultimately led beyond Judaism.

In tracing the impact of Spinoza's Jewishness, the novel highlights elements within the Jewish literary tradition that foreshadow his eventual
dissent. In an early scene the young Baruch fervently recites the first verse
of the Shema, affirming the oneness of God in a clear portent of his future
monism; later he studies the commentary of Ibn Ezra, where he discovers
implicit support for both his growing doubt about the Mosaic authorship of
the biblical text and his unified theory of substance; later still, he immerses
himself in an investigation of the Kabbalah, finding in its emanationist doctrines kernels of a pantheist theology.

By making Spinoza's native literature and society an embryo for his Bildung, Auerbach implies that his eventual heresy is not a simple betrayal
of his Jewish heritage but rather a development of earlier paradigms and
precedents. And indeed, in Spinoza's later encounters with freethinkers
from outside the community, he stands out for his relative moderation. He
rejects the suggestion of Ludwig Meyer, one of his Christian peers, that
"rationalism must strive to eliminate all positive faith and in particular all
biblical authority," arguing instead, in good Idealist fashion, that revelation and philosophy need not be at odds with each other, the former often
anticipating through the imagination what the latter arrives at via logical
demonstration.[68] Indeed, throughout the novel, Spinoza often resorts to the
use of a fragment from the Jewish tradition—not merely from the Bible,
but also from the Talmud and Jewish folklore—to illustrate a philosophical
truth. The most dramatic example of this comes in a chapter on Descartes,
where Spinoza employs a legend related by "old Chaje," his family's illiterate Ashkenazic maid, to point out the problems of Cartesian dualism.[69] Spi-

noza, then, models an orientation toward scripture and tradition that avoids the complete negativity of a ruthless materialism, but instead appreciates how kernels of both can be lifted and guided in the direction of greater cosmopolitanism.

In this light, the figure of Spinoza would appear to be a prototype of the "practical liberalism" sympathetic to religious traditions that Auerbach had commended in his previous essay. And this is indeed the claim of Jonathan Skolnik, a scholar of German Jewish literature, who takes Auerbach's image of Spinoza as fully in line with the reformist posture put forward in his own name in *Das Judenthum*. Countering the more common perception of Auerbach's *Spinoza* as a plea for Enlightenment universalism against all forms of religious particularism—a view encapsulated in one portrayal of the novel as a "utopia of total assimilation"[70]—Skolnik argues that such a zero-sum vision of the universal-particular relationship is in fact rejected in the work. Instead of flatly refuting the legacy of the historical religions, Auerbach's Spinoza combs them for elements of worldly value, seeking to liberate the universal potential that is lodged within the particular. "The factors so decisive for Auerbach in 'Das Judenthum und die neueste Literatur' remain operative," Skolnik concludes.[71]

Without denying such continuities between Auerbach's earlier statements and the Spinoza character of his novel, I want to analyze one scene that I believe complicates their resemblance. Just prior to his excommunication, Spinoza is visited in the novel by one of the luminaries of the Jewish community, Salomon da Silva. Historically, Da Silva, whose real first name was Samuel, was a Marrano physician from Portugal who became an apologist for rabbinic Judaism, best known for his official rebuttal to Uriel da Costa's heresy.[72] Though in fact Da Silva settled in Hamburg, Auerbach includes him here among Amsterdam Jewry, probably because of his association with Acosta. Within the novel, the erudite and polished Da Silva serves, like Manasseh ben Israel, as an exemplar of an openness toward general culture that stays within the bounds of rabbinic law. Early on, Da Silva facilitates the young Baruch's intellectual development by securing for him a teacher in Latin; now, he visits Spinoza in a desperate effort to prevent him from seceding:

> I confess . . . that Judaism has plenty of abuses and abnormal growths that must be done away with. When I was your age, I was also very troubled by this. The hotheaded youth always want to quickly lop off these growths, but that doesn't work. You must first seek to win the confidence of the people and not offend them, then eventually you may be able to achieve something and, little by little, carry out your plans. But the first rule is, whoever wishes to effect a transforma-

tion of any community in keeping with reason and the times, must never place himself outside it. So, my advice to you is—come back. Think, there are others upon whom the light of reason has dawned who nevertheless don't throw the old rites overboard at once. Much has happened in recent times: fifty years ago, anyone who would have said this would have been stoned. And thus it shall always be. If you return, you can help reform Judaism along with many bright minds, perhaps as their leader.[73]

Though Auerbach's portrait of this confrontation derives from the early biographies of Spinoza, which claimed that the Jewish leadership made numerous attempts to dissuade Spinoza from airing his heretical opinions—a claim that would be vindicated with the discovery of the actual text of the ban in the early 1860s—the content of his invented dialogue is clearly anachronistic. Jewish Reform, after all, was not an ideological option available in seventeenth-century Amsterdam, and thus Auerbach is truly "appropriating" these figures from their historical context to air a very contemporary dilemma.

Da Silva implores Spinoza to adopt a moderate as opposed to revolutionary approach to modernization. Yet Spinoza will have none of this gradualism: "Who told you, then," he replies to Da Silva, "that I want this? Maybe even a purified Judaism doesn't suit me, maybe I can't agree with its fundamental doctrines."[74] None of Da Silva's other arguments prove able to convince Spinoza to defer to the communal powers-that-be. Unsuccessful in his mission, Da Silva parts with tears in his eyes, while even Spinoza is described as "deeply shaken" and distressed.

When this exchange is read against the backdrop of Auerbach's prior work, we realize that clarifying where the author "stands" on the issues discussed here may not be as simple as identifying him with the philosopher he so obviously adores. The parallels between the sentiments ascribed to Da Silva and Auerbach's own arguments of a year before are striking, particularly in a novel where the relationship between author and hero appears otherwise so close. Da Silva begs Spinoza to settle for patiently guiding the *Volk* in the direction of greater universalism. Auerbach, in his earlier tract, had praised Lessing and Schiller—arguably the two German authors most beloved by nineteenth-century German Jews—for having done just that. They avoided the "elitist obscurity" of the French philosophes who "soared well beyond the emotions and inclinations of the so-called masses"; instead they "moved with loving modesty from hut to hut, admiring the upright virtue of the plainspoken *Bürger*, seeking little by little to weed out superstition and in the inwardness of faith to establish a boundless tolerance."[75] They exemplified, in other words, the "practical liberalism" lauded by Auerbach in *Das Judenthum*, and whose exponent here appears to be not Spinoza, but Da Silva. There is good reason to suspect that, in this scene, Auerbach is airing a very personal ambiguity over modern Jewish identity. Should one pursue the path of reform, working patiently and tactically for change even if it means accepting a certain *doubleness* between conviction and conduct? Or should one imitate the more categorical individualism of a Spinoza, emulating his efforts to attain total freedom and integrity, but at the expense of a nomadic and isolated existence?

The novel does not end with this confrontation. In the ensuing chapter about the excommunication, Spinoza—cast as a Jewish Luther, only without the support enjoyed by his sixteenth-century precursor—appears before a rabbinic court to answer charges against him. Instead of simply turning his back on the court, which is how Spinoza most likely responded, Auerbach's hero remonstrates with his accusers, contesting their allegations of heresy on the basis of his own reading of traditional sources.[76] He cites select biblical passages, along with medieval Jewish philosophers such as Ibn Ezra and Joseph Albo, to vindicate his argument for the sacred prerogative of natural reason vis-à-vis all other forms of knowledge. "In our reason," he claims, "on the heights of pure divine thought, here is Sinai."[77] If earlier, in his clash with Da Silva, Spinoza raised the possibility of a total rupture with Judaism, his method of disputation with his rabbinic interrogators suggests that his rationalism might indeed be viewed as a reinterpretation, and not simply a rejection, of his Jewish inheritance. One might conclude that Auerbach wishes to appropriate Spinoza here for the liberal Jewish theology he had advanced previously.[78] Yet even if this is so, it should be noted that the conception of reform appears to have shifted. Whereas in his earlier treatise, Auerbach vouches for a reform moored in the spiritual history of a Jewish *collectivity*, Spinoza, in this passage, grants authority solely to the realm of *individual* reason and conscience. If there is a reformist view here, then it is only a schismatic one—more reflective of the radical reform position later articulated by the nineteenth-century German rabbi Samuel Holdheim (1806–1860) than of the "historical Judaism" that Auerbach had defended in *Das Judenthum*.[79]

The book ends with a climactic confrontation meant to erase any doubt about the prototypical status of its hero. On the night before Spinoza is to leave Amsterdam for Rijnsburg, he is visited in a dream by Ahasverus, the Wandering Jew. According to a much-traveled Christian myth whose prominence in European literature dated back to Reformation Germany, the hoary figure of Ahasverus had been a living witness to the crucifixion of Jesus. His unnatural survival was a punishment for having taunted the Christian savior en route to the cross, as a result of which Jesus condemned him to roam the earth, without peace or rest, for eternity. Appearing to Spinoza here, Ahasverus narrates his tragic story and deplorable situation, before concluding by abruptly proclaiming the philosopher to be the long-awaited messiah: "You have come to be a redeemer of mankind; me too shall you redeem."[80] Though Auerbach was not shy about inventing episodes in his novel that could speak to contemporary dilemmas of Jewish integration and identity, here he abandons any pretense of historical realism in favor of a blatantly allegorical portrayal of Spinoza. To Christianity, the homeless-ness of the Jews was their punishment for the rejection and crucifixion of Jesus, a yoke that would be lifted only upon their conversion at the end of days. By casting Spinoza as the savior of the Wandering Jew, Auerbach sub-verts this expectation, ascribing to the Amsterdam heretic the redemptive function associated in Christianity with the second coming of Christ. In this new secular messianic myth, the isolation of the Jews would end not via conversion, but as a result of the emancipation from traditional religion set into motion by Spinoza, the first modern Jew.

One might view this ending as an effort to repair the various fissures exposed in the course of the narrative—between Spinoza and Da Silva, and the radical and reform-minded approaches to Jewish modernization they instance, and by extension between this novel and *Das Judenthum*. For in his redemption of Ahasverus, the ultimate symbol of Jewish particularity in Christian legend, Spinoza promises an end to the inescapable stigma of Jewishness, one of the foremost concerns of Auerbach's earlier essay. Still, the question of whether Judaism has a place in this prophecy, and if so what that place might be, goes unanswered. We are left to wonder: Is the enlight-ened and emancipated society imagined here as Spinoza's legacy compatible with an ongoing and positively affirmed Jewish difference—with the view expressed in *Das Judentum* that "Judaism can and will satisfy every need of mankind for all time"? Or is Spinoza being invoked as the forerunner of a fully assimilationist vision of the future that will climax in the dissolution of *all* confessional identities in a universal community of humanity?

V.

What I have tried to argue in this chapter is that Auerbach's pioneering portrayal of Spinoza as a progenitor of the modern, emancipated Jew, when examined up close and in the context of his earlier intellectual biography, contains a fundamental ambivalence over what it means to be a modern, emancipated Jew. For all the temporal and thematic proximity between *Das*

Judenthum and *Spinoza*, they are in many ways difficult to reconcile in their vision of Jewish modernity. One possibility for resolving this tension might be to suggest different target audiences for the two works. Jacob Katz, for instance, maintains that whereas the earlier *Das Judentum* defends the notion of a "modernized Judaism against external objectors," in *Spinoza* Auerbach writes "in the face of internal resistance."[81] Yet this contention is consistently vitiated in the course of the novel, starting with the preface, where Auerbach presents his book as a corrective to the silly and stereotypical image of Jews in German literature. The pronounced intertextuality of the 1837 novel vis-à-vis other works of German literature—something that is most strongly felt in the finale, which develops Goethe's never-realized literary ambition of staging an encounter between Spinoza and the Wandering Jew—speaks further to the implausibility of this suggested divide between an "internal" and "external" addressee.[82]

Alternatively, we might reason that Auerbach changed his mind with respect to the future of Judaism, and that he conveyed this reversal through his appropriation of Spinoza. These were years of decision for Auerbach. His former aspiration to become a liberal reformer working within the community appeared to have been dashed. A letter written by Auerbach to his cousin in the fall of 1836, between the publication of *Das Judenthum* and *Spinoza*, suggests that he was indeed grappling with the idea of a drastic aboutface: "Practically every morning I negate all my ideas and all my external attachments, in order to construct them afresh. I must do this if I am ever to achieve autonomy and independence from all and everything."[83] Over the course of his life, though Auerbach never repudiated his Judaism, it became more an expression of loyalty to personal origins—a matter of honor—than a strongly held religious identity. After writing one more "Jewish novel" about Haskalah poet Ephraim Kuh, Auerbach abandoned Jewish subject matter to focus primarily on Christian peasants, and presented in his wildly successful *Black Forest Village Stories* and later novels a more sanguine view of the tension between the individual and the community.[84]

Yet I would argue for another reading, one that does not try to remove the ambiguity in Auerbach's position by retrojecting later commitments onto the twenty-five-year-old author, but instead regards the clash between Da Silva and Spinoza as illustrative of a conflict found in many liberal Jewish thinkers during that decade. Indeed, the same Geiger who rejected the path of a "violent and ruthless break with tradition" in both his sermons and scholarship—and so deeply influenced the young Auerbach in this respect—sounded a very different tune in many of his personal letters to his friend Joseph Dernburg in the 1830s. "There is hardly any time left for a reformation; the only course possible now is revolution—and God grant that something new may then come forth."[85] These were Geiger's own words in June 1836, and their impatience and despair about the possibility of *any* reform of Judaism are echoed in other letters to Dernburg from this period. By appreciating this tension within Geiger, and seeing the 1830s as a decade when the course Jewish modernization would take—whether that of "reformation" or "revolution"—was still very much in question, we can better understand how Spinoza might be reclaimed in 1837 not in clear-cut support of one possibility against the other, but in a vacillation between both.

The friction between these two paths of modernization—reform and revolution—gains added resonance in the second, revised edition of the novel from 1854, where the standoff between Spinoza and Da Silva is expanded. Here, Auerbach drops a hint as to who the model for Da Silva might be. The issue at stake is Spinoza's pursuit of a single, absolute truth. Da Silva criticizes this quest, arguing, "God himself vouchsafes the multiplicity of truth."[86] Might there be an echo here of the conclusion of Mendelssohn's *Jerusalem*, with its rejection of a union of faiths on the grounds that "diversity is evidently the plan and purpose of Providence"?[87] Could it be that through this fictional quarrel, in addition to playing out his own identity crisis, Auerbach was in effect staging a debate between Spinoza and Mendelssohn, both candidates for the title of first modern Jew, rivals over what this entailed?

VI.

Auerbach's 1837 novel attracted relatively little notice. It received positive mention in Philippson's *Allgemeine Zeitung des Judenthums* by a reviewer who lauded "Herr Berthold Auerbach" for "giving us the first Jewish novel."[88] It received considerably less applause from David F. Strauss, Auerbach's mentor from his Tübingen days. Strauss may have been one of the inspirations for Auerbach's engagement with the Amsterdam philosopher, and from his later correspondence with his cousin, it is clear that Auerbach admired Strauss (with whom he remained lifelong friends) as something of a modern-day Spinoza, possessed with the same unyielding devotion to the "naked truth" as his seventeenth-century prototype.[89] His review of the *Spinoza* novel must therefore have come as a disappointment to Auerbach. While offering modest praise for Auerbach's evocation of the "local color" of Jewish life and even the external events of Spinoza's youthful experience, Strauss criticized the novel for failing to provide an aesthetically persuasive account of the inner life of Spinoza and its connection to his philosophical genius. Comparing the portrait of the hero to a sculpture hewn from marble, Strauss concluded that the author "had diligently chiseled the body of Spinoza with appropriate bearing and handsome attire; but in place of the head he had placed an edition of the complete works of the philosopher."[90] In any event, the book appears to have found few readers, and as such enjoyed no reprint, accounting for its extreme rareness today.

The fortunes of the second, revised edition of the *Spinoza* novel, of 1854, proved quite different.[91] By then, Auerbach was a celebrated author renowned for his "village stories" and for his German translation of Spinoza's collected works. The higher profile of the author, coupled with the continued mainstreaming of the philosopher in nineteenth-century liberal bourgeois culture, made for a much larger audience. Retitled *Spinoza: Ein Denkersleben* [Spinoza: A Thinker's Life], shorn of the elaborate footnotes of the original and of the general frame as a "Ghettoroman," this new version "proved to be one of Auerbach's most enduring works," undergoing some thirty editions by 1907.[92] Several translations followed, including into Dutch (1856), French (1858–59), English (1882), Hebrew (1898), and Yiddish (1917). Evidence of the impact of the novel on nineteenth- and even early-twentieth-century popular perceptions of the philosopher leads to more trails than can be followed. One finds Auerbach's portrait supplying the basis for the first biographical tribute to Spinoza in the Yiddish press in 1886.[93] In a very different setting, the distinguished English jurist and Spinoza aficionado Sir Frederick Pollock (1845–1937), in his *Spinoza: His Life and Philosophy* (1882), gave a glowing endorsement of Auerbach's historical novel, going so far as to assert that for those who "fear to attack technical works on philosophy, there can be no better introduction to Spinoza."[94]

More immediately, the ripples of Auerbach's novel were felt in the mid-century Hebrew Enlightenment of Central and Eastern Europe. In 1856, some four decades before the "official" translation of *Spinoza: Ein Denkersleben* into Hebrew, lengthy excerpts of the novel (no doubt, without subsidiary rights) were incorporated in the first work to call for the translation of Spinoza's oeuvre into the sacred tongue. Its publication would cause a ruckus without parallel in Spinoza's Jewish reception in nineteenth-century Europe. Let us turn, now, from Germany to Galicia, and more specifically to Salomon Rubin's *New Guide to the Perplexed*.

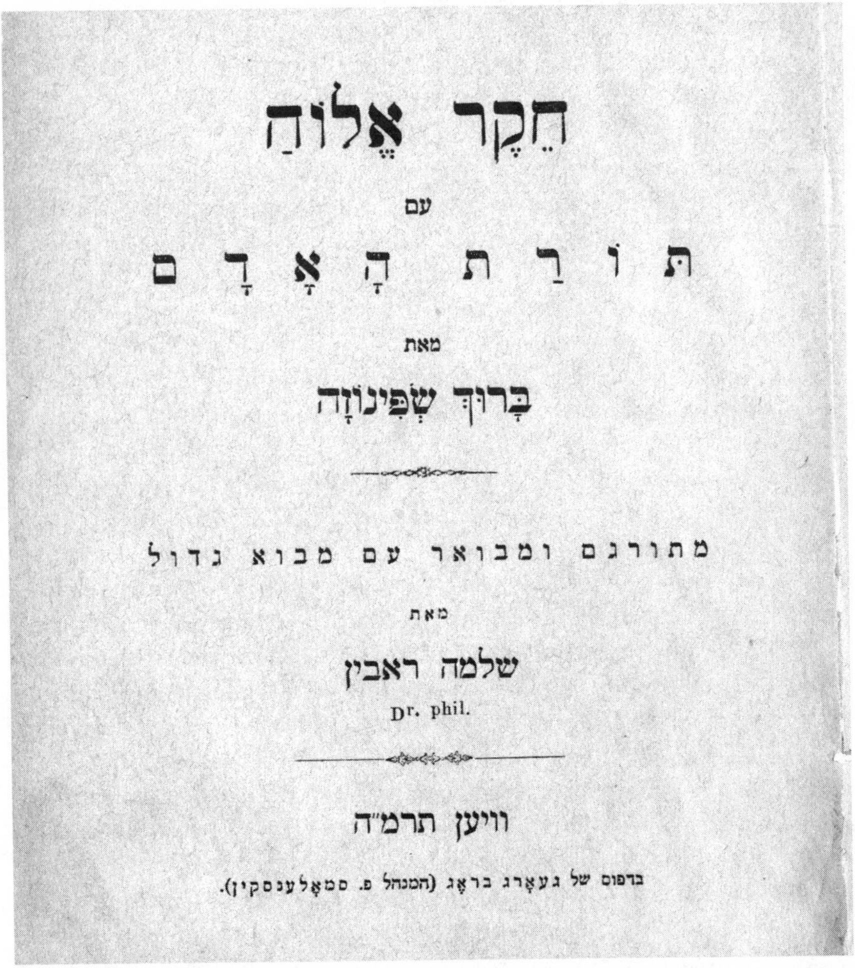

חֵקֶר אֱלוֹהַ

עם

תּ וֹ רַ ת הָ אָ דָ ם

מאת

בָּרוּךְ שְׁפִּינוֹזָה

―――⋆―――

מתורגם ומבואר עם מבוא גדול

מאת

שלמה ראבין

Dr. phil.

―――⋆―――

וויען תרמ"ה

בדפוס של געאָרג בראָג (המנהל פ. סמאָלענסקין).

---

*FIGURE. 4.1. Title page, S. Rubin's Hebrew translation of Spinoza's *Ethics* (Vienna, 1885). Courtesy of the Library at the Herbert E. Katz Center for Advanced Judaic Studies, University of Pennsylvania.

CHAPTER 4

A Rebel against the Past, A Revealer of Secrets

Salomon Rubin and the East European Maskilic Spinoza

I.

In 1856, exactly two hundred years after his excommunication by the Sephardic community of Amsterdam, Spinoza was reappropriated in Hebrew literature as the second coming of Maimonides. That fall, there appeared the first volume of a work named *Moreh nevukhim he-hadash* [The New Guide to the Perplexed].[1] Its author was Salomon Rubin, a native of Habsburg Galicia and relative newcomer to the Hebrew Enlightenment. Fresh from translating Karl Gutzkow's well-known drama *Uriel Acosta* into Hebrew, Rubin turned his attention in *The New Guide* to the other legendary Jewish heretic of seventeenth-century Amsterdam. In two volumes of roughly thirty pages each, Rubin provided a rambling apologia for an audacious venture—a proposal to translate Spinoza's two most famous works, the *Ethics* and the *Treatise*, into Hebrew. Yet the justification for this scheme was in fact already inherent in Rubin's title, which conferred on Spinoza's philosophical system the arresting label of a "new guide to the perplexed."

With this work, Rubin made a brash entrance into a controversy over Spinoza that had been simmering for just over a decade in Central and Eastern European Jewish culture. The opening salvo in this dispute had come back in 1845, with the publication by the Galician maskil Meir Halevi Letteris (1800–1871) of a flattering portrait of the Amsterdam philosopher in a Hebrew periodical.[2] Titled "The Life of the Wise Scholar Baruch de Spinoza," replete with the eulogistic phrase "may his memory be for a blessing" (*zikhrono li-berakhah*, or *z'l*) traditionally appended to the names of the departed, the article was the first ever to be devoted to Spinoza in Hebrew literature.[3] The hagiographic nature of this short profile, which went so far as to assert that the *Treatise* contained "not a whit of heresy" and that Spinoza's pantheism "rested on the foundations of our Sages" drew an angry response from two scholars from Northern Italy (then part of the Habsburg

Empire) who, like Letteris, were veteran affiliates of the Hebrew Enlightenment: Isaac Samuel Reggio (1784–1855) of Gorizia and Samuel David Luzzatto (1800–1865) of Padua.[4] Reggio and Luzzatto disagreed about much: The former was a committed rationalist and the latter an avowed antirationalist with regard to biblical exegesis, yet they shared an aversion to the effort to recover Spinoza for Judaism. Reggio, the editor of the journal in which Letteris's article had appeared, expressed his dismay in a footnote to the piece, asserting a "total contradiction" between the *Treatise* and the "fundamentals of the Torah."[5] Luzzatto was even more scathing in his criticism. As one who considered philosophic speculation to be utterly foreign to authentic Judaism, Luzzatto had previously protested the maskilic hero-worship of Maimonides and Ibn Ezra.[6] With Spinoza now ostensibly on the verge of being added to this canon, he once again entered the fray. In 1847 he opened a work of biblical commentary with a sharp attack on Spinoza, branding him an atheist undeserving of rehabilitation in any language, not to mention in the "holy vestments" of Hebrew. He implied that Spinoza's thought was responsible for all the ills of modern society and, without mentioning Letteris by name, accused him of misrepresenting the facts by "Judaizing" a traitor who "distanced himself from [his people], and neither lived with them nor died in their midst."[7]

If Luzzatto hoped his polemic might stem the growing attraction to Spinoza within the Haskalah, he was to be disappointed. In 1850 the Lithuanian-born Hebrew scholar Senior (Sheneur) Sachs (1816–1892) lent support to Letteris's blanket claim of a Jewish lineage for Spinoza's philosophy. In a collection of dense essays based for the most part on his research on the eleventh-century Andalusian poet and philosopher Solomon ibn Gabirol (Avicebron) and Ibn Ezra, Sachs situated Spinoza's pantheism within a line of development immanent to medieval Jewish Neoplatonism and the later Kabbalah.[8] Though Sachs did not shower the Amsterdam heretic with accolades, Luzzatto saw his writings as yet another sign of the creeping domestication of Spinoza's heresy, and once again he issued a livid rejoinder.[9]

Then came Rubin's *New Guide to the Perplexed* of 1856. If not the first attempt to reclaim Spinoza within the nineteenth-century Haskalah, this was easily the most far-reaching. By casting him as the heir to a now outdated Maimonides, Rubin was in effect vaulting Spinoza to the top of the Haskalah pantheon. Criticizing the continued veneration of antiquated models of philosophizing within the Haskalah, Rubin reserved his praise for those who "believed in the Lord and in His servant *Baruch*, and not in Aristotle and in *Moses* [i.e., Maimonides] his pupil."[10] With this wry twist on the biblical verse from Exodus 14 regarding the crossing of the sea—"and they believed in the Lord and in His servant *Moses*"—Rubin seemed to be suggesting that even the original Moses was not immune to being supplanted by the philosopher Baruch.

Rubin's plan to translate Spinoza into Hebrew left the already agitated Luzzatto apoplectic. That same year, he published a broadside against Spinoza and his youthful partisans in a Hebrew periodical; Rubin fired back with a stinging rebuke of Luzzatto; and so it went, back and forth, in both letters and articles, until Luzzatto's death in 1865.[11] At this point, Rubin's study of Spinoza had only begun to bear fruit. Before his death in 1910 at the age of eighty-seven, he would complete pioneering Hebrew translations of both the *Ethics*[12] and the *Compendium of Hebrew Grammar*,[13] a German dissertation contrasting Spinoza to Maimonides[14], and a few general introductions to Spinoza's thought in Hebrew.[15] These constituted only a portion of a vast scholarly and journalistic oeuvre, spanning six decades, whose main concerns included mysticism, folklore, and superstition, among both Jews and other peoples from the ancient Near East to present-day Eastern Europe.

The historian Jonathan Israel has become well known for arguing that the reception of Spinoza played a major part in the emergence and evolution of the so-called Radical Enlightenment of seventeenth- and eighteenth-century Europe. What distinguished this militant fringe from the "mainstream moderate Enlightenment," according to Israel, was its attitude toward tradition. Whereas the latter sought to "preserve and safeguard what were judged essential elements of the older structures, effecting a viable synthesis of old and new," the Radical Enlightenment "rejected all compromise with the past and sought to sweep away existing structures entirely."[16] Spinoza and Spinozism, moreover, were "the intellectual backbone of the European Radical Enlightenment everywhere," the symbol par excellence of this wing of the movement to sympathizers and opponents alike.[17]

This chapter probes the relationship between Spinoza and the radicalizing of Enlightenment in nineteenth-century Eastern European Jewish culture.[18] My focus is on the image of Spinoza in the work of Rubin, the greatest advocate of the dissident thinker within the Haskalah. One of the main dilemmas confronted by maskilim in their attempt to articulate a self-consciously modern Jewish identity concerned the perception of change. The questions that hovered over their polemical and pedagogical writings included: What kind of bond should the Haskalah maintain toward venerable Jewish texts and methods of study? How far should the movement go in accommodating novel ideas to classical exemplars so as to avoid the suggestion of a rupture with the past? What were the limits of innovation? These issues were at the core of Rubin's engagement with Spinoza. The Israeli historian Shmuel Feiner, in his book *Haskalah and History*, writes that Rubin's Spinoza "was not a legitimate bearer of Jewish tradition but a religious revolutionary relying solely on his intelligence . . . an example of Kantian man, proclaiming his own full freedom."[19] Feiner sees this appropriation as symptomatic of a growing militancy in the East European Haskalah at midcentury—the emergence of a rebellious orientation no longer obsessed with presenting itself as "the authentic heir of the Jewish past," but openly committed to the modern and secular as such.

That Rubin intended to radicalize the Haskalah by hailing Spinoza over Maimonides is clear. Yet the relationship between Spinoza and the Jewish past, as represented by Rubin, is in fact more complicated than Feiner concedes. For all his emphasis on the trailblazing nature of Spinoza—the "new guide to the perplexed"—in contrast to Maimonides, Rubin also portrays the heretic as the offspring of an esoteric legacy of speculation embedded within Jewish thought. A rebel against Jewish tradition, and a revealer of its secrets: An appreciation of this tension within Rubin's Spinoza is vital, as it not only provides a key to the nineteenth-century East European Jewish reception of the philosopher in a broader sense, but also suggests ambivalence to the modernizing thrust of the Jewish version of radical Enlightenment.

II.

The attraction to Spinoza on the part of East European Hebraists such as Rubin and Letteris was similar to that of the German Jewish thinkers of the 1830s and 1840s. Both groups saw Spinoza as a champion of such liberal values as rationality, individuality, freedom of thought, and intellectual daring. Both drew inspiration for celebrating the Amsterdam heretic by the fact of his reclamation within German philosophy starting in the late eighteenth century. And both, finally, felt a special kinship with Spinoza as a Jew who had asserted his independence from tradition without converting to another religion. Nevertheless, nineteenth-century German Jewish culture and the Eastern European Haskalah diverged in both context and sensibility—and the recovery of Spinoza in these two settings, notwithstanding the proximity in time and common motivations in each, differed accordingly.

Letteris and Rubin belonged to the first and second generations, respectively, of the Galician Haskalah.[20] The Haskalah emerged in the once Polish territory of Galicia in the first decades of the nineteenth century, at exactly the same time as the movement was petering out in its original Prussian context. Its migration to Galicia came on the heels of the ceding of the province to the Central European Habsburgs in the first Polish partition of 1772, as a result of which Galician Jewry would ultimately be included within the Enlightenment reforms of the Emperor Joseph II.[21] From Austrian Galicia, the Haskalah eventually spread into the Jewish communities of the Russian Empire in the 1830s and 1840s. In both these locations, which together housed the vast majority of what once had been Polish Jewry, the Jewish Enlightenment remained an active cultural current through most of the nineteenth century. Its chief language of expression was Hebrew, with the result that the East European Haskalah is sometimes called the Hebrew Enlightenment. This Hebraic character was critical in distinguishing the reception of Spinoza by the maskilim from that within German Jewry. In part, the use of Hebrew was a tactical move, a way of broadening the cultural horizons of young Jewish males (and a smaller number of females) in a language that would be familiar to them, while avoiding a Yiddish vernacular seen as irremediably corrupt. Yet it was also supported by a genuine, if rudimentary ideology of Hebraism, which drew on the traditional sanctity of the language and imagined Hebrew as a formative and organic factor in Jewish peoplehood.

We find this reasoning in Rubin's defense of his plan to render Spinoza in Hebrew:

> It is incumbent upon every language, new or old, Western or Eastern, living or dead, to gather into her store of rhetoric the choicest, most noble and useful works of all her sister tongues . . . and to nestle them in her bosom like the fruit of her womb, so that they become to her like her own favorite children.
>
> Surely, then, every language enjoys an added birthright [*mishpat ha-bekhorah*] in repossessing her lost children, who were taken from her breasts and given over to the embrace of a foreign bosom. . . .
>
> Who, then, will deny to our holy language the right to restore to her bosom the words of Spinoza, her *Hebrew son*, in whom she enjoyed no pleasure all the days of his life, so that she should at least after his death rejoice in his philosophy that was founded on the sacred mountain of Scripture, in the Torah of her prophets and teachers, whose banner she has waved over centuries . . . ?[22]

Thirty years later Rubin would reiterate this rationale for translating Spinoza's *Ethics* into Hebrew with the blunt assertion that "ours is the birthright" (*lanu mishpat ha-bekhorah*).[23] There is a Hebraic origin to the philosophy of Spinoza—an origin that in the Romantic logic employed here is the mark of true essence. Hebrew serves here as the ultimate mark of Jewishness, though this secularizing impulse is checked by Rubin's suggestion of a bond between "our holy language" and a specific religious content: the "sacred mountain of Scripture," the "Torah of her prophets and teachers."

This was a rather different tack toward reclaiming Spinoza than had been taken by the German Jewish intellectuals of the previous chapter. Berthold Auerbach, for instance, approached Spinoza through the eyes of one who saw himself as Jewish by confession and German by nationality.[24] He viewed the German high culture in which the seventeenth-century philosopher had been absorbed—his embrace by Lessing, Herder, and Goethe—as his *own* patrimony, and he both wrote about and translated Spinoza with the aim of introducing him to German readers of any religious background. In line with the evolutionary model of Abraham Geiger's Reform philosophy, Auerbach sought to highlight the role played by usable precedents in the Jewish past in Spinoza's self-formation; he also finished his novel with an image of Spinoza as a prototype of the modern Jew's break with the constraints of rabbinic law and assimilation into the surrounding culture sans conversion. Yet he certainly did not write to assert a uniquely Jewish hold on Spinoza; on the contrary, he viewed efforts to "Judaize" the Amsterdam philosopher with suspicion, equating them with a betrayal of the Enlightenment ideals of universal reason and common humanity. Rubin was not bothered by this concern. Like most other Hebrew maskilim who lived in the multinational empires of nineteenth-century Eastern Europe, even those who were most critical of tradition, he saw no contradiction between a continued affirmation of Jewish linguistic and cultural particularism and the entry of Jews into European culture and society. Rubin could claim Spinoza—the "Hebrew son"—specifically for Jewish culture, without, in his mind, violating the integrationist spirit of the maskilic project.

One key aspect of the Hebraizing of Spinoza in the East European Jewish Enlightenment, then, was the ethnic self-assertion this appropriation revealed. Another element that must be considered is the rhetorical nature of Haskalah Hebrew. The maskilim tended toward a highly florid and allusive Hebrew known as *melitsah*. This form favored the use of biblical and, to a lesser extent, rabbinic phrases, so as to create a virtual echo chamber of canonical references within the text.[25] There was a double-edged thrust to this maskilic strategy. On one hand, the heavy dose of citations might serve as a bridge between traditional Jewish literature (itself laden with intertextuality) and Haskalah writing, obscuring the novelty that characterized the latter. Yet this essentially classicizing impulse could easily be adapted for seditious ends, since it abetted the transposing of deviant subject matter into a familiar register. Moreover, it did this often in a veiled and indirect manner, without clearly delineating for the reader the passage being quoted or parallel being drawn. Haskalah Hebrew thus facilitated a recovery of Spinoza for Judaism at the level of style alone, over and beyond any explicit rationale detailed on the surface of the text. The splicing of sacred, or at least venerable texts into the Hebrew appropriations of Spinoza lent them a fundamentally different inflection than anything written in a non-Jewish language. For those opposed to Spinoza, like Luzzatto, the assimilation of his image and thought to Judaism via Hebrew melitsah could not be anything but heretical. Still, the question of intent—whether an individual maskil, in enveloping his reclamation of Spinoza with biblical and medieval allusions, did so sincerely or subversively—cannot be answered in the abstract. In the same work, the invocation of classical phrases or exemplars might be meant to anchor Spinoza in Jewish sources in one place, and to rattle the tradition in another. In using the vocabulary of medieval Jewish thought to depict Spinoza, Rubin was being sincere. There are other instances, however, where his use of melitsah is clearly ironic. In one of his many flourishes, he writes that "everyone, young and old, cleric and layman, rabbi and philosopher now supplicate before the dust of Baruch, and to his name and memory *all say: 'Glory.'*"[26] The final snippet comes from the ninth verse of Psalm 29, where it denotes the universal acknowledgment of the glory of God in his temple. To write Spinoza into the tradition of Jewish philosophical speculation was one thing, to surreptitiously equate him with the God of the Bible quite another. The familiarity of this psalm to any Hebrew reader, moreover, given its regular recitation in the Sabbath liturgy, would have made this example of melitsah all the more mischievous.

A blurring of the boundaries between the old and new was thus one of the by-products of maskilic Hebrew. It was also characteristic of the incipient critical study of the past in the Hebrew Enlightenment. In the 1820s and 1830s, soon after Wissenschaft des Judentums originated in the German Jewish milieu, a modern Jewish scholarship in Hebrew emerged in the periodical literature of the Galician Haskalah. In time, this Hebrew discourse became known as Hokhmat Yisrael, literally the "wisdom of Israel." Its leading early practitioners included the Galician thinkers Shlomo J. L. Rapoport (1790–1867) and Nahman Krochmal (1785–1840), along with the aforementioned Italians Luzzatto and Reggio. Despite appearing at roughly the same historical moment as Jewish research in German, and ultimately coming to serve as the term most commonly used to render Wissenschaft des Judentums in Hebrew, Hokhmat Yisrael differed from its German Jewish equivalent in ways that have become the subject of growing attention.[27] Generally speaking, Hokhmat Yisrael was marked by a much closer tie to traditional methods and sources than was Jewish Wissenschaft. Whereas the founders of Wissenschaft, including Leopold Zunz, Eduard Gans, and

Immanuel Wolf, were fresh from a university education that had exposed
them to cutting-edge methods of historical and philological criticism as
well as to an overall ethos of freedom of inquiry, the pioneers of Hokhmat
Yisrael were autodidacts whose models for research stemmed, to a much
greater extent, from within their Jewish intellectual heritage. Rapoport, for
instance, whose bibliographic essays on the Gaonim (or heads of the medieval Babylonian Talmudic academies) are generally considered the starting
point for the critical study of this subject, derived methodological inspiration from lexicons and biographical indices within rabbinic literature.[28]
Luzzatto, meanwhile, identified his willingness to interpret the Bible con-
textually, even when this yielded a reading contrary to rabbinic tradition,
with medieval practitioners of literal exegesis such as Rashi and his grand-
son Samuel ben Meir.[29] And if the early Wissenschaft figures were typically
reformers who sought to historicize Jewish writing and praxis as part of an
agenda of far-reaching religious change, scholars such as Rapoport, Krochmal, and Luzzatto, for all their forays into textual and even historical criticism, remained fundamentally dedicated to the authority of Jewish law.

The difference between these two discourses shines through in the
phrases that were adopted to designate them. The term *Wissenschaft* implied
a basic watershed in the view of Jewish tradition—the ideal of evaluating its
entirety from a standpoint of pure objectivity. The Hebrew expression of
Hokhmat Yisrael had a much different resonance. First mentioned in a rabbinic midrash, the phrase eludes precise definition.[30] What is clear, however,
is that throughout the nineteenth century, Hokhmat Yisrael signified not
merely the new critical inquiry that was taking shape in the Hebrew Haskalah, but a much more expansive sense of an intellectual tradition immanent to Judaism. The question of how to demarcate this tradition provoked
fierce controversy in the Galician Haskalah. If the originators of modern
scholarship in Hebrew—Luzzatto, Krochmal, and Rapoport—were, as I
mentioned before, united in their commitment to Halakhah, they clashed
bitterly over which legacies from the spectrum of Jewish literature should
be considered legitimate and normative. Was Hokhmat Yisrael synonymous
with the elitist rationalism of Maimonides and the medieval philosophers?
Did the Jewish Neoplatonism found in Ibn Ezra and the later Kabbalah have
a place in this orbit? Or, as Luzzatto argued against Rapoport and Krochmal, did these speculative and allegorizing currents represent a Greek, or
"Atticist," perversion of the historical Judaism upheld by such thinkers as
Yehudah Halevi? Here, I wish only to underscore that however Hokhmat
Yisrael was circumscribed, the underlying assumption was of a continuum
linking the medieval to the modern. When Letteris, then, labeled Spinoza
"one of the *hakhme yisrael*" in his groundbreaking article of 1845, this had

reverberations that went well beyond the literal sense of "sages of Israel." In the jargon of the Hebrew Enlightenment, he was situating Spinoza in an authentic tradition of Jewish thought even before spelling out any concrete linkage.

To sum up, the Hebrew Enlightenment of Central and Eastern Europe formed a distinct paradigm of reception for a figure like Spinoza. The perception of tension between the old and the new was less acute within the Haskalah than in nineteenth-century German Jewish culture, or at least there was a penchant toward disguising innovation as tradition. In that case, what are we to make of Rubin's presentation of Spinoza in 1856 as the *New Guide to the Perplexed*?

III.

Rubin was born in 1823 in the small town of Dolina in eastern Galicia. The story told by his biographers—the doyen of Hebrew literary history, Yosef Klausner, and the German rabbi turned social democrat, Jakob Stern— deviates little from what might be considered the template of Haskalah narratives about the making of a maskil.[31] The typical stages of development are all there: his schooling in the traditional heder and yeshiva of Eastern Europe; his arranged marriage while still in adolescence; his resistance to following the rabbinic path urged upon him by his elders; his discovery of critical perspectives in Hebrew texts (the commentary of Ibn Ezra, the medieval treatises on Hebrew grammar, and so forth) that had been marginalized in his Talmudic education; his subsequent acquisition of German, French, and Latin and perusal of foreign works; his wandering from place to place to eke out a modest living.

It was not until the 1850s that Rubin became an active contributor to the Hebrew Haskalah. His entry into the public sphere came at a time of growing radicalization in the Galician branch of the Jewish Enlightenment. Under the banner of Joshua Heschel Schorr (1818–1895), there rose around midcentury a young and iconoclastic generation of maskilim imbued with the revolutionary spirit of 1848 and impatient with the cautious approach to historical criticism of tradition exhibited by the elders of the movement, such as Reggio and Rapoport. The periodical *He-Haluts* [The Pioneer], founded by Schorr in 1852, became the principal organ of these religious radicals. In a mix of scholarly and satirical essays, Schorr subjected rabbinic interpretations of the Torah and the legislation to which they gave rise to withering critique.[32] Moreover, inspired by the example of Abraham Geiger, he fixed his arrows not just on the Oral Law but, increasingly, on the Written Law itself, becoming the first Hebrew writer to embrace a historical-critical approach to the Pentateuch and, without repudiating the *idea* of Revelation, to treat at least the *text* of the Torah as an essentially human document. In place of the Halakhah, whose authority for the present he plainly rejected, Schorr maintained that the essence of Judaism was monotheism, the "pure belief" in God's oneness and unity. Here, then, was an ideological break with Jewish law in Hebrew literature that, like the Reform movement in Germany, declared itself neither heresy nor apostasy, but authentic Judaism.

Rubin never published in Schorr's journal; nor did he make the campaign for religious reform a centerpiece of his writing. Yet his sympathy with the openly defiant ethos of *He-Haluts* was made clear beginning with his 1856 Hebrew translation of Karl Gutzkow's decade-old German play *Uriel Acosta*.[33] Gutzkow was one of the original members of Young Germany, the left-wing movement that had roiled German letters in the 1830s with its scathing attacks on revealed religion. In *Uriel Acosta*, a political drama cum romantic tragedy that was an adaptation of a novella he had written over ten years earlier, Gutzkow cast the excommunicated Jewish freethinker of seventeenth-century Amsterdam as a martyr in the struggle for religious liberty.[34] Debuting not long before the revolutions of 1848, the play proved far more successful than Gutzkow's earlier novella, becoming almost overnight a symbol of the cause of liberal nationalists throughout Europe. Interest surged in the life and writings of the ill-fated Acosta.[35] Meanwhile, the Hebrew version of *Uriel Acosta* produced by Rubin was one of several translations of Gutzkow's work in the second half of the nineteenth century.[36]

Merely the decision to render this play in Hebrew, and thereby reclaim a notorious critic of biblical infallibility and talmudic law for modern Jewish culture, could have sufficed to cement a reputation for Rubin as one of the newly emergent maskilic rebels.[37] If there were any doubts about his alliance with this camp, he erased them in a long foreword "to the enlightened and critical reader," where he sought to make the contemporary relevance of Acosta's plight perfectly transparent.

Part of this resonance, we learn here, was quite personal. At the time Rubin published his translation, he was living alone in the Romanian city of Galatz (Galati), working as a bookkeeper for a large firm while his wife and children remained over the border in his native Galicia. Four years earlier, he had left the Galician townlet of Zhuravne (Zurawno), where he had been employed as a tutor in foreign languages, after running afoul of the Hasidic majority. After word circulated of a manuscript Rubin had written harshly critical of Hasidism, the communal authorities placed him in herem. In a small town heavily populated by Hasidim, where job opportunities for a maskilic tutor were already limited, this was enough to drive Rubin to leave and find work elsewhere.

That this excommunication shaped Rubin's identification with Gutz-kow's Acosta is clear from his preface. In a segment denouncing Jewish priests and rabbis throughout the ages for their autocratic behavior, Rubin, in typical maskilic fashion, provides a genealogy of their alleged victims. Beginning with Moses and the biblical prophets, he mentions the two classic heroes of the Haskalah, Maimonides and Mendelssohn, before proceeding to lament the recent demise of the Galician reformer Abraham Kohn, a liberal rabbi in Lemberg (Lviv) who had been poisoned to death by his Hasidic opponents back in 1848.[38] His list of casualties concludes as follows:

> My heart burns like a raging fire when I recall how in my destitute, rebellious days in the land of my birth Galicia, in that smallest of towns Zhuravne, the rabbis, judges, and Hasidim, like a colony of locusts, gathered against me to destroy me. They sounded the *shofar* and humiliated me, shouting *Herem!*—all on account of my book *Spider's Web*, in which I admonished their crooked ways, and explained a mere trifle of their obscure doctrines, and roused my brothers to open their eyes and hearken to what the new times demand of them!
>
> Uriel too, this Uriel Acosta, is not a fresh creation of this poet, but in fact lived some two hundred years ago in the city of Amsterdam.[39]

The juxtaposition of his ban with that of Acosta suggests that, whatever the differences in their practical ramifications, for Rubin they were one and the same, an expression of the despotic nature of rabbinic authority from time immemorial. Indeed, we find here a biographical dimension to the East European attraction to heretics like Acosta and Spinoza—a common experience of excommunication, however distinct in form and context—that was absent in the case of the German Jewish intellectuals of chapter 3.

In addition to stressing his own bond with Acosta, Rubin identified each of the play's characters with a distinctive social type "in the congregation of Israel in our days." Uriel, not surprisingly, he called the "standard-bearer of the young, honest, and enlightened faction of our people, sifting and sounding out the certainties of faith, bringing the meditations of scholars of other nations to bear upon the Torah and Talmud, slow to believe and quick to put into question . . . a painful thorn and stinging barb in the eyes of the rabbis."[40] He was, in other words, a "Young Hebrew" along the lines of Schorr and the other radical maskilim, waving the flag for unfettered freedom of thought. The total integrity of Acosta is put into relief by Rubin's profile of another of the dramatis personae, the figure of Da Silva. Da

Silva, it will be recalled from the previous chapter, was the author of the Portuguese *Treatise on the Immortality of the Soul*, the main treatise defending the rabbinic doctrine of immortality of the soul against Acosta. Though this former Marrano physician from Portugal in fact settled in Hamburg, Gutzkow—like Auerbach in his *Spinoza*—took the license of placing him in Amsterdam.[41] Da Silva, Rubin wrote, bore the mark of

> the moderates among our people: an expert in Torah and Talmud as well as an investigator into the wisdom of the nations, a student of the ancient philosophers— Plato, Aristotle, and their peers—a product of the *bet midrash* of the Arabs in Spain. Such a man is similar to the enlightened Talmudists in our times, proficient in the Talmud and its commentaries in addition to the *Book of Doctrines and Beliefs*,[42] the *Guide to the Perplexed*, the *Akedah*,[43] the *Principles*[44] and other scholarly and scientific works composed from the period of the Geonim to the fourth century of this millennium.[45] Such a man has a hand everywhere—he is with both the rabbis and the *maskilim*, abandoning neither camp. He knows how to compromise in everything; in his heart he is a *scholar* and on the outside a *rabbi*. He flatters the beliefs and customs of the masses, currying favor among them for the sake of his present welfare and livelihood, even though he is supposed to be a healer. Such a man is like "a lodge in a garden of cucumbers,"[46] tossed about by every wind, never standing firm.[47]

According to the translator, Da Silva and Acosta were in fact prototypes of the current clash of generations between the old and new guards of the Galician Haskalah. In Da Silva's equivocation, in his stale philosophical knowledge, in his unwillingness to risk anything for the sake of freedom of thought, Rubin saw the quintessence of the maskilic middle. In the skeptical, searching, instinctively sincere Acosta—whom in a later article Rubin would compare to the medieval Jewish martyrs of cherished memory—he saw the epitome of the Jewish Enlightenment ideal of *hakirah*, or critical inquiry.[48]

Soon after translating *Uriel Acosta*, Rubin came out with the first volume of his book on Spinoza. Possibly, it was his reading of Gutzkow that motivated this progression from one Amsterdam heretic to another. Near the end of Gutzkow's play, a young Baruch strolls with Acosta (portrayed here as his uncle) in a garden, working out the rudiments of his future philosophy while his despondent predecessor contemplates suicide. The torch is thus figuratively passed from the herald of modernity to its secular messiah. Rubin's title for his translation, however, suggested a different trajectory for his road to Spinoza, one originating not in another radical dissenter, but in the veritable dean of Haskalah cultural heroes—Maimonides.

IV.

The title alone of Rubin's *The New Guide of the Perplexed* was, to use Erich Auerbach's phrase, "fraught with background." First, there was the obvious reference to Maimonides, and to the role both his image and his philosophical tour de force had played in the history of the Jewish Enlightenment. The title also carried echoes of *Moreh nevukhe ha-zeman* [The Guide to the Perplexed of the Time (1851)], the unfinished opus of Jewish philosophy authored by one of the luminaries of the Galician Haskalah, Nahman Krochmal.[49] Finally, there was the adjective "new," with all the weight this term carried in a movement where innovation was often presented as tradition rightly understood.

One of the hallmarks of the Haskalah was its attempt to revive the legacy of medieval Sephardic rationalism.[50] This inheritance functioned as a "usable past," providing an internally derived license for the effort to extend the scope of Jewish education beyond its largely talmudic focus in "baroque" Ashkenazic culture. In addition to the study of the Bible and of Hebrew grammar, the maskilim encouraged a renewal of the medieval philosophic tradition that had flourished in the Sephardic milieu. They recovered and reprinted philosophical and literary texts that had been marginalized for centuries, drew heroic portraits of exemplars of premodern rationalism in the new Hebrew press, and frequently used the language and genres characteristic of earlier Jewish philosophy (to wit, the commentary) for the dissemination of their own thought.

The prime beneficiary of this reclamation of medieval philosophy was, not surprisingly, the individual most synonymous with this heritage, a figure whose preeminence was reflected in his common designation in Jewish sources as the "great eagle"—Maimonides. Within the Haskalah, only Moses Mendelssohn himself could match the Rambam (the acronym for Rabbi Moses ben Maimon by which Maimonides was conventionally known) in symbolic clout. In the pages of *Ha-me'asef* [The Gatherer], the groundbreaking Haskalah periodical of the 1780s, a Maimonides myth took shape that enlisted the philosopher as a prototype of the values most dear to the Jewish Enlightenment, celebrating such features as his rationalism, his distinction beyond the limits of Jewish society, his achievement of a fruitful synthesis of Jewish and secular knowledge, and (most problematically) his commitment to universalism and tolerance. This iconic image of Maimonides (the Rambam) was entwined with that of Mendelssohn (the Rambaman, or Rabbi Moses ben Menahem-Mendel) to form a composite ideal of the rational and cultivated Jew, encapsulated in the familiar adage "from Moses to Moses, there was no one like Moses."[51]

The cult of Maimonides within the Haskalah extended to his masterwork of medieval rationalist exegesis, *The Guide of the Perplexed*. Mendelssohn, it will be recalled, was said by his maskilic biographer to have attributed his famous humpback to days and nights spent hunched over the *Guide* in his youthful zeal to understand it.[52] The more radical Jewish thinker Salomon Maimon (1754–1800) paid even greater tribute to Maimonides, adopting the surname Maimon to express his indebtedness to the *Guide* for its direction on the road to enlightenment. In addition to devoting most of the second part of his *Autobiography* to an exposition of the *Guide* for a largely non-Jewish readership, Maimon composed an anonymous Hebrew commentary to the first part of the work for the benefit of the Berlin Haskalah.[53]

The passion for Maimonides and the *Guide* was arguably even more earnest in the Haskalah of Eastern Europe to which Rubin was heir. This popularity had much to do with demographics. The struggle against Hasidism that occupied center stage in this outpost of the Jewish Enlightenment, coupled with the marginality and alienation of the maskilim in East European Jewish society, made their rationalism all the more militant.[54] This was one factor in the intensity of the attachment to Maimonides among these modernists. The Galician Haskalah yielded both a new Hebrew translation of Maimonides' *Guide* and numerous appropriations of the twelfth-century philosopher as a symbol of reason and enlightenment against Hasidic folly.[55] A glimpse of the stature enjoyed by the *Guide* is afforded by a letter published in the first edition of *Kerem Hemed*, the leading journal of the Galician Haskalah in the 1830s. Presumably written by Rapoport, the missive prescribes a strict regimen of readings of Maimonides for a friend wavering in his commitment to Haskalah, beginning with the legal works and culminating in the *Guide*: "Give this [i.e., the *Moreh*] your complete attention, and do not stop until you have finished. Do not let a difficult chapter keep you from moving onward, for sometimes a later [section] will shed light on an earlier [one]. Besides, even the little you grasp on first reading will delight you like one who discovers a great bounty, and soon, as your eyes are further opened, you will come to understand everything therein."[56]

Well into the nineteenth century, then, grounding in the *Guide* continued to be seen by many as a crucial part of the education of the would-be maskil. This was so notwithstanding the considerable friction between the medieval Aristotelian framework of Maimonides and the methods and parameters of modern science and philosophy. From both the biographical sketch of the Rambam printed in *Ha-me'asef* and the diverse commentaries written on the *Guide*, it is clear that even those Hebrew authors most committed to revitalizing the Maimonidean legacy were often aware of this gap. Their response was generally to seek to reinterpret Maimonides to accommodate him to contemporary intellectual trends.[57] At its most extreme, this led to the omission or outright deletion of those aspects of Maimonides' life and thought that clashed with the zeitgeist. We find this approach in the Galician maskil Mendel Lefin's commentary on the *Guide*. Writing in the wake of Kant, Lefin emphasized the epistemologically modest strands in Maimonides (for instance, his "negative theology") while ignoring the more boldly speculative ones.[58] Others, even in appropriating Maimonides, more openly acknowledged their rejection of various elements of his philosophy. Salomon Maimon exhibited this tack in his *Givat Ha-moreh* [Hill of the Guide].[59] Unlike most traditional commentators, Maimon acknowledged his intent to evaluate Maimonides' *Guide* from the vantage point of current knowledge.[60] At times he tried to save Maimonides by indicating how his arguments, read selectively and between the lines, could be reconciled with modern science; at other times he frankly dismissed Maimonides' proofs as outmoded. Still, the mere fact that he expressed his reservations as part of a chapter-by-chapter exegesis indicates a desire to bridge the gap between Maimonides and recent philosophy, wherever possible. By working within the framework of the *Guide* he implied that it was still relevant, particularly for the didactic aims of the Jewish Enlightenment.

The maskilim, then, not only celebrated Maimonides as a model of intellectual harmonization, but often put this ideal into practice in their interpretations of his life and work. They did so in part to anchor their innovations in an august figure whose *Guide*, at least in the Haskalah if not necessarily in traditional society, was widely regarded as on the safe side of heresy. Rubin balked at this deference, yet he was not the first to see the need for a *Guide to the Perplexed* better suited to the age; Nahman Krochmal had already composed a work in this vein, *The Guide to the Perplexed of the Time*. What relevance did this exemplar of nineteenth-century Jewish religious thought have to Rubin's project of reclaiming Spinoza? Was there a deliberate echo in Rubin's choice of title—not only of Maimonides' *Guide*, but also of Krochmal's updated version of this classic?

Born in 1785 Krochmal spent all fifty-five years of his life in Galicia, mostly in the cities of Brody and Zolkiew.[61] Despite publishing very little, he influenced successive generations of the Galician Haskalah through his private mentoring and correspondence and had many who considered themselves his disciples. He died in 1840 before completing his *Guide to the Perplexed of the Time*. First published in 1851, eleven years after his death, Krochmal's seventeen-chapter opus was a dense mélange of metaphysical speculation, idealistic philosophy of Jewish history, and historical criticism of Jewish religious literature. Through his *Guide*, Krochmal, an instinctive moderate, sought to help the contemporary maskil confront the challenges of the modern age without losing his balance and seeking refuge in either secular heresy or religious fanactisim. His strategy was to initiate the reader into a deeper understanding of Jewish sources, "in the manner of Maimonides in his book *Moreh nevukhim* . . . yet with deviations large and small in both subject and syntax, in line with the demands of the perplexities of the time in which we are living."[62]

Briefly, I want to identify some key aspects of Krochmal's *Guide* that would reverberate in Rubin's later project:

The ambivalent use of Maimonides. As is evident from the excerpt cited above, Krochmal felt that a *Guide to the Perplexed* modeled after that of Maimonides could speak to the crisis within nineteenth-century Judaism. At the same time, the original was no longer sufficient to the task. That Krochmal opted to bridge the divide between Maimonides' *Guide* and the current state of affairs by writing what amounted to a "new guide" and *not* through a commentary—the genre that earlier maskilim as opposite in temperament and ideology as the cautious Lefin and the radical Maimon had employed in their own efforts to modernize Maimonides—is a mark of the boldness of his design. Most important, Krochmal took from Maimonides the general aim of seeking to extrapolate a philosophy from Jewish sources that could resolve the ostensible contradiction between Judaism and contemporary thought.[63] What he explicitly eschewed was the Aristotelian metaphysics of Maimonides and his school.[64] While appropriate to its time, the stark dualism of the Maimonidean concept of the relationship between God and the universe, as derived from Aristotelianism, was incompatible with the emphasis on the *immanence* of God within nature and history in nineteenth-century German Idealism.[65] To find a pedigree for this development within the gamut of Jewish religious thought, Krochmal had to look elsewhere.

The appropriation of Jewish Neoplatonism and Kabbalah. Krochmal discovered a "usable past" in the speculative mysticism known in Hebrew as *torat ha-nistar*, or recondite knowledge.[66] In the Hebrew Enlightenment, this was a break from the norm. The East European rationalists of the 1820s and 1830s, locked in battle with Hasidism, generally viewed the Kabbalah as a bizarre and treacherous deformation of "normative" Judaism; some went so far as to equate it with pagan idolatry.[67] The idea that one might affirm the legacy of both Maimonides *and* the Zohar [Book of Splendor] would have struck the typical maskil as outlandish. Yet, to Krochmal, Jewish Neoplatonism and the early Kabbalah contained the seeds of a metaphysics that could answer the challenge of German Idealism. Particularly in Ibn Ezra, of all the medieval Jewish thinkers the one with whom the nineteenth-century

philosopher most identified, Krochmal found insinuations of an immanentist doctrine of God's creation and providence. In line with the "great chain
of being" in Neoplatonism, Ibn Ezra (per Krochmal) understood all of reality (the Many, or *ha-kol*) to be the manifestation of a continuous flow of
divine emanations ultimately originating in the hidden God (the One, or
'ehad).[68] Though the hidden God remained beyond comprehension, this
One constituted the absolute unity prior to all form and matter. In this
scheme, there was no abyss between God and the world, no concept of a
creation "from nothing," as existed in Maimonides. Rather, for Ibn Ezra
and his spiritual heirs, the world inheres *within* God, as one possible *limitation* of His infinite intellect. From this, Krochmal derived a distinctively
Jewish lineage for panentheism, the view that all being exists within God,
but—unlike in strict pantheism—God is still transcendent to being. "This,"
Krochmal wrote, "is the true meaning (or *sod*) of the verse, 'I am first, I am
last, and other than myself, there is no God.'"[69]

   *The task of the modern Jewish philosopher as that of revealing the metaphysi-
cal truth concealed in Jewish sources.* Krochmal's method for firming up "the
perplexed of the time"—namely, to study the history of Jewish religious
philosophy in sweeping and contextualized fashion and then tease solutions to the current crisis out of the resources of Judaism—rested on two
main assumptions. First, there was a conviction that this textual heritage
contained a deeper import than was apparent on the surface. Against Luzzatto, Krochmal defended a modified version of the allegorical approach to
interpretation central to medieval Jewish thought.[70] The foundation of this
hermeneutic, present in both philosophy and the Kabbalah, was the belief
that texts contained both an exoteric sense (*nigleh*) and an esoteric truth
(*nistar*); the mark of enlightenment was the ability to penetrate through
the literal, exterior meaning to the inner core.[71] This outlook had to be
adapted to square with nineteenth-century German philosophy, as the notion that there was a static truth embedded in texts like "apples of gold in
settings of silver"[72] was incompatible with the historicist character of Hegelian metaphysics. Krochmal's solution was to treat this polarity between the
exoteric and the esoteric as a dynamic unfolding both in the individual and
in history—a teleological progression in which the concealed truth of God's
absolute oneness is gradually made manifest.[73] Whence the second of the
two assumptions: that the proper objective of the modern Jewish thinker
was to accelerate this process, by bringing to light the "purified faith" (*emunah tserufah*) already anticipated in *potentia* within classical Jewish sources.

   Spinoza is mentioned only once in Krochmal's work, in chapter 12, in
the remarks that preface his discussion of Alexandrian Jewish thought of
the Second Temple period. To justify his historical method in general, and

possibly his treatment of this particular legacy marginalized by rabbinic Judaism, Krochmal writes:

> And know, it is a fundamental and honored principle that it is proper, indeed, obligatory, for us to investigate the ideas, mores, and characteristics that have emerged from within our nation over the course of time, throughout our history. [We must study] the bonds and associations we have developed with others to a greater extent than any other people, albeit with limitations. [We must study] the way we have related to—and been transformed by—these ideas, mores, and characteristics, and how, on their basis, we have interacted with others—those who were distant from us and have come closer to some extent, borrowing from our ways, such as the Greeks at the time of Plotinus and Proclus, and, in a different way, Mohammed, as well as those who were close to us and distanced themselves such as the early Christians, or *the philosopher Baruch* and his followers.[74]

Krochmal thus indicates his own knowledge of Spinoza's writings as well as his belief that such inquiry is appropriate to the study of Jewish history. It is also clear from this passage that "the philosopher Baruch" would have been recognized within his circle as a reference to Spinoza. For all this suggested familiarity, he says nothing to absolve Spinoza of heresy, and by grouping him with the early Christians as "those who were close to us and distanced themselves," he does little to mitigate Spinoza's rupture from Judaism. All in all, his *Guide* reads like an apology for Judaism *against* Spinoza's thought and example. Krochmal defends, however unconventionally, the basic principles that Spinoza had undermined, from the metaphysical chosenness of Israel to the spiritual content of Jewish law, from the belief that the Bible contains esoteric truth to the integration of religion and philosophy. He *reinterprets* the tradition instead of rejecting it, choosing Maimonides over Spinoza as his guide.[75]

In spite of this, the individuals most responsible for rehabilitating Spinoza within the Hebrew Enlightenment were largely his disciples. Letteris was one of Krochmal's earliest devotees; in addition to the first Hebrew article about Spinoza, he also wrote the original biography of Krochmal, which appeared as a foreword to the second, 1863, edition of *The Guide of the Perplexed of the Time.*[76] Sachs, whose essays of the 1850s built on Krochmal's revitalization of medieval Jewish Neoplatonism, had briefly studied with the Galician philosopher near the end of his life.[77] Then there was Abraham Krochmal (c. 1818–1888), the son of the philosopher, who became a leading advocate for religious reform in the Hebrew press and served briefly as Schorr's coeditor of *He-Haluts.*[78] Starting in the 1870s he published a few works aimed at reconciling aspects of the philosophy and biblical criticism of Spinoza (whom he labeled "Rabbi Baruch") with Judaism.[79] Significantly, all three of these thinkers invoked the authority of the elder Krochmal for their inclusion of the Amsterdam heretic within the canon of *Hokhmat Yisrael*. His son Abraham went the furthest in this regard. In his *Even Ha-Roshah* [Foundation Stone] of 1871, a loose translation of Herder's *God; Some Conversations*, one of the key texts in the German Spinoza renaissance of the late eighteenth century, he cast his father in the role of Spinoza's defender (if occasionally also critic), and another Galician rabbi and maskil, Tsvi Hirsch Chajes (1805–1855), as the initially skeptical interlocutor eventually won over.[80]

Rubin had not been one of Krochmal's students; his association with the Haskalah began in the 1840s, after the philosopher had died. Nevertheless, it is clear that he had read Krochmal and, like the thinkers mentioned above, believed that the "Socrates of Galicia" had pointed the way toward a new reception of the Amsterdam heretic. Even by titling his work as he did, Rubin may have hinted at this link to Krochmal and not only to Maimonides, signaling that what had been only gingerly implied in *The Guide to the Perplexed of the Time* would be taken to its radical conclusions in his own *New Guide to the Perplexed*.

V.

The title of Rubin's book was *The New Guide to the Perplexed, Including Two Books of the Great and Noble Thinker Baruch de Spinoza According to the French Translation of Emile Saisset*[81] *with a Life of the Philosopher*. It appeared in two volumes, the first in 1856 and the second in 1857. The first and the beginning of the second volume consist of an introduction to Spinoza. After an opening tribute that embraces Spinoza as an exemplar of freedom of thought and pure reason, Rubin proceeds to explain his reasons for rendering the *Ethics* and the *Treatise* into Hebrew and to justify the chosen title of his translation:

> In their endeavor to scale the heights of wisdom, the *maskilic* youth of our people have traditionally begun their ascent with the learned works of the sages of Spain and Arabia, works that have become wizened with age. . . . The *Guide* has been to them the cornerstone . . . on which they have established the foundations of their intellect before proceeding onto the wisdom and philosophy of the nations. Yet the philosophy of the *Guide*, with its reliance on the doctrines of Aristotle, is as remote from the truth as east from west, as the days of yore from the present; it is very distant from the system of modern philosophy. . . .

Thus from the bottom of my heart I say to the youths of Jeshurun, those who have left the traditional House of Study [*bet midrash*] as a result of their fervent desire for wisdom, who yearn to delve into philosophy yet still lack the strength to persevere in the study of works in different languages and of different nations: let them first look intently in this new guide. It will speak to them in the language of their parents and teachers, which they have been used to hearing from the time they first thought to consult books. And so it shall lead them to the gates of the temple of the new philosophy that is built on its foundations.[82]

If others before Rubin in the Hebrew Enlightenment had acknowledged the obsolescence of Maimonides' Aristotelianism, few had done so in as cutting a fashion. Against the earlier maskilic strategy of bringing Maimonides' *Guide* into step with the present—even, in the case of Krochmal, of renewing the genre, yet doing so with deep reverence for the *Moreh* of the Rambam—Rubin called for a clean break. By titling Spinoza the *New Guide to the Perplexed*, he came, in essence, not to praise Maimonides but to bury him. Just as Spinoza, in the *Treatise*, cast his repudiation of the rationalist interpretation of the Bible as a break with Maimonides in particular, so too Rubin equated his repossession of Spinoza with the liberation of the Haskalah from the shadow of the "great eagle" of medieval Jewish philosophy.[83] Rather than starting with Maimonides, the young scholar alienated from the *bet midrash* should begin his intellectual journey with Spinoza, via the familiar Hebrew of Rubin's promised translation. As one of the founders of modern philosophy, it was Spinoza, not Maimonides, who was best suited for the role of "guide of the perplexed."

The problem with Maimonides, however, was not just the dated quality of his metaphysics. Rubin also finds him wanting as a model for the Haskalah. In a comparison of Spinoza and Maimonides, Rubin begins by duly acknowledging what he sees as their similarities: a rational, nonanthropomorphic understanding of God, a suspicion of the masses, the use of a foreign language for their speculative literature, their excommunication by fanatical rabbis.[84] But the differences that Rubin highlights are more telling. Maimonides was a product of diverse travels, experiences, and encounters, Rubin argues, whereas Spinoza was fundamentally a hermit shielded from outside influence. Maimonides was a communal leader and ambassador, a figure close to kings who sought both wisdom and glory—a twelfth-century "court Jew," Rubin seems to be implying. Maimonides' concern for his reputation among the common people led him to tailor his message to his audience, as demonstrated by the very different character of his *Guide of the Perplexed* and his *Mishneh Torah*. Spinoza, by contrast, was poor and averse to the masses; he cared not a whit for appearances but for truth alone.

Maimonides, as a result of his natural caution, was cagey and deliberately obscure in his writing; Spinoza, on the other hand, was completely frank and uninhibited in his writing, difficult for the masses to understand but for the wise of heart utterly lucid. Finally, Maimonides relied on Aristotelian philosophy, which was already somewhat obsolete in his time and was all the more so in Rubin's time; "not so Baruch: he forged a new path that our forefathers could not have imagined."[85]

No one, I think, would confuse this for a fair and balanced comparison of the two philosophers. Just as he had done with the characters of Gutzkow's *Uriel Acosta*, Rubin projects onto Maimonides and Spinoza a contemporary tension within the Hebrew Enlightenment, as seen from the point of view of one of its rival factions. Maimonides, drawn here after Gutzkow's Da Silva, has all the stereotypical features of the dithering moderate in the eyes of the ideological purist. He is antiquated, derivative, lacking in boldness, desperate to please everyone; above all, he is internally divided, ever the scholar-rabbi, the philosopher-politician. Spinoza, on the other hand, is the ideal fantasy of the radical maskil. He represents a fresh type of Haskalah hero, one beholden to no wealthy patron or religious authority and aspiring only to the "liberty to philosophize." Marginal and impoverished, like many a Galician maskil, he is for this very reason intellectually free—and thus able to become the founder of "a new path that our forefathers could not have imagined."

It would appear that one source for Rubin's trailblazing view of the Amsterdam heretic was his familiarity with the work of his fellow Spinoza admirer and translator Berthold Auerbach. In 1854 Auerbach, by now a celebrated author within German literature, had come out with a revised edition of his 1837 *Spinoza* novel.[86] Rubin was evidently one of its readers. In the second volume of Rubin's *New Guide to the Perplexed*, he supplements his own abbreviated narration of the life of the seventeenth-century thinker with various excerpts from Auerbach's fictional portrait in footnotes.[87] Most notably, Rubin includes a translation (some forty years before the Hebrew version of Auerbach's *Spinoza* was published) of the triumphalist epilogue from Auerbach's novel, which portrays Spinoza as the redeemer of Ahasverus, the Wandering Jew.[88] In Rubin's otherwise close rendition of this segment, the identity of Ahasverus—a familiar symbol of Jewishness within West European and particularly German literature but not within East European Jewish society—is not clearly marked. Auerbach finishes the scene with an image of the Wandering Jew leaning over to kiss Spinoza, writing "[i]t was the kiss of the dying Ahasverus, who bore the fate that Jesus Christ on the cross had laid upon Israel"; Rubin converts this into "[i]t was the kiss of Jeshurun," employing the poetic name used to designate the Israelites on rare occasion in the Bible, and always in an affectionate manner.[89] What drew Rubin to this scene was likely neither the pejorative vision of the Jewish past that Ahasverus connoted in the German context, nor what the historian Jacob Katz has called with reference to this passage "the utopia of a total assimilation of the Jews."[90] He probably found Auerbach's epilogue appealing because its poetic beatification of Spinoza into a hero of watershed significance—a prototype of the "new Jew"—echoed his own construction of the Amsterdam philosopher as the modern Maimonides.

The image of Spinoza presented by Rubin is thus, on the one hand, quite revolutionary. In the context of a Hebrew Enlightenment traditionally anxious about embracing innovation too openly, Rubin's Spinoza—for all his residual ties to Maimonides—appears bluntly novel. Witness how Rubin introduces the *Treatise* to the reader: "[T]here," he writes, Spinoza "demonstrates that all the prophecies were only imaginary visions, and all the miracles mere exaggerations hanging by a thin hair on the laws of nature, and Moses only a sage politician who was great in his time."[91] This summary does little to disabuse the pioneering biblical critic of radical heresy. It is passages like this that led Shmuel Feiner to claim that the Spinoza of the *New Guide of the Perplexed* exemplifies a rejectionist attitude to the Jewish past.[92] In this view, rousting Maimonides from his perch in the maskilic pantheon and installment of Spinoza in his place is a challenge to the Haskalah to grow up—to wean itself from the old in favor of the *new*.

Yet, on the other hand, alongside the image of Spinoza as a figure of rupture with the past, there exists another view of the seventeenth-century heretic in Rubin's account, that of an heir to a subterranean legacy of philosophic speculation *within* Judaism. This perception is most acute in the section "On God" devoted to Spinoza's metaphysical monism, which begins as follows:

> Like God concealed in his lair, invisible to all flesh and incomprehensible to all life; yet revealed in his brilliant glory by the heavenly bodies, the celestial hosts telling of his feats throughout the earth . . . and like the human soul hidden in the innermost recesses, beyond the reach of all matter and corporeality, but glimpsed fleetingly through the window-lattices before she turns away; and like nature in her holy palace, her face cloaked in mystery and her image concealed from every penetrating eye; yet, from behind the veil, clear and manifest to every noble spirit and precious soul who knows how to embrace her as a whole—so too is the system of Spinoza in its investigation of the secrets of God, the soul, and nature: elusive in a web woven of fixed logic, moving about under the cover of geometrical laws sturdy as a polished mirror yet also hard as barren rock, sealed and implicit.[93]

As indicated by the language used in this passage, the path that Rubin charts for his reader into the Spinozan *Deus sive natura* is thoroughly mystical, pivoting on the tension between the hidden and the revealed. The God of Spinoza, according to Rubin, is both fully manifest in the universe and at the same time "concealed in his lair," bringing to mind the ultimately ineffable deity of Neoplatonism. By maintaining this concept of divine transcendence, Rubin signals his departure from a strict pantheist interpretation of Spinoza's metaphysics. In fact, he immediately goes on to define Spinoza's pantheism as "psychological pantheism," or *panentheism*. By identifying Spinoza with the Platonic notion that "[n]ature is the body of the divine spirit," or conversely, that God is the soul of the world, its eternal and indispensable source of life, Rubin appears to lend support to an idealist reading of the seventeenth-century philosopher that would ascribe priority to spirit over matter in his metaphysical system. This would at least partly restore the mind-body hierarchy ostensibly undermined by Spinoza's doctrine of the strict identity of thought and extension, encapsulated in the famous seventh proposition of Book II of the *Ethics* stating that "[t]he order and connection of ideas is the same as the order and connection of things."

After defining Spinozism as a version of panentheism, Rubin proceeds to elaborate on the precedents for this idea of God in the history of religion. "Glimpses of this system," he writes, "appeared in the light clouds of dawn in antiquity."[94] Rubin casts a wide net, alluding to sources from Greco-Roman thought to Norse mythology, but most of his references are to Jewish literature. Starting with one piece of evidence from the Torah itself—the fact that the "master of the prophets (i.e., Moses) would occasionally call a *natural* act a *divine* decree"[95]—Rubin then scours rabbinic, philosophical, and kabbalistic texts for suggestions of the view that all is in God. Sayings and legends of the Sages [Hazal][96] bump up against mystical numerologies,[97] while citations from Maimonides' *Guide*[98] stand alongside paraphrases from the kabbalistic Zohar[99] and Sefer Yetsirah [Book of Creation].[100] All these excerpts speak to the notion of a monistic undercurrent pulsing through Judaism. If on a merely exoteric plane Judaism mandates a separation between God and his creation, the implication of the fragments quoted here is that there is a hidden, esoteric interpretation, or *sod*, attesting to their ultimate unity.

Having begun, then, by accentuating the radical and innovative nature of Spinoza, Rubin mitigated this picture by excavating precedents for his "heresy" within "tradition." In doing so, he suggested a bond between his reclamation of Spinoza and the Galician philosopher whose method of assimilating novel ideas to an esoteric dynamic within Judaism had left an imprint on so many nineteenth-century maskilim—namely, Krochmal. That

Krochmal lurked in the background of this reception was made clear in Rubin's subsequent work in defense of Spinoza, *Teshuvah Nitsahat* [A Victorious Reply], written to rebut the criticism of Luzzatto in particular. In this forty-five-page treatise, Rubin expands on his earlier presentation of the Jewish foundations for Spinoza's pantheism while simultaneously muting the revolutionary zeal that was so much a part of the *New Guide*. Krochmal receives honorable mention for having demonstrated the Jewishness of Spinozism as part of his lengthy exposition of the "poor man's wisdom" of Ibn Ezra.[101] After explaining how various statements made by Krochmal can be explicated in a Spinozist light, Rubin writes: "You have shown the discerning reader that our philosopher is blessed [*barukh*] and his source is blessed—he is our brother, our kith and kin even in his outlook. His words are all words of tradition, the foundations of his thought are in the mountains of Zion, and the axioms of his system rest on the pillars of the wisdom of our people from antiquity to the present."[102] Krochmal, in other words, had laid the groundwork for the restoration of Spinoza to his Hebraic inheritance that Rubin was proposing. In his *Guide to the Perplexed of the Time*—first by sidestepping the theism of Maimonides, then by revitalizing the panentheism of Ibn Ezra—he had implanted a seed that would blossom in Rubin's suggestively entitled *New Guide to the Perplexed*. If Krochmal had shown that an immanentist theology could be developed more convincingly from Jewish sources than from the Christian symbols relied on by the German Idealists Schelling and Hegel, Rubin would prove Spinoza—the figure trumpeted by the German post-Kantians as one of the founders of modern thought—the consummator of this tradition within Hokhmat Yisrael. Spinoza's modernity, in this view, was a function of his having exposed a heretofore latent metaphysical content within Jewish texts. His novelty lay in translating into the "clear and distinct" language of seventeenth-century rationalism what premodern Jewish thinkers had only intimated in an allusive and figurative manner. But for his having written the *Ethics* in Latin instead of Hebrew, Spinoza's position toward his Jewish sources was not far removed from that of Krochmal toward Ibn Ezra. Both were disclosing what had been concealed—the esoteric interpretation of Jewish monotheism as radical monism, or Krochmal's "purified faith."[103]

This was likewise the stance adopted by Rubin toward Krochmal—the militant to the middle-of-the-road maskil, or the *New Guide* vis-à-vis the *Guide of the Perplexed of the Time*. The radical maskil, in this view, would neither cling to tradition, even if only for show, nor unmoor himself entirely from the Jewish past. Rather, modeling himself after Spinoza, the "new guide" for the modern Jew, he would bring light to dark places, guide underground traditions from the periphery to the center of Jewish cultural memory. In short, he would act as a revealer of secrets. Heine, writing in the mid-1830s, had famously called pantheism (in the context of discussing Spinoza) "the secret religion of Germany."[104] For Rubin, as for many of his nineteenth-century East European contemporaries enamored of the heretic from Amsterdam, this secret was equally at home within Judaism.

VI.

In 1885 Rubin's translation of Spinoza's *Ethics* into Hebrew finally appeared in print.[105] By now, the Galician upstart who had brashly defied the old guard of the Jewish Enlightenment with his iconization of Spinoza and Acosta three decades before was, at age sixty-two, one of the elder statesmen of secular Hebrew literature. Ever since his conflict with Luzzatto over Spinoza, Rubin had kept a distance from literary polemics. In his choice of subjects he remained quite daring, challenging the traditional religious perception of Jewish uniqueness with books on such things as parallel creation myths in the ancient Near East.[106] The tenor of his writings, however, was sober and scholarly, often reminding his admirers of the legendary evenness of his favorite thinker.[107] And at a time when materialist, positivist, and atheistic ideas were beginning to make inroads among the Eastern European Jewish intelligentsia, the philosophical idealism to which Rubin remained devoted was comparatively moderate and even old-fashioned.

This idealism was immediately evident in the idiosyncratic Hebrew title of Rubin's translation. On the first of the two title pages, which furnished the Latin and German titles of Spinoza's *Ethics* using the Roman alphabet, the given name prevailed: *Ethica* in the former, *Die Ethik (Tugendlehre)* in the latter. On the second, Hebrew title page, one encountered an altogether different title: *Heker 'Elohah 'im torat ha-'adam*, or *The Investigation of God with the Science of Man*. By emending the title so, Rubin indicated that, in his reading, the ethics of Spinoza was effectively subordinate to his immanentist theology. Rubin's Spinoza was, at bottom, a religious thinker, a quasi-mystical "God-intoxicated man" in the *Hen kai pan* (One and All) mold of his German Romantic appropriators, only with a distinctively Jewish intellectual pedigree.

That Spinoza could still fire Rubin's Hebraist passion was clear from his long introduction to *The Investigation of God*, in which he sounded the same determination to reclaim the Amsterdam heretic for Judaism and Hebrew literature and to exculpate him of all wrongdoing that he had demonstrated in his first apology for Spinoza. "Now that all the peoples of the earth have come around to pay homage to the stone of Spinoza . . . now it is our birthright to repatriate him within our Hebrew literature."[108] Had Spinoza not been excommunicated, he might have written in the language of Gersonides and Crescas, exemplars of the medieval Jewish philosophy that had left traces on his thought; "for the Hebrew tongue was very dear and beloved to him and only death came between them"—a reference to Spinoza's unfinished book on Hebrew grammar.[109] Indeed, Rubin argued that it was only the need to write in a foreign language for a non-Jewish audience, and not any grudge toward the community that expelled him, that led Spinoza to refer to earlier Jewish philosophers as "Pharisees" and to feign a preference for the New Testament over the Hebrew Bible.[110] The "spirit of Jewish thought [*hokhmat yisrael*] spoke through him" and enabled him to supply a monistic alternative to Cartesian dualism.[111] Spinozism, in short, was "fundamentally Jewish from beginning to end."[112]

The appearance, in Hebrew, of Spinoza's most significant philosophical work reverberated widely. From one of his earliest extant letters, a missive to a friend from July 1904, touching on a lecture about Spinoza he had recently given to a Zionist organization in his hometown of Plonsk, it is clear that David Grin—soon to be known as David Ben-Gurion (1886–1973)—first encountered the *Ethics* via Rubin's translation.[113] Micah Josef Berdichevsky (1865–1921), in a remarkable diary entry from 1900, describes being transformed by the mere purchase of the translated *Ethics* ten years earlier, when he was not yet known as the Nietzschean heretic par excellence in fin-de-siècle Hebrew literature. He prefaces his reconstruction of that moment with a striking confession:

> There are a select few among the heroes of the spirit whose stature is so lofty and the power of their personality so absolute that even without being familiar with their work . . . you tremble merely upon hearing uttered their Holy Name [*shemam ha-meforash*, a term that refers to the divine Tetragrammaton].
>
> . . . And I will not err if I say that this was the case with Spinoza. He touched me to the heart, and I set his image before me even prior to looking at his Holy Tablets [*luhot-ha-berit*, the tablets on which were inscribed the Ten Commandments revealed at Sinai].

Here we are given a glimpse into what a reception theorist might call the "horizon of interpretation" for the budding author's exposure to Spinoza's thought.[114] Berdichevsky concedes that the name and image of the Amsterdam philosopher had a potent, mystical charge for him *before* he read a word of the "Holy Tablets" (i.e., the *Ethics*)—an indication of the near sacred aura that Spinoza already enjoyed in East European secular Jewish culture. After opening with this reflection, Berdichevsky recalls having bought "the Eth-

ics in a beautiful Hebrew edition" ten years earlier while living in Odessa. By then, he writes, "I had rejected the God of my fathers and my heart was filled with anger and sadness." Yet shortly after buying Rubin's Hebrew translation of the *Ethics*, he experiences something resembling a call to prophecy:

> I stood for a moment in the middle of the road. Suddenly, everything changed before me; mountains surrounded me and lo and behold! The body of Spinoza touched my own and a voice cried inside me: the book in your hands is the answer to the mystery of the universe! And once again, I had a vision of this majestic figure in all his solitude. A feeling of reverence grabbed me; a hallowed torrent of ideas rained down upon me; thousands upon thousands of words of truth lit up my mind, and it seemed as if everything had become clear. Here I was sitting at the feet of my teacher and rabbi, lonely like him, and like him cut off from Israel. The voice of the Reproof sounded in my ear: cursed shall you be in getting up and cursed shall you be in going out. Yet I was blessed and favored in that moment, and I felt a revelation of the spirit in all the strings of my soul. I had taken on a different form.

Berdichevsky closes with the admission that, following this rapture, "a few years passed until I read Spinoza. But his great benevolence was disclosed to me from the moment I received his book and held it in my hand."[115]

To be sure, the text of Rubin's translation plays only an indirect role in Berdichevsky's recounting of his discovery of Spinoza. Whatever rhetorical embellishment this episode underwent in the retelling, the point Berdichevsky wishes to convey is that the epiphany preceded the real encounter; Spinoza "touched him to the heart" before any serious engagement with his writings. Still, the echoes, even exaggeration of a major trope in the maskilic reaction to Spinoza—the image of the Amsterdam philosopher as a "new guide to the perplexed," an initiator into the "mystery of the universe"— are unmistakable. For all his secularism ("I had rejected the God of my fathers"), Berdichevsky drenches his reminiscence in theological language, reconstructing his earliest reception of Spinoza as a great and redemptive ecstasy, a sudden insight into esoteric truths (the *nistar*) gifted from on high. The Spinoza of this diary entry is, in short, a revealer of secrets. At least in this respect, Berdichevsky proves himself here to be Rubin's heir.

In the last decades of the nineteenth century, the East European maskilic Spinoza that Rubin had done so much to fashion was fast becoming a theme of Jewish visual culture as well. At the vanguard of this development was the Lodz-born Polish Jewish artist Samuel Hirszenberg (1865–1908).[116] In 1888 Hirszenberg completed the first of his historical works, an oil-on-canvas entitled *Uriel Acosta and Spinoza*. The painting portrays Spinoza as a young boy of no more than ten, sitting on the lap of his mentor Da Costa. The contrast between the two figures could not be starker. Baruch has long, golden curls and soft, cherubic features; he wears an elegant, perfectly tailored mauve-colored coat over an ivory, wide-collared chemise; and his face, tilted back ever so slightly and turned to the massive tome that sits open on the desk before him, is aglow with a serene rapture. Da Costa, on the other hand, is gaunt, bearded, and brooding; he is dressed all in black, from his large skullcap to his long, shapeless caftan; and his posture is as stiff and tightly coiled (witness the fingers gripping the armrest) as Spinoza's is relaxed, even languorous. Hirszenberg based this painting on a scene from the last act of Gutzkow's *Uriel Acosta* already described in this chapter, in which a young and happy Baruch walks in a leafy park together with his distracted "uncle" Uriel, who (in the conceit of the play) is devastated by the loss of his betrothed to another man on account of his scandalous heresy. The pink flowers resting on the open book on the table in Hirszenberg's painting have their roots in this episode: As Spinoza collects flowers, a chastened Da Costa urges that he "sleep, like flowers, content to enjoy their loveliness," without embarking, like him, on a path of restless inquiry into the true nature of things that will only lead to ruin. Yet before leaving Da Costa, for the last time, Baruch cannot help but use the flowers for a philosophical analogy, by comparing the fresh ones to the eternal, infinite attribute of Thought, and their faded counterparts to finite modes.

Was Hirszenberg familiar with Rubin's Hebrew adaptation of Gutzkow's *Uriel Acosta*? Did his depiction of Spinoza and Da Costa in 1888 have anything to do with Rubin's translation of the *Ethics* of three years earlier? At present there is nothing to suggest he was acquainted with either. Still, *Uriel Acosta and Spinoza* can justly be considered part of a pattern of rehabilitation of Spinoza both inaugurated and exemplified by Rubin. First, nearly everything about the painting suggests an East European Jewish frame of reference. The setting is no longer a verdant city garden but a small, austere room that has the feel of a claustrophobic space; the plainness of the background wall, bare of all ornament, is interrupted only by an unruly stack of books on a nearby shelf. With his long black coat and untrimmed beard, Da Costa looks more like an Ashkenazi rabbi than a seventeenth-century Portuguese Jew. Only the child Spinoza, with his brightly colored clothing and fair expression, is an exception to the general drabness and darkness of his surroundings. Moreover, by picturing Da Costa and Spinoza in what appears to be a master and disciple relationship, Hirszenberg, deliberately or not, echoes the image of the seventeenth-century pantheist fostered by Rubin and other East European maskilim, as heir to a freethinking legacy opposed to talmudic orthodoxy yet seeded in Judaism, and conveyed from

FIGURE. 4.2. Samuel Hirszenberg, Uriel Acosta and Spinoza, 1888. Photo from postcard. The Jewish Theological Seminary, New York.

rav to *talmid* via an underground "chain of tradition." Here too, in other words, there are intimations of a Spinoza who is a recipient, and eventually a revealer of secrets.

Uriel Acosta and Spinoza was one of Hirszenberg's first paintings; his *Spinoza* (1907) of two decades later was one of his last. No longer a boy in the lap of his heterodox tutor, the Spinoza of this mature work is an excommunicated heretic. Hirszenberg portrays Spinoza, dressed like a Dutchman, walking composedly in the foreground of a cobblestone street, rapt in a book he is reading. To all appearances, he is utterly unperturbed by the scowls and menacing glares of the bearded brood all in black behind him. While one of the men kneels down, perhaps to pick up a stone to throw at Spinoza, the rest simply recoil, packing ever closer together in herdlike fashion, and in so doing underscoring the degree to which Spinoza stands abandoned and alone, apart from the crowd. If Hirszenberg's earlier opus had hinted at a Jewish countertradition of dissent to which Spinoza belonged, here the emphasis was exclusively on rupture. This too, however, was a crucial aspect of the maskilic Spinoza—the "rebel against the past," the "founder of a new path that our forefathers could not have imagined," the hero of freedom and solitude.

The response to Rubin's translation was far from universally positive. One detractor was the Polish Jewish writer Nahum Sokolow (1859–1936),

FIGURE. 4.3. Samuel Hirszenberg, Spinoza, 1907. A. A. Deineka Picture Gallery of Kursk, Russia.

who by the 1880s had become arguably the most wellknown Hebrew journalist in all of Eastern Europe.[117] Reviewing *Heker 'Elohah* shortly after its
appearance, the Warsaw-based Sokolow scoffed at Rubin's attempt in his
preface to equate Spinozism with Judaism. "It is true," he conceded, "that
Judaism is not uniform among us . . . and perhaps Spinoza had his own
peculiar Judaism, but in the conventional sense, as we are accustomed to
understand Judaism, it is as far from Spinoza as east from west." Spinoza, he
pointed out, denies free will and replaces it with an absolute determinism.
He denies the immortality of the soul by dissolving it in the immortality of
the *En-sof*, in the general eternity of the universe and its forces. The God
of Spinoza is so boundless that ultimately, at least from the vantage of the
human intellect, He is everything; there is nothing else.

> This is philosophy, but why should we deceive ourselves into saying that this
> is Judaism? By means of rhetoric (*melitsah*) and casuistry (*pilpul*) one can prove
> anything; one can extract some isolated saying from the *Guide* or from Kab-
> balistic books, find similar wording between it and a statement of Spinoza, and
> declare the two kin! . . . But can the foundations of Judaism—the creation of
> the heavens and the earth, general and special providence, immortality of the

soul, reward and punishment, the divinity of the Torah and the [authority of] the non-cognitive commandments—be sustained on the basis of the philosophy of Spinoza?

Put simply, Sokolow concluded—sounding very much like Luzzatto years earlier—"Judaism and Spinozism do not make a good match."[118]

This was Sokolow's position on the "Judaizing" of Spinoza in 1886. Yet some four decades later, without in any way retracting his earlier criticism of Rubin, Sokolow would write *Barukh Shpinozah u-zemano: Midrash be-filosofyah uve-korot ha-'itim* [Baruch Spinoza and His Time: A Study in Philosophy and History], a massive Hebrew intellectual biography whose overriding aim was to reclaim Spinoza for modern Jewish culture. In the intervening years, Sokolow had become a Zionist—indeed, not just any Zionist but a major leader and emissary in the annals of political Zionism prior to the creation of the State of Israel. How Zionism, and a secular nationalist conception of Jewishness to be more exact, afforded a new platform for receiving, and rehabilitating, Spinoza is the subject of my next chapter.

*Figure. 5.1. Photograph of Yosef Klausner, 1911. The National Library of Israel, Jerusalem.

CHAPTER 5

From the Heights of Mount Scopus

Yosef Klausner and the Zionist Rehabilitation of Spinoza

I.

On February 21, 1927, the Hebrew University of Jerusalem, then in only its third year of existence, commemorated Spinoza on the two-hundred-fiftieth anniversary of his death. Its afternoon assembly was one of several tributes held around the globe to mark the occasion, the grandest of which was clearly a four-day conference in The Hague, the city where Spinoza had died in 1677. Modest in comparison, the Jerusalem event nevertheless packed the main auditorium on Mount Scopus with an audience that, in addition to the expected mix of students, lecturers, professors, and university officials, contained many leading figures in the Jewish community of Palestine (known as the Yishuv). Sitting at the dais next to Rabbi Judah L. Magnes, the American-born chancellor, were the acclaimed Hebrew poets Hayyim Nahman Bialik and Ya'akov Cahan, as well as the veteran Russian Zionist Menahem Ussishkin, a member of the Executive Committee of the university.[1] It was Magnes who opened the event, by reading aloud a missive in both Hebrew and Latin that had been sent by the university to the gathering in The Hague. In the letter, he praised Spinoza as "a son of his people in both his religious enthusiasm and bold knowledge of God" and declared this day of remembrance a university holiday.[2]

Next to speak was Professor Yosef Klausner, who recently had been hired by the university to serve as the first chair of Hebrew literature. A longtime member of the Zionist intellectual elite, the Russian-born Klausner had three decades of Hebrew writing and editing behind him, and a litany of scholarly and publicistic works to his name—perhaps most germanely, his biography of Jesus of Nazareth, the first of its kind in Hebrew, and a subject of international controversy among both Jews and Christians from its publication in 1922.[3] Over his career, he had written profiles of many past and present Hebrew authors, among them S. D. Luzzatto and Salomon

Rubin, who had butted heads over Spinoza in the middle of the previous century.[4] This, however, was to be his first opportunity to treat Spinoza directly. Klausner introduced his speech, later published under the title "The Jewish Character of Spinoza's Philosophy," as an attempt to give a strictly objective assessment of a topic long distorted by myth and misrepresentation.[5] Throughout, he zigzagged between negative and affirmative opinions of the Jewishness of Spinoza and his system, at one minute criticizing the effort to paper over differences between Judaism and Spinozism, at another appearing to do just that. Yet it was not this ambivalence, but the exuberance of his finale that would be remembered:

> To Spinoza the Jew, it is declared two-hundred-fifty years after his death, from the heights of Mount Scopus, from our Temple in miniature (*mikdash-ha-me'at*)—the Hebrew University in Jerusalem:
>   . . . The ban (*herem*) is nullified! The sin of Judaism against you is removed and your offense against her atoned for! Our brother are you, our brother are you, our brother are you (*'ahinu 'atah, 'ahinu 'atah, 'ahinu 'atah*)![6]

To close, Klausner invoked the phrase traditionally used to rescind a rabbinic ban—"Our brother are you"—and applied it to Spinoza. The secular and right-leaning Zionist ideologue had usurped the role of the *bet din* (or rabbinical court) in Jewish law, symbolically lifting the stigma of heresy from the seventeenth-century philosopher.

Whatever the seriousness with which this annulment was uttered, it made a fast impression. Gershom Scholem, watching from the audience that day, would later recall that "when we left the hall, some people laughed at his [Klausner's] emotional performance (Our brother are you! . . .) and said that under Jewish law it was sheer nonsense and proved only that Klausner was ignorant of the Law."[7] Hugo Bergmann, the head of the Jewish National Library and future professor of philosophy at Hebrew University, who spoke after Klausner on more general themes in Spinoza's thought, penned a brief note to a friend that same evening, writing: "Delivered the Spinoza lecture in the university. Beforehand Klausner's lecture, which concluded with the words repealing the ban: Our brother are you!"[8] The Hebrew press in Mandate Palestine reporting on the event singled out the same line for mention. By the end of the week, Klausner's statement was sufficiently well-known that a column for the Hebrew daily *Haaretz* could begin: "At about the same hour as Professor Klausner stood on Mount Scopus in Jerusalem and abrogated the herem on the Jewish philosopher Baruch Spinoza . . . I went to find the street named after Spinoza in Tel-Aviv."[9] News of what had happened eventually reached America, leading one Reform rabbi to complain about the "the incident of the formal removal of the ban, an incident reported to have taken place on the hallowed heights of Mt. Scopus and in which a preeminent scholar figured as master of ceremonies."[10] Even the *New York Times* reported on the event in Jerusalem in a brief article whose headline read: "Ban Against Spinoza Revoked by Jews."[11] Klausner's amnesty has since served as a landmark in the story of Spinoza's Jewish reception, eliciting a range of reactions from approbation to refutation to ridicule.[12]

However over-the-top in its symbolism, this public reprieve belonged to a century-old campaign on the part of Jews to reclaim Spinoza. Klausner hinted at this in later protesting that his "pardoning" of Spinoza had been misunderstood. The excommunication had "expired of its own accord," he would insist, as demonstrated by the packed house on hand at the Hebrew University to recall the legacy of the seventeenth-century heretic. The ban imposed by the Amsterdam Sephardim on Spinoza had sought total extirpation of his memory, including among its list of forbidden things the reading of "anything composed or written by him." It went without saying that a jubilee commemoration wasn't kosher either. In his own eyes, all Klausner had done was acknowledge a decline in the authority of the herem that had already taken place de facto.[13]

Yet there was more to this pardon of Spinoza than perhaps Klausner realized. By conjuring the classical rabbinic formula for lifting the herem, Klausner implied that his was not a mere personal rapprochement with Spinoza, but one that bore the imprimatur of Judaism and the Jewish people as a whole. Even if Klausner lacked the passionate attachment to Spinoza that Auerbach and Rubin (for whom the encounter with the philosopher was truly formative) had experienced, the implication of his rhetoric was that he could offer something that they could not: the embrace of a broad national movement that presumed to represent *all* Jews, including the most distant and alienated. "From the heights of Mount Scopus"—and not from Germany or Galicia, or from Amsterdam for that matter—would come an end to the estrangement between Spinoza and Judaism, with all accounts settled and all sins forgiven. Zionism, with its belief in "the centripetal force of Jewish peoplehood," a collective and essentialist Jewishness overlying individual and regional differences, seemed to provide one basis for reclaiming Spinoza.[14] It also presented a set of obstacles. For how could a commitment to national unity and solidarity be squared with the domestication of a renegade like Spinoza? Could Spinoza—the same Spinoza whom Berthold Auerbach had depicted as the herald of a Diaspora-oriented cosmopolitanism the Spinoza who appeared to have turned his back not only on his religion but on his people—seriously be deemed an asset to a separatist movement that ascribed pivotal meaning to ethnic ties?[15]

Klausner, who throughout his career clamored for a national culture that would fuse "Judaism" (*yahadut*) and "humanism" (*'enoshiyut*), believed that under the right conditions, national cohesion and individual liberty—the "freedom to philosophize"—could complement each other. He conveyed this confidence through his attempt to repair the breach between Spinoza and his native people. Other nationalist intellectuals, both for and against Spinoza, were less sanguine about the possibility of such reconciliation.

In what follows, before circling back to the 1927 commemoration on Mount Scopus, I will examine three contexts for Klausner's appropriation of Spinoza. I will begin by tracing the origins and early development of the Zionist recovery of Spinoza, with a focus on the major trends and ideological frames in this reception to which Klausner was heir.[16] I will then turn to Klausner's own intellectual biography, focusing in particular on his conflicted feelings over the course a secularization of Hebrew culture should take. Finally, I will study the shadow cast on Klausner's lifting of the herem by concomitant developments in the reception of Spinoza outside the realm of Jewish nationalism. Ultimately, I contend that the issue of Spinoza's Jewish or even proto-Zionist credentials was only the surface of the debate over the appropriation of him for Jewish nationalism. At a more fundamental level, this was a debate over the meaning of Zionist secularism—its parameters, its pantheon of heroes, and its relationship to Jewish religion and the Jewish past.

II.

The Zionist objection to the liberal integrationist approach to the "Jewish Question" was divided between two main ideological currents. One, which became known as political Zionism, took its point of departure from the demonstrated failure of liberal enlightenment to eliminate anti-Semitism and "normalize" the condition of the Jews. In this view, assimilation into the Diaspora might have been a worthy goal, but it had been rendered impossible by recalcitrant Gentile hostility. This animosity, moreover, was increasingly based not on religious but on racial and biological differences, implying that total integration was in principle unattainable. The upshot was that the Jewish Question would be remedied only if Jews stopped waiting in vain for their situation to ameliorate through general progress and instead actively sought to transform their circumstances, pursuing what the early Russian Zionist Leo Pinsker famously called *autoemancipation*. Those who shared this reasoning took as their chief aim the acquisition of a state or at least homeland for the Jews that would be capable of accommodating the vast and disenfranchised Jewish population of the Russian Empire in particular. Though there were others prior to him who espoused a Jewish nationalism with territorial ambitions, this position eventually became synonymous with the charismatic Austro-Hungarian journalist and founder of the Zionist movement Theodor Herzl (1860–1904).

"Cultural" or "spiritual" Zionism offered a separate critique. The founder of this variety of Jewish nationalism was the Russian Zionist Asher Ginzberg (1856–1927), who went by the pseudonym Ahad Ha'am. Here, the issue with the Diaspora-oriented response to the Jewish problem was not so much its feasibility as the threat it allegedly posed to the survival of Judaism. While rejecting traditional Judaism and conceding that Western emancipation had brought many benefits, this camp saw the privatization of Jewish identity as a religious confession, a kind of false consciousness.[17] Judaism was not a matter of personal choice, nor was it a label determined by others; it was an inherited, organic identity of descent. Cultural Zionists thus concerned themselves primarily with a reshaping of Judaism from a covenantal religion of laws and commandments into a rich, vibrant, and life-affirming secular culture.

The division between political and cultural Zionism roughly corresponds to the two primary frames that shaped the Zionist recovery of Spinoza from its nineteenth-century beginnings. The first and more "politically" focused of the two was the tradition of *mevasre ha-tsiyonut*, or the "forerunners of Zionism." The second, more "culturally" oriented of the two was the principle of "national pantheism," a vitalist ideal that attributed all manifestations of Jewish life, however ostensibly unrelated, to an immanent national spirit, or *Volksgeist*. In what follows, before turning to Klausner, I will discuss these paradigms in turn, tracing the role of each in the Zionist reception of Spinoza.

The "Forerunners of Zionism"

The search for precursors of Zionism has ranged from a serious historiographic enterprise to an exercise in nationalist mythmaking and the creation of a "usable past."[18] Some have restricted the label of forerunner to those who sought to translate words and ideas into action; others have opted for a maximalist definition capable of reeling in makers of even the most oblique references to Jewish national revival and territorial independence. Spinoza, not surprisingly, entered the ranks of the "forerunners of Zionism" through the second door.

The case for including Spinoza in the prehistory of political Zionism rested ultimately on an enigmatic passage at the end of the third chapter of the *Treatise*, "Of the Election of the Hebrews." There, Spinoza provides his famous treatment of the biblical concept of the divine election of the Jews. Without flatly repudiating the fact of "God's choosing," he secularizes this doctrine in accordance with his pantheism, reasoning that "since no one acts except by the predetermined order of Nature—that is, from God's eternal direction and decree—it follows that no one chooses a way of life for himself or accomplishes anything except by the special vocation of God." In other words, the "chosenness" of Israel denoted *post facto* the natural merit that the Hebrews had achieved in ancient times. What was this mark of distinction? Spinoza held that nations could be differentiated only "in respect of the kind of society and laws under which they live and are governed," that is, on political grounds.[19] Starting from this premise, and supporting his case through biblical citations, he argued that the chosenness of the Hebrews was a reflection of their having established a secure and prosperous state (the tribal federation of Joshua and Judges more so than the later monarchy) on the basis of Mosaic Law. But this was only a fleeting accomplishment; eventually the state was overrun, the people were exiled, and the Hebrews lost their sovereignty—which was the same as saying that they ceased to be "chosen." The election of the Hebrews was thus a temporal and political, not an eternal and spiritual phenomenon, and no longer applied to a scattered and dispossessed Diaspora Jewry who "at the present time," had "nothing whatsoever" that they could "arrogate to themselves above other nations."[20]

Why, then, had the Jewish nation endured in the Diaspora? In medieval Jewish apologetics, this seeming miracle was commonly cited as evidence that the Jews remained "chosen" by God and would ultimately regain their political independence with the coming of messianic redemption. And while Christianity purported to have inherited the mantle of the "true Israel," it too understood the survival of the Jews to be a supernatural phenomenon, a result of God's having set apart the "people of the Book" for a special purpose. Spinoza rejected this reasoning. "As to their continued existence for so many years when scattered and stateless," he wrote, "this is in no way surprising, since they have separated themselves from other nations to such a degree as to incur the hatred of all, and this not only through external rites alien to the rites of other nations but also through the mark of circumcision, which they most religiously observe."[21] What had cemented and preserved the national identity of the Jews, in spite of their dispersion, was a purely natural cause: namely, the interaction between their self-isolation via peculiar rituals (in particular that of circumcision) and the hatred this insularity bred in others. Spinoza then turns to the experience of forced Jewish converts to Catholicism in Spain and Portugal to bear out this argument.

In Spain, where New Christians were offered "full civic rights," they were rapidly integrated and their former Jewishness stamped out; in Portugal, on the other hand, where they were denied the same liberties, they continued to practice Judaism in secret. This contrast has been shown to be wrong and inverted, and particularly odd coming from one, like Spinoza, who would have known better.[22] Yet historicity is not our concern here. Spinoza's point is that ostracism is the only thing holding the Jews together. Once measures discriminating against Jews are lifted, they follow their individual self-interest and blend in completely with the rest of the population.

It is this argument that proponents of Jewish assimilation would often cite in appropriating Spinoza as a prophet of their own favored solution to the "Jewish Question."[23] The segment that immediately follows, however, complicates Spinoza's position on the survival of the Jews:

> The mark of circumcision, too, I consider to be such an important factor in this matter that I am convinced that this by itself will preserve their nation forever. Indeed, were it not that the fundamental principles of their religion discourage manliness, I would not hesitate to believe that they will one day, given the opportunity—such is the mutability of human affairs—establish once more their independent state, and that God will again choose them.[24]

Spinoza appears to reverse himself in this passage, by suggesting that there is something about the intensity with which Jews observe circumcision that would be sufficient to safeguard Jewish identity "by itself," regardless of the attitudes of other nations. And this leads him to speculate about an alternative future for the Jews, one that would involve not their disappearance but their reclamation of sovereignty.

Viewed in context, it is clear that Spinoza is not endorsing or even predicting the revival of Jewish statehood. At most, he is vouching for its possibility. Yet the "proto-Zionist" potential (if not intent) of this passage was not exhausted by the reference to the re-creation of a Jewish state. Of equal import was the condition attached: that the Jews first overcome the emasculating effects of their religion. As the Jewish cultural historian Jay Geller has written, "this passage's combination of Jewish body, gender, statelessness, and survival insinuated the specter of Jewish persistence and—particularly with its assertion that 'the principles of their religion make them effeminate'—the equally uncanny ascription of embodied Jewish gender identity: the feminized male Jew."[25] From its inception, Zionism was rhetorically linked with the recovery not only of land and language, but also of virility.[26] And the Zionist axiom of "Negation of the Exile" (*shelilat ha-golah*) meant rejection not only of continued Jewish existence in the Diaspora, but of a "Ghetto Jew" long stigmatized as timid, sickly, effeminate, even homosexual in antisemitic discourse.[27] This preoccupation with masculinity was perhaps most pronounced in the early Zionist leader Max Nordau's (1849–1923) call for the creation of a "Jewry of muscle" (*Muskel-judentum*), who would be distinguished by brawn as much as bookishness and brainpower.[28] "Let us take up our oldest traditions," Nordau beseeched, harking back in a 1903 article to the ancient legacy of Jewish gymnasts in Hellenistic times; "let us once more become deep-chested, sturdy, sharp-eyed men."[29] Yet the "muscle-Jew" fantasy of Nordau and other Western Zionists was only one instance of an ideal type—the "New Hebrew Man"— whose incarnations ranged from the *haluts* (pioneer) to the sabra (native-born member of the Yishuv or the State of Israel) to the Jewish paramilitary or soldier, and whose cultivation was a goal of practically every stream and stage within the movement.[30] With his famously soft and pale features and, in the words of his early biographer Colerus, "very weak constitution," Spinoza would seem a very unlikely poster child for the "New Hebrew Man." Moreover, his criticism of Jewish effeminacy in this passage appears more an indictment of the political quietism of rabbinic Judaism ("did not the principles of their religion make them effeminate") than of the "Diaspora Jew" or the Jewish body per se. Yet this emphasis on Jewish passivity would, as we will see, resonate with those who advocated self-emancipation as the solution to the so-called Jewish Question. Whatever he meant by the use of the Latin *effeminare*, Spinoza may be said to have anticipated with this choice of words the gendered dimension of the future quest for Jewish na-tional revival.[31]

The first to use this passage to support the view that Spinoza was a Jew-ish nationalist *avant la lettre* was the pioneering German socialist turned pioneering Jewish nationalist Moses Hess.[32] In 1862 Hess published *Rome and Jerusalem*, a short book justly considered the first sustained argument for a modern, secular Jewish nationalism. Prior to this manifesto, the left-wing German Jew—a self-proclaimed "Young Spinozist" in his youth—had been estranged from Judaism for decades.[33] In his early works from the late 1830s and early 1840s, he had espoused a messianic socialism that seemed to render outdated even a weakened form of Jewish separation. He foresaw the replacement of both Judaism and Christianity with a global and panthe-ist religion of reason, in which the alienation between spirit and matter, and the social hierarchy and inequality that was the necessary counterpart of this divide, would be permanently overcome. In *Rome and Jerusalem*, he switched course dramatically, beginning the work by declaring himself "back with my people." He passionately affirmed the Jewishness he had once repudiated, yet advanced a revolutionary interpretation of this identity as, at root, a nationality as opposed to a religion. The solution to the Jewish Question, he averred, was neither the radical cosmopolitanism he had for-

merly advocated nor the confessionalization of Jewish identity promoted by
Reform Judaism, but rather the embrace of a humanitarian Jewish nationalism in the spirit of Herder and Mazzini.

And, one might add, Spinoza; for if earlier in his career he had identified
Spinoza as the prototype of a universal human brotherhood, in *Rome and
Jerusalem* he transposed the monistic philosophy of his favorite philosopher
to an emphatically Jewish key. In the third letter of *Rome and Jerusalem*,
while criticizing the Jewish "Reformers" for renouncing the national character of Judaism, Hess writes, "Spinoza conceived Judaism as a nationality
(see the end of the third chapter of his theological tractate) and held that the
restoration of the Jewish kingdom depends entirely on the courage of the
Jewish people."[34] To be sure, Hess makes note of this in a somewhat offhand
manner; his interest in Spinoza lies more in the metaphysical unity doctrine
of the *Ethics* than in the critique of religion of the *Treatise*. Still, it would be
fair to say that the appropriation of this passage for a Jewish national ideology began with a German Jew himself later canonized in the pantheon of
Zionist forerunners.[35]

Though widely reviewed in the Jewish press upon its appearance, *Rome
and Jerusalem* did not spawn a movement and was rather quickly forgotten.[36] The responses, moreover, understandably tended to focus on what
was most strikingly novel in Hess's treatise—the argument for a modern
Jewish nationality—and to pay little attention to his use of Spinoza, with
some exceptions.[37] Exactly twenty years later, a Russian-Jewish physician
from Odessa named Leo Pinsker (1821–1891) published a German pamphlet entitled *Autoemanzipation* [Self-Emancipation], in which he urged
European Jewry to seek a homeland of its own.[38] Like Hess, the highly
Russified Pinsker had previously been a staunch advocate of Jewish integration, albeit one more closely affiliated than the German socialist with the
organized Jewish community. The 1881 pogroms that spread through the
southern areas of the Russian Pale of Settlement, including into Odessa,
robbed him of the faith that emancipation alone would solve the Jewish
Question. *Autoemanzipation* marked his volte-face. Regarding this pioneering tract of political Zionism, Klausner would later close a lecture on Spinoza from 1932, commemorating the three-hundredth anniversary of his
birth, with the following anecdote:

> And in connection with these marvelous words [i.e., the conclusion to chapter 3
> of the *Treatise*] I have something to relate that has been unknown to anyone but
> me to date:
>
>   An old Lover of Zion,[39] the late physician Dr. Zvi Himmelfarb, who for many
> years was a member of the committee of the Lovers of Zion in Odessa, told me
> in 1917, that in 1881, when the idea arose of founding the Love of Zion in order

to establish a Jewish state in the Land of Israel, Dr. J. L. Pinsker was hesitant, as in the Sixties and Seventies he had been a complete assimilationist and Russifier. The pogroms of 1881 shocked and terrified him; but, at first, he saw the idea of a Jewish state as a dream of the young and delirious.

One time, on a winter afternoon, this Himmelfarb, who was still a young student, came to see Dr. Pinsker along with another student, who was close in outlook to the Biluim.[40] They showed him this passage in the *Theological-Political Treatise*. It was close to dusk. Pinsker pondered these marvelous words of Spinoza for a long while—until it grew completely dark. Then he rose from his place and said with evident emotion:

"Yes, if Spinoza, a man of careful and measured intelligence, Spinoza who treats everything with caution and Judaism—without much love,—if he could believe in the possibility that the Jews 'will one day establish their own state and God will again choose them,' it is a sign, that it is not just a dream of the delirious!"

And thus was sealed the fate of his treatise *Autoemancipation*, which Pinsker wrote not only under the influence of the pogroms, but also because of the strong impact of these words of Spinoza.

And in this way Spinoza prompted—to be sure, not intentionally—the movement of Hebrew revival.[41]

This secondhand testimony is rather too neat and melodramatic to be entirely credible. But whether history or myth, or something in between, the account suggests that an interest in reading Spinoza into the chain of tradition for political Zionism emerged early on in the history of the movement—among the pioneering Lovers of Zion, who regarded Pinsker as a mentor.

With the publication of Theodor Herzl's *The Jewish State* [*Der Judenstaat*] in 1896 and the convening of the First Zionist Congress in Basel the following year under his leadership, this passage from the *Treatise* drew increased attention. In 1897 David Neumark, writing in the second volume of Ahad Ha'am's cultural Zionist periodical *Ha-Shiloah* [The Spring], produced the first Hebrew translation of Spinoza's fragment. Neumark (1866–1924), a Reform rabbi in Bohemia who was also a Zionist—an unusual combination in that era—was not overly enamored of Spinoza; as one committed to a theology of a continued Jewish "mission," he resented the *Treatise*'s depiction of the Jews as a people frozen in time. He cast his translation as a response to the frenetic efforts of "our nationalists and Zionists" to find statements by "righteous Gentiles" foretelling the revival of Jewish nationalism, which they prefer to texts from their own people. The excerpt from Spinoza, he noted, represented a third category: "one who is not of them and not of us."[42] Two years later, the German Zionist newspaper *Die Welt* printed this passage under the heading "Spinoza on Zionism," concluding with the question: "Will this sublime philosopher prove also to be a prophet?"[43]

A major development in the Zionist history of this passage would come in 1938, with the publication of the first volume of Ben-Zion Dinur's (Dinaburg) compendium of Zionist sources *Sefer ha-Tsiyonut* [The Book of Zionism]. Dinur (1884–1973), then a lecturer in modern Jewish history at Hebrew University, explained that his purpose in putting together this work—one of the many "anthology projects" undertaken by Zionist intellectuals between 1920 and 1960—was "to gather the best of Zionist literature as well as documents pertaining to the movement and its endeavors . . . in historical chronology."[44] He devoted his first volume to what he called the "*mevasre ha-tsiyonut*," or "forerunners of Zionism." Dinur defined this category broadly, designating as a harbinger any expression of even a loosely secular conception of the Jewish people combined with a belief that the redemption would occur through natural means. Most famously in this respect, he argued that the Jewish Enlightenment, whose integrationist ethos made it ostensibly the antithesis of Zionism, in fact represented an embryonic stage of the movement—particularly in Eastern Europe, where a Hebraist revival coincided with the first hints of a secular national consciousness.

At the very beginning of this development he located Spinoza. By interpreting "chosenness" as a civic instead of spiritual capacity, Spinoza became the first to secularize the messianic idea and to secure Jewish uniqueness on purely immanent as opposed to transcendent foundations. Spinoza was a Zionist precursor, in other words, because he intuited the intrinsically political character of the Jewish nation that had long lain dormant under the "effeminate" exterior of rabbinic religion. "The Amsterdam philosopher," Dinur writes, "who was almost completely cut off from his Jewish surroundings and who, at first glance, looks upon the fate of his people with the indifference of a foreigner, nevertheless is wholly permeated with a feeling of the majestic national being of the Jewish people and with a recognition of the forces of renewal latent in this being."[45] Therefore, Dinur concludes, "one must see in Spinoza's views on the possibility of a fulfillment of the redemption . . . the *first* revelation of several *foundations of modern Zionism*, expressed here as a result of patterns of life and of thought close to those of later generations."[46] Accordingly, it was with two excerpts from chapter 3 of the *Treatise*—one of them being, of course, the passage on the revival of Jewish statehood—that Dinur opened the section devoted to "forerunners of Zionism" from the Jewish Enlightenment.[47]

After the founding of the State of Israel in 1948, the proto-Zionist reading of this extract from Spinoza became a good deal more aggressive. Hess had understood the end of the third chapter as saying only that the reclamation of Jewish sovereignty would depend on an assertion of popular will and a manly "courage." Dinur had identified Spinoza's reformulation of "chosenness" from a spiritual into a political principle as the start of an attempt to explain the national individuality of the Jews without recourse to religious modes of thought. However, the Amsterdam philosopher's most renowned advocate in Israel's first decade of statehood—Prime Minister David Ben-Gurion—never tired of claiming that Spinoza had *predicted* the reestablishment of a Jewish state.[48] "He [Spinoza] was in a certain sense the first Zionist of the last three hundred years," Ben-Gurion wrote in 1953. "Through keen insight into Jewish and world history he prophesied the rebirth of the State of Israel."[49] With Ben-Gurion, the effort to cast Spinoza as not simply a "forerunner" of Zionism, but as one of its "founding fathers," reached a level never seen before or since. Yet the Spinoza-as-precursor argument represented only one of the roads taken in reclaiming Spinoza for a Zionist weltanschauung. Another basis for his appropriation was the expansive view of Jewishness that grew out of the spiritual Zionist project of restructuring Judaism into a secular national culture—a view that Ahad Ha'am, the leading spirit of cultural Zionism, called "national pantheism." Here, the ramifications of Spinoza for Zionism represented only one side of the equation. The other was the ramification of a Zionist perspective on understanding Spinoza. Otherwise put: what was at stake was not simply what Spinoza could do for Zionism, but what Zionism could do for Spinoza.

"National Pantheism"

Behind the campaign to reconstruct Jewish culture and identity along secular national lines lay a simple yet revolutionary inversion in Jewish self-understanding. Traditionally, Jewish peoplehood was believed to be a function of a special revelation embodied in the Torah. At Sinai the Jews had *become* a nation, and their continued existence as such depended on their adherence to the covenantal law. This interrelationship was perhaps most famously expressed by the tenth-century thinker Rav Saadia Ga'on in his classic work *The Book of Beliefs and Opinions*, where he writes, "Our nation of the children of Israel is a nation only by virtue of its laws."[50] Nearly a millennium later, Rabbi Yehiel Michel Pines (1842–1913), an early exponent of religious Zionism, echoed Saadia, arguing that "Israel is not a natural nation in origin, for its peoplehood from the beginning was not born naturally, that is to say, as a result of a common race and territory, but rather out of the Torah and the covenant of faith."[51] Put simply, Jewish nationality rested on a fundamentally religious base.

Secular Zionism—or cultural Zionism, to be more specific—reversed this hierarchy. The Jews were and had always been a natural, ethnic nation. Like all peoples, they possessed a unique national spirit. Religion had long been the dominant mode of this *Volksgeist*, but it did not exhaust its essence. Rather, it was part of a much broader realm of Jewish *culture*, a complex of values, laws, customs, and traditions ultimately created by the people themselves. The Torah was not a gift of a transcendent God, but an inspired product of the Jewish genius. Moreover, while the Jewish national character was, in a sense, timeless, a constant amid the vicissitudes of history, the religious and ethical outlook that characterized the people was subject to evolution. In short, the Jews were akin to a historical organism with an instinctive will to life, always adapting to changing circumstances in order to persevere in its being.

Ahad Ha'am, the theorist of cultural Zionism who would become most synonymous with the inversion of nationality and religion in Jewish identity, coined the phrase *national pantheism* to describe this belief in an immanent national matrix that underlay all the *modi* of Jewish expression throughout the centuries. In a published response to an 1898 letter from one of the "Lovers of Zion," asking whether an atheist who nevertheless loved his people and its cultural heritage and wished for a national revival of the Jews in the land of their forefathers could be considered "one of us," Ahad Ha'am answered yes, arguing that such a Jew should be considered a "national pantheist." Just as a pantheist, Ha'am argued, finds the "spirit of God" in the deep structure of reality rather than beyond nature, the "national pantheist . . . sees the *creative power of the spirit of the people from within*."[52] Ha'am did not cite Spinoza, though in the following excerpt from the Zionist thinker Moshe Glickson (1878–1939), whose work was above all concerned with the relationship between the individual and the community, we see how echoes of Spinoza might attend constructions of a "national pantheism":

> The nation is not a metaphysical entity, not a mystical ethereal thing that exists outside of the tangible existence of Reuben, Simon, and Levy etc; nor is it merely a logical abstraction. . . . [T]he nation is inside Reuben and Simon etc, it is Reuben and Simon themselves insofar as they are more than only a personality. . . . As Spinoza would put it: these two are not different substances, but rather two "descriptions of substance," that may be likened to two measures in geometry, length and width.[53]

Here, the substance-attribute distinction in Spinozan metaphysics is adduced only for the purpose of analogy (and a rather poor one at that) to the organic relationship between the Jew and his national community. Yet it is not far-fetched to reason that this resemblance struck a chord with other "national pantheists" in the mold of Ahad Ha'am, one of whom, as we will see, was Yosef Klausner.

Could Spinoza—clearly a nonbeliever, though one who demonstrated little affection for his people—be considered, on Ahad Ha'am's terms, a "national pantheist"? Those, like Dinur, who saw in Spinoza's secularization of Jewish "chosenness" an acknowledgment of latent "forces of renewal" (read Ha'am's *creative power of the spirit of the people from within*), might well have assented to this label. The problem of national solidarity would, as we will see, pose greater, though not insurmountable difficulties for some Zionists. Yet the unifying logic of "national pantheism" facilitated a recouping of Spinoza independent of any "national feeling" of which the Amsterdam heretic might be aware. In chapter 4, we saw how Rubin portrayed Spinoza as heir to an esoteric tradition of Jewish speculation, as part of the effort to reclaim Spinozism as a distinctively Jewish philosophy. While an equation of Spinozism and Judaism was asserted by some Zionist thinkers, most dismissed this parallel while seeking to place the Jewishness of Spinoza on a more cultural, linguistic, and ethnic footing.

One of the first to take this route was Hillel Zeitlin (1871–1942), in his 1900 monograph *Baruch Shpinozah: Hayav, sefarav, u-shitato ha-filosofit* [Baruch Spinoza: His Life, Works, and Philosophy]. A fascinating figure in modern Jewish intellectual history, Zeitlin, over the course of his life, went from orthodoxy to the secular ideologies of Zionism and territorialism before ultimately returning to orthodoxy.[54] Born in czarist Belorussia and raised as a Habad Hasid, Zeitlin claimed to have lost his faith as a result of his self-education in philosophy.[55] When he wrote his book on Spinoza, Zeitlin was living in the Belorussian city of Homel, where he was part of a circle influenced by the ideas of Schopenhauer and Nietzsche that included the Hebrew author Yosef Haim Brenner (1881–1921). He had not yet become an active Zionist—that would occur in 1901, after he attended the Fifth Zionist Congress and was won over by Herzl—yet he was already wrestling with the questions that were being debated both between, and within, political and cultural Zionism.

As a result of his own estrangement from the piety of his youth, Zeitlin strongly identified with Spinoza. Nevertheless, he presented his biography as an attempt to explain the conflict between Spinoza and the Jewish community of Amsterdam in a more balanced fashion than had previous maskilic treatments of the subject. In the twelfth and final chapter of the book, Zeitlin took up the question of the relationship between Spinoza and Judaism that had preoccupied Hebrew literature in the second half of the nineteenth century. On the one hand, he rejected the argument of thinkers like Rubin, who claimed that Spinozism was an authentic stream within Jewish philosophy. On the other hand, he maintained that it did not follow that Spinoza was "not one of us," as Luzzatto and his admirers had asserted. Instead, he adopted a third position, which he outlined as follows: "*Consciously*, Spinoza was opposed to Judaism, but *he was a Jew without knowing it*. His theory is not the faith of Judaism, nor is it the philosophy of Judaism. What it is, if one can say this, is the *ultimate tendency* of Judaism. It conforms not to Judaism in itself, but to the eternal *ideals* of Judaism in the *purest sense*: absolute justice, absolute peace, absolute love."[56] Zeitlin thus inaugurated an important shift in the rehabilitation of Spinoza, affirming the Jewishness of Spinoza's thought without trying to harmonize his pantheism with Jewish monotheism. What is particularly noteworthy in this excerpt is the claim that Spinoza "*consciously*" sought to break with Judaism yet "*was a Jew without knowing it*." Whereas Rubin had portrayed Spinoza as a proud Jew convinced that he was part of an elite chain of tradition within Jewish thought, Zeitlin interpreted his Jewishness as something reflexive and involuntary—an inheritance of the prophetic ideals of justice, peace, and love. One finds traces here of the cultural Zionist philosophy of Ahad Ha'am, for whom Jewishness was an organic national identity distinguished by a unique ethical outlook rooted in the prophets.[57]

In the early 1920s, the Zionist philosopher Jakob Klatzkin (1882–1948) began to make a more rigorous argument for the impact on Spinoza of Jewish cultural forms. The son of a famous Lithuanian rabbi, Klatzkin abandoned orthodoxy in his twenties and spent most of his life in Central Europe, where he was active in Zionist cultural projects. Within Zionist ideology, he was distinguished by the extremity of his repudiation of Diaspora Judaism. He was particularly critical of Ahad Ha'am's attempt to construct a cultural Jewish identity that would be defined by a particular ethical content. What would ensure Jewish continuity, he argued, was not the secularization of the Jewish religious heritage encouraged by Ahad Ha'am and his "spiritual Zionist" disciples, but the acquisition of the two concrete "forms" necessary for survival in the modern world—namely, land and language.

Though Klatzkin did not overtly link his Zionist outlook to his research in Jewish philosophy, traces of his "formalist" nationalism can be seen in his novel approach to the question of Spinoza's Jewishness. In 1923 Klatzkin published a Hebrew biography of Spinoza, which he followed up a year later with a new translation of the *Ethics*.[58] While he, like his maskilic predecessors, argued for the Hebraic foundations of Spinoza's magnum opus, what he meant by this was something entirely different. Rubin had stressed ideational parallels between Spinozism and the Jewish speculative tradition. Klatzkin disagreed with this line of reasoning, contending that there was an essential difference between Jewish monotheism and Spinozist pantheism that Rubin had misrepresented.[59] The influence on Spinoza of medieval Jewish philosophy was not one of *ideas*, but of *language*. Klatzkin identified specific Latin terms in the *Ethics* that posed difficulties when translated into most languages yet were illuminated once rendered into their medieval Hebrew equivalent.[60] This led him to argue for a kind of linguistic determinism at work in the composition of the *Ethics*. Spinoza, having been raised on the canon of medieval Jewish thought, could only go so far in escaping the clutches of its Hebrew idiom. If, for Rubin, the *content* of medieval Jewish thought constituted the hidden Jewish kernel in the *Ethics*, for Klatzkin, it was the Hebrew language itself, that is, the *form* of Spinoza's philosophy, that lay beneath the surface. "A good Hebrew translation," Klatzkin thus concluded, "would be, in many a sense, more accurate, indeed more original than the Latin original."[61]

In Nahum Sokolow's *Baruch Shpinozah u-zemano: midrash be–filosofyah u-be-korot ha-'itim* [Baruch Spinoza and His Time: A Study of Philosophy and History] from 1929, the reappropriation of Spinoza for modern Jewish culture reveals "national pantheist" thinking at its most inclusive. Sokolow was one of the most versatile figures in the history of Zionism. Before becoming a leader and envoy for the World Zionist Congress, who played no small role in successfully advocating for England's Balfour Declaration in 1917, Sokolow had been a renowned Hebrew author, journalist, and translator, and he continued to juggle writing and diplomacy right up to his death in 1936.[62] His first contribution to Spinoza's Jewish reception occurred in 1885, in a hostile review of Rubin's preface to Rubin's translation of the *Ethics*. Sokolow, like both Zeitlin and Klatzkin, rejected the analogy of Spinozism and Judaism. But whereas in 1885 this appeared to represent his final word on the conundrum of Spinoza's Jewishness, over forty years later, amid the general hoopla surrounding the bisesquentennial of the death of the Amsterdam philosopher, Sokolow sounded a very different tune. While rebuking Spinoza for his acerbic treatment of Judaism in the *Treatise* and even sympathizing with the Amsterdam Mahamad for imposing the ban, Sokolow insisted that no judgment on its part could decide the issue of Spinoza's identity. "Whether or not he was excommunicated or considered himself Jewish" was immaterial, Sokolow wrote; for "[o]ne does not become a Jew via the shofar, nor does one cease to be a Jew via the shofar. Jewish existence is a fact of nature, of birth. Spinoza only withdrew or was withdrawn from the religious community; he could never have abandoned or been excommunicated from his people."[63] The more specific unconscious legacies singled out by Zeitlin and Klatzkin give way here to a veritable torrent of inherited characteristics: "his blood, his brain, every capillary of his heart, his temperament, his spiritual being—none of these could cease to be what they were."[64] Spinoza, in short, bore the permanent imprint of a particular Jewish national type, with all its biological, ethnic, and cultural determinants. He was a single manifestation, albeit a highly distinctive and influential one, of "the power of the Hebrew spirit and the glory of the Israelite genius" over time. Sokolow—perhaps the "national pantheist" par excellence—made clear that his interest in historical recuperation did not stop with Spinoza. "Spinoza is ours and the excommunicators are ours," he concluded. "All is tied and connected together."[65]

The perspectives of Zeitlin, Klatzkin, and Sokolow offer three examples of a paradigm shift from the nineteenth-century Haskalah to secular Zionism. Their interpretations of Spinoza's Jewishness as a kind of cultural, linguistic, even racial inheritance—a birthright unbeknownst to the philosopher himself—illustrate the immanentist impulse characteristic of "national pantheism." What still remains to be more fully considered is the overarching framework in which these appropriations of Spinoza occurred—the project to create a national Jewish culture. A belief widely shared among the writers who contributed to media such as Ahad Ha'am's cultural Zionist journal *Ha-Shiloah* or the German monthly *Ost und West* (whose original guiding light was the young Zionist Martin Buber) was that there had to be a "Jewish renaissance."[66] There was broad disagreement, however, over what this would entail. Indeed, the questions that preoccupied the Zionist intelligentsia at the turn of the century were the same ones, *mutadis mutandis*, that we have encountered in the previous chapters on German liberal Judaism and the East European Haskalah—namely, what should be the relationship between the old and the new? What events, personalities, places, or movements from the Jewish past should be viewed as exemplary for the present? What balance, if any, was to be struck between the "Jewish" and the "universal" in this cultural renaissance? How were these categories to be understood in the first place? What was Jewish art, music, literature? Could Jewishness be ascribed only to something with allegedly Jewish content? Or did writing in Hebrew automatically confer Jewishness on its subject matter?

Above all, there was the problem of how the architects of a secular national revival should relate to Jewish religion, particularly as this remained a vital part of the Jewish identity of most East European Jews, the raw materials for the cultural Zionists' vision of the future. Ahad Ha'am represented one side of the spectrum of opinion on this issue. Ha'am, on the one hand, was an adamant freethinker who rejected literal belief in a personal and transcendent God, special providence, and the giving of the Torah at Sinai. In his famous short essay excoriating emancipated French Jewry for their "Slavery within Freedom" (1891)—a "slavery" implicit in their need to hold fast to outmoded religious beliefs, lest the basis for their continued existence as Jews under the terms of their "freedom," namely by "Mosaic faith" alone, crumble—Ha'am boasted, "I at least can speak my mind concerning the beliefs and the opinions which I have inherited from my ancestors, without fearing to snap the branch that unites me to my people, I can even adopt that 'scientific heresy which bears the name of Darwin,' without any danger to my Judaism."[67] Nevertheless, for all his religious agnosticism and even atheism, Ha'am sought to instill secular Jewish nationalism with a loving appreciation for the cornerstones of traditional religion, now regarded as "spiritual assets" of the Jewish people as opposed to revealed articles of faith.[68] Writing about the meaning of the Sabbath in 1898, the originator of cultural Zionism famously quipped that, "more than Israel has kept the Sabbath, the Sabbath has kept Israel," and he, moreover, insisted that "[w]hoever feels in his heart a true connection with the life of the nation in each of its generations, will be utterly unable— even if he does not believe in the World to Come or in a Jewish state—to imagine a reality of a Jewish people without the 'Sabbath Queen.'"[69] What was needed, Ahad Ha'am stressed, was "rebirth—not creation," a cultural renaissance that would remain moored in the deep wellsprings of Jewish collective memory.[70]

If Ahad Ha'am represented one pole, the other was occupied by the iconoclasts known as the "young Hebrews," whose chief inspiration was the enfant terrible of fin-de-siècle Hebrew literature, Micah Yosef Berdichevsky. Echoing Nietzsche, the philosopher who most spoke to their desire for a radical break from the past, this band of Zionist intellectuals called for a "transvaluation of values" (shinui 'arakhin). Ahad Ha'am's attempt to construct a secular Jewish culture that would hold on to the "spiritual assets" of Judaism met largely with scorn from figures like Berdichevsky, for whom not just rabbinic Judaism but also prophetic religion, indeed the very symbols of Torah and covenant at times appeared to be one great error. "Our hearts, ardent for life," Berdichevsky wrote at the turn of the century, "sense that the resurrection of Israel depends on a revolution—the Jews must come first, before Judaism—the living man, before the legacy of his ancestors."[71] Secular Jewish nationalism had to be a true liberation of the individual from the constraints of religion, including from the vague "ethical culture" promulgated by Ahad Ha'am. The times demanded a stark choice: "to be the last Jews or the first Hebrews."[72]

Berdichevsky's defiance of "Ahad Ha'amism" was, in fact, a refutation of the very idea of "national pantheism," with its concept of a secular yet eternal Jewish national essence that endured amid the flux of history and permeated even those renegades who refused to bow to the will of the collective. From chapter 4, we know that Berdichevsky's discovery of Spinoza via Salomon Rubin's translation was a revelatory experience, one this icon of Jewish revolutionary secularism recounted in the language of prophecy and a "road to Damascus"-style conversion. Yet Berdichevsky would have nothing to do with the posthumous efforts to bring Spinoza home by way of cultural nationalism. Hillel Zeitlin's Hebrew biography of Spinoza from 1900 thus met with a scorching review from Berdichevsky's pen. Berdichevsky found especially irksome the suggestion of a rapprochement between Spinoza and the community that drove him out. For "we cannot forgive the persecutors, these men, who rejected this hero of the spirit among us completely," he protested.[73] Commenting on the passage in which Zeitlin had linked Spinoza with "the ultimate tendency of Judaism," Berdichevsky sneered, "And they utterly rejected this very man, who had inherited the ultimate tendency of Judaism!" The rupture between Spinoza and Jewry could not be whitewashed: The Jews expelled him, and he in turn made his mark in Western thought and literature—and not in Judaism.

For Berdichevsky, then, there was to be no gloating about Spinoza being "one of us," no attempt to domesticate his heresy by spiriting him back into the fold through the back door. Above all, there was to be no appeal to a unifying element in Jewish life that linked all Jews past and present and overcame the entropic forces of history. While he died six years before Klausner's speech on Mount Scopus, he undoubtedly would have disapproved.

The running feud between these two forms of Jewish secularism—the basically conservative model of Ahad Ha'am and the acutely critical brand of Berdichevsky—came to a head in a controversy over Christianity that erupted in 1910, involving the already mentioned Hebrew author Yosef Haim Brenner. Brenner had moved from Eastern Europe to Palestine in 1909 as part of the wave of Jewish immigration from 1903 to the end of World War I known as the Second Aliyah. The settlers of the Second Aliyah were famous for their religious irreverence, and Brenner, a great admirer of Berdichevsky, was one of the most freethinking among them.[74] In essays first published in the Palestinian socialist journal *Ha-Poel ha-Tsa'ir*, Brenner called for a complete emancipation of Jewish nationality from Judaism. To show the lengths to which he was willing to go in severing the two, he argued in one of his pieces that it was possible "to be a good Jew and, at the same time, to be thrilled by the Christian legend of the son-of-God who was sent to mankind, and who atoned with his life for the sins of all the ages."[75] This inflammatory comment, with its implication that one could be nationally Jewish and religiously, for all it mattered, Christian, scandalized the Hebrew-reading public and elicited a number of polemical responses.

One such rejoinder appeared in the 1911 volume of *Ha-Shiloah* under the title "Freedom and Heresy" [*Herut ve-Apikorsut*]. The author of the piece, identifying himself by the pen name "Hebrew Man," which he commonly used, sought to discriminate between true "freethinking" and "heresy." While admitting that personal liberty and creativity were prerequisites for a Hebrew cultural renaissance, he contended that these had to be balanced with "a feeling of awe for the venerable and sacred possessions of the nation, on which Jewish existence relied for several thousand of years." Appreciation of this religious heritage, "which is dear and beloved to the greater part [of the nation] still," would ensure that the builders of the new national culture remained connected to the Jewish masses and would also imbue their work with the "spirit of holiness and celebration that always accompanies anything on which generations of lives have depended." Brenner, with his callous dismissal of the problem of apostasy and, by extension, the cause for which countless Jews had martyred themselves throughout history, had demonstrated not genuine "freethinking" but an "ugly" and gratuitous disrespect worthy of the description "heresy": "No! One who is truly free and enlightened, who has a place in his heart for holiness and is capable of appreciating the value of holiness in the eyes of others, would never speak with such levity on things sacred to millions of people, and all the more so on things that the life of his nation depends on!"[76] The author of this plea for sensitivity to tradition and respect for the martyrs was the same person who would formally reclaim the prototype of the modern Jewish secular heretic in a public ceremony sixteen years later—Yosef Klausner.

III.

All his life, Klausner maneuvered between the moderate and militant visions of renaissance outlined above, at times tilting toward one, at times toward the other.[77] Born near Vilna in 1874, at the age of eleven he moved with his family to the southern metropolis of Odessa, which, at the time, contained the second largest Jewish community in the Russian Empire. In these years Odessa—long at the vanguard of modern Jewish ideologies in Eastern Europe—was becoming a center of the proto-Zionist Lovers of Zion movement and of an efflorescence of Hebrew literature.[78] Among the residents of Odessa in the 1880s were Moses I. Lilienblum and Leo Pinsker, early leaders of the drive for Jewish settlement in Palestine, as well as Ahad Ha'am, who would emerge by the end of the decade as one of the sharpest critics of the Lovers of Zion. Once in Odessa, Klausner enrolled in one of the modern Hebrew day schools that had recently opened and tended to be staffed by Hebraist sympathizers with the Lovers of Zion. By his teens he was already a part of the Hebrew nationalist intelligentsia of the city, becoming the youngest member of a pioneering society devoted to the revival of Hebrew as a spoken tongue. In the late 1890s, while studying Semitic and modern languages, history, and philosophy at Heidelberg, he began contributing to various Hebrew periodicals—including Ahad Ha'am's newly founded *Ha-Shiloah*. He also became active in Herzl's world Zionist movement from the outset, attending the First Zionist Congress in Basel in 1896 and each one thereafter until 1913.

In 1903 Klausner replaced Ahad Ha'am as editor of *Ha-Shiloah*, in which capacity he would endure, in spite of several disruptions in its publication, through the final issue in 1926. Under Ahad Ha'am, *Ha-Shiloah* had become the most distinguished periodical in Hebrew journalism, renowned for its literary quality as well as its strong opposition to political Zionism and to the militant secularism of Berdichevsky. The assumption of its editorship thus gave Klausner a platform to become an opinion molder. From the tenor of his aforementioned criticism during the "Brenner controversy" of 1910, it should be clear that Klausner was in several respects a loyal Ahad Ha'amist, convinced, like his mentor, that secular Jewish culture had to maintain an organic link to its religious past and avoid the temptation of what he called "de-historicization."[79] To the end of his life he rejected the path of a total "normalization" of Jewry, the oft-expressed Zionist aspiration to become "a nation like all the others." True to the credo of Ahad Ha'am, he would always maintain that Judaism was a "national *Weltanschauung* built on religio-ethical foundations."[80] The Jewish national impulse, he insisted, exhibited "two fundamental aims" rooted in the prophetic legacy—the demand for "the unity of God and the reign of absolute justice." His exaltation of the biblical prophets was most emphatically conveyed in his essays on the Jewish messianic idea. In the "original" form of this belief, which he identified with the prophetic works of First Isaiah and Micah, he found the perfect synthesis of national and universal ideals—and one of the main "gifts which the people Israel have left as an inheritance to the entire world."[81]

Over his first decade as editor of *Ha-Shiloah*, Klausner issued frequent criticism of the rebel camp in Hebrew literature, whom he branded "sophists" (with Berdichevsky the "greatest" among them) for their extreme relativism and consequent rejection of the idea of a "unique 'essence' of Judaism."[82] A "national pantheist," Klausner contended that however different the Judaism of the Bible was from that of the Talmud, the Judaism of the Talmud from that of Maimonides, the Judaism of Maimonides from that of the Ba'al Shem Tov, or the Judaism of the Ba'al Shem Tov from that of Ahad Ha'am, each was a stage in the development of one historical organism. As for the present, he viewed with alarm the increasingly "areligious" character of the typical "young Hebrew" in Palestine, for whom Judaism was only "the Hebrew language and the Land of Israel."[83] Arguing against an association of the tradition with the *Shulhan Arukh* alone—the sixteenth-century code of Jewish law that had become the detested symbol of talmudic Judaism among modern reformers—Klausner urged upon the "young Hebrews" a different approach to religion:

> Renaissance is a return to the good in the old. And in our old religion there are many lovely customs. I don't know, if I can see anyone reviving the practical commandments like *tefillin* (phylacteries), *tsisit* (ritual fringes), or *mezuzah*. But it is possible and desirable to revive the Sabbath banquet with its glorious serenity, the Passover "*seder*" with its pleasant air of festivity, the *etrog* and *lulav* and the *Hoshana* prayer of Sukkot, the greenery of Shavuot, the blasting of the *Shofar* on Rosh Hashanah, the sublime and sacred *Neilah* (concluding) prayer of Yom Kippur.[84]

Klausner went on to add that only if Zionism maintained a connection to religion and faith would it be able to become a truly mass movement. "The young Hebrew," he concluded, "must become a creator not only with regard to the *language* of Israel and the *land* of Israel, but also with regard to the *faith* of Israel!"[85]

This was one side of Klausner—the moderate reformer, the champion of historical continuity, the advocate for the nation as a whole. Yet there was another dimension to his personality as well—the part that was impatient for a razing of the walls between Hebrew literature and universal culture, that admired the greatness he believed came only from far-reaching innovation, and that celebrated those who went against the grain. Whereas the one feared revolution and warned against "heresy," the other was strongly drawn to them. From the first issue of *Ha-Shiloah* he edited, Klausner signaled that he would depart from his predecessor's practice of printing material only on Jewish subjects. He promised "*to remove completely the boundaries separating 'Hebraism' from 'universalism'*" and thereby broaden the scope of Hebrew literature to include "all that is true, good, and beautiful in all the national literature."[86] This, in turn, would guarantee that modern Hebrew literature would eventually take its rightful place in general humanistic culture. "We do not consider ourselves to be beneath the Norwegians," Klausner concluded, no doubt alluding to the contemporary popularity of Henrik Ibsen and Knut Hamsun. Thus, on one of the major issues that had divided Ahad Ha'am and Berdichevsky, Klausner sided with the latter.

Klausner's attraction to "heretical" figures would be most dramatically exemplified by his Hebrew inquiry into the "historical Jesus." Yet I would argue that we can gain equal if not greater insight into his attraction to Spinoza via his commentary on the contemporary Hebrew writer he admired most, the poet Saul Tchernichowsky. A friend from their years growing up together in Odessa and attending university in Heidelberg, Tchernichowsky epitomized for Klausner the glorious potential of the "New Hebrew man." The mix of nostalgia for, and estrangement from the receding world of the shtetl found in the work of the more celebrated Hebrew poet Haim Nahman Bialik was totally absent in Tchernichowsky. Born in a Russian village, to a family that was religious without being overly fastidious, Tchernichowsky was blessedly free of the ambivalence, secretiveness, guilt, and pedantry that Klausner associated with the stereotypical maskil. He wrote not about talmudic prodigies losing their faith, but about universal themes such as nature, love, the body. The knowledge of nature that the poet had gained by training in medicine at Heidelberg, Klausner claimed,

> had not killed his love of nature, but just the opposite: it broadened and deepened this love and produced that *pantheist* philosophic-poetic world-view, which had already budded in his poem *Nocturno*, which he wrote while still in Odessa, yet which became more profound in Heidelberg from his intense study of science. This perception is: that man, fauna, and flora have one exalted source, they sprout forth from one exalted root.[87]

The unity and wholeness Tchernikhowsky found in nature also typified his person. "For him, in truth," Klausner wrote in 1907, "there is no Judaism at all—his humanity is his Judaism, and he Judaizes everything through his language and will."[88] While Klausner would occasionally express reservations about the Nietzschean flavor of much of Tchernichowsky's poetry and its paucity of Jewish content, his admiration for the vital, original, nature-affirming character of his oeuvre outweighed his misgivings. Tchernichowsky, he concluded, was by nature and outlook "the *complete* opposite" of Ahad Ha'am—and at the same time Klausner's favorite poet.[89]

Ultimately, the ideal that guided Klausner through all his attempts to construct a national culture was the integration of "Judaism" and "humanism." He wavered over how to achieve this synthesis: At times, in the spirit of Ahad Ha'am, he emphasized an adaptation of global values to the Jewish national character; at others, in the spirit of Berdichevsky and Tchernichowsky, he demanded that the partitions between the "Jewish" and the

"universal" be overthrown entirely.[90] The goal, however, was complete
identity—a culture that would be "universal-human and national-Hebraic
as one," without any compartmentalization between the two. In this fantasy,
the individual Jew would never have to escape from Jewishness to develop
all his or her capacities and become whole. The pursuit of Bildung, which
required that Auerbach's Spinoza depart from his native community, could
be carried out at home.

IV.

The tribute at the Hebrew University in February 1927 took place in the
near aftermath of the most scathing and sustained attack on Spinoza by a
Jewish thinker since the nineteenth-century Luzzatto at least and perhaps
dating back to the writ of excommunication itself. Klausner, it will be recalled, later justified his lifting of the ban as the ratification of a posthumous recuperation of the Amsterdam philosopher that had already taken
place in practice. If he believed this, his memory was short, or at the very
least selective. Twelve years earlier, in 1915, the distinguished neo-Kantian
philosopher and German Jewish liberal theologian Hermann Cohen had
published a lengthy essay on Spinoza entitled "Spinoza über Staat und Religion, Judentum und Christentum" [Spinoza on Religion and State, Judaism
and Christianity].[91] The prosaic title gave little indication of the vitriol of
the polemic to follow. As a stalwart Kantian, Cohen had long objected to
Spinoza's pantheism, which by collapsing all reality into God-or-Nature
rendered the distinction between the "Is" and the "Ought" meaningless and
thus left no room for a transcendental and prophetic ethics.[92] Yet it was
the critique of Judaism in the *Treatise* more than the philosophical system
of the *Ethics* that drew the heaviest fire in Cohen's 1915 attack. The bill of
indictment drawn up by Cohen was long and diverse, beginning with the
charge that Spinoza had prefaced his *Treatise* with biblical criticism solely
out of spite toward the community that had expelled him, and not because
it had any logical connection to the work's primary task of defending the
Dutch republican government of Jan de Witt and the "freedom to philosophize." Motivated by bile alone, his "Bible science" was consequently as
unscrupulous as it was tendentious. Spinoza was accused of intentionally
misrepresenting the Mosaic revelation as purely political and particularist,
knowingly attributing to ancient Israel and their "Pharisaic" descendents a
hatred of the rest of humankind belied by countless statements in biblical
and rabbinic literature, purposefully exempting the New Testament from

the arrows he fixed on the Hebrew Bible, and extolling Jesus over Moses, the latter out of a genuine preference for Christianity over Judaism. For Cohen, Spinoza was more rightly considered the founder of modern antisemitism than of modern Judaism: "The pithy slogans," Cohen wrote, "in which Spinoza vented his hatred of the Jews can be found today almost verbatim in the newspapers of that [i.e., the anti-Semitic] political orientation."[93] Ultimately, Spinoza's many offenses derived from a single, unspeakable crime, his "humanly incomprehensible betrayal" of his religion and people.[94] Far from deserving to be "decorated with flowers," as the young Mendelssohn had urged, Spinoza deserved to be remembered as the "enemy" of Judaism and ethical idealism par excellence.

Cohen's fiery rebuke did little to stem the Jewish cult of Spinoza. In 1927, at any rate, it was largely drowned out by the unprecedented show of affection for the Amsterdam philosopher throughout the West to mark the two-hundred-fiftieth anniversary of his death. In France there was a celebration at the Sorbonne, presided over by the poet Paul Valéry and featuring a letter written by the most famous French philosopher of the day, Henri Bergson, declaring that "today everyone has in essence two philosophies, his own and that of Spinoza."[95] The Soviet Union honored Spinoza with its greatest of accolades, displacing Kantianism from its accustomed perch in the "prehistory" of dialectical materialism and putting Spinozism in its place.[96] Books and articles in French, Russian, English, German, Dutch, Spanish, Italian, Portuguese, Polish, Yiddish, and Hebrew were published to mark the occasion. The Liberal Synagogue of London held a memorial with the English Jewish metaphysician Samuel Alexander as its keynote speaker; the Biblioteca Israelita of Lisbon hosted its own commemoration; and numerous Jewish periodicals ran special editions with cover stories about Spinoza.[97]

For the most lavish spectacle, however, one had to travel to The Hague. In 1877 the Dutch capital had been the site of the first major public salute to the memory of Spinoza, on the two-hundredth anniversary of his death. At that affair, the French Semiticist Ernest Renan had delivered his legendary paean to the Amsterdam philosopher, pointing to the house on the Paviljoensgracht where Spinoza had died and famously suggesting that "[i]t was here, perhaps, that God was most nearly seen."[98] The two-hundred-fiftieth anniversary was to be the occasion for an even bigger party. Hosting the tribute was the Societas Spinozana (the Spinoza Society), an international consortium that had been established in 1920 to "promote the study of the philosophy of Benedictus de Spinoza, and of its value in relation to human life, among men of all nations and creeds."[99] The founders of the society—a distinguished and cosmopolitan group that included the French Jewish philosopher Léon Brunschvicg, the German art critic and Spinoza scholar and

translator Carl Gebhardt, and the English jurist Sir Frederick Pollock—
were all noted experts in the life and thought of Spinoza. For seven years,
the Societas Spinozana had worked to revive interest in Spinoza and his
philosophy among both academics and laypersons. In its brochures as well
as in many of the articles that appeared in the elegant *Chronicon Spinozanum*, the annual journal published by the society, Spinoza was depicted not
simply as a thinker of great historical stature but as a prophet of sorts, car-
rying a message of peace and universalism to a Europe bloodied by national
hatreds. The two-hundred-fiftieth jubilee marked the pinnacle of their efforts to that point. Starting on February 21—the actual date of Spinoza's
death—with a convocation in the venerable Rolzaal, where the States General had decreed the original ban on the *Treatise* and the *Opera posthuma*, the
festivities spanned four days of speeches and discussions on the legacy and
essential problems of Spinozism.[100] The highlight came on the second day,
with the dedication of the house on the Paviljoensgracht where Spinoza had
died, and which the Societas Spinozana had recently purchased to serve,
once restored, as its base. In the words of Adolph S. Oko, the American
Jewish librarian of Hebrew Union College in Cincinnati and the secretary
of the Societas Spinozana, the site would be a "shrine" like "Shakespeare's
house in Stratford, the grave of Voltaire, the home of Goethe, [and] Dante's
cell," places where "the reverent soul feels itself somehow standing in genius' own presence."[101] In acquiring the house, the society was acting in
behalf of the "rightful owner, Humanity—consecrated as it is by Spinoza's
philosophy and his death."[102]

Of the members of the society, it was Gebhardt who was the driving
force behind the campaign to revitalize Spinozism. A resident of Frankfurt am Main, Gebhardt had produced the still definitive critical edition of
Spinoza's *Opera posthuma* in addition to German translations of each of his
works. He had also made a significant contribution to the historical understanding of Spinoza in his writing, one that would be recognized in hindsight as the start of a new line of inquiry. While the Jewish origins of the
philosopher had long figured prominently in his mythic image in European
culture—and more recently had acquired an important place in historiography as well, in the scholarship of Manuel Joël, Jakob Freudenthal, and Stan-
islaus von Dunin-Borkowski—Gebhardt was the first to treat the Marrano
background of seventeenth-century Sephardic Amsterdam as the most seminal context for Spinoza's heresy and thought. "Spinoza," Gebhardt wrote
in 1921, "was a Marrano. Whoever calls him a Jew applies an imprecise um-
brella concept to him, encouraging false connections of ideas."[103] Indeed,
it was Gebhardt who was imprecise with this statement—not Spinoza but
his parents had been conversos—yet his point was clear enough: Spinoza's

uniqueness was not a function of his Jewishness *tout court* but of his having been a descendant of a special kind of Jew, a Marrano.

In support of this thesis, Gebhardt cited seventeenth-century documents from within the Sephardic community of Amsterdam that spoke to the influence of specific channels of converso influence on Spinoza prior to his excommunication. Yet this tangible evidence was only the surface of an argument that at bottom rested on an essentialist concept of the Marrano psyche as a house divided against itself. To be a Marrano, Gebhardt argued, was to be tragically caught between the historical religions at a time when these were the dominant criteria of identity. But this very alienation prepared the way for the discovery of a secular and universal religion beyond the traditional categories, one that, after the abortive efforts of Uriel da Costa, would be introduced by Spinoza. "The world-historical mission of the Marranos," Gebhardt wrote with a Hegelian flourish, "was to bring forth Spinoza. Out of their split consciousness emerged modern consciousness."[104] Gebhardt thus claimed Spinoza as "the first European . . . our guide, after calamitous strife, to a new and unified world, belonging to every people and reminding each to realize a culture of humanity within national culture."[105]

Three weeks after the Spinoza celebration in The Hague, Gebhardt gave the keynote address at a tribute to the philosopher held by the Jewish Academic Union of Philosophers at the University of Vienna. Speaking on the theme of "Spinoza, Judaism, and Baroque," he identified cosmopolitanism with what he called "Galuth":

> Since the destruction of the Second Temple, Jewry has lived in Galuth. Abandoning the plaintive sense of the word and aiming only at its essence, we may translate Galuth for us as: symbiosis. Judaism, whether national religion or religious nationality, has not lived apart within regional borders, but rather, has lived for two thousand years among other peoples, among other religions. Thus, whereas others may live according to the laws of inner causality, Judaism is primarily determined by the law of interaction. If the Greek were Greek and the Roman Roman, the German German and the English English, the Jew was and is shot through with a double life-stream, first the Jewish and then the life-stream of the people, in whose cultural community he resides.[106]

Against "Galuth," Gebhardt introduced a binary opposite he termed "Ghetto," or "the isolation from the other cultural community, the constriction of the other life-stream."[107] Of these two alleged *Tendenzen* in exilic Judaism, his sympathies, as expected, were with the former:

> The greatest of the Galuth affirmed their fate of symbiosis, by living equally in two worlds. Thus Philo was both Jew and Hellenist, Ibn Gebirol and Jehuda ha

Levi lived in both the world of Torah and of Islamic culture, Maimonides, in Spain and in Cairo, belonged also to Gothic scholasticism, and Leone Ebreo, the son of the last great biblical commentator Abarbanel, entered the Renaissance as a Jew. But Spinoza was perhaps the greatest product of a Judaism that was a Judaism of Galuth, yet a Judaism without Ghetto.[108]

If elsewhere Gebhardt had underscored the proto-Europeanness of Spinoza, before an audience of Viennese Jews, he was an exemplar of the combinatory possibilities of Diaspora Jewish identity. Echoes of Spinoza's ascription of greater capacity to complex than to simple bodies in the fourteenth proposition of the second book of the *Ethics*—"[t]he human mind is capable of perceiving a great many things, and is the more capable, the more its body can be disposed in a great many ways"—can be heard in this praise for the symbiosis signified by "Galuth."[109] This symbiosis, Gebhardt went on to note, was not only cultural but racial. "No people of world history are as diversely mixed as the Jews."

Whether Gebhardt meant deliberately to criticize Zionist constructions of Jewishness with this homage to hybrid identities is unclear. Perhaps he was just playing to the likely resonance of the ideal of "German Jewish symbiosis" amid a group of Austrian Jews. Klausner, moreover, could not have known of this lecture prior to his reclamation of Spinoza because it was delivered three weeks afterward. Nevertheless, Gebhardt's speech in Vienna offers an example of the competing models of modern Jewish identity for which Spinoza was being appropriated in the very same year. Gebhardt had argued that "Spinoza belongs, like the greats of all religions, to all people equally."[110] Could Klausner show that he belonged doubly to Jewry?

V.

In 1919, after the Bolshevik Revolution had brought Odessa's "Golden Age" of Hebrew literature to an abrupt end, Klausner and his family moved to Jerusalem. With the opening of the Hebrew University in 1925, Klausner hoped to be appointed to the chair of Jewish history, in light of his growing body of work on Second Temple Judaism in particular. But his training was not held in high regard by the German Jewish scholars who dominated the early faculty of the university. They viewed Klausner as essentially a publicist and popularizer, whose increasing sympathy for Vladimir Jabotinsky's right-wing Revisionist party made him even more suspect.[111] Klausner was thus given the less sought-after position of chair of Hebrew literature.

Certainly, the international to-do about Spinoza in the postwar period was, by itself, a strong enticement for a nationalist like Klausner to reclaim him. As one Jewish scholar wrote with regard to the three-hundredth anniversary of Spinoza's birth in 1932—an occasion even more widely celebrated than the previous jubilee five years earlier—"the national feeling does not permit them [i.e., the Zionists] to surrender one of the greats of philosophy, to whom all of humanity shows respect."[112] Yet Klausner, in the 1920s, was also beginning to devote more attention to Jewish philosophy, in particular to the stream influenced more by Platonic than Aristotelian ideas. In 1926 he composed the introduction to the first translation of Solomon ibn Gabirol's *Fons Vitae* into Hebrew.[113] There, he argued for the origins in Ibn Gabirol's thought of a uniquely "Jewish pantheism," which combined a transcendent God possessing free will with an emanationist view of nature. Some eighty years earlier, the discovery of Ibn Gabirol's immanentist metaphysics had served the Hebrew maskil Senior (Shneuer) Sachs as a stepping-stone toward Spinoza. Klausner had less need of this intermediary, yet, as we will see, his interest in Spinoza and Ibn Gabirol had a common motivation.

Klausner called his lecture "The Spirit of Judaism and the Philosophy of Spinoza," a title that was changed in its published form to "The Jewish Character of the Philosophy of Spinoza."[114] "I will not speak about Spinoza's personal or philosophical relationship to Judaism and the Jews," he begins, only to expound on this question for five pages, and with a great deal of ambivalence. He starts with the issue of the herem, the primal scene in the Spinoza myth dating back to the first biographies of the philosopher. Thanks to the historiography of "the Jew Freudenthal" and "the Christian Dunin-Borkowski," Klausner claims, the stereotypes surrounding this event have been dismantled. "The *herem* of the Amsterdam rabbis and oligarchs was, to be sure, not a desirable act from our point of view today; yet it was not a *dreadful* act."[115] Excommunication was not a tool peculiar to the Jewish community; it had a place even among Protestant dissident sects as progressive as the "Collegiants," with whom Spinoza was on good terms. Moreover, Spinoza showed no great courage in not deferring to the Mahamad, for in truth he had left the community before it expelled him. The image that Auerbach had drawn in his historical novel, of Spinoza as a seventeenth-century Luther, disputing with his rabbinic prosecutors in a public forum, was sheer fantasy. After the excommunication, moreover, "no injury was done to Spinoza by Judaism," dispelling the fictions that Spinoza had to escape Amsterdam because of fear for his safety, or that the Jewish community had petitioned the Amsterdam stadtholders to ban him from the city. Remarkably, he footnotes this assertion by crediting Luzzatto—the chief antagonist of Spinoza within the nineteenth-century Haskalah—for having been the first "to assess the life of Spinoza in Hebrew with sobriety and from a Jewish point of view."[116] From an essay beginning with such praise for Luzzatto, one would be hard-pressed to anticipate a concluding embrace of Spinoza as "our brother."

Klausner proceeds to the various injuries done by Spinoza to Judaism in the *Treatise*, among them his favoring of Christianity, his treatment of the biblical prophets as inferior to Jesus and the apostles, and his crude dubbing of Jews as "Pharisees." These features had all figured prominently in Cohen's caustic critique of Spinoza and vindication of the herem a little over a decade earlier.[117] "He [Cohen] clearly showed," Klausner wrote, "the contradictions in the judgements of Spinoza about the great Jewish thinkers in every generation, his crooked judgement about the image of the God of Israel according to the teaching of Moses and the prophets, and in general his unjust attitude to Judaism."[118] Yet Klausner also faulted Cohen for engaging with Spinoza as a contemporary and failing to appreciate the historical context for the *Treatise*—a tack similar to that taken by Leo Strauss in his 1924 analysis of Cohen's attitude toward Spinoza.[119] Moreover, he cited an example from Spinoza's correspondence that would become a favorite prooftext of the Zionists. The letter concerned was epistle 76, in which Spinoza rebutted the attempts of one of his former acquaintances to convert him to Catholicism. Countering the line of reasoning that the spread and prosperity of Christianity attested to its truthfulness, Spinoza ventured that one could argue that the endurance of Judaism through thousands of years of persecution gave it equal claim to this mantle. And if Christianity had its martyrs, so did Judaism, Spinoza maintained, recalling an anecdote he had heard about a certain Judah "the Believer" who in the midst of being burnt to death by the Inquisition in an auto-da-fé, uttered a verse from Psalms that one of the Gospels had attributed to Jesus during his crucifixion. Spinoza thus showed, says Klausner, "that Christianity had no advantage over Judaism from the side of ethics, constancy, and self-sacrifice."[120]

After dispensing with the question of Spinoza's attitude to Jewry and Judasim, Klausner explains that he also does not intend to deal with the relationship between Spinoza and previous Jewish thought. Here too, however, this appears to be mere posturing. The large corpus of research on this topic, Klausner writes, has shown how important thinkers such as Maimonides, Hasdai Crescas, Ibn Ezra, Gersonides, Ibn Gabirol, and Leone Ebreo were to the philosophical oeuvre of Spinoza. In a bizarre calculation, he states that 80 percent of the *Treatise* deals with "Jewish" matters and only 20 percent with "non-Jewish" ones. Even those works, moreover, less overtly Jewish than the *Treatise*, still contain substantial evidence of Jewish influence. "Thus Spinoza belongs not just to humanity as a whole," Klausner deduces, "but to Judaism in particular."[121] Indeed, he speculates that if the *Treatise* or the *Ethics* had been written in Hebrew, they would certainly have caused a ruckus similar to those about Maimonides and Gersonides in the history of Jewish thought, yet ultimately they would have come to be considered part of this legacy.

Did the presence of so many Jewish traces in Spinoza's philosophy support the notion of a basic agreement between Judaism and Spinozism? On this question, which threw the nineteenth-century Hebrew Enlightenment into controversy, Klausner finds in favor of Luzzatto. The pantheist rationalism of Spinoza and the prophetic monotheism of the Jewish people are fundamentally opposed to each other. Rejecting the panentheist interpretation that had originated in German Idealism and been taken up by the maskilim, Klausner maintains that, for Spinoza, God is totally identical with nature, whereas even the most abstract and depersonalized forms of Jewish monotheism in medieval Jewish thought always remained true to the belief that God exceeded the universe. Klausner also endorses another of Luzzatto's criticisms, namely that the rational and utilitarian ethics of Spinoza, which rest entirely on maximizing the capacity (*virtu*) of the individual, cannot be squared with Judaism. "Prophetic Judaism," he concludes, "whose crown is the messianic idea with its communal vision of the kingdom of heaven, can never be harmonized with this perspective. Spinozism is *not* Judaism in the purest sense of the term."[122]

This brings Klausner to the pivot in his argument. Turning to the "national pantheist" rationale of Ahad Ha'am, Klausner lays the foundation for reappropriating Spinoza for Jewish *Geistesgeschichte*. "Judaism is not solely a religion just as it is not solely a nation"; it is the product of a natural *Volk* with an immanent tendency toward a particular religious and ethical outlook that informs its national consciousness.[123] Like any historical organism, it is full of internal variety and incongruity. The discrepancies between the "Judaisms" of Spinoza and the prophets, then, need not be resolved for the former to be reclaimed for Jewish identity. The unifying characteristic of Judaism is not any single abstract teaching or idea, such as the "pure faith" (*emunah tserufah*) sought by the nineteenth-century Reformers; rather it is "[t]he consciousness that all [the multiple Judaisms] are simply part of an uninterrupted chain . . . to our generation and until the end of all generations."[124] In short, the unity of Judaism was its consciousness of historical continuity amid so much diversity.

"From this vantage point," Klausner reasons, "Spinoza was a complete Jew and his teaching contained an absolutely Jewish character."[125] Not only was his system a product of the Jewish national impulse; it was also, like Judaism, in essence a *torat hayim*, a philosophy of life, and thus similarly rife with contradictions. On the one hand, Spinoza's philosophy was atheistic, materialistic, mechanistic, deterministic, utilitarian, and Machiavellian. On the other hand, it was "God-intoxicated," idealistic, teleological, obsessed with freedom, concerned with community, and committed to the proposition that "man is God to man." Most important, the Spinoza who deprecated Judaism in the *Treatise* also claimed the ultimate aim of the Bible to be "righteousness and justice" and predicted the possibility of a future restoration of Jewish sovereignty.

This image of a Spinoza torn between extremes, and in this respect quintessentially Jewish, culminates in an unexpected historical analogy:

> *Jakob Klatzkin* compared the *Ethics* of Spinoza to the *Shulhan-Arukh* of Rabbi Yosef Karo: arid laws on the outside and a blazing faith within. I have another comparison that appears to me more fitting: *a soldier from the ranks* of *Judah Maccabee*. On the outside—a soldier like any soldier: crude, armed, fighting with cruelty, killing and trampling the enemy, and on the inside—a deeply pious man, fighting to save his people, his God and his Torah. . . . So too is Spinoza like this: cold, dry, geometrical at first glance, yet within—a burning faith, the religion of his people, the religious spirit of his ancestors, who gave their lives in martyrdom—the same burning spirit of that "Believer," whom Spinoza knew and recalled warmly, the one who sang with the expiration of his soul on the burning stake of the *auto-da-fé* of the Inquisition: "In your hands, O Lord, I place my spirit."[126]

To compare Spinoza to a Maccabee soldier, however absurd on its face, was equivalent to ranking him among the elite of the Zionist pantheon. Along with such events as the mass suicide of the zealots at Masada in 73 C.E. and the failed Bar-Kochba uprising of 132–35 C.E., the Hasmonean revolt of the second century B.C.E. was one of the most central *lieux de mémoire* in Zionism, and one with which Klausner was well familiar through his studies of Second Temple Judaism.[127] In this context it serves as evidence of how far Klausner was willing to go to merge Spinoza with Zionist imagery.

Yet Klausner's effort to expose "Jewish" characteristics allegedly inherited by Spinoza should not be taken as the main motivation for this appropriation. What drew Klausner to Spinoza in the first place was less any visibly Jewish element to Spinoza's person or thought than the possibility of naturalizing Spinoza's perceived "universal-human" significance. In other words, if Klausner invokes a line of reasoning characteristic of Ahad Ha'am to establish how Spinoza *belongs* to Judaism, Klausner's admiration for Spinoza is more closely related to this Russian Zionist critic's literary infatuation with Tchernichowsky.

Klausner edges toward an acknowledgment of this near the end of his lecture. Spinoza, he writes, was the fourth in a chain of Jewish thinkers—after Philo, Ibn Gabirol, and Don Judah Abarbanel (Leone Ebreo)—who had a much stronger impact on Western civilization in general than on Jewish philosophy. The first-century Alexandrian Jew Philo would not be clearly mentioned in any Hebrew work until the sixteenth-century *Me'or 'enayim* [Light of the Eyes] of Azariah de Rossi. The eleventh-century Ibn Gabirol would be celebrated within Jewish liturgy for his Hebrew poetry, yet would not even be recognized as the author of the *Fons vitae* until the 1840s. The sixteenth-century Leone Ebreo's *Dialoghi d'amore* would have a profound influence on Renaissance thought and would be translated soon after its appearance into several European languages, yet despite being rendered into Hebrew in the seventeenth century the book remained little known in the Jewish world until "our time," Klausner writes. Spinoza, meanwhile, would be excommunicated. What these thinkers had in common was the fact that they were all influenced by Platonist and Neoplatonist philosophy, with its pantheist leanings. "And so the matter is clear," Klausner claims: "[A]s long as Judaism was sustained on religion alone, without land, without language, without a national foundation, it is possible that all those who wished to graft onto it a Platonic or Neoplatonic pantheism were in fact a danger."[128]

Their pure or quasi pantheism was not the only thing that made them a hazard. In a later essay from 1932 entitled "Tradition and Innovation in Jewish Literature," with which he prefaced his collection of studies of the aforementioned Jewish Platonists, Klausner highlighted an even greater departure from the norm in medieval Jewish thought on the part of Ibn Gabirol, Leone Ebreo, and Spinoza. None of their three major metaphysical works—the *Fons vitae*, the *Dialoghi d'amore*, and the *Ethics*—were written in the guise of interpretation of sacred scripture; they contained no cited verses, no sayings of the sages, indeed no identifiably Jewish content at all. At a time when Jewish continuity was dependent on masking innovation as tradition, the neglect of these texts was perhaps understandable. But now the continued tendency to regard works as Jewish only if they deal with a specifically Jewish problematic has become an impediment to a much-needed freshness and creativity in Jewish culture. This meant that

We have to devote special attention to those Hebrew poets or thinkers who up
to now have been considered a "foreign branch" in the vineyard of our literature:
to *Immanuel of Rome*[129] *more* than to Rabbi *Judah ha-Levi*, to *Tchernichowsky* more
than to *Bialik*. This way, perhaps, our children will see that there is innovation in
our "House of Study"—in an original Hebrew literature, and thus they will not
go to seek nourishment in other literatures or only in Hebrew translations of
superficial works in other languages.[130]

If one step toward "universalizing" a national culture was to shift the scale
of attention from authors like Bialik to Tchernichowsky in contemporary
Hebrew literature, another, even more basic step was "to restore our ban-
ished greats: all the Jewish works that are genuinely novel, which survived
for us in foreign languages and until recent times were 'exceptional' in the
chain of Jewish tradition."[131]

And such was the case with Spinoza. If his pantheism and bold innovation had once been a threat to Judaism, now they constituted a national
asset, as we hear once again in Klausner's abrogation of Spinoza's herem:

> Now everything has changed. Judaism has ceased to be solely or even especially
> a religion—as *Moses Mendelssohn* and *Hermann Cohen*, enemies of Spinoza, de-
> picted it—and it is also not—and shall never be!—a nation alone: it shall be a
> *nation-religion in one*. It has begun to acquire land and a national language, and at
> the same time a territorial and political foundation along with them. . . . [A]nd,
> in the marvelous words of Spinoza, "given the opportunity—such is the mutabil-
> ity of human affairs—they may establish once more their independent state, and
> God will again choose them." In this situation the four philosophers estranged
> from Israel are no longer a threat to her: they will bring not danger, but encour-
> agement and invigoration to her spirit. Judaism will be enhanced and enriched
> by all her great sons—including the lost and rejected ones. To Spinoza, however,
> whose *Ethics, Treatise on the Improvement of the Intellect*, and *Hebrew Grammar*
> have been translated into Hebrew, with only the *Theological-Political Treatise*, his
> short works, and correspondence still missing—it is declared in recognition of
> the great sin that his people perpetrated against him, and the likewise not trivial
> sin that he perpetrated against his people, but also in recognition of his human
> greatness and the Jewish character of his teaching— To Spinoza the Jew, it is
> declared two-hundred-fifty years after his death, from the heights of Mount Sco-
> pus, from our Temple-in-miniature (*mikdash-ha-me'at*)—the Hebrew University
> in Jerusalem:
>
> . . . The *herem* is nullified! The sin of Judaism against you is removed and your
> offense against her atoned for! Our brother are you, our brother are you, our
> brother are you![132]

VI.

The international buzz created by Klausner's lifting of the ban on Spinoza "from the heights of Mount Scopus" quickly dissipated. Though he included his "Our brother are you!" flourish in the published versions of his speech, Klausner—perhaps because of the criticism and even mockery his "amnesty" elicited, perhaps because he was never so wedded to it in the first place—never pressed the issue of a formal pardon for Spinoza any further. In later addresses he gave on Spinoza—including another tribute in the old "People's House" (*Bet ha-'am*) in Tel Aviv to mark the tercentenary year of Spinoza's birth in 1932—he mostly shied from theatrics, arguing for the Jewishness of Spinoza without resorting to rabbinic formulas.[133] There was every reason to think the matter of a public reprieve for Spinoza all but dead, a case of bloated rhetoric now deflated.

Twenty-seven years later, this death proved only to have been a prolonged hibernation. On December 25, 1953, Israel's labor union newspaper *Davar* ran a front-page article with the headline, "Let Us Amend the Injustice." The specific "injustice" involved none of the most obvious controversies of the day besetting the five-year-old Jewish state: the fallout from Israel's bloody raid two months earlier on the West Bank village of Qibya, the continued housing of tens of thousands of Jewish immigrants from the Middle East in shantytowns, the Palestinian refugee crisis. Rather, this was a brief for Spinoza, an appeal to right the wrong to Jewish culture as long as the herem on the philosopher retained any authority. In essence the author was continuing Klausner's quest to see the works of great Jewish thinkers like Philo and Spinoza added to the treasury of Hebrew literature. The circumstances, however, were quite different. For the Jewish Yishuv of 1927 was now a Jewish state, the infant university on Mount Scopus an internationally prestigious research institution with its own press. And the author was not just one Zionist intellectual but a man widely regarded as the "founding father" of modern Israel: David Ben-Gurion, then in between stints as prime minister.

The "Old Man" of Yishuv and Israeli politics was an ardent admirer of the Amsterdam philosopher. Spinoza, in the eyes of Ben-Gurion, had inaugurated the breakthrough of the scientific spirit into modern Judaism, all the while rejecting a purely mechanical and materialist view of nature, upholding in its stead the biblical view that mind and body, spirit and matter were "manifestations of a higher unity."[134] He had founded a biblical hermeneutic that rejected spiritual allegory and demanded that all knowledge of Scripture "be sought from Scripture alone," thereby inadvertently laying the foundation for the prime minister's dream of transforming the Hebrew Bible from a work of transcendent revelation into a national epic of Israel's origins.[135] Indeed, for Ben-Gurion, Spinoza had anticipated not only Jewish secularism, but a specifically Zionist secularism. The prime minister's obsession with Spinoza's "proto-Zionism" was everywhere in evidence in the early years of statehood, from his address to the 1951 Zionist congress, where he cited Spinoza's "prophecy" of a restoration of Jewish sovereignty, to his diary from August of that same year, where he recorded, in Latin, the exact wording of that pregnant passage of the *Treatise* that begins "were it not that the principles of their religion discourage manliness . . ."[136]

Ben-Gurion's transcription of this excerpt in his journal followed his agreement a month earlier to become a friend of the first society devoted to Spinoza in the Jewish state.[137] In 1950 Georg Herz-Shikmoni (1885–1976), a German Jewish Zionist—and an even more avid Spinozist—who had immigrated to Palestine twenty-five years earlier, founded the Bet Shpinozah (Spinoza House) in the coastal city of Haifa.[138] His Spinozaeum, as it was also known, was a little center on Mount Carmel for which he had large ambitions that are almost laughable in retrospect. In both literature distributed by the center and in letters seeking dues-paying members and donations, Herz-Shikmoni described a campaign to make Spinoza and his thought cornerstones of the new Jewish culture in Israel. He envisioned daily recitations on Israeli state radio of passages from Spinoza's *Ethics*; special "Spinoza Days" dedicated to the study of his philosophy that would become part of the official school curriculum; and, ultimately, a center for the "Spinoza House" on Mount Carmel, whose exterior would be modeled after the *Spinozahuis* in The Hague.[139] While the Spinozaeum, from its founding to its closing in 1973, was largely kept alive by Herz-Shikmoni alone, it nevertheless—especially in its early years—managed to attract several distinguished members. In addition to Ben-Gurion, the roster included Klausner and the British-born Leon Roth, the first chair of the philosophy department at the Hebrew University.[140] Manfred George, the New York–based editor of the German Jewish newspaper *Der Aufbau*, was a member, as was the renowned Yiddish poet Melech Ravitch. But the biggest star among the friends of the Spinozaeum was clearly Albert Einstein, a longtime Spinoza enthusiast, who when asked by the *New York Times* in 1929 if he believed in God had responded, "I believe in Spinoza's God who reveals himself in the orderly harmony of what exists, not in a God who concerns himself with fates and actions of human beings."

In his positive reply to Herz-Shikmoni's letter of invitation, Ben-Gurion suggested that the "*Bet Shpinozah* take upon itself the publication of Spino-

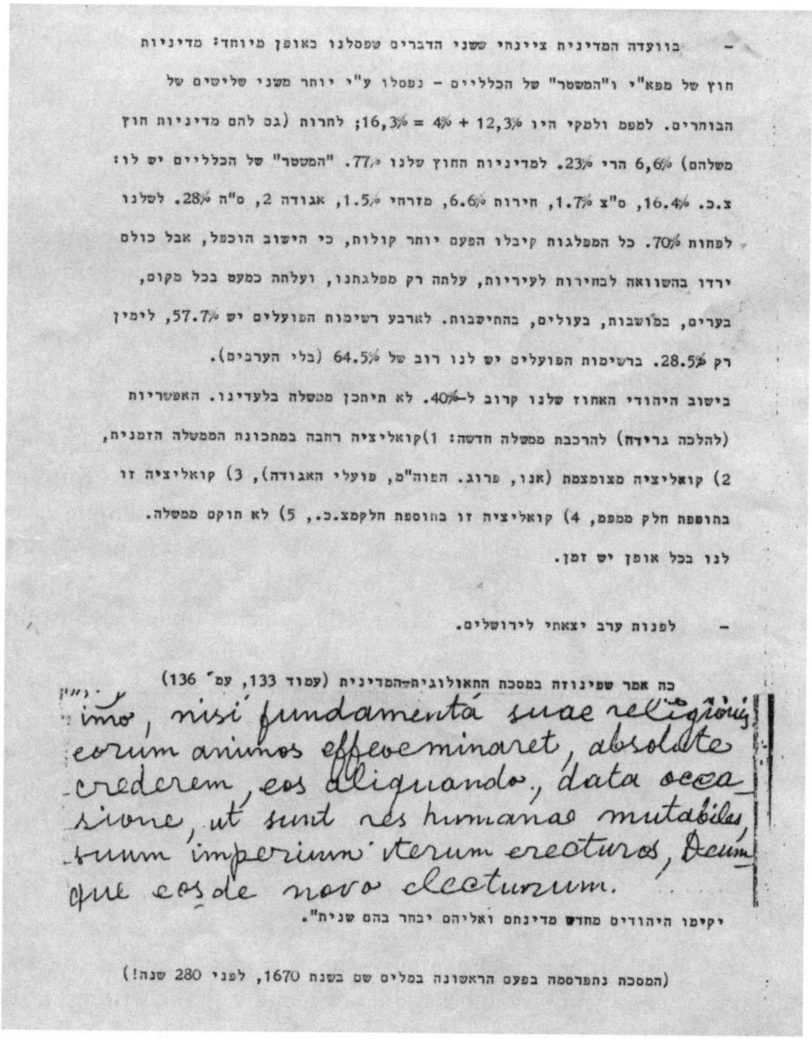

בועדה המדינית ציינתי ששני הדברים שמפסלנו באופן פיוחד: מדיניות

חוץ של מפא"י ו"המסתר" של הכלליים – נפסלו ע"י יותר משני שלישים של

הבוחרים. למפם ולמקי היו 12,3% + 4% = 16,3%; לחרות (גם להם מדיניות חוץ

משלהם) 6,6% הרי 23%. למדיניות החוץ שלנו 77%. "המסתר" של הכלליים יש לו:

צ.כ. 16,4%, ס"ז 1.7%, חירות 6.6%, מזרחי 1.5%, אגודה 2, ס"ה 28%. לשלנו

לפחות 70%. כל המפלגות קיבלו הפעם יותר קולות, כי הישוב הוכפל, אבל כולם

ירדו בהשוואה לבחירות לעיריות, עלתה רק מפלגתנו, ועלתה כמעט בכל מקום,

בערים, במושבות, בעולים, בהחיבבות. לארבע רשימות הפועלים יש 57.7%, לימין

רק 28.5%. ברשימות הפועלים יש לנו רוב של 64.5% (בלי הערבים).

בישוב היהודי האחוז שלנו קרוב ל—40%. לא תיתכן ממשלה בלעדינו. האפשריות

(להלכה גרידה) להרכבת ממשלה חדשה: 1)קואליציה רחבה במתכונת הממשלה הזמנית,

2) קואליציה מצומצמת (אנו, פרוג. הפוה"מ, פועלי האגודה), 3) קואליציה זו

בתוספת חלק ממפם, 4) קואליציה זו בתוספת חלקמצ.כ., 5) לא תוקם ממשלה.

לנו בכל אופן יש זמן.

– לפנות ערב יצאתי לירושלים.

כה אמר שפינוזה במסכת התאולוגיה-המדינית (עמוד 133, עמ' 136)

...imo, nisi fundamenta suae religionis eorum animos effoeminaret, absolute crederem, eos aliquando, data occasione, ut sunt res humanae mutabiles, suum imperium iterum erecturos, Deumque eos de novo electurum.

יקימו היהודים מחדש מדינתם ואליהם יבחר בהם שנית".

(המסכה נתפרסמה בפעם הראשונה במלים שם בשנת 1670, לפני 280 שנה!)

FIGURE. 5.2. David Ben-Gurion's diary for August 7, 1951, containing, in the prime minister's handwriting, his transcription, in the original Latin, of the passage from chapter 3 of Spinoza's *Theological-Political Treatise* that begins "were it not that the principles of their religion discourage manliness . . ." The Ben-Gurion Archives, Be'ersheva, Israel.

za's books and letters in Hebrew," stating his readiness "to try to find all the assistance necessary for the task."[141] True to his word, the prime minister, when not busy with matters of state, began seeking out translators, publishers, and financial backing for this endeavor, assisted by his minister of education, who happened to be none other than Ben-Zion Dinur.[142] It was Ben-Gurion's hope that the Hebrew University would publish the complete

works of Spinoza in Hebrew all at once, and in time to mark the tercentenary of Spinoza's excommunication in 1956.[143]

Such was the backdrop to Ben-Gurion's appeal to "amend the injustice."
Like many a Zionist thinker before him—Klatzkin, Sokolow, Klausner—
Ben-Gurion allowed that the Jewish community of Amsterdam had sufficient reason three centuries earlier to expel Spinoza. "Amsterdam Jewry
of that time, however, is not Jewry, nor is the seventeenth century the eternity of the eternal people," he insisted, adding that "[i]t was not within the
authority or the power of the Jews of Amsterdam in the year 1656 . . . to
exclude the immortal Spinoza from the community of Israel for all time."[144]
The Athenian people condemned Socrates to death in antiquity, yet Socrates
was never written out of the history of Greek thought; why, then, should a
Jewish court in Amsterdam be able to do to Spinoza what the judgment of
the Athenians could not do to Socrates? At the present moment, with Jewish sovereignty restored, the conditions for an "ingathering" of Spinoza and
his works were ripe. Lauding Spinoza as "the most original thinker and the
most profound philosopher that Jewry has produced in the past two thousand years," Ben-Gurion concluded that "[t]here is no longer any justification for the spiritual 'bereavement' of the Exile in the State of Israel. *The
publication of a complete and critical edition of Baruch Spinoza's writings by the
Hebrew University of Jerusalem* is a debt of honor to ourselves from the national and cultural point of view, and it should not be put off."[145] A rehabilitation that, however zealously pursued, had long served as a counterweight
to the historical memory of traditional Judaism—as a *countermemory*, so to
speak—seemed well on its way to acquiring official legitimacy in the State
of Israel.[146]

In his article, Ben-Gurion was careful to note that the injustice demanding redress was cultural, not religious—the fact that "Hebrew literature
would not be complete, so long as it did not include all the writings of Baruch Spinoza." He was not calling for an annulment of the herem. Yet this
qualification, to his alleged chagrin, went entirely unnoticed. Ben-Gurion,
it was (and, to a striking degree, still is) widely believed, had proposed that
the ban on Spinoza be officially lifted. And a controversy that had seemingly ended years before now returned at an even higher pitch. Already
in 1953 Herz-Shikmoni had written the chief rabbi of Israel, Isaac Halevi Herzog, to determine whether, from the perspective of Jewish law, the
herem on Spinoza still held. That September, shortly after the Jewish New
Year of 5714, he received an encouraging letter in response. While denying Herz-Shikmoni the formal invalidation of the ban he no doubt wanted,
Rabbi Herzog nevertheless suggested, based on a close exegesis of the writ
of excommunication, that the anathema could be read as applying only to

Spinoza's lifetime. "It seems," he concluded, "that the ban on the reading of Spinoza's books and essays no longer stands."[147]

On the other hand, the chief rabbi of the Sephardic community of Amsterdam, Salomon Rodrigues Pereira, refused to grant a similar ruling, invoking the well-known dictum from Jewish law that "[n]o rabbinate has the right to review a decision of previous rabbinates, unless it is greater in number and wiser."[148] Meanwhile, from the halls of the Israeli Parliament to the pages of the worldwide Jewish press, debate raged over Ben-Gurion's article. The nonpartisan Hebrew daily *Ma'ariv* opined: "The man was great. He was a spiritual giant, and he was Jewish. Why shouldn't he belong to us? Why shouldn't his work be considered a part of Hebrew writing?" Predictably, the orthodox camp was less enthused. On the floor of the Knesset, Eliyahu-Moshe Ganhuvsky, an MK from the religious Zionist Ha-po'el ha-Mizrahi party, warned that canceling the herem on Spinoza would open the floodgates to naturalizing "countless individuals established by history as traitors." The Mizrahi (religious Zionist) newspaper *Ha-Tsofeh* [The Watchman] sarcastically labeled Shikmoni's group in Haifa Spinoza's *Hasidim*, and it castigated them for "introducing into the temple of Jewish thought a new idolatry that was liable to ruin the spiritual and cultural character of the State of Israel."[149]

Yet the most sustained attack on the repatriation of Spinoza came not from a religious Jew but from a secularist. Rising to challenge Ben-Gurion was Yehoshua Manoah, an Eastern European Jew who had been among the founders of Deganyah, the first kibbutz. From 1954 to 1956, Manoah and Ben-Gurion engaged in a dialogue in the Hebrew press over the propriety of celebrating Spinoza from a national Jewish perspective, with occasional contributions to the debate by other Israeli intellectuals. Here I wish to highlight only a central—and indeed familiar—aspect of Manoah's argument against Spinoza:

> I am not religiously observant, but nevertheless I can say wholeheartedly that I take pride in the belief in one God (monotheism), the most magnificent creation of our people, which conquered a large number of the peoples of this earth and ever since has been an unfailing source of consolation, deliverance, and mercy, for which until today no substitute has been found. But I will admit that in truth, I don't have the strength to enter into arguments and controversies over this noble and glorious creation. As a national Jew, who sees an ironclad need that the materials for the construction of the present and the future be taken from the tradition of the past and its sacred possessions—there are things for me that, once touched, immediately cause offense. Regarding these things there can be no compromise! They are, to my mind taboo. Even somebody completely secu-

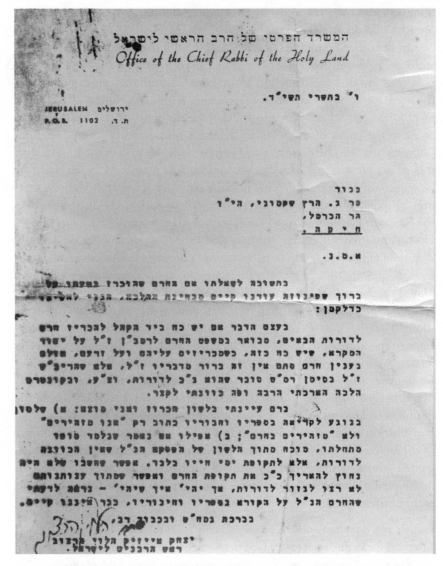

FIGURE. 5.3. Letter from the chief rabbi of Israel, Isaac Halevi Herzog to G. Herz-Shikmoni, 6 Tishre 5714 (September 15, 1953), suggesting that the rabbinic ban on Spinoza's writings no longer applies. G. Herz-Shikmoni Papers, Abba Khoushy Archive, University of Haifa Library, Haifa, Israel.

lar, but nationalistic, must have something like this (one might call it "holy"). . . .
For me (and I don't care what others think) anybody who belittles the stature
of Moses, our teacher (*Moshe rabenu*), speaks ill of the Prophets of Israel, shows
disrespect to the Hebrew Bible, our book of books, which in my eyes has no
equal—I want nothing to do with his philosophy.[150]

Manoah gives the secular-national rationale for keeping Spinoza out. Like
Spinoza, he does not feel bound by the Law, and while he "takes pride" in
the monotheistic idea, he has no interest in religious disputations. But in
attacking Moses, the prophets, the Bible, Spinoza was not just attacking the
Jewish religion; he was undermining the "sacred possessions" of the Jewish
people, the building blocks on which any future national Jewish culture had
to be constructed. To honor such a traitor—to say to him "Our brother are
you!"—would be to show an appalling disrespect to our forebearers. And
respect, Manoah concludes, is precisely what is missing in contemporary
Israeli secularism.

Contra Ben-Gurion—but also contra Klausner—Manoah insists that
one cannot enter Spinoza into the cultural pantheon and also extol the values of Jewish unity and solidarity. These cannot be brought together as part
of a single "imagined community," as it were. Yet what leaps out most in this
protest is how closely it resembles Klausner's scolding of Brenner and the
"Young Hebrews" from 1911. The need for respect for the "great values" of
our ancestors urged by an openly nonobservant Jew, the fear of total rupture from the religious past, the insistence that there are certain lines that
cannot be crossed without committing national treason—all these emphases in Manoah have their counterpart in Klausner. One of the great secular
champions of the reappropriation of the Amsterdam philosopher for Hebrew culture shared with one of its vehement secular critics a nearly verbatim concern over unchecked secularization. By going beyond attention-
grabbing gestures like Klausner's lifting of the herem, and appreciating the
anxiety over where to draw the line between "freedom" and "heresy" they
obscure, we gain more complex insight not only into the Zionist use of
Spinoza, but into an essential tension within the Zionist formation of the
secular.

*Figure. 6.1. Photo of I. B. Singer as a young man. Isaac Bashevis Singer Papers, Harry Ransom Center, The University of Texas at Austin.

CHAPTER 6

Farewell, Spinoza

I. B. Singer and the Tragicomedy of the Jewish Spinozist

I.

Mention the making of Spinoza into a modern Jewish culture hero and the author most likely to come to mind is Isaac Bashevis Singer. Like dybbuk possessions and love triangles, Spinoza casts a long shadow in Singer's vast oeuvre. He figures most conspicuously in "The Spinoza of Market Street," a widely acknowledged masterpiece of Singer's short fiction that portrays a would-be Spinoza in early twentieth-century Jewish Warsaw. Yet the Amsterdam philosopher is also a mainstay of several of Singer's novels and of his copious autobiographical writings (the lines between which are often deliberately blurred), where an at least temporary veneration of Spinoza and the *Ethics* often serves as a *rite de passage* in the protagonist's journey from traditionalism to secularism. Reflecting on the emergence of Spinoza as an icon for nineteenth- and twentieth-century Jewish iconoclasts, historian David Biale writes, "One thinks of Isaac Bashevis Singer's characters who obsessively read Spinoza, a practice that Singer borrowed from earlier Yiddish and Hebrew writers."[1] Others preceded (and succeeded) him, but it is Singer who, over time, has become the most readily invoked example for Spinoza's rehabilitation from heretic to hero, as "the first modern Jew."

In fact, the twinning of Singer with this rehabilitation is rife with irony. At one level, this is because Singer—unlike Berthold Auerbach, Israel Zangwill, Melech Ravitch, and others—never fictionalized or poeticized Spinoza himself, but Spinoza's Jewish reception. In Singer's writing, there is no return to the scene of seventeenth-century Amsterdam, no reconstruction of Spinoza's Sephardic upbringing and estrangement from Judaism, no reprise of the excommunication.[2] The setting for the Spinoza theme in his work is prewar and interwar Eastern Europe—specifically Warsaw and its environs—and, to a lesser extent, Singer's later American home. The subject is the intimate link between the encounter with Spinoza's rationalist and pantheist heresy and the peculiarities of East European Jewish enlightenment and secularization. Indeed, as Biale intimates, the whole basis for Singer's appropriation of Spinoza is the earlier appropriation (and adulation) of him by modern Jewish secularists. With a mixture of wry humor and occasional pathos, Singer dramatizes the overwrought nature of this appropriation, the intensity of the identification with Spinoza among many a talmudic prodigy turned secular intellectual. *We might call Singer the great ironist of Jewish Spinozism.* And yet, Singer is not only a satirist of the modern Jewish fixation with Spinoza. He is also a critic. The pinnacle of Spinoza's system—the ideal of the *amor dei intellectualis*—could not provide satisfactory answers to what were, for Singer, the perennial truths of human existence: the power of the emotions, the problem of evil, the pangs of homelessness. Herein lies an even more fundamental paradox to the association of Singer with the Jewish cultural reclamation of the Amsterdam rebel—the fact that his appropriation is essentially an argument with Spinoza, a critique of the Enlightenment legacy of secular rationalism he embodied. But because of its repetitive character, it is a rebuke, even repudiation that only furthers the cause of rehabilitation, cementing the bond between Spinoza and the *oyfgeklerte yid*, the "enlightened Jew."

This chapter will analyze the Spinoza image in Singer's work in three stages.[3] First, relying primarily on Singer's autobiographical writings, I will chart Singer's path from worship to wariness of Spinoza in Warsaw between the wars, the very period that witnessed a broad and ecumenical revival of the Amsterdam philosopher and a veritable explosion of his popularity within Yiddish literature.[4] I will then turn to an analysis of the two works in Singer's canon most pivotal to his use of Spinoza, "The Spinoza of Market Street" and *The Family Moskat*. Written in close proximity—"The Spinoza of Market Street" was originally titled "*Der Shpinozist*" and published in *Di tsukunft* [The Future] in 1944, while *The Family Moskat* [*Di familye mushkat*] was serialized in *Der forverts* [The Forward] from 1945 to 1948—these two works reflect the range of the Spinoza theme in Singer, from the miniature scale of the short story to the multigenerational novel, and from gentle comedy to harsh post-Holocaust tragedy.

II.

I used to carry around Spinoza's *Ethics* wherever I went.[5]

It is perhaps a further irony that Singer came under the spell of Spinoza not in worldly, cosmopolitan Warsaw, his home for nearly ten years of his youth and then for much of his twenties and early thirties, but in the secluded shtetl of Bilgoray (Bilgoraj) in southeastern Poland. In 1917 Isaac and his mother Bathsheba, fleeing the extreme hardships and shortages of wartime Warsaw, returned to her hometown. He spent four years in this traditional Jewish town, separated from both his father Pinhos Menahem, a Hasidic rabbi exacting in his faith and religious discipline, and hostile to anything smacking of secular modernity, and his elder brother Israel Joshua, an artist-novelist who was already an "enlightened" heretic. While Bilgoray was a bastion of "old Jewishness," it was not immune from "the new winds" of modern Jewish politics and culture, and it was in the context of his compulsive reading of "original works in Yiddish" and "translations of European writers" that Singer discovered "Stupnicki's book on Spinoza."[6]

One can safely assume that few readers of Singer's *In My Father's Court* in translation today have ever heard of this book or, for that matter, Stupnicki. Shaul Stupnicki (1876–1942) was a well-known Yiddish journalist in Poland and a prominent supporter of the Folkspartei, the movement and political party, inspired by the Jewish historian Simon Dubnow, that sought national-cultural autonomy for Jews in Eastern Europe. His greatest legacy was as one of the leading intellectuals of the Warsaw ghetto, where he contributed to Emmanuel Ringelblum's Oyneg Shabes archive.[7] Yet in the history of Spinoza's Jewish reception, he also looms large. In 1917—the same year Singer moved to Bilgoray—Stupnicki published *Borukh Shpinoza: Zayn filozofye, bibel-kritik, shtatslere un zayn badaytung in der antviklung fun mentshlikhen denken* [Baruch Spinoza: His Philosophy, Biblical Criticism, Political Theory, and Import for the Development of Human Thought]. The Yiddish library on Spinoza as of 1917 was still extremely modest. It consisted mostly of a smattering of articles, the first of which had appeared in a St. Petersburg weekly in 1886; a translation of Berthold Auerbach's *Spinoza* novel by the Lithuanian-born playwright Bernard Gorin; and a slender primer on Spinoza's life and philosophy by the American Yiddish journalist and socialist Philip Krantz (Jacob Rombro).[8] Stupnicki's volume was something new, a book of over one hundred sixty pages that was the first attempt at a scholarly and comprehensive introduction to Spinoza in Yiddish. "For the first time," Stupnicki wrote in his introduction, "the Jewish reader has in hand the complete Spinoza, his *philosophy*, his *biblical criticism*, his *political theory*."[9] Acknowledging that for many, Spinoza's teachings—in particular his biblical criticism—would be "new and startling," the author maintained that "the Jewish reader is, by now, sufficiently grown up" to cope with the challenge to his inherited beliefs.

"The Spinoza book created a turmoil in my brain," Singer writes. The biblical criticism that Stupnicki felt necessary to caution against seems barely to have attracted notice. It was instead the pantheist philosophy of the *Ethics* and Spinoza's God that instantly absorbed him:

His concept that God is a substance with infinite attributes, that divinity itself must be true to its laws, that there is no free will, no absolute morality and purpose—fascinated and bewildered me. As I read this book, I felt intoxicated, inspired as I never had been before. It seemed to me that the truths I had been seeking since childhood had at last become apparent. Everything was God— Warsaw, Bilgoray, the spider in the attic, the water in the well, the clouds in the sky, and the book on my knees. . . . I too was a modus, which explained my indecision, my restlessness, my passionate nature, my doubts and fears.[10]

This was Singer's "Spinoza moment," and for all the singularity of its description in his memoirs, it shares the features of many a similar first encounter with the Amsterdam philosopher in the modern Jewish experience: the sense of wondrous discovery, the feeling of having serendipitously stumbled upon the long elusive truth, the intuition of the oneness of all being. The notion that even his "tangled thoughts were divine" seemed to untangle everything, to invest his turbulent, wandering thoughts with necessity and thus stability. "I was exalted," he concludes; "everything seemed good."

If the Stupnicki book was what lit the flame and converted the teenage Singer for a time into a young Spinozist and devotee of the *Ethics*, it was not his first exposure to the philosophy of Spinoza. One of the arguments, apparently, that raged in the Singer household between Israel Joshua and his parents concerned Spinoza's heresy. As he describes elsewhere in his autobiographical writings, Isaac first learned of Spinoza from his elder brother.[11] His father, meanwhile, countered that "Spinoza's name should be blotted out," though he curiously mitigated his heresy by adding "Spinoza had contributed nothing" that was not already recognized by the Hasidic masters.[12] "There was an interpretation by the famous Baal Shem," Singer writes, paraphrasing his father, "who also identified the world with the Godhead. True, the Baal Shem had lived after Spinoza, but my father argued that Spinoza had drawn from ancient sources, which no Spinoza disciple could deny."[13]

Pinhos Menahem's "ancient sources" were the teachings of Jewish mysticism, and from Singer's closing comment it is clear he thought this nexus between Spinozism and Kabbalah was irrefutable. Much of *A Little Boy in Search of God*, one of his later memoirs, is devoted to his youthful discovery of—and enthrallment with—the "cabala books in my father's bookcase." His father cautioned that "you couldn't take to the cabala before you reached thirty" or "[o]ne could drift into heresy." Isaac Bashevis ignored these warnings and read these works furtively—his first experience of literature as forbidden fruit. Their crux, as Singer perceived it, was pantheism: the "concept that everything is God and God is everything; that the stone in the street, the mouse in its hole, the fly on the wall, and the shoes on my feet were all fashioned from the Divinity."[14] In one volume in particular, *The Pillar of Service* by the eighteenth-century Hasidic kabbalist Reb Baruch Kossover (d. 1779), Isaac claimed to find proofs for the existence of God akin to the "arguments I found later in Spinoza's *Ethics*." "My later interest in Spinoza," the older I. B. Singer reminisced, "stemmed from studying the cabala."[15]

With this admission, Singer stands in a chain of tradition stretching back to Salomon Maimon, the eighteenth-century thinker who was, arguably, the first Jewish Spinozist. In his classic *Autobiography*, Maimon had similarly transposed the Lurianic myth of creation to a Spinozist key: "[T]he Cabbalah is nothing but an expanded Spinozism," he famously explained, "in which not only is the origin of the world explained by the limitation of the divine being, but also the origin of every kind of being, and its relation to the rest, are derived from a separate attribute of God."[16] Moreover, when Maimon finally came to read Spinoza for the first time after fleeing Poland for Berlin, he claimed that "his system had already been suggested to me by the Cabbalistic writings."[17] Singer never alludes to Maimon as a precursor. Perhaps he was genuinely unaware of the echoes of the earlier *Autobiography* in his own self-fashioning, but they are striking. Like Maimon, Singer not only highlights the similarities between Spinozism and the Kabbalah. He also implies that his early study of the Kabbalah gave him a grasp of Spinozism even before he read Spinoza.

What is clear is that, for Singer, the allure of Spinozism lay in its demonstration of a total immanence of God that could be found, in more cryptic form, in the Kabbalah. The Spinoza whom Singer would come to adore was clearly the "God-intoxicated man" of Novalis and the German Romantics. Indeed, though his father would undoubtedly have seen red if he knew his son Isaac was reading secular literature of any kind, not to mention the "horrible heresies" of the Amsterdam philosopher, the Spinoza admired by Singer was, in a way, also a testament to the strength of this paternal legacy—with its heightened spirituality and Hasidic ecstasy—even in its defiance.

Yet Singer could not entirely commit to this religious Spinoza. The other Spinoza—the atheist and materialist par excellence hated by orthodox theologians and heralded by radical secularists—hovered close by. It was as if Spinoza stood at a crossroads, where one path led homeward, back toward the secret pantheism of Kabbalah, while the other drifted in the direction of the modern evolutionary philosophies of Malthus and Darwin.

Recalling his discovery of Malthus—again, through a pamphlet supplied by Israel Joshua—Singer writes that he "proved in a way that couldn't be clearer that countless creatures were born to die, for otherwise the world would fill with so many creatures that everyone would starve to death or simply be crushed."[18] Darwin, he added, "went even further and maintained the continuous struggle for food or sex is the origin of all species." In these thinkers, Singer found a fundamentally pessimistic outlook. The notion of a "natural selection" governed by no higher metaphysical plan or purpose appeared to render both individual strivings and suffering meaningless. And the young Isaac, trying to digest such ideas while still in his early teens, was gripped by the thought that the seeds of this godless philosophy lay in the God of Spinoza:

> Spinoza attributed to God merely the capacity to extend and to think. The anguish of people and animals did not concern Spinoza's God even in the slightest. He had no feelings at all concerning justice or freedom. The Baal Shem and the murderer were of equal importance to Him. Everything was preordained, and no change whatsoever could affect Spinoza's God or the things that were part of Him. . . . This philosophy exuded a chill, though still I felt that it might contain more truth (bitter truth) than the cabala. If God were indeed full of mercy and benevolence, He wouldn't have allowed starvation, plagues, and pogroms. *Spinoza's God merely fortified the contentions of Malthus.*[19]

Interestingly, if, in my reading, his pious father Pinhos Menahem was the invisible (and ironic) inspiration behind Singer's mystical Spinoza, his freethinking elder brother—who had introduced Isaac to the Spinozan heresy in the first place—became, for a time at least, synonymous with Spinoza the cold rationalist, the Spinoza who seemed only a step from Malthus and Darwin. "All existence is nature, and nature knows of no pity," Singer quotes Isaac Joshua as having said in response to his moral anguish over the killing of animals for meat.[20] Or, as he argued to his mother amid the harsh deprivations of the First World War, "There is no Almighty. Man is an animal like all other animals."[21]

Out of this tug-of-war came Singer's own stab at a "refined Spinozism." His starting point was Spinoza's sixth definition in the first part of the *Ethics*, "On God," which states: "By God I understand a being absolutely infinite, that is, a substance consisting of an infinity of attributes, of which each one expresses an eternal and infinite essence."[22] This sentence has long bedeviled Spinoza scholars: Did the seventeenth-century philosopher mean to say that there were other, infinite attributes of God beyond Thought and Extension?[23] Whatever the answer to this age-old ambiguity, Singer, in admittedly idiosyncratic fashion, pounced on it:

Since according to Spinoza substance contained an endless number of attributes, this left some room for fantasy. I even toyed with the notion of changing some of Spinoza's axioms and definitions and bringing out a new *Ethics*. You could easily say that time was one of God's attributes, too, as well as purpose, creativeness, and growth.[24] I had read somewhere about Lobachevski's non-Euclidean geometry, and I wanted to create a non-Spinozan pantheism, or whatever it might be called. I was ready to make will a divine attribute, too. This kind of revisionist Spinozism would come very close to the cabala.[25]

That this "revisionist Spinozism" was indeed central to Singer's thinking in late adolescence is clear from his account of his first stab at becoming a published writer. In 1923, while staying, temporarily, with Israel Joshua and his wife, in-laws, and newborn son in a small flat just outside Warsaw—desperate to find work and avoid having to return to his parents then living in Galicia—Singer wrote his very first manuscript on Spinoza and the Kabbalah. Blithely unaware of any previous scholarship on this topic, Singer composed a little book on the subject in a mere two weeks. His main argument was that "Spinoza had not enriched and expanded the idea of the Kabbalah with his philosophy"; on the contrary, "he had narrowed them, stripped them of their magnificent stature," such that "Spinozism [was] nothing more than an abridged and shriveled Kabbalah."[26] One is immediately arrested by the inversion of Maimon's formulation of the relationship between Spinozism and the Kabbalah in his *Autobiography*, though once again this link goes unacknowledged. Maimon called the Kabbalah "an expanded Spinozism," suggesting that the pruning of the mythological excesses of Lurianic acosmism as part of its translation into Spinozan rationalism was a positive development in the history of thought. Singer, on the other hand, laments the compression of Jewish mysticism in Spinozism, its yielding of "an abridged and shriveled Kabbalah."

Pressed by his brother to travel to Warsaw to do something productive, the younger Singer resolved to see if he could get his work published. Arriving by train, still dressed in his long gaberdine coat and sporting sidelocks, he went first to the Warsaw Synagogue on Tlomackie Street. Its elderly secretary, Hayim Yehiel Bernstein (1845–1928), was a noted authority on the Jewish calendar as well as an expert on Spinoza and Jewish philosophy in general. Singer thought Bernstein might recommend a suitable forum for his study of Spinoza and the Kabbalah. But the meeting with the wizened scholar—echoes of which would find their way into Singer's later fiction, including *The Family Moskat*—did not go as hoped. After allowing Singer to expound at length on "Spinoza, the Kabbalah, similarities, influences," the secretary deflected all his requests for guidance. The help he could offer amounted to "*gornisht, absolut gornisht.*" And so, after helping the nearly blind Bernstein leave his office and cross the street, Singer—tired and hungry, and suddenly seized by a loathing of his brochure and of philosophizing in a broader sense—walked into the nearest courtyard, opened the garbage can, and threw away his manuscript.[27]

Some twenty years later in the mid-1940s, I. B. Singer, now living in New York, would write a few articles explaining Spinoza's philosophy for the readers of *Der Forverts*.[28] Around the same time, he was also beginning to make use of Spinoza—or the ghost of Spinoza—as a fictional theme in his writing.[29] By then, the one-time romance had largely faded.

III.

Q: Did you begin to move away from Spinoza before you came to this country or later?

A: Before.[30]

What had begun as a trickle prior to and during the First World War became a flood in its wake. In 1923 the first Yiddish translation of the *Treatise* appeared in print—nearly four decades before Spinoza's devastating secular critique of religion (and Judaism in particular) was finally translated into Hebrew.[31] That same year, two separate presses—one in Warsaw and one in Chicago—published William Nathanson's pioneering Yiddish rendition of the *Ethics*; by 1927 the Warsaw imprint was already in its third edition.[32] Stupnicki's groundbreaking effort to create a Yiddish-language *vissenshaft* on Spinoza was taken to new heights by the New York–based Yiddish philosopher Jacob Shatzky. His *Spinoza un zayn svivoh* [Spinoza and His Environment], published in 1927 (along with 1932, one of the two major Spinoza jubilee years of the interwar period)—a work consciously modeled on the magisterial fin-de-siècle Spinoza biographies of Jakob Freudenthal and K. O. Meinsma—was reviewed in practically every Yiddish newspaper and journal of significance.[33] To this day, it remains the most significant exemplar of a Yiddish scholarly account of the life and times of the Amsterdam philosopher. Meanwhile, at the same time that Hebraists in Palestine were claiming Spinoza for secular Zionism, Yiddish socialists—from Bundist social democrats to Soviet Trotskyists and even Stalinists—were busy appropriating Spinoza as as a precursor of Marxist liberation and dialectical materialism.[34] In 1932 Leo Finkelstein delivered a tribute, in Yiddish, at the international Spinoza congress held in The Hague to commemorate the three-hundredth birthday of the philosopher—the first instance in which Yiddish was ever publicly represented at one of these multilingual symposia.[35] Yet the highlight of the Spinoza renaissance in Yiddish between the wars was, without question, the *Spinoza bukh* of 1932. Edited by Shatzky and published by the Jewish division of the short-lived Spinoza Institute of America, the *Spinoza bukh* was an anthology of Yiddish essays on topics ranging from Spinoza and Kant to Spinoza and Marx, and from the problem of free will in philosophy from Spinoza to Bergson to the relationship between Spinoza's thought and Judaism.[36] The collection—however uneven in the quality of its articles—was a landmark, proof positive that the competition between Yiddish and Hebrew (which produced no similar Spinoza Festschrift in 1932) now extended to the representation of Spinoza as well. Hebrew clearly had enjoyed a considerable head start, but Yiddish was now catching up, and in some cases even surpassing its rival.[37]

The Yiddish Spinoza renaissance spanned countries and even continents. But Warsaw, where the nineteen-year-old Singer arrived in 1923, was certainly one of its main centers. And the poet and editor Melekh Ravitch (1893–1976), who quickly took Singer under his wing, was one of its main champions. Many Yiddish poets—from H. Leyvick to Abraham Sutzkever—would in time write verse about Spinoza.[38] Ravitch (né Zekharye Chone Bergner), originally of Galicia, was the first, and arguably the most ardent. In 1919 the first edition of his famed Spinoza cycle of poems appeared.[39] Written from 1916 to 1918, while Ravitch was a foot soldier in the Austro-Hungarian army, the four-part poem (much like the *Societas Spinozana* founded by Carl Gebhardt shortly thereafter) images the rationalist Spinoza as, in essence, the answer to the blood-soaked passions of the Great War. The first section—*Der mentsh*—portrays Spinoza from birth to death, devoting special attention to his excommunication. The second—*Dos verk*—muses on Spinoza's metaphysics and biblical criticism. The third and fourth sections—*Di shpin* [The Spider] and *Ktoyres* [Incense], respectively—contain meditations on everything from Spinoza's stoic example to his role as a kind of eternal flame for the poet throughout his wanderings.[40]

Ravitch's *Shpinoza* is a fascinating paradox: a lyrical poem, characterized by vivid, even graphic imagery and a striving for emotional effect that is at the same time a paean to the most rationalist element of Spinoza's system. The geometrical method—the very aspect of Spinoza's *Ethics* that nearly all his admirers, since the German Romantics, had scotched—is here the subject of the deepest reverence. In the "Geometrical Form of the *Ethics*," one of three poems devoted to the *Ethics* in the section *Dos verk*, Ravitch traces his infatuation with the Amsterdam philosopher to the precise definitions and strict deductions of his masterwork:

> It was not your deep loneliness,
> nor the endless sorrow in your face,
> nor even your infinite tranquility
> that built the high airy bridge
> of the silent night watches of my soul
> in your land, Spinoza . . .
> And what my soul plumbed down to bedrock
> was often no more than a simple axiom
> a formula, an adjective or proof
> a parable with a ruler, a parable with a drawn line,
> or your eternal parable about the sum of the angles of the triangle.[41]

The notion that the emotions could be pinned down with the exactitude of "the sum of the angles of the triangle" was, for Ravitch, neither a pipe dream nor a type of crude reductionism, but a source of consolation in the face of chaos and immense suffering. In Spinoza, Ravitch—like the "young Spinozist" Moses Hess nearly a century earlier—found a new millennial prophet to succeed Moses (his "tablets turned to dust") and Jesus (the "crucified one" who was "just a dead image").[42] In the necessitarianism and non-sectarianism of the *Ethics*, he saw a foundation stone for rebuilding on the ruins left by war.

Ravitch viewed Spinoza as a figure of total rupture. Contrary to East European Hebraists like Rubin, who aimed to "Judaize" Spinoza by linking him to a subterranean tradition of Jewish pantheism, or like Klausner, who wished to declare an end to the conflict between Spinoza and Judaism with a general "amnesty," Ravitch—at least the young Ravitch—rejected the path of reconciliation.[43] Spinoza's break from his "own blood," however painful, had been entirely mutual: Spinoza craved freedom from the "five cells [i.e., books]" of the Torah and the start of a "new life" as Benedictus, not Borukh; the whole of Amsterdam Jewry, meanwhile—as described in two poems devoted to the *herem*—drove him out with a barrage of insults and curses ("D'Espinoza, fool, *meshugener*, Borukh, accursed, throw him to the mad dogs / Benedictus, *treyf* skull, thief, die, *gehenm* [hell], beat him, skin him, tie him up').[44] The narrowing of this breach, the masking of Spinoza's innovation as tradition—a tack taken even by radical maskilim like Rubin in the effort to reclaim him—was not for Ravitch. It was the uncompromising Spinoza whom Ravitch adored, for, within Yiddish poetry, Ravitch too hoped to be a groundbreaker, with the Amsterdam philosopher as his lodestar:

> Perhaps I am destined to be a candle
> for my generation,
> a trailblazer, at a crossroads,
> on the endless path to God—
> but you are the light of my light
> the torch of my own night.[45]

Ravitch moved to Warsaw in 1921 and rapidly became one of the leading members of the Yiddish Warsaw avant-garde. With Spinoza as his guiding light, Ravitch was determined to bury the old and usher in the new, only in poetry—Yiddish poetry—and not in philosophy. In 1922 he, along with fellow twentysomething radicals Peretz Markish and Uri Zvi Greenberg, founded a journal, *Di Khalyastre* [The Gang], expressly devoted to the promotion of a revolutionary poetics in Yiddish.[46] Not the religious and regional particulars of Jewish Eastern Europe, but the dominant European aesthetic movements of the day, from proletarianism to futurism to expressionism, would take center stage. For a time, it included among its contributors Israel Joshua Singer. The periodical was defunct after only two years, but the label *Khalyastre* endured as a byword for a defiantly modernist and antireligious impulse in twentieth-century Yiddish writing.[47] In its wake, Ravitch went on to found and edit *Literarishe bleter* [Literary Pages], one of the most prominent Yiddish literary journals in interwar Poland. He also became secretary of the famed Yiddish Writers' Union on Tlomackie 13, before leaving Warsaw for good in 1934 for a decade of worldwide travel.

If I have gone on about Ravitch at more length than seems warranted, it is not only because he, more than anyone else in the world of Yiddish literature, furnished Singer with the ideal type of the Jewish Spinozist. It is also because of his personal influence on the late adolescent who arrived in Jewish Warsaw as a would-be Yiddish writer. Early on, Ravitch took on the role of Singer's guide and guardian, greeting him with free temporary accommodations, providing him with some much needed polish, and, in general, introducing him to the world of Yiddish literary Warsaw. In *A Little Boy in Search of God*, Singer writes of the discussions they had in Ravitch's garret apartment, in which his host would proclaim his "absolute faith" in a "world of justice that could come today or tomorrow" and would contain neither Jew nor Gentile, but "only a single united mankind."[48] One can safely assume that these discussions at some point touched on the philosopher from Amsterdam. And Singer's first low-paying job in Warsaw would be as a proofreader for the *Literarishe bleter* of which Ravitch (as well as, for a time, Israel Joshua) was editor. Yet Bashevis would ultimately reject the Spinoza worship of Ravitch, just as he turned his back on the utopian radicalism and socialism of *Di Khalyastre* and its successor, the *Literarishe bleter*.[49] While it is impossible to pinpoint the precise moment of this reversal—Singer himself in one of his later interviews mentioned only that it came "before" he left Warsaw for New York in 1935—it would appear that a crucial role in this change of heart was played by another Warsaw Yiddish and Hebrew writer: the poet and essayist Aaron Zeitlin (1898–1973).

Zeitlin was a son of Hillel Zeitlin, whom we first encountered in chapter 5 as the author of a turn-of-the-century Hebrew critical study of Spinoza written from the perspective of a Jewish secularist and Zionist. By the 1920s the elder Zeitlin was no longer either. He had "returned" to a pious, if still idiosyncratic version of the Hasidic spirituality and *halakhic* observance of his youth. As Singer described him, "[t]he father, Hillel Zeitlin, who was learned in philosophy and a cabalist, had come to the early conclusion that a modern Jewishness (whether in nationalistic or socialistic form) that lacked religion was a paradox and absurdity."[50] Not only did he castigate the "radical, atheistic atmosphere" of Yiddish literature between the wars (it was actually Zeitlin who coined the label "*di Khalyastre*," originally as an epithet); he also opposed the more appreciative stance vis-à-vis traditional religion of writers and poets like I. L. Peretz and H. N. Bialik, whose work—even if often saturated with nostalgia for the shtetl—hinged, nevertheless, on a cultural nationalist understanding of Jewishness. Within interwar Warsaw, a circle formed around Zeitlin that in many ways functioned as a counterpoint to the Yiddish PEN Club.[51] "He rarely entered the Writers' Union," Singer would later write, "but his home was itself a kind of writers' union. . . . His house was always filled with writers, some just starting out, as well as with other remarkable personages. Every young man who lifted a pen sooner or later called on Hillel Zeitlin." Moreover, despite his newfound orthodoxy, he "had patience for all: for kabbalists seeking clues about the Messiah and the End of Days and for scoffers who came to debate the existence of God."[52]

Isaac's introduction to the open house of Hillel Zeitlin came as a result of an acquaintance struck with his son Aaron. Only six years Singer's senior, the younger Zeitlin was already an accomplished poet when the two first met by chance in the Writers' Union on 13 Tlomackie in 1924. Aaron shared his father's mystical sensibility as well as contempt for the revolutionary politics and infatuation with various isms of the Yiddish avant-garde. Like many postwar intellectuals, he was also fascinated with spiritualism and occultism.[53] "Both Zeitlin and I were deeply interested in psychic research," Singer later recalled. "We often sat for hours then—and years later too—conversing. We both believed in God, in demons, evil spirits, in all kinds of ghosts and phantoms."[54]

The acquaintance between the younger Singer and the younger Zeitlin quickly turned into a deep friendship that eventually culminated in a literary collaboration. In 1932 they cofounded *Globus*, a Yiddish journal that was determined to shun the leftism of Yiddish literature and its politicization in a broader sense.[55] The periodical survived for only three years, and its significance in the history of Yiddish literature is largely a product of its serialization of Bashevis's debut novel, *Der sotn in Goray* [Satan in Goray].[56] A dark portrait of a seventeenth-century Polish shtetl decimated first by the 1648–49 Chmielnitski massacres, then plunged into even greater devastation by the false hopes raised by the seventeenth-century messianic movement of Shabbetai Zevi, the novel—blending "history" with frank description of supernatural phenomena and personae—was an implicit condemnation of what Bashevis would later brand the "literary Sabbateanism" of the interwar period, with its determination to cast aside the yoke of the past and its dreams of a utopian future. We will have to consider the relevance of Singer's early literary fascination with the Sabbatean heresy to his later introduction of the Spinoza theme in his writing. But for our purposes here, what is most important about *Globus* is that it became a forum for Zeitlin to profile—and attack—the Spinoza craze that crested in the tercentenary year of 1932.

Zeitlin's *"Perushim oyf toyres-Spinoza"* [Comments on the Teachings of Spinoza] was, loosely speaking, a review of the *Spinoza bukh* of 1932, but as the author himself admitted, it was "a review of *ideas*, not simply a book review."[57] After initially offering mild praise for the inclusion of such a volume in the still slight library of Yiddish literature, Zeitlin issued a critique as blistering of appropriations of Spinoza, whether for Judaism or Marxism, as of the ideas of Spinoza himself. While Zeitlin's bill of indictment was long, his main charge was that Spinoza's philosophy was utterly inadequate to the problem of human suffering—"the Job-experience of modern man." This inadequacy stemmed from its very character *as* philosophy, at least as a philosophizing about the nature of God. For such philosophy, especially when driven to the extremes of Spinozism, ultimately reduced God to the affectless *causa sui* of the natural order and all human suffering to the infinite chain of causes of deductive reasoning. The contrast with Ravitch could not be starker. Ravitch viewed the *more geometrico* as the most suitable response to the chaos and carnage of war. Zeitlin saw this same method as the ultimate tragedy of Spinoza—that he had no answer to human tragedy save necessity. "Who knows?," Zeitlin asked. "Perhaps it is sheer madness that so many minds have sought and continue to seek consolation precisely from the lonely man from Amsterdam?"[58] In place of Spinoza's God, Zeitlin called for a return to the living, personal, suffering, responsive, choosing, indeed highly anthropomorphized God of the Bible and the Kabbalah—the God who answered Job out of the whirlwind, and even in chiding consoled him. And in place of the philosophical pursuit of intellectual perfection (*shlemus*)—reflected in the Spinozan ideal of the *amor dei intellectualis*—he envisioned a human encounter with God that would be intimate, at times angry and argumentative, but always impassioned. For it was through feeling and suffering, not through contemplative reason, that man came closest to God. With a closing flourish that deliberately mimicked the trinitarian formula, Zeitlin wrote: "*Let us overthrow the God of the philosophers in the name of the three: in the name of suffering, in the name of will, and in the name of faith.*"[59]

To what degree his relationship with Zeitlin spurred Singer to spurn the Spinoza enthusiasm of his youth is impossible to determine with any certainty. No doubt, his own attraction to mystical, supernatural forces played a part in this break. Nevertheless, the similarity between the views expressed by Zeitlin regarding Spinoza, and Singer's later reflections on the philosopher in his memoirs, is striking. Zeitlin stresses, as Singer later would, *free will* as the crux of Judaism and the key issue dividing it from Spinozism.[60] He also explicitly distinguishes between the "mystical" and the "rationalist" Spinoza, arguing that while the first ascribes to God infinite attributes, the latter limits human apprehension to two, thought and extension.[61] Given that Zeitlin was already a forceful voice and a recognized poet by the time Singer met him, it is certainly plausible that he exercised great influence on Singer's developing opinions of the Amsterdam heretic. Indeed, it is even possible that Singer, in his memoirs, retrojected ideas about Spinoza formed at a later period—and perhaps under Zeitlin's guidance—onto his adolescent musings.

But Singer would become best known not for his essayistic reflections on Spinoza and Judaism but for his fashioning of the Spinoza-obsessed secular Jewish intellectual into a recurring type in his fiction. In this respect he would prove a true original.

IV.

I recalled Spinoza's words to the effect that everything could become a passion. I had resolved beforehand to become a narrator of human passion rather than of a placid lifestyle.[62]

Spinozism was the first heresy to intrigue and, for a time, win over the young Bashevis. A little over two decades after tossing his "Spinoza and the Kabbalah" essay into a garbage bin on Tlomackie Street in Warsaw, Singer would revisit this early enthusiasm in his famous short story "The

Spinoza of Market Street," published in Yiddish in 1944 under the title "*Der Shpinozist.*" Yet it was a different Jewish heresy that first ignited his literary imagination. From 1932 to 1944—a period interrupted by his wrenching, albeit in retrospect lifesaving move to New York in 1935—Singer wrote, in addition to his acclaimed novel *Satan in Goray*, several stories and another serialized novel dedicated to the messianic movements of Shabbetai Zvi and his "successor" Jacob Frank.[63] Critics have commonly explained these works—*Satan in Goray* especially—as thinly veiled warnings about the secular messianisms of the 1920s and 1930s, from fascism to communism, and an added jab at the Jewish attraction to the latter.[64] Yet there was more to Singer's fascination with this heresy than mere contemporary critique. Singer was drawn to the very same aspect of Sabbatean theology that Gershom Scholem would immortalize in the title of his groundbreaking 1937 essay "Redemption through Sin."[65] This was the idea that the road to redemption lay not in the time-honored posture of patiently waiting for God to act, in submission to the yoke of the Law as interpreted and enforced by the rabbinic and lay leadership of the community, in the careful control and sublimation of the passions, but in just the opposite—in giving vent to desire, in sinning with full intent. Where Singer differed markedly from Scholem was in his willingness to ascribe ultimate agency to Satan and his entourage in luring Jews to succumb to this heresy. Several of his early stories are actually narrated by "the Primeval Snake, the Evil One, Satan," who, through his chosen human agents, manipulates the God-fearing into believing "that there was no such thing as a sin" and that "it is preferable for a man to commit a sin with fervor, than a good deed without enthusiasm."[66]

Dating back to Heinrich Graetz's history, the rationalist Spinoza and irrationalist Shabbetai Zvi had often been bracketed together in Jewish consciousness as contemporary, though so strikingly different precursors of the modern revolt against rabbinic authority and the Judaism of the "ghetto."[67] Of both the Spinozan and Sabbatean heresies, it could be said, at the very least, "that there was no such thing as a sin." Yet, for Singer, it would appear that the difference between them far exceeded any superficial resemblance. In his writings Spinozism is in fact far more evocative of rabbinic Judaism than Sabbateanism. Each in its own way seeks a bridling of the passions: rabbinic Judaism on the basis of the revealed Law and communal coercion, Spinozism through reliance on pure and autonomous reason. It is the very ideal (or illusion) that rational enlightenment, as symbolized by Spinoza's *Ethics*, might inoculate us against the storm and stress of the passions that Singer would question in his fiction. This questioning begins with "The Spinoza of Market Street."

V.

Above everyone there hovers an image of what he should be. As long as he is not
that, he will not be in full peace with himself.[68]

At least with regard to the title, "The Spinoza of Market Street" is one of
the rare cases where the translation is an improvement on the original.[69]
The Yiddish version, as already mentioned, is called simply "*Der Shpinozist*"
[The Spinozist]. But the hero of the short story—Dr. Nahum Fischelson—is
not simply a student and follower of the Amsterdam philosopher. He is a
copyist, who has striven to emulate his exemplar in every way possible. Like
Spinoza, Fischelson—"a short, hunched man with a grayish beard"—is a
lifelong bachelor and recluse.[70] Like Spinoza—at least in his years in The
Hague at the home of the Van den Spycks—Fischelson lives in a garret
apartment on Market Street in Warsaw. After earning a doctorate in philosophy in Zurich and returning to Warsaw, he had been made the head
librarian at the Warsaw synagogue. To say that he was "excommunicated"
would be too strong; nevertheless, he "had wanted to be as independent as
Spinoza himself" and was thus forced to step down because of his "heretical
ideas." Ever since, he has subsisted on a small subsidy provided by the Berlin
Jewish community thanks to the intervention of a sympathetic member—
just like Spinoza, who was supported for a time by a pension from one of his
patrons and close friends, the Dutch republican Jan de Witt. His main task,
still unconsummated after years of work, is to compose a commentary on
the *Ethics*. More fundamentally, his ambition is to live a life based on sober
reason alone.

What Singer does with brilliant effect in this story is invert the conventional Spinoza topos in Jewish culture. Traditionally, Spinoza had served as
a symbol of the radical maskilic break with the Written and Oral Law, as
part of an embrace of secularism. Yet here the focus in not on the betrayal
of Torah, but on Spinoza's *Ethics*, which is, in effect, Fischelson's surrogate
holy writ. Having studied it for the last thirty years, "[h]e knew every proof,
every corollary, every note by heart." Yet the more he studied, "the more
puzzling sentences, unclear passages, and cryptic remarks he found. Each
sentence contained hints unfathomed by any of the students of Spinoza."[71]
Like the first-century sage Ben Bag-Bag, who said of the Torah, "Turn it,
turn it, for everything is in it," Fischelson finds in the *Ethics* a bottomless pit
of meaning and interpretation.[72] On the rare occasions he leaves his apartment, he brings the *Ethics* with him and devotes any spare time to reading it. He displays a constant, almost fanatical recourse to passages from
the *Ethics* to justify his stated positions (his refusal to fear death) and make

sense of his experience (the joy caused by a cool evening breeze through his attic window)—as if justification can come only within the four cubits of Spinoza's system. His greatest pleasure comes in looking out his window at night and observing the planets and constellations through his telescope, which provides him with the reassurance that "although he was only a weak, puny man . . . he was nevertheless a part of the cosmos, made of the same matter as the celestial bodies." "In such moments," the narrator continues, "Dr. Fischelson experienced the *Amor dei intellectualis* which is, according to the philosopher from Amsterdam, the highest perfection of the mind." The Book of Nature—"the earth, the sun, the stars of the Milky Way, and the infinite host of galaxies known only to infinite thought"—appears to stand as open to the ecstatic Fischelson as the Book of Revelation: Spinoza's *Ethics*.[73]

Yet, in ways both marked and subtle, even mischievous on the author's part, Fischelson invariably falls well short of his lodestar. Singer hints at this incongruity between the hero and *his* intellectual hero even before mentioning the name Spinoza, starting with his very first sentence: "Dr. Nahum Fischelson paced back and forth in his garret room in Market Street." The cause of his distress is the stifling summer heat, but already we know that Fischelson suffers from a very un-Spinozan restlessness and agitation. Further intimations of Fischelson's deviation from his exemplar come toward the end of the first paragraph, once more before any reference to Spinoza:

> A candle in a brass holder was burning on the table and a variety of insects buzzed around the flame. Now and again one of the creatures would fly too close to the fire and sear its wings, or one would ignite and glow on the wick for an instant. At such moments Dr. Fischelson grimaced. His wrinkled face would twitch and beneath his disheveled mustache he would bite his lips. Finally he took a handkerchief from his pocket and waved it at the insects.
>
> "Away from there, fools and imbeciles," he scolded. "You won't get warm here; you'll only burn yourself."[74]

To the reader directly or indirectly familiar with the early biography of Spinoza by Johannes Colerus, this little episode is an unmistakable wink. According to the Lutheran preacher, on the rare occasion Spinoza took a break from lens grinding or writing, one of his hobbies was to look for spiders and make them fight together, or throw flies into a cobweb, "and [he] was so well pleased with that Batttle, that he would sometimes break into laughter."[75] Fischelson, on the other hand, observes flies about to burn themselves and impulsively swats at them. His curmudgeonly tone notwithstanding, he seems to care that these insects might suffer pain and even death. On this point, Singer makes a revealing confession in the introduction to his collection of memoirs *Love and Exile*:

There was a time when I used to catch flies, tear off their wings, and put them into boxes of matches with a drop of water and a grain of sugar for nourishment. Suddenly, it occurred to me that I was committing terrible crimes against those creatures just because I was bigger than they, stronger, and defter. While I was always angry with the wicked, I was wicked myself toward those who were weaker than I.[76]

Juxtaposing these passages, we realize that if—by virtue of his inability to watch the death of the flies with indifference and even enjoyment—there is something defective in Fischelson's efforts to emulate Spinoza, for Singer this is to his credit, even if this moral advantage goes unrecognized by Fischelson himself.

The rest of the story narrates Fischelson's continued fall from the Spinozan ideal. Like Spinoza, he is beset with maladies, in his case not a life-threatening tuberculosis but a stomach ailment that causes pain "after only a few mouthfuls of oatmeal." Yet instead of bearing his lot stoically, he bemoans it, even instinctively crying out "God in Heaven, it's difficult, difficult" to a supernatural deity he presumably denies. When, from his attic window, he looks down from the heavens to behold the bedlam of Jewish Warsaw, with all its sounds and smells, its mixture of the sacred and the profane, the calm of his *amor dei intellectualis* is rudely interrupted. "He knew that the behavior of this rabble was the very antithesis of reason. These people were immersed in the vainest of passions, were drunk with emotions, and according to Spinoza, emotion was never good."[77] Fischelson experiences a quasi-religious feeling at the thought that he is made of the same substance as the "celestial bodies," but he literally cannot stomach that he is made of the same matter as Warsaw's "rabble."[78] Nor, as the author makes clear, is he free of its irrationalism:

Even the cats which loitered on the roofs here seemed more savage and passionate than those in other parts of the town. They caterwauled with the voices of women in labor, and like demons scampered up walls and leaped into eaves and balconies. One of the toms paused at Dr. Fischelson's window and let out a howl which made Dr. Fischelson shudder. The doctor stepped from the window and, picking up a broom, brandished it in front of the black beast's glowing, green eyes. "Scat, begone, you ignorant savage!"—and he rapped the broom handle against the roof until the tom ran off.[79]

Who is it that perceives the cats as "demons," and the one at the window as a "black beast" with "glowing, green eyes"? Though related in the third person, the point of view appears to be that of Fischelson himself—again, the Fischelson who presumably is not superstitious and does not believe in devils. Regardless, the same Fischelson who starts by castigating the crowd for their immersion "in the vainest of passions" is overcome, as he chases away the tomcat, by a moment of passion.

With the failure of his pension to arrive on time, followed by the sudden outbreak of the First World War, Fischelson reaches a point of near total unraveling. The chaos on the streets, the unavailability of food or anyone who can help him, sends him into a nervous spell. He drags himself home and lies down in bed, convinced he is dying, and falls into a deep sleep with vivid, mysterious dreams. On awaking, "[h]e tried to meditate about his extraordinary dream, to find its rational connection with what was happening to him and to comprehend *sub specie eternitatis*, but none of it made sense."

Then comes the moment of *renversement*. "The eternal laws, apparently, had not yet ordained Dr. Fischelson's end." Enter Black Dobbe, a homely spinster who lives next door. She is "tall and lean, and as black as a baker's shovel." Her nose is broken, she has "a mustache on her upper lip," she speaks "with the hoarse voice of a man," and wears "men's shoes." Put simply, she is physically repulsive and even ridiculous. She is a poor and simple Warsaw Jew, uneducated, illiterate, superstitious by nature. She used to sell bread and bagels she bought from a baker but now has been reduced to selling "wrinklers"—that is, "cracked eggs"—in the marketplace.[80] About all that she has in common with Fischelson is that she too is unmarried and alone. This was not her choice, though: Engaged several times, on each occasion the groom-to-be jilted her.

The plot device that brings the two together is a letter. Black Dobbe needs a letter from her American cousin to be read for her and, finding no one else around, reluctantly knocks on the door of the heretic. But the door has been left slightly ajar, and opens to reveal Fischelson lying in bed unconscious. Black Dobbe revives him with water, helps him up, smooths down his blanket, and prepares a meal for him. Fischelson, in turn, reads the letter to her and disabuses her of the notion that he is a convert and that the *Ethics* must be a "gentile prayer book" by insisting to be "a Jew like any other Jew."

Despite his temporary recovery, Fischelson remains certain he is on death's door and prepares a will. "But death did not come. Rather his health improved." Meanwhile, he begins to spend more time with Black Dobbe. She cooks for him and tells him the word on the street about the war; he shows her his telescope and regales her with stories of his years in Switzerland and other European cities. The final hook comes when Black Dobbe brings out her trousseau from one of her earlier engagements. "And she began to spread out, on the chair, dresses—woolen, silk, velvet. Taking each dress up in turn, she held it to her body. She gave him an account of every item in her trousseau—underwear, shoes, stockings." She turns silent, her face "brick-red," while "Dr. Fischelson's body suddenly began to shake as if he had the chills." "Very nice, beautiful things," are the only words he can manage to utter.

Fischelson's betrayal of Spinoza continues with the wedding to Black Dobbe that immediately follows—a betrayal only heightened by the fact that it is conducted "according to the law," with a rabbi officiating, the groom wearing the traditional white robe (or *kitel*), and Black Dobbe circling him seven times "as custom required." Dobbe is like a woman transformed—beaming and all decked out in "a wide-brimmed hat" adorned with fruit, a dress of "white silk," high-heeled shoes, and ample jewelry—but Fischelson remains weak, frail, even gloomy. He is "scarcely able to walk" and too weak to break the goblet at the end of the ceremony with his foot. All in all, he is "anxious to return as quickly as possible to his attic room," and to get back to the *Ethics*.

But the final surprise in a string of them—a surprise that never could have been derived at according to the geometric method—occurs that night in the marital bed. Interrupting Fischelson in his reading of the *Ethics*, Dobbe appears "wearing a silk nightgown, slippers with pompoms, and with her hair hanging over her shoulders." Fischelson, in turn, drops the *Ethics* from his hands. Intense, passionate lovemaking follows. "What happened that night," the narrator suggests, "could be called a miracle. If Dr. Fischelson hadn't been convinced that every occurrence is in accordance with the laws of nature he would have thought that Black Dobbe bewitched him. Powers long dormant awakened in him. . . . Although he had only a sip of the benediction wine, he was as if intoxicated." The word *intoxicated* (*vi a shikur*) is perhaps a sly allusion to Spinoza, the "God-intoxicated man," only here the intoxication comes from great, revitalizing sex. Fischelson is "again a man as in his youth," his pains alleviated, his health and virility restored.

Is this consummation of the marriage—a consummation in stark contrast to the unfinished commentary on the *Ethics*—in fact a miracle, no matter what Fischelson thinks? Is Fischelson's sudden Viagra-like potency a product of supernatural intervention? Here we might benefit from stepping back to consider "The Destruction of Kreshev" (1943), one of Singer's "devil" stories written only a year before "The Spinoza of Market Street." The story begins:

> I AM the Primeval Snake, the Evil One, Satan. The cabala refers to me as Samael and the Jews sometimes call me merely, "that one."
>
> It is well-known that I love to arrange strange marriages, delighting in such mismatings as an old man with a young girl, an unattractive widow with a youth in his prime, a cripple with great beauty, a mute with a braggart.[81]

The mismatch here is between Lise, the devoted daughter of Reb Bunim, the richest man in the Polish shtetl of Kreshev and a generous, upstanding pillar of the community, and a brilliant, "extremely clever" yeshiva student, Shloimele, who is a secret follower of Shabbtai Zvi, the false messiah. Shloimele lures her, with elaborate theological justifications, into acts of ever greater sexual deviance, culminating in his persuading her to have sex with an ox of a man, her father's ignorant coachman Mendel. Shloimele's subsequent admission of the havoc he has wrought brings apocalpyse down on Kreshev: Lise is formally divorced from Shloimele and publicly humiliated, driving her to suicide; Mendel is flogged and imprisoned and, once freed, torches the town in revenge.

No supernatural voice narrates "The Spinoza of Market Street." And yet, here too we have what can only be described as a "strange marriage"— the coupling of an intellectual with an illiterate, an expert in Spinoza's *Ethics* with a seller of cracked eggs. Here too, moreover, the moment of truth occurs in the bedchamber. In this case, however, the marriage of Nahum Fischelson and Black Dobbe yields a kind of salvation instead of damnation, a comic rather than tragic ending. The implication of the story is that the "eternal laws" that "had not yet ordained Nahum Fischelson's end" are not Spinoza's ironclad laws of nature but the whims of uncanny, vitalistic forces, which here lead to life, not death; joy, not destruction.[82]

This insight, however, is denied Fischelson. No sooner has he risen from bed at dawn than he quickly regrets his opting for carnal knowledge over the *amor dei intellectualis*:

> Dr. Fischelson looked up at the sky. The black arch was thickly sown with stars— there were green, red, yellow, blue stars; there were large ones and small ones, winking and steady ones. There were those that were clustered in dense groups and those that were alone. In the higher sphere, apparently, little notice was taken of the fact that a certain Dr. Fischelson had in his declining days married someone called Black Dobbe. Seen from above, even the Great War was nothing but a temporary play of the modes. The myriads of fixed stars continued to travel their destined courses in unbounded space. The comets, planets, satellites, asteroids kept circling these shining centers. Worlds were born and died in cosmic upheavals. In the chaos of nebulae, primeval matter was being formed . . . and he Dr. Fischelson, with his unavoidable fate, was a part of this. The doctor closed his eyelids and allowed the breeze to cool the sweat of his forehead and stir the hair of his beard. He breathed deeply of the midnight air, supported his shaky hands on the window sill and murmured, "Divine Spinoza, forgive me I have become a fool."[83]

The philosopher and Spinoza scholar Steven B. Smith has questioned whether Fischelson's lament in his famous last words—"Divine Spinoza,

forgive me I have become a fool"—reflects an accurate understanding of
Spinoza's philosophy of the passions. "Fischelson believes that erotic love
is at odds with the life of reason," Smith writes, "but Spinoza constantly
reminds us that mind and body are not two substances at war with one another, but two aspects of the same individual. The passions are not at odds
with reason, but 'inadequate ideas' waiting to be developed."[84] Despite his
encyclopedic knowledge of the *Ethics*, Fischelson has forgotten the crucial
third proposition of the fifth book, *Of Human Freedom*: "An affect which is
a passion ceases to be a passion as soon as we form a clear and distinct idea
of it." For Smith, this raises the question whether Singer is satirizing Spinoza, or only Fischelson's idolatrous yet imperfect understanding of him.
Smith leans toward the latter. My own reading is that he is mocking both.
One need only consult one of his later interviews, where he admitted that
"what I wanted to say [in "The Spinoza of Market Street"] was that if you
are a human being, if you are alive, you cannot live according to Spinoza,"
to realize that Singer *did* view passionate love as a betrayal of Spinoza—but
a worthy betrayal.[85] (Smith may be right about Spinoza, but in that case,
both Fischelson and Singer himself are fools.) In this reading, Fischelson is
a fool for thinking himself a fool simply for having married and slept with
a woman—and having been as if reborn in the process. He is a fool for failing to appreciate the miracle of an aging, decrepit scholar discovering the
fountain of youth.

Fischelson may think he has betrayed Spinoza by succumbing to passion.
But the problematic passion, Singer suggests, lies in his obsessive attachment to the *Ethics* and the elusive *amor dei intellectualis*, an attachment that
even true love cannot break.

VI.

I convinced myself that philosophy can never reveal anything. It can tell us what we
cannot do, but it can never tell us what we can do.[86]

Sixteen months after the publication of "*Der Shpinozist*" in *Di tsukunft*,
Singer transposed the Spinoza theme from the short story form to the se-
rialized novel. In November, 1945—six months after the end of the war
against Germany and the revelation of the full catastrophe of European
Jewry—*Der Forverts* printed the first installment of *Di familye Mushkat* [The
Family Moskat]. It ran for nearly three years.[87] In 1950 it became the first of
Singer's novels to be translated into English, albeit in substantially abridged

form. Set largely in Warsaw and its environs and stretching from prewar czarist Poland to Hitler's invasion in September 1939, the novel traces the demise of East European Jewry through the prism of four generations of a particular family, ruled at the beginning by its wealthy patriarch, Reb Meshulam Moskat. In Singer's artistic vision, the ruination of the Moskat family transpires on two planes. On one hand, it is a product of the entropic and corrosive forces of modernity. The sacred canopy of the Law, with its multiple fences and restrictions, steadily recedes. The authority of rabbis and patriarchs alike withers. Romantic love preempts arranged marriages and wrecks existing ones; new, secular political ideologies, from Zionism to socialism, become surrogates for traditional faith; and migration to America threatens to sever connection to Yiddishkayt altogether. Yet all this fragmentation is ultimately trumped by the tragic fate they share—the looming destruction of the Moskats, and of East European Jewry as a whole, at the hands of the Nazis.

In *The Family Moskat*, Spinoza functions as the signature of a single character, albeit one of the most central in a book swarming with them—the figure of Asa (Oyzer) Heshel Bannet. We meet him for the first time at the start of the second chapter:

> A few weeks after Meshulam Moskat returned to Warsaw another traveler arrived at the station in the northern part of the capital. He climbed down from a third-class car carrying an oblong metal-bound basket locked with a double lock. He was a young man, about nineteen. His name was Asa Heshel Bannet. On his mother's side he was the grandson of Reb Dan Katzenellenbogen, the rabbi of Tereshpol Minor. He had with him a letter of recommendation to the learned Dr. Shmaryahu Jacobi, secretary of the Great Synagogue of Warsaw. In his pocket rested a worn volume, the *Ethics* of Spinoza in Hebrew translation (*ibergezetzt in loshn-koydesh*).[88]

Our earlier discussion of Singer's autobiographical writings suggests that the resemblance between author and character is more than accidental. Yet the genealogy of this figure clearly is meant to extend further back. Though he arrives in Warsaw still wearing sidelocks and a gaberdine coat, Asa Heshel is the proverbial talmudic prodigy turned maskil, a type familiar since Salomon Maimon. In describing the intellectual journey of the young heretic the narrator furnishes us with the arc of Spinoza's Jewish rehabilitation, in miniature:

> He attended cheder for only half a day. He quickly got the reputation of a prodigy. At five he was studying Talmud, at six he began the Talmudic commentators, at eight the teacher had no more to give him. At the age of nine he delivered

a discourse in the synagogue, and at twelve he was writing learned letters to rabbis in other towns. . . . Matchmakers flooded the family with matrimonial offers; the townsfolk predicted that he was sure, in God's good time, to inherit his grandfather's rabbinical chair. . . . And then what does the promising youth do but abandon the roads of righteousness and join the ranks of the "moderns"? He would start endless disputes with the others . . . in the study house and criticize the rabbis. He prayed without putting on the customary prayer sash, scribbled on the margins of the sacred books, made mock of the pious. Instead of studying the Commentaries he delved into Maimonides's *Guide for the Perplexed* and Jehuda Halevi's *Khuzari*. Somwhere he got hold of the writings of the heretic Salomon Maimon.[89]

In short, Asa Heshel has traveled the road from the *beys medresh* to Maimonides to Spinoza, with the assistance of Rubin's Hebrew translation of the *Ethics*. He arrives in Warsaw with barely a possession to his name, but he has his "new" guide to the perplexed, he has his Spinoza.

According to his letter of recommendation, written by the head of the modern Jewish school in Zamosc, Asa Heshel has come to Warsaw "because of his thirst for enlightenment," more specifically with the aim of acquiring a formal high school and university education and an "honorable livelihood." Yet this sense of purpose is belied by the previous depiction of Asa Heshel before leaving home. On one hand, he is consumed by "eternal questions" about the existence of God, the responsibility of man, and the immortality of the soul. On the other, he is congenitally passive, undisciplined, and resigned, more strung along by events than working to shape them.[90] He begins courses of study without completing them. He reads without method. "Each day he would make up his mind anew to leave the town, and each day he stayed." In the end, the truth of the matter is that he leaves the shtetl of Tereshpol Minor for Warsaw not "because of his thirst for enlightenment"—as a boy from the provinces determined to "make it" in the big city—but because he is compelled to by circumstances. The man who proposes marriage to Asa Heshel's mother hinges his offer on her heretical son's leaving town. And so doubts are sown, from the very outset, as to whether Asa will be able to resist the temptations of Warsaw and commit to the pursuit of secular learning that is his putative aim.

The Family Moskat contains a reprise, on an operatic scale, of the main question of "The Spinoza of Market Street": namely, is the contemplative ideal of the "intellectual love of God" any match for the passions? The answer is an even more emphatic no. A chance encounter with Abram Shapiro, the sybaritic son-in-law of Reb Meshulem, gives Asa Heshel entrée into the

Moskat family. There, he meets Hadassah, the granddaughter of Meshulem, and the two immediately fall for each other. Yet Meshulem is determined that Hadassah marry Fishele Kuttner, a scion of a wealthy family who is, to boot, a pious follower of the same Hasidic rebbe of the Moskat patriarch. In a passage found in the original Yiddish but scrubbed from the English translation of the book, Singer makes palpable the tension between Asa's Spinozism and romantic obsession:

> Asa Heshel tried to console himself with the thought that he, Hadassah, Fishele, and Reb Meshulem were all motions of the infinite substance, bubbles in the sea of the Godhead. Everything that had happened to him today and would happen in the future was necessary, determined according to the eternal laws, unchangeable. But Spinoza's thought did not help with his anxiety. He was still far from the level of loving God with an intellectual love, independent of everyday events. He was full of affects and had no idea how to expel them and what to supplant them with.[91]

Needless to say, the affects win out. His continued visits to the Moskat family, ostensibly for tutoring in Polish and Russian by Hadassah (whose education in non-Jewish schools is an early symptom of the fraying of Meshulem's authority), quickly become a pretext for an affair between them. Reb Meshulem's discovery of their goings-on leads him to press hard for an arranged marriage to Fishele. Hadassah and Asa Heshel elope as a result, with the aim of absconding to Switzerland, but they are apprehended at the Austrian border, and while Asa manages to escape, Hadassah is arrested and, after brief internment, is returned to her parents in a sorry state. At this point the twosome becomes a foursome. Asa, now living in Switzerland, agrees—for unexplained reasons—to marry a woman he does not love: Adele, the daughter of Meshulem's third wife, who has been infatuated with Asa from the very start. Hadassah, meanwhile, accedes to her family's demand that she marry Fishele. Yet the magnetic attraction between the two lovers does not ebb. Returning to Warsaw, Asa resumes his now adulterous affair with Hadassah, the two engaging in ever more brazen acts of lust— from sadomasochistic fantasy to fornicating on Yom Kippur, the Day of Atonement. Their respective spouses eventually grant them divorces, and Asa and Hadassah, now ostracized by most of the branches of the Moskat family, finally enter into marriage. Yet it does not prove a consummation devoutly to be wished for. After marrying Hadassah and having a child with her, Asa loses all romantic interest. By the end of the book—when Hadassah is killed in the Nazi bombardment of Warsaw—Asa has already taken up with a new consort, a Communist-party functionary named Barbara. As

Spinoza predicted, a life devoted to the pursuit of happiness via passionate love leads only to sadness, but his proposed alternative—the *amor dei intellectualis*—offers only puny opposition.

To this tension between Spinozan equilibrium and the turbulence of the emotional life that was so central to "The Spinoza of Market Street," Singer adds another key layer to the Spinoza theme in *The Family Moskat*—the conflict between Enlightenment rationalism and orthodoxy. This conflict is dramatized in the relationship between, and the often revealing doubling of, Asa Heshel and his elderly maternal granfather, Rabbi Dan Katzenellenbogen, the rabbi of Tereshpol Minor. Rabbi Dan is a thoroughgoing traditionalist, an ascetic by nature who is a harsh critic of "Jewish modernity" in all its forms. When Asa Heshel, drawing on his reading of the *Ethics*, tries to explain to his grandfather that he does not "deny the existence of God," Rabbi Dan promptly rejects the deist and pantheist heresies: "I know, I know. All the arguments of the heretics; there is a Creator, but he has revealed Himself to no one; Moses lied. And others maintain that Nature is God. I know, I know. The sum and substance of it all is that any sin is permitted. That's the truth of the matter."[92] He rejects all Jewish adaptations to modernity, from liberal Judaism to nationalism. When Asa Heshel ventures a halfhearted defense of secular Zionists, claiming that "Jews were a people like every other people, and . . . were demanding that the nations of the world should return the Holy Land to them," his grandfather scoffs: "If . . . they had no further belief in the Bible, then why should they have any longing for the biblical land of the Jews? Why not some other country? Any country?"[93]

The conflict between the two characters becomes more striking with the outbreak of the First World War, when the Russian soldiers drive all the Jews out of Tereshpol Minor, and Reb Dan is forced to lead his flock into exile. Among the few communal possessions the town Jews bring with them are "the scrolls of the law from the synagogue . . . carefully placed on beds of straw in a wagon, the holy objects covered with prayer shawls and Ark curtains." Reb Dan, meanwhile, totes "his prayershawl bag and a couple of cherished volumes" while burning forty years' worth of manuscripts and letters. The chaos of the evacuation, coupled with scenes en route of Russian soldiers brutalizing Jewish refugees, and wounded soldiers being brought back from the front, causes Reb Dan to lose his bearings:

> Here, stumbling along the wanderer's path, the rabbi met the powers of evil face to face. It was as though the noise and the stench of corruption and death had extinguished in him the spark of godliness. He had lost the pillar he leaned against for support. He wanted to pray, but his lips were powerless to form the words.

He closed his eyes. He felt that he was falling into an abyss. He gripped the sides of the wagon and began to recite the afternoon prayer, but in his confusion he forgot how the words went. Over and over he found himself repeating the same phrase, "Happy are they that dwell in Thy house."[94]

Reb Dan, ironically, finds himself in a situation much like Nahum Fischelson in "The Spinoza of Market Street." Unable to recall the words to one of the most commonly repeated (and thereby memorized) prayers in the liturgy—the Ashre prayer, composed largely of Psalm 145, which opens the daily afternoon service—he reminds the reader of Singer's earlier story of Fischelson's sudden incapacity to remember the axioms of the *Ethics* amid war, sickness, and passion.

Yet Reb Dan is able to recompose himself when he has a moment, in his cart, to read a page of Talmud, or when the procession arrives in a nearby village and he is escorted to the synagogue. He can withstand even the mayhem of Warsaw, his ultimate destination, when he sits in synagogue on the night of Yom Kippur:

> As he sat there in his prayer shawl and white robe Reb Dan could forget that he had been driven out of Tereshpol Minor. He was in a sanctuary, among his own people and among the familiar volumes of the law. No, he was not alone. There was still a God in heaven, angels, seraphim, a throne of grace. All that he needed was to stretch out his hand and he would touch one of the holy volumes whose words were the voice of the living God, the letters with which God had created the world. A sudden wave of pity swept over him for the unbelievers who wandered about in outer darkness, shooting and killing one another, looting, stealing, raping. What were they seeking? What would be the outcome of their endless wars? How long would they go on sinking into the morass of iniquity?[95]

Whether Reb Dan's continued belief in an omnipotent "God in heaven" whose will is revealed in the "familiar volumes of the law," who is capable of bringing about miracles and who will ultimately reward good and punish evil—whether this is, ultimately, a convincing response to the "shooting and killing . . . looting, stealing, and raping" he has witnessed remains open to doubt. This is not an endorsement of Reb Dan's orthodoxy. An earlier exchange between Reb Dan and the town maskil Jekutiel the watchmaker, in the midst of the evacuation from Tereshpol Minor, has already put the tenability of both the "traditional" and "modern" answers to antisemitism into question:

> "*Nu*, rabbi?" he said.
>
> It was clear what he meant was: Where is your Lord of the Universe now? Where are His miracles? Where is your faith in Torah and prayer?

"*Nu*, Jekutiel," the rabbi answered. What he was saying was: Where are your worldly remedies? Where is your trust in the gentiles? What have you accomplished by aping Esau?[96]

Yet the persuasiveness of his strong theism aside, what is striking is that Reb Dan—the *golus* (exilic) Jew personified—can be driven from home, bullied and humiliated en route, even momentarily shaken in his faith, and still regain his equilibrium. He does not need an actual home to feel at home: Place him in a shul, amid "the familiar volumes of sacred law," and he will, however briefly, experience the warmth and protection of a second home.

Can the secular Jew exposed to the same turmoil and tragedy as Reb Dan find a second home in—Spinoza? Like Reb Dan, Asa Heshel—in part because of circumstances, in part because of his own ingrained passivity—is a peripatetic figure, a wandering Jew. The one constant by his side—whether he is in Warsaw or Tereshpol Minor, a student in Switzerland or a soldier on the eastern front in World War One—is Spinoza's *Ethics*, which he reads and rereads with the same fanatical devoutness as Nahum Fischelson. While serving in the Russian army, to the mockery of his fellow soldiers, Asa sneaks in a few pages of the *Ethics* whenever possible:

> He sat here in the barracks before taps and carried on a dispute with Spinoza. Well, then, let it be admitted that everything that was happening was necessary. That the entire war was nothing but a play of modes in the infinite ocean of the Substance. But for what reason has the divine nature required all of this? Why should he not put an end to the entire tragicomedy? He read from the Fifth Part of the *Ethics*, where Spinoza discussed the intellectual love of God.
>
> Proposition 35: God loves Himself with infinite intellectual love.
>
> Proposition 37: There is nothing in nature that is contrary to this intellectual love of God or that can remove it.
>
> Asa Heshel raised his eyes from the page. Was it really so? Could one in truth love all these Ivans? Even this one with the pockmarked face and the shifty piggish eyes?[97]

Doubts such as these dog Asa Heshel and he proves unable to resist the slide into ever increasing skepticism, misanthropy, and even nihilism. Returning from war, he confesses to Abram, "I have no philosophy," and "I've made up my mind that the human race is no more important than flies or bedbugs."[98] Without abandoning Spinoza, Asa becomes convinced that the only way to "save" him is to reconcile Spinoza's egoistic ethics ("the idea that happiness and morality are identical") with the pessimistic philosophy of Malthus. Asa's (unsurprisingly) never-finished dissertation, "The Laboratory of Happiness"—with its ludicrous proposal of "the establishment of a research laboratory for experimentation in pure happiness"—ultimately amounts to an argument for birth control, "more sex and fewer children."[99]

The contrast, then, between Reb Dan and Asa Heshel is quite stark. The proximity of the "familiar volumes of the law" provides Reb Dan with a reliable pillar of support, however tenuous that support will ultimately prove come the Nazi invasion. The *Ethics*—for all its original promise in Asa Heshel's eyes—appears capable of offering no such mooring. Ironically, one of the rare times in the novel Asa enjoys a moment of "at-homeness" comes during his brief return home to Tereshpol Minor, when he accompanies his grandfather to synaogue for evening prayers. Surrounded by yeshiva students "reading in the dim light" and worshippers "softly chanting," standing in front of the Ark and inhaling the "heavy odor that seemed . . . to be compounded of candle wax, dust, fast days, and eternity," Asa Heshel is suddenly (if evanescently) seized with the thought that "everything he had experienced in alien places seemed to be without meaning. Time had flown like an illusion. This was his true home, this was where he belonged. Here was where he would come for refuge when everything else failed."[100] But even after his ambitions to become a professor of philosophy have collapsed, even after his divorce from Adele and the failure of his marriage to Hadassah, indeed even after the imminence of the Nazi attack has become evident, it is the system of Spinoza to which Asa consistently turns and returns. While gazing through his window at "the sky, the stars, the planets, the Milky Way," he coolly ponders the thought that "the same laws which controlled the sun and the moon, the comets and the nebulae, also governed life and death, Mussolini, Hitler, every Nazi lout who lustily sang the *Horst Wessel* song and howled for Jewish blood to spurt from the knife."[101] Not even the blitzkrieg, when it comes, can initially shake his absorption in the rationalism of the *Ethics*: "Between bombardments he made calculations in pencil. . . . Where was one to seek refuge from this chaos if not in the realm of 'adequate ideas'? A triangle still contained two right angles. Even Hitler could not change that."[102]

VII.

The differences between the English and Yiddish versions of *The Family Moskat* are most glaring in their respective endings. The former concludes with what is the penultimate chapter in the Yiddish original. There, the last word is given to Hertz Yanovar, a "secular" intellectual who nevertheless throughout the novel is obsessed with the occult. Standing amid the Nazi devastation of Warsaw, a bedraggled Yanovar blurts out in Polish that the Messiah will soon come. Pressed by Asa Heshel to explain his meaning, he answers, "Death is the Messiah. That's the real truth!" For the English reader, then, the book closes on a note of nihilistic resignation that appears to reflect Asa Heshel's own outlook by novel's end.

Not so the Yiddish edition, which includes an additional chapter (chapter 65) of eleven pages. Here, after depicting the observance of the Jewish New Year among the surviving members of the Moskat clan, the narrative abruptly shifts to a "pine forest" far from Warsaw, where a small group of "would-be pioneers" celebrate Rosh Hashanah, taking a brief respite in their desperate efforts to escape the Germans and "reach the land of Israel." The omniscient narrator makes clear that they are not the only ones: "From every town, young men and women, Zionist and otherwise, started out with the same desire: to reach the far-off promised land, Jerusalem, Tel Aviv, Jaffa, and Haifa, the colonies and the kibbutzim."[103] And whereas the English ending equates messianism with death and catastrophe, the Yiddish version connects the Zionist emigration to the traditional belief in messianic restoration: "Rise up, oh, remnants of Israel, and prepare for the final battle. Like a torch is the House of Jacob and the House of Esau is straw. Rise up and fear not. Yours is the final victory. Unto you will come the Messiah."[104] A stark gap thus separates the two endings, a near polar opposition between hopelessness and hope.

Critics familiar with the Yiddish edition have long clashed over the literary merits of the original ending. Some argue that its inclusion was little more than an attempt to console the contemporary Yiddish reader—a reader likely to have lost scores of loved ones, relatives, friends, and acquaintances in the recent destruction—by providing an optimistic conclusion altogether discordant with the general mood of the book. In this view, the darkness of the English ending—"Death is the Messiah"—forms a more appropriate resolution.[105] Others insist on the integral connection of the final chapter to the overall thematic framework of the novel and on the consequent incomplete character of the English edition.[106]

What is indisputable is that one cannot appreciate the centrality of the Spinoza theme to *The Family Moskat*, and to the figure of Asa Heshel in particular, without reading chapter 65 of the Yiddish original. The chapter begins with a description of Asa Heshel gathering his things, preparing to move in with his sister's family on a street in Warsaw thus far spared the worst of the bombardment. In addition to packing "a few shirts, underwear, a sweater, socks, and some books," Asa also stuffs his copy of Spinoza's *Ethics* into his pocket. An extended argument with Spinoza ensues, as Asa, his previous detachment wavering, struggles to make sense of Hadassah's death and the devastation all around him:

He stood near the boarded-up doorway of a shop in the glare of a burning sun-
set and took stock of his life. Is there a God? Yes, there is. He is everything: the
earth, the sky, the milky way, the crying of a child, the Nazi bomb, Einstein's
theory, Hitler's *Mein Kampf*. The smoke rising there is He, too. He is One, He
is Eternal. My body is an infinitely small part of His body. My spirit is a drop in
the ocean of His spirit. Who is killing whom? Who hates whom? All answers rest
in God. We have one aim here: to continue existence as long as possible; to be
happy as much as one can. If you can't, let His will be done. Is this Spinoza? Yes,
that's the whole of him. Can one die with such a philosophy? There's no choice.
What do the others say that's different? God's ways are hidden.

But no, no! It isn't so! There is another credo: God is a fighter, a warrior. God
is on the side of the righteous. He gave free will to choose between good and evil.
Every hour. Every second. What kind of God is that? The Jewish God, the Judge
of all the earth, the God who is jealous and vengeful. He wages war against Ama-
lek. He is neither Hitler's *Mein Kampf* nor the Nazi bomb. Nature is His work
but is not He. He created evil to provide a choice. He sent Hitler as a trial and a
punishment. Is God to blame if we sat by with folded hands and let the wicked
rise up? If we are all lazy, why should He be diligent? Why should not the wicked
triumph if the righteous wait for miracles? How could I have forgotten this pre-
cept? Did I not learn it in religious school, studying Deuteronomy? I forgot it
because I wanted to cast off every yoke, because I wanted to yield to every lust
and close an eye while men of power robbed, killed, raped, incited. What better
excuse for tolerating evil than to blame God for everything?[107]

Earlier, Asa contemplated the leveling thrust of Spinoza's metaphysical monism, its reduction of the "crying of a child" and "Hitler's *Mein Kampf*" to
modes of a single substance, with quiet acquiescence. Now, at least momentarily, he recoils from such resignation, recalling "another credo" (*emunah*):
the belief in the personal, transcendent, even anthropomorphic God of the
Bible, "[t]he Jewish God . . . who is jealous and vengeful" and "gave free will
to choose between good and evil."

Torn between these alternatives, Asa Heshel abruptly gives up committing to either ("What's the use of all these speculations?"), yet later in
the chapter this same internal tug-of-war between the Spinozan and the
biblical God repeats itself. While his sister and her family go off to High
Holiday prayers, Asa stays home, adamant that "[i]f you live as an unbeliever (*apikores*), you should die as an unbeliever." As if by rote, he begins to
browse the pages of Spinoza's *Ethics*, yet, like Dr. Fischelson, quickly loses
his bearings:

What did he want, that Amsterdam philosopher? Did he know what he was talk-
ing about, or was he simply splitting hairs? What is it, this substance and its
endless attributes? Whom does he call God? What is thought? What is spirit?

What are ideas? What sort of spider's web has he woven here? Asa Heshel tried to run quickly through all the theorems, but the more he studied, the more confused he became. Some sentences were obvious; others now seemed to him unclear, ambiguous, a game of words. In essence, one could be both a Nazi and a Spinozist. True, the fascists were opposed to Spinoza, but only because he was a Jew. The professors of philosophy in Berlin, Leipzig, Bonn, are no doubt analyzing Spinoza now, just as the poets there are still writing poems, and the essayists are chattering about culture, aesthetics, ethics, personality. They had divided the roles among themselves. You fight and you sing; you philosophize and you rob; you slaughter children and you write history.[108]

Putting the *Ethics* aside, Asa Heshel grabs a Bible from the bookcase. Still racked with theological questions and misgivings, he nevertheless finds in the clarity of its commandments, prohibitions, and promises something sturdy to grasp hold of:

Suppose there is no God! Suppose the murderers are right! Suppose God himself is on Hitler's side! Suppose Moses is a liar! His words are thereby not diminished but more exalted. One Jew, Moses ben Amram, stood up in opposition to nature, to man, to history and let his voice be heard: I am the Lord Thy God who brought thee out of the land of Egypt, out of the house of slavery. . . . Thou shalt not kill. Thou shalt not commit adultery. Thous shalt not steal. Thou shalt not bear false witness against thy neighbor. . . . Be holy, for I, the Lord thy God, am holy. . . . Thou must not steal nor deal deceitfully nor fraudulently with thy neighbor. . . . Thou must not oppress nor rob they neighbor. . . . Thou must not be guilty of unjust verdicts. Thou must neither favor the little man nor be awed by the great. . . . Thou must not slander thy people. . . . Thou must not bear hatred for thy brother in thy heart. Thou must openly tell him of his offense, thus not take a sin upon yourself. Thou must not exact vengeance nor bear a grudge against thy people. Thou shalt love thy neighbor as thyself. . . . Thou shalt not follow the laws of the nations that I expel to make way for thee, because they have practiced all these things and I have come to detest them. And I say unto thee: thou shalt take possession of their soil. I myself will give it to thee, a land flowing with milk and honey. . . . And I will set thee apart from all these peoples to be mine . . . to be high above the other peoples I have made, in praise, in renown, and in honor, to be a nation consecrated to the Lord, your God. . . .

In the street, bombs kept exploding. Fires flamed. Cannons cracked. But Asa Heshel did not interrupt his reading. These words, indeed, are neither unclear nor ambiguous. The Nazi could not adopt them. These are not words but flames that the eternal Jew has flung at eternal evil.[109]

VIII.

Up until his death in 1991, I. B. Singer would continue to people his novels and short stories, particularly those of a semiautobiographical and non-supernatural character, with intellectuals intermittently drawn to and repelled by Spinoza.[110] The seventeenth-century philosopher remained code in his work for the illusory assumption of many a secular Jewish intellectual that the *Ethics* could be a new "tree of life," a Spinozan Torah of rationalist self-government that might substitute for the Mosaic Torah of divine revelation and imperative. Never again, however, would Singer pen so scorching, indeed Zeiltinesque an indictment of Spinoza as one finds in the original Yiddish ending to *The Family Moskat*. True, the diatribe is given to an invented character, leaving the notoriously slippery Singer plausible deniability that Asa Heshel is simply a mouthpiece for his own ideas. Yet the fact that nowhere else in Singer's work do we find so stinging and sustained a rebuke of Spinoza suggests that the author was indeed airing a very personal and sincere animus toward the "beyond good and evil" ethics and toward the leveling pantheism of Spinoza in the aftermath of the Shoah. Still, the exclusion of this coda from the English translation of *The Family Moskat* meant that most later readers were not privy to this fury. And the much greater readership for "The Spinoza of Market Street" following its translation in 1961 meant that Singer's Spinoza image in the popular mind would ultimately owe more to the lighthearted caricature of Nahum Fischelson than to the much darker view of the Jewish Spinozist in the case of Asa Heshel. Perhaps this is how Singer—whose criticisms of Spinoza in later writings and interviews contained little in the way of invective—would have wanted it.[111]

Be that as it may, Singer clearly judged the modern Jewish attachment to Spinoza to be a path wrongly taken, a source not merely of comedy, but of tragedy. Contrary to the images from previous chapters in this book, Singer's Spinoza was neither a secular messiah come to liberate the Jews from the ghetto and usher in a religion of humanity; nor was he a prototype of, and posthumous returnee to, a revived Jewish political and ethnic nation. Above all, for the emancipated Jew alienated from orthodoxy and the law and in search of a new safe harbor, Spinoza was no "new" guide to the perplexed.

Epilogue

Spinoza *Redivivus* in the Twenty-First Century

I.

Six weeks before he died, Irving Howe (1920–1993) delivered his last lecture in front of an audience at Hunter College. Fittingly, it was a eulogy, albeit one he had been giving, in one form or another, for nearly two decades, starting with his magisterial history of the East European Jewish immigrant experience, *World of Our Fathers* (1976). In this talk, entitled "The End of Jewish Secularism," the renowned critic, editor, and socialist paid final respects to Yiddishkayt, that amalgam of Yiddishism, leftism, and this-worldly messianism that had flourished in the heyday of East European Jewish immigration to America but that, two generations later had largely run its course. "I think," he lamented, "we are reaching a dead end." With Yiddish culture, the Jewish labor movement, and socialist politics in terminal decline, secular Jewishness in America had lost its moorings, and what had emerged in the postwar era as substitutes—the memory of the Holocaust and solidarity with Israel—would not be enough to sustain it. The one task left was to "say farewell with love and gratitude" to the "world that made us," Howe claimed—to give the remains not of Judaism, but of Jewish secularism, a decent burial.[1]

Howe's eulogy was focused on North America alone, but late twentieth-century pessimism about the future of cultural Judaism was hardly limited to the Jewish Diaspora. Within the State of Israel as well—the "grandest creation of nineteenth-century Jewish secularism," in the words of one scholar—its prospects were in doubt.[2] By the 1990s the foothold that the Labor party—the founding party of the state—had long held in Israeli politics was a thing of the past, the hegemony of its socialist-Zionist ethos an even more distant memory. The old spiritual Zionist ideal of a Hebrew culture that would be at once universal and yet affirmatively and knowledgably Jewish, expressed through words, concepts, and symbols originating in the Jewish tradition but transposed to a secular key, was falling victim, in the eyes of many, to a pincer movement. On one flank it was threatened by a resurgent, increasingly politicized orthodoxy, in both its religious-Zionist and *haredi* (Ultraorthodox) varieties, which rejected the very notion of a secular Judaism and claimed a monopoly on the definition of Jewishness. On the other flank it was confronted by a rising generation of "new Israelis" who were either ideologically opposed, or, more frequently, simply indifferent to a Jewishness they deemed insufferably parochial.[3] Indeed, it was this latter "post-Zionist" trend, characterized (and, for the most part, celebrated) by the Israeli journalist Tom Segev in *Elvis in Jerusalem* (2002), that appeared to have the wind at its back by the turn of the millennium, reflected in the ever-mounting number of Israelis, motivated primarily by the individualist and consumerist values of the modern West, who showed little of the interest of their Ashkenazi Zionist elders in justifying their secularism in Jewish terms.[4] Squeezed by these two demographic trends, Jewish secularism, in Israel as in other centers of Jewish life, seemed to many to be in a terminal state, destined for a slow but inexorable decline.

Judged from the perspective of a decade into the new century, the obituaries of Howe and others were, perhaps, premature. No less an authority on American Jewish history than Jonathan Sarna has claimed that, "in our own day, almost like the proverbial phoenix, Jewish secularism has made something of a comeback," defying Howe's bleak diagnosis which "at the time, most observers agreed with."[5] As evidence of this "unexpected rebirth," Sarna points to the amazing success of the National Yiddish Book Center in Amherst, Massachusetts, whose mission of rescuing Yiddish books, which seemed to many quixotic when the organization was founded in 1980, today seems clairvoyant with the recent vogue of klezmer music and Yiddish culture. He points to the group Reboot (also, interestingly enough, based in Amherst), a self-proclaimed vanguard of "thought-leaders and tastemakers" that runs invitation-only annual conferences that are a kind of Davos for well-connected Jewish thirtysomethings to think of creative ways to "reboot" the "culture, rituals, and traditions" of Judaism for Generations X and Y through projects like the recent architectural competition Sukkah City. He points to the overtly heretical and anti-establishment (and now discontinued) magazine *Heeb: The New Jew Review*, described in its original 2002 mission statement as a "take-no prisoners quarterly for the plugged-in and preached-out," and to the more mainstream American Jewish World Service, founded in 1985, which stands apart from most American Jewish charitable organizations in its focus on global rather than specifically Jewish causes.

None of the above, however, has made as concerted an effort to reinvigorate secular Jewish culture and identity in the past decade as the last organization Sarna singles out, the Center for Cultural Judaism (CCJ) and its parent institution the Posen Foundation. Established in 2003 with a mission of bringing Jewish secularism to the nearly one-half of American Jews who described themselves as "secular" or "somewhat secular" in a 2001 survey, the CCJ has had an especially noticeable—and controversial—impact on Jewish studies programs on college campuses.[6] Since 2003 more than thirty of some of the finest universities in North America, including Harvard and Brown, have received grants from the CCJ on the basis of proposals to expand course offerings related to the study of Jewish secularism and secularization.[7]

Standing behind this sharp secular turn in Jewish studies is Felix Posen, a British Jewish energy magnate, philanthropist, and self-described "cultural Jew" with a calling. Now in his eighties, Posen has emerged in the past decade as the patron par excellence of secular Jewish education. Before being badly hurt by the Bernard Madoff scandal that broke out in late 2008, the Swiss-based Posen Foundation, run jointly by Posen and his son Daniel, had been donating over four million dollars each year to finance educational projects and curricula related to secular Judaism.[8] Moreover, while its affiliate, the CCJ, focuses on North America, the Posen Foundation directs its efforts worldwide, and in fact began its work in 2000 by awarding grant money to universities in Israel, where its influence has been particularly profound. With the exception of Bar-Ilan, Israel's flagship religious-Zionist university, nearly every major university in Israel contains Posen-seeded courses (in the case of Tel Aviv University, even an academic program) related to secular Jewish culture and identity. The Posen Foundation is also responsible for the recent publication of *Zeman yehudi hadash: Tarbut yehudit be-'idan hiloni* [New Jewish Time: Jewish Culture in a Secular Age], a five-volume encyclopedia on the subject of Jewish secularism and secularization with contributions from some of the leading scholars of Jewish studies in both the United States and Israel.[9] Meanwhile, the first of ten volumes of the Posen Library of Jewish Culture and Civilization, an "anthology of important literary works produced primarily by Jews from the biblical period to the end of 2002," is slated to appear sometime in 2012 under the imprint of Yale University Press.

Are these developments evidence of a genuine revival of Jewish secularism? Or is it merely the perception of crisis that is fueling a flurry of efforts at cultural reconstruction, while the long-term indicators remain decidedly bearish? I will qualify my impressions with the trite but true claim that (to borrow from *Star Trek*'s Dr. McCoy) "I'm a historian, not a fortune-teller." The dubious record of mid-twentieth-century secularization theorists in predicting the inevitable decline of religion in the developed world should caution those who make similar predictions regarding secularism. That said, I remain skeptical that a secular Jewish culture of any real coherence, robustness, and depth, especially in the Diaspora, can survive the loss of what was once, in essence, a surrogate *religion* of Jewish secularism. Reports of the demise of the latter were not, to my mind, premature. I would also submit that if, as Yosef Yerushalmi writes, the "blandly generic term *secular Jew* gives no indication of the richly nuanced variety of the species," we can expect this variety to grow exponentially—and the label "secular Jew" to turn even more "blandly generic"—as hybrid identities become increasingly the norm.[10]

Whatever the future of secular Judaism, the various projects for revitalizing it in the present—as the Posen encyclopedias and myriad course syllabi and book lists make clear—have boosted an interest in retracing its past. And this genealogical imperative has given new life to an old controversy: Spinoza's Jewishness, and more specifically the issue of whether he was the "first secular Jew."

II.

Periodizations are notoriously arbitrary and subjective, and in the case of contemporary developments typically premature as well. Nevertheless, a strong argument can be made for opening the latest chapter in Spinoza's Jewish reception in 1988. In that year there appeared in Israel a thick volume on the sources and reverberations of Spinoza's philosophical revolution entitled *Shpinozah ve-kofrim 'aherim* [Spinoza and Other Heretics].[11] Its author was Yirmiyahu Yovel, then a professor of philosophy at the Hebrew University in Jerusalem. Yovel was already associated with Spinoza: Four years earlier, in 1984, he had founded the Jerusalem Spinoza Institute, only the second society in the history of Israel devoted to promoting the study and diffusion of Spinoza's thought.[12] Yet it was the publication of *Spinoza and Other Heretics* that made Yovel, almost overnight, into something of a celebrity intellectual in Israel, while at the same time signaling, if only in hindsight, the renewal of an obsession with Spinoza's Jewish legacy and identity that, two decades later, shows no signs of abating.

The immediate success enjoyed by Yovel's Spinoza book in Israel was astounding. By early 1989 this nearly six-hundred-page tome (it would be translated as two volumes in English) had run through four editions with over five thousand copies sold.[13] Incredibly, in December 1988 *Spinoza and Other Heretics* was the top-selling book in Israel. Public discussions of the book at universities—the kind of seminars that typically managed to attract "a few university eggheads and maybe a casual drop-in or two looking for a place to snooze," wrote one American reporter—proved to be standing-room-only affairs. "Newspapers that usually show more interest in British soccer scores than Dutch liberal ideas," he added, "devoted columns to the long-dead thinker. A soft-porn magazine coupled a portrait of Spinoza, who was known for living a saintly life, with a cheesecake cover picture. He wore a frock, she a tattoo."[14]

The extraordinary interest elicited by Yovel's book generated extraordinary interest in its own right. Why, critics and pundits debated, would an academic book on Spinoza, however readable, rise to the best-seller list? Spinoza's great innovation, Yovel argued, was his "philosophy of immanence," with its emphasis on the fact that "this-worldly existence [is] all there is . . . the only actual being and the sole source of ethical value."[15] Most of *Spinoza and Other Heretics* was dedicated to tracing this "radically new philosophical principle" backward and forward in time: In the first volume of the English translation, entitled *The Marrano of Reason* (1989), Yovel underscored the crucial importance of Spinoza's Marrano lineage in the Amsterdam philosopher's conflating of God with nature; in the second, *The Adventures of Immanence* (1992), he charted the peregrinations of this allegedly major strain of modern philosophy in the work of Kant, Hegel, Marx, Nietzsche, and Freud.

Yet Yovel's book did not become a cultural phenomenon on account of its theses concerning transcendence and immanence. Nor would an argument for Spinoza's pioneering modernity alone have been enough to make this book a surprise best seller. Its broad appeal was a symptom of something else, as even the author admitted. The first full year of the first Palestinian intifada in the occupied territories was 1988; it was also a year racked by the "who is a Jew?" question, when Orthodox parties came close to succeeding in their campaign to amend the Law of Return to exclude from automatic citizenship anyone converted to Judaism under non-Orthodox supervision. "People here do not know what they have in common," claimed one professor of Jewish history. "It is supposed to be their Jewishness, but what is Jewishness?"[16]

Appearing amid what he called "renewed identity issues in the homeland," Yovel's book put forward a resolutely "secular" definition of Jewishness while providing this definition with a precursor.[17] "A philosopher of immanence and secularization," Yovel wrote, in the epilogue to volume one, "was he [Spinoza] also the first secular Jew?"[18] While paying lip service to the anachronism of this classification in the context of the seventeenth century, Yovel opined that Spinoza, who "left the Jewish congregation but did not enter the church," was indeed a harbinger of "what later generations would call 'Jewish secularism.'"[19] He was a forerunner not simply because of what he renounced—namely, commitment to Halakhah and deference to rabbinic authority on the one hand, and conversion to another religion on the other—but because of what he was one of the first, allegedly, to realize could not be so easily renounced: namely, one's Jewishness as a purely existential identity. According to Yovel, this insight stemmed from Spinoza's reflections on the experience of his Marrano forebears and contemporaries in Spain and Portugal. The stubbornness of Jewish self-identification within the ranks of the conversos, fueled in part by the emergence of a "new, existential kind of anti-Semitism" on the Iberian Peninsula that impeded the absorption of even the most sincere "New Christians," made the Amsterdam freethinker aware of a gap "between the religion of the Jews and their actual, more fundamental existence."[20] Jewishness was not exhausted by belief or practice; left over was "a basic and collective dimension of Jewish identity" that linked "Jews, Marranos, and a nonbeliever like himself," a secular peoplehood that Spinoza intuited without being able fully to articulate.[21] For Yovel, Spinoza thus contemplated (without ever endorsing) another remedy to what would become known as the "Jewish Question"— the reclamation of Jewish sovereignty within an independent state. Yovel entertains the possibility that Spinoza was a "closet Zionist." He "may not have defined Zionism as a goal"—for this was "an anachronistic solution," one that "[i]n Spinoza's time, had no social basis and was not even a glimmer on the horizon of consciousness"—but "he pointed out the methodological approach": namely, "an utterly prosaic, natural, and secular" interpretation of Judaism.[22]

Eight years after Yovel's book appeared, Yale University political theorist Steven B. Smith delivered his own brief for Spinoza's prophetic relevance for Judaism and liberalism in *Spinoza, Liberalism, and the Question of Jewish Identity* (1997). While acknowledging that Spinoza, "if he was an advocate of a religiously tolerant liberal state as one solution to the Jewish Question . . . was also a founder, perhaps *the* founder, of political Zionism," Smith nevertheless put him squarely in the assimilationist camp. "Spinoza's solution to the theologico-political problem can be summarized in a single word: assimilation."[23] The thrust of the *Treatise* was a strategy for "dissolving group identities, not accommodating them," since, for Spinoza, only by suppressing "the politics of group identity" could individual freedom and intellectual independence be safeguarded.[24] To the extent that Judaism would survive in Spinoza's ideal polity, it would be as a privatized confession in harmony with the liberal civil religion of the secular state, not as a separate ethnic minority or subculture. Indeed, Smith's Spinoza is ultimately a contemporary culture warrior, called on to fight the American postmodernists and communitarians who would elevate diversity, multiculturalism, and identity politics over the "older idea of a common citizenship." Like Yovel, Smith endorsed the view of Spinoza as a "prototype of the emancipated Jew" and forerunner of Jewish secularism, but what he meant by this is somewhat different. For whereas the Israeli Yovel diagnosed in Spinoza a deep if inchoate sense of Jewish peoplehood, the American Smith construed Spinoza's secular Jewishness as a commitment to the liberal values of reason, cosmopolitanism, and individual freedom over any corporate ties.

The years since have seen a proliferation of works that follow in the footsteps of Yovel and Smith by asserting Spinoza's pertinence to problems of Jewish identity in the present. An inventory of such works would include several academic books, which often make the case for Spinoza's Jewish modernity in ways quite different from the arguments of Smith and Yovel.[25] It would include Rebecca Goldstein's whimsical *Betraying Spinoza: The Renegade Jew Who Gave Us Modernity* (2006), a personal memoir-cum-philosophical meditation on Spinoza's Jewishness, in which the quest for a Jewish impulse buried beneath the geometrical proofs of Spinoza's rationalism serves quite explicitly as a vehicle for wrestling with dilemmas of Jewish identity at the turn of the twenty-first century.[26] It would include, by my count, two plays, in Hebrew and English, that center on the excommunication of Spinoza, as well as an Israeli film that imagines a Spinoza reborn in late-twentieth-century Tel Aviv.[27] Finally, it would include further contributions by both Smith and Yovel to this literature, most notably the latter's translation of the *Ethics* into Hebrew in 2003, only the second Hebrew translation of Spinoza's magnum opus since Jacob Klatzkin's of the mid-1920s.[28] In his introduction to the translation, Yovel justifies it on explicitly populist grounds, claiming that the "majority of [Hebrew] readers in our time, students and others, bemoan the difficulty of understanding the Hebrew version of Klatzkin" and require a more familiar idiom.[29] And to come full circle, Yovel served earlier in the last decade as editor in chief for the Posen encyclopedia on Jewish secularization, thus clearly emerging as the person in whom the revived interest in Spinoza and the broader campaign to rejuvenate Jewish secularism are most intimately conjoined.

This new wave of appropriations of Spinoza as a prototype of the modern, secular Jew, however, has not gone unchallenged. One of the first to issue a rebuttal was Richard Popkin, the late historian of early-modern Western European thought. In a lacerating review of the first volume of Yovel's diptych in *The New Republic*, Popkin derided his claim that Spinoza was "in some meaningful way, both a secularist *and* a Jew" as a "cliché . . . based on only a few morsels of evidence."[30] In one of his last published essays, Popkin went so far as to question the historical significance of the excommunication itself, claiming that its fashioning into a milestone in the confrontation between orthodoxy and modernity, and eventually into a "turning point" in Jewish history itself, was a myth propagated by later writers. All in all, he concludes, the herem, at least in context, "was a minor, local event in the Amsterdam community, one that was never discussed later on."[31] More recently, Steven Nadler, the author of *Spinoza: A Life* (1999), the preeminent biography of Spinoza in English, has issued his own refutation of the view that traces Jewish secularism back to Spinoza. Nadler insists that the adult Spinoza "seems to have had practically no sense of Jewish identity," in part because being Jewish, for Spinoza, was totally bound up with observance of the Halakhah, which he had famously rejected. Contra Yovel, Nadler maintains that Spinoza had no concept whatsoever, not even a vague premonition, of Jewishness as an existential identity. It might, then, make sense to consider Spinoza as "perhaps the most prominent early modern model of the secular individual," yet he was "not the first secular Jew, for he was not a secular Jew at all."[32] Finally, in a piqued rejoinder in *Commentary* to Goldstein's book, Allan Nadler calls for an end to "two centuries of determined Jewish efforts to restore the wayward heretic to the bosom of his people," noting "how little Spinoza has to contribute to current debates over Jewish identity and Jewish destiny."[33] At the heart of this backlash is the belief that Spinoza must be set loose from his legion of Jewish invokers, reclaimers, and, yes, betrayers, and returned to his seventeenth-century context, where he can be, simply, Spinoza.

III.

Broadly speaking, then, we find in the recent literature two basic positions on Spinoza's place in the world of Jewish secularism. In one corner stand those—let us, a bit crudely, call them the "presentists"—who seek to draw Spinoza nearer to us, by vouching for his anticipation of the modern, secular Jew and driving home his relevance to the contemporary culture wars. In the other corner stand those—let us, a bit less crudely, call them the "contextualists"—who look askance at interpretations of Spinoza as a Jewish precursor, judging such readings guilty of everything from historical anachronism at the very least to a groundless "Judaizing" of the Amsterdam philosopher more problematically.

In this book, I have argued for a different way of conceiving the relationship between Spinoza and secular Jewish identity. Like the "contextualists," I am deeply skeptical of the claim that Spinoza was the first secular Jew, and not just because the emphasis on a single progenitor lies suspiciously close to myth. It is, of course, impossible to know what unexpressed and perhaps unconscious thoughts and feelings lurked in the psyche of the Amsterdam philosopher. We cannot rule out the possibility that Jewishness continued to figure in his self-concept, however elusively. The absence of evidence is not necessarily the evidence of absence. But this absence should neverthe-less give us pause. All too often, expansive claims for Spinoza's initiation or even simply anticipation of a secular Jewish outlook are found to rest on table scraps: a fragment from a letter here, a book excerpt ripped out of context there, even passages with no clear allusions to Jewishness at all beyond those read into them. Historicizing the idea of Spinoza's break with Amsterdam Jewry as a "turning point" between the old and the new, as we have done here, providing this notion of a beginning with its own beginning and charting some of its most salient iterations in Jewish cultural memory reveals how much retrojection has been involved in making Spinoza a fore-runner and exemplar of the "secular Jew." Dilemmas of identity of later vintage are referred back to the Amsterdam heretic, even as he is wrested from his seventeenth-century milieu and forced into the present to serve as a mouthpiece for some version or another of secular Jewishness. Seen in the *longue durée* of Spinoza's reception, it becomes clear that the efforts of aforementioned "presentists" to link up with Spinoza has a history that stops well short of the philosopher himself. Their true "precursors," I would submit, are the nineteenth-century Jewish intellectuals who were the first to resurrect Spinoza as their standard-bearer.

To claim that Spinoza was not the originator of Jewish secularism, how-ever, is not to say that he was immaterial to its origins. There may be no causal nexus or even strong connection between the seventeenth-century philosopher and the rise of secular Jewish identity, but we would be ill advised to separate them entirely. What this book has shown is that whatever Spi-noza, the Spinoza of history, may have intended, the Spinoza of memory has been crucial to constructions of nontraditional Jewishness—assimilationist, cosmopolitan, and national—from the nineteenth century to the present. Between the *reception* of Spinoza and the formation of secular Jewish iden-tity (or identities), in other words, an intimate link most certainly exists. Obviously, there have been many self-described Jewish secularists who have defined their Jewishness without reference to Spinoza. By no means was the reception of Spinoza a necessary cause of Jewish intellectual secularization. That said, no other cultural icon has figured as prominently, as diversely, and as recurrently in fantasies of the modern, secular Jew as Spinoza.

We can thus agree with the "contextualists" that the common percep-tion of Spinoza as the first secular Jew is a myth that has more to do with fantasy than reality without rejecting it out of hand. Dispelling myths is one of the principal tasks of historical criticism; understanding their effects, however, is too. As Peter Novick has written, "A central problem for any new cognitive structure is to legitimize its epistemological foundation. This may involve a myth of an individual genius or hero whose personal qualities exemplify the way in which the new knowledge is acquired. . . . Without some such myth, cognitive structures lack grounding and authority."[34] What Novick asserts with regard to the professionalization of history holds equally true of what Yosef Yerushalmi called "the historically problematic and not self-evident" condition of being "a Jew without God."[35] In both cases, the quest for legitimacy for ideas, practices, and ways of being in the world without clear precedent generated new foundation myths, from the myth of "historical objectivity" as embodied in the figure of Leopold von Ranke to the myth of Spinoza, the first "secular Jew."

Another advantage of treating as myth Spinoza's pioneering reputation is that it reveals the complex interplay of the secular and the sacred in the fashioning of Spinoza and, by extension, in modern Jewish self-fashioning. As a window into the effort to transform Jewishness by freeing it from a *halakhic* framework, the Jewish rehabilitation of Spinoza is rightly considered a barometer of secularization. Yet this process is seen through a glass darkly if perceived only as a one-way street from the holy to the profane. The rhetoric of this recovery—its dominant metaphors, schemata, and tropes—suggests that the "religious" is not so much displaced in the drive to create a new Jewish culture (or "new Hebrew man") as it is deployed in a new context. Examined up close, each of the appropriations analyzed in this book—from Auerbach's rendering of Spinoza as the "redeemer of mankind" to efforts of Klausner and other Zionists to redeem Spinoza by rescinding the ban—contains notes of both sacralization and secularization. Indeed, the brilliance of I. B. Singer's parody derives precisely from its laying bare the rabbinic, exegetical mindset that continues to haunt the Nahum Fischelsons and Asa Heshels for whom the *Ethics* has simply replaced the Talmud, and who respond to life's challenges not with the bold *Selbstdenken* of a Spinoza, but by asking, in essence, "what would Spinoza do?" For all its caricature, Singer's portrait of the Jewish Spinozist poses a serious question: Namely, if Spinoza has served as a charismatic *rebbe* and *moreh* for generations of Jewish freethinkers, how freethinking have the latter been really? If one of the most common techniques for creating a secular Jewish culture has been, historically, the canonization of classic heretics like Spinoza, does the use of the adjective *secular* to characterize this culture conceal as much as it reveals? Is a label along the lines of "first secular Jew" even truly secular?

IV.

On the surface, there is little about the contemporary revival of Spinoza in modern Jewish culture that is original. The perception of Spinoza as the first modern or secular Jew, the tension between assimilationist and ethnic or national interpretations of this identity, the extent to which the rising interest in the Amsterdam philosopher cuts across disciplines and genres to the point that it constitutes a genuine cultural phenomenon: As has been shown, precedents can be found for all these features of the current moment in the prior history of Spinoza's Jewish reception. Above all, I would argue, the wave of Jewish appropriations of Spinoza in the present is driven by the same all-too-human need that has motivated such appropriations in the past: It is the need to imagine origins, to develop a sense of a beginning, all as part of the struggle over where to draw the boundaries of Jewishness and whether a secular Jewish identity is even possible. To close, however, I would like to offer some thoughts, admittedly quite speculative, about two aspects of the most recent chapter in Spinoza's Jewish reception that strike me as new, if not in an absolute sense at least in their overall prominence.

The first involves the nature of the awareness behind appropriation. Throughout this book, I have stressed that the concept of Spinoza as the first modern or secular Jew is a constructed image that tells us more about the appropriators of the seventeenth-century heretic than about the heretic himself. If I may give a playful misreading of that wonderful epigraph from William Wordsworth's "Ode: Intimations of Immortality"—"The Child Is Father of the Man"—we might say that the intellectual "children" of Spinoza have been, in effect, "father" to their own "founding father." They have claimed descent from a progenitor they themselves created. This was as true of Auerbach in the nineteenth century as it was of Singer in the twentieth. In each of the case studies, we found that it was problems of identity in the present—the need to provide a secular Jewish existence with both cover and content—that underlay the birth of Spinoza as a modern Jewish prototype and sustained this image throughout its many iterations. Nevertheless, the participants in this formation of a precursor generally did so naively. They transposed Spinoza to their own frames of reference with at most a fleeting idea of the distance being eclipsed.

In one of the most recent additions to the Jewish cult of Spinoza, Goldstein's *Betraying Spinoza*, this lack of irony about his appropriation is the first thing to go. A novelist and philosopher, Goldstein begins her book with an account of her adolescent introduction to Spinoza in a Jewish history class at her strictly Orthodox, all-girls high school on Manhattan's Lower East

Side. Her teacher's deprecating (if surprisingly well-informed) discussion of the life of this *apikores* notwithstanding, the author, a budding skeptic herself, identified with Spinoza. "There was a moment long ago," she writes, recounting this discovery, "when I knew next to nothing about the magnificent reconfiguration of reality laid out in the system of Spinoza, and yet when I felt I knew something about what it was like to have been him, the former yeshiva student, Baruch Spinoza."[36] As this book has shown, moments like the one Goldstein describes have a time-honored place in the Jewish reception of Spinoza. Her response echoes that of the eighteen-year-old Auerbach, declaring in 1830 after reading about Spinoza for the first time, "I shall now be called Moses Baruch Berthold Benedict Auerbach." For both, a certain kinship with Spinoza—a sense of inhabiting a similar if not identical predicament—occurred at a decisive stage in their intellectual maturation, providing them with an exemplar for constructing a new identity. But this teenage infatuation is punctured in Goldstein's case by the philosophical understanding of Spinoza acquired in later years. A serious engagement with the rationalist metaphysics found in the *Ethics* causes her to question whether reading its author as a model Jewish thinker, even a heretical one, amounts to "betraying Spinoza," straying from his utterly impersonal vision of reality through a fixation on identity. From there, much of the rest of *Betraying Spinoza* consists of a rather derivative explanation of why Jewish concerns in fact *were* a determining factor in the genesis of Spinoza's philosophy. Still, one wonders whether Goldstein's method of drawing attention to the act of appropriation itself, questioning the "Judaizing" of Spinoza even while proceeding to do just that, marks a new, postmodern turn in the Jewish cult of the Amsterdam heretic, wherein lighthearted betrayal is generally fine, so long as it is conscious.

The second novelty has to do with a change in the vector of Jewish reclamations of Spinoza. For virtually all the thinkers profiled in this study, the attraction to Spinoza was part of a basic biographical arc from a traditional upbringing toward a modern, secular Jewish identity. Over the course of the nineteenth century, an encounter with Spinoza became a rite of passage in the maturation of the secular Jewish intellectual. The "conversion" story of the radical maskil came to include a de rigueur brush with the biblical criticism and repudiation of the Law of the *Treatise*, the *Deus sive Natura* of the *Ethics*, and the myth of a martyr for intellectual independence and integrity above all else. The degree to which this "narrative" became a stereotype of the culture is reflected and ironized in I. B. Singer's fiction, which takes for granted an understanding of Spinoza as a code for secular heresy and rejection of halakhic authority. This is how the terse observation that Asa Heshel arrives in Warsaw from the shtetl with a worn Hebrew translation of the *Ethics* is able to convey so much about his character, even before we gain any substantial knowledge of him.

Certainly, Spinoza has not ceased to appeal to rebels in the mold of the classical Jewish heretic who rejects the very tradition in which he or she has learned; this is confirmed by Goldstein's own autobiographical account of her path to secular Jewish identity via Spinoza. And the popularity of recent books like Shalom Auslander's *Foreskin's Lament: A Memoir* (2007) suggests that one of the most archetypal plotlines in the literature of Jewish secularism—the story of the Orthodox Jewish boy turned enfant terrible who angrily and dramatically breaks with his religious past, struggling to free himself of an ancestral God and law that for all his efforts, he is unable entirely to shake—continues to resonate. As stated, however, the threat to secular Jewishness today comes not only from the religious Right but from the swelling ranks of nominally "secular" Jews for whom estrangement from Judaism is an inheritance rather than a lived experience and who have little need to struggle against a tradition they are too far removed from to fight. More and more, it seems, the nontraditional Jew as *apikores*, even as self-consciously "wicked son," has given way to the "one who does not even know how to ask." Could it be that for this "lost" soul, the turn to the prototype of the secular Jewish intellectual allegedly "lost" to Jewish culture might also be understood as a *return* to identity? For the perplexed of our own day, it would seem that Spinoza has moved beyond his customary role in the modern Jewish imagination as a guide beyond Judaism. Perhaps, paradoxically, through his very marginality, he has also come to represent the hope of a way back.

Notes

Preface

1. Philip Weiss, "Baruch Spinoza Goes into Rehab at Yivo Institute," *Mondoweiss*, November 1, 2006, http://mondoweiss.net/2006/11/baruch_spinoza_.html.
2. Steven Nadler, "The Jewish Spinoza," in *Journal of the History of Ideas* 70, no. 3 (2009): 506.
3. Roger-Pol Droit, "Spinoza: L'homme qui a révolutionné la philosophie," in *Le Point*, July 12, 2007. The issue contained a few other short articles on Spinoza in addition to the cover story.
4. "New Jerusalem Press Round Up to Date," *The Theater J Blog*, July 6, 2010, http://theaterjblogs.wordpress.com/2010/07/06/new-jerusalem-press-round-up -to-date/. The play proved such a hit at the box office that Theater J has already scheduled a return engagement for its 2011–2012 season.

Introduction: Spinoza's Jewish Modernities

1. Yosef H. Yerushalmi, *Freud's Moses: Judaism Terminable and Interminable* (New Haven, 1993), 10.
2. See Steven B. Smith, *Spinoza, Liberalism, and the Question of Jewish Identity* (New Haven, 1997); Jonathan I. Israel, *Radical Enlightenment: Philosophy and the Making of Modernity, 1650–1750* (Oxford, 2001); Yirmiyahu Yovel, *Spinoza and Other Heretics*, vol. 2, *The Adventures of Immanence* (Princeton, 1992); Michael Hardt and Antonio Negri, *Empire* (Cambridge, MA, 2000); Antonio Damasio, *Looking for Spinoza: Joy, Sorrow, and the Feeling Brain* (New York, 2003).
3. See Frederick C. Beiser, *The Romantic Imperative: The Concept of Early German Romanticism* (Cambridge, MA, 2005), 171–88; Eccy de Jonge, *Spinoza and Deep Ecology: Challenging Traditional Approaches to Environmentalism* (Farnham, UK, 2004).
4. David Biale, "Historical Heresies and Modern Jewish Identity," in *Jewish Social Studies* 8 (2002): 115. The "non-Jewish Jew" label was coined by the British Marxist historian of Polish Jewish origin Isaac Deutscher. See *The Non-Jewish Jew and Other Essays* (London, 1968).
5. Yirmiyahu Yovel's *Spinoza and Other Heretics, vol. 1: The Marrano of Reason* and Steven B. Smith's *Spinoza, Liberalism, and the Question of Jewish Identity* are two of

the most important "master narratives" of Jewish secularization of recent vintage to begin with Spinoza. On the other side of the fence are scholars such as Steven Nadler and the late Richard Popkin, who while acknowledging that Spinoza drew on Jewish sources in the development of his philosophy, deny that he either envisioned, or would conceivably have endorsed, a specifically and self-consciously *Jewish* secularism. See Popkin, "Notes from Underground," *The New Republic 202*, no. 21 (May 21, 1990): 41; Nadler, *Spinoza: A Life* (Cambridge, UK, 1999), and more recently "Spinoza and the Origins of Jewish Secularism," in *Religion and Ethnicity? Jewish Identities in Evolution* (New Brunswick, NJ, 2009), 59–68. I discuss these authors and the ongoing debate over whether Spinoza was the first "secular Jew" at greater length in my Epilogue.

6. There is still no book-length study, in English, expressly devoted to the Jewish reception of Spinoza. The Israeli philosophers Eliezer Schweid and Ze'ev Levy have written voluminously in Hebrew (and, in Levy's case, occasionally in German, his native tongue) about Jewish responses to Spinoza. Schweid, the 1994 Israel Prize laureate, is particularly well known for interpreting virtually the entirety of modern Jewish thought as a response to the Spinozan challenge. Yet both Schweid and Levy approach this topic as philosophers, not historians. Their chief concern is what place, if any, to assign Spinoza in Jewish thought—the question of whether he *was* a Jewish philosopher. I come at this subject from a very different angle, as I explain below. See Eliezer Schweid, *Ha-yehudi ha-boded veha-Yahadut* (Tel Aviv, 1974); idem, *Toledot ha-filosofyah ha-yehudit: Ha-me'ah ha-tesha 'esreh* (Jerusalem, 1977); Ze'ev Levy, *Shpinozah u-musag ha-yahadut: Tefisah ve-gilguleha* (Tel Aviv, 1972) and *Baruch Spinoza—seine Aufnahme durch die jüdischen Denker in Deutschland* (2001).

7. Jan Assmann, *Moses the Egyptian: The Memory of Egypt in Western Monotheism* (Cambridge, MA, 1997), 8–9.

8. My comments here are in line with those of Steven Aschheim in his examination of the reception and reworking of Nietzsche's thought in twentieth-century Germany. See *The Nietzsche Legacy in Germany, 1890–1990* (Berkeley, 1994), 4–5.

9. Moshe Idel, *Ascensions on High in Jewish Mysticism: Pillars, Lines, Ladders* (Budapest, 2005), 11.

10. For an analysis of how one of the quintessential symbols of the Revolution—the storming of the Bastille—became a cultural paradigm with shifting meanings over time, see Hans-Joseph Lüsebrink and Rolf Reichardt, *The Bastille: A History of a Symbol of Despotism and Freedom*, trans. Norbert Schürer (Durham, NC, 1997).

11. For the now classic account of secularization as a "rupture," see Hans Blumenberg, *The Legitimacy of the Modern Age*, trans. Robert M. Wallace (Cambridge, MA, 1985). Jonathan I. Israel's multivolume revision of the historiography of the Enlightenment, beginning with his *Radical Enlightenment*, is one of the most emphatic recent arguments for modernity as a rupture with the past.

12. This perspective has traditionally been associated with critics of modernity determined to expose the theological atavisms within discourse deemed "secular" and thereby puncture the Enlightenment "grand narrative" of modernity as a progressive break from a religious past. See, for example, Carl Schmidt, *Political Theology: Four Chapters on the Concept of Sovereignty* (Chicago, 2006 [1923]); Karl Löwith, *Meaning in History: The Theological Implications of the Philosophy of History* (Chicago, 1957). Yet studies in this vein are not ipso facto hostile to modernity.

For recent works that stress religious lineages for modernity and the Enlightenment, see Charles Taylor, *A Secular Age* (Cambridge, MA, 2007); Michael A. Gillespie, *The Theological Origins of Modernity* (Chicago, 2008); and David Sorkin, *The Religious Enlightenment: Protestants, Jews, and Catholics from London to Vienna* (Princeton, 2008).

13. Manuel Joël, *Spinoza's Theologisch-politischer Traktat auf seine Quellen geprüft* (Breslau, 1870); Harry A. Wolfson, *The Philosophy of Spinoza: Unfolding the Latent Processes of His Reasoning* (Cambridge, MA, 1983 [1934]); Steven Nadler, *Spinoza's Heresy: Immortality and the Jewish Mind* (Oxford, 2001).

14. Israel's Spinoza was the "intellectual backbone" of the Radical Enlightenment, which—according to Israel—"rejected all compromise with the past and sought to sweep away existing structures entirely." See *Radical Enlightenment*, 11.

15. On this, see also Adam Sutcliffe, *Judaism and Enlightenment* (Cambridge, UK, 2003).

16. Ben Halpern, "Secularism," in Arthur A. Cohen and Paul Mendes-Flohr (eds.), *Contemporary Jewish Religious Thought* (New York, 1987), 863. For a new history of Jewish secular thought that stresses its inflection by rabbinic and medieval Jewish philosophical concepts of God, Torah, and Israel, see David Biale, *Not in the Heavens: The Tradition of Jewish Secular Thought* (Princeton, 2010).

17. See Israel, *Radical Enlightenment*; *Enlightenment Contested: Philosophy, Modernity, and the Emancipation of Man, 1670–1752* (Oxford, 2006); and *A Revolution of the Mind: Radical Enlightenment and the Intellectual Origins of Modern Democracy* (Princeton, 2009).

18. See Georg G. Iggers, *Historiography in the Twentieth Century: From Scientific Objectivity to the Postmodern Challenge* (Middletown, CT, 2005).

19. Steven Nadler, "The Jewish Spinoza": 491–510.

20. Yerushalmi, *Freud's Moses*, 9.

Chapter 1: Ex-Jew, Eternal Jew

1. On the early publication history of the *Theological-Political Treatise*, see Israel, *Radical Enlightenment*, 275–85. For brevity's sake I will mostly refer to the *Theological-Political Treatise* as simply the *Treatise* throughout the rest of this book.

2. The phrase appeared in an April 1671 letter from J. G. Graevius to the philosopher Leibniz and is discussed below. See Jakob Freudenthal, ed., *Die Lebensgeschichte Spinoza's in Quellenschriften, Urkunden, und nichtamtlichen Nachrichten* (Leipzig, 1899), 193; Ernst Altkirch, ed., *Maledictus und Benedictus: Spinoza im Urteil des Volkes und der Geistigen bis auf Constantin Brunner* (Leipzig, 1924), 29.

3. Freudenthal, 192; Altkirch, 26.

4. Freudenthal, 193; Altkirch, 29.

5. Spinoza, "Letter 45," in *Completed Works*, trans. Samuel Shirley, ed. Michael L. Morgan (Indianapolis, 2002), 884.

6. Freudenthal, 174; Altkirch, 51.

7. The Catholic Church placed the *Treatise* on the index of forbidden books in 1679 and added the *Opera posthuma* in 1691. See Altkirch, 54.

8. A leading early spokesperson for the moderate Cartesian attack on Spinoza was Regner à Mansvelt, a professor of theology at the University of Utrecht. See Altkirch, 34.

9. This gibe appeared in Kortholt's *De tribus impostoribus* (1680), a rejoinder to the radical deist branding of Moses, Jesus, and Mohammed as "impostors" that applied this same moniker to Hobbes, Herbert of Cherbury, and Spinoza. See Altkirch, 61.

10. See Kortholt: "Benedictus Spinoza, who should more rightly be named Maledictus; for the earth, full of thorns [*spinosa terra*] as a result of the divine curse [Gen. 3:17–18], has never borne a more accursed man, nor one whose writings are strewn with so many thorns." In Altkirch, 61.

11. This came in a poem by Joachim Oudann, which appeared in Adriaen Verwer's *Mom-aensicht der atheistery afgerukt* (Amsterdam, 1683). See Altkirch, 64–65.

12. *Fuerstellung vier neuer Welt-Weisen, nahmentlich I. Renati Des Cartes, II. Thomae Hobbes, III. Benedicti Spinosa, IV. Balthasar Beckers, nach ihrem Leben und fuernehmsten Irrthuemern* (Koethen, 1702), 2. Qtd. in Altkirch, 77.

13. For a copy of this image, see E. Altkirch, *Spinoza im Porträt* (Jena, 1913), 90.

14. On Orobio, see Yosef Kaplan, *From Christianity to Judaism: The Story of Isaac Orobio de Castro*, trans. Rafael Loewe (Oxford, 1989), 1. Though originally published in 1684, the first extant edition of Orobio's polemic is from 1703. See Fritz Bamberger, *Spinoza and Anti-Spinoza Literature* (Cincinnati, 2003), 88. The significance of this tract both at the time and well into the eighteenth century has often led scholars to exaggerate the Jewish contribution to the emerging anti-Spinoza movement. Following the ban of all editions of the *Opera posthuma* by the states of Holland in June 1678, Jonathan Israel writes, "[t]he barrage of refutations from Voetian, Cocceian, Anabaptist, and Jewish quarters continued unabated," though the only Jewish contribution to this barrage was that of Orobio. See Israel, *The Dutch Republic: Its Rise, Greatness, and Fall, 1477–1806* (Oxford, 1995), 922.

15. The Dutch Collegiant in question was Johannes Bredenburg, a merchant from Rotterdam who had written a rejoinder to Spinoza's *Treatise* in 1675 that tried and failed to demolish Spinoza's proofs for an inexorable determinism. On his *Enervatio tractatus theologico-politici* (Rotterdam, 1675), see Bamberger, *Spinoza and Anti-Spinoza Literature*, 46. For an analysis of Orobio's *Certamen philosophicum*, see Seymour Feldman, "Ha-bikoret ha-yehudit ha-rishonah neged Shpinozah," in *Iyyun* 37 (1988): 222–37.

16. Qtd. in Paul R. Mendes-Flohr and Jehuda Reinharz, eds., *The Jew in the Modern World: A Documentary History*, 3rd edition (New York, 2010), 57. The writ of excommunication found here is translated from the Portuguese by Rita Mendes-Flohr and is reprinted by permission of Oxford University Press, Inc.

17. The text was unearthed by the Dutch researcher Johannes van Vloten (1818–83), an important figure in nineteenth-century Spinoza scholarship. See B. de Spinoza, *Benedicti de Spinoza opera quae supersunt omnia. Supplementum*, ed. J. van Vloten (Amsterdam, 1862), 290–93.

18. From the late seventeenth century onward it has been widely presumed that around the time of his herem, Spinoza wrote an apologia in Spanish vindicating his rupture with the Jewish community on ideological grounds. Though never published, this work, it is said, contained *in nuce* the arguments of the *Treatise*. There is

certainly plausibility to this rumor, yet proof remains elusive. The person who first asserted the existence of this precursor to the *Treatise*—a Dutch Cartesian at the University of Leiden named Salomon van Til (1643–1713)—is still the only one ever to claim to have actually *seen* it. See Van Til, *Het Voorhof der heydnen* (Dordrecht, 1694–96).

19. For two radically different hypotheses of recent years—one emphasizing Spinoza's refutation of the immortality of the soul, the other a financial conflict between the Mahamad and Spinoza concerning his late father's estate—see Steven Nadler, *Spinoza's Heresy: Immortality and the Jewish Mind* (Cambridge, UK, 2001); Odette Vlessing, "The Excommunication of Spinoza: A Conflict Between Jewish and Dutch Law," *Studia Spinozana* 13 (2003): 15–47. For a somewhat dated overview of various theories for Spinoza's expulsion, see Asa Kasher and Shlomo Biderman, "Why Was Baruch de Spinoza Excommunicated?" in *Skeptics, Millenarians, and Jews*, eds. David Katz and Jonathan Israel (Leiden, 1990), 98–141.

20. The exception occurred in 1712, when the Portuguese Jewish community of Amsterdam excommunicated three heretics for "following the sect of the Karaites, acting as they do, and entirely denying the Oral Law, which is the foundation and underpinning of our Holy Law." In expelling these three "Karaites" (an epithet in rabbinic apologetics of the era for anyone who renounced the legitimacy of the Oral Law), the communal syndics resorted to an excommunication formula that had been used on only one other occasion in the history of the congregation—namely, with Spinoza. On this episode, see Yosef Kaplan, "'Karaites' in the Early Eighteenth Century," in *An Alternative Path to Modernity: The Sephardi Diaspora in Western Europe* (Leiden, 2000).

21. Israel S. Révah, a French Jewish historian of the conversos and the Western Sephardic Diaspora, unearthed this datum. While doing research in the archives of the Inquisition in Madrid in the mid-1950s, he came upon two affidavits from August 1659 that yielded startling information. Two men, an Augustinian monk originally of Columbia and a Spanish sea captain, had presented themselves before the Inquisition for questioning after returning to Madrid from time spent abroad, including in Amsterdam, where their paths had crossed. While in Amsterdam, they became acquainted with Spinoza and Dr. Juan de Prado, and heard then "that they had previously been Jews and had observed their law, but . . . had distanced themselves from it because it was not good, but a fabrication, and for that reason they had been excommunicated." See Révah, *Spinoza et le Dr. Juan de Prado* (Paris, 1959), 66–68; Kaplan, *From Christianity to Judaism*, 134.

22. On this subculture of libertinism and skepticism, see Jonathan Israel, "Philosophy, Deism, and the Early Sephardic Enlightenment," in *The Dutch Intersection: The Jews and the Netherlands in Modern History*, ed. Yosef Kaplan (Leiden, 2008), 173–201. For a recent study that argues for a substantial degree of secularization and religious laxity among Sephardim and Ashkenazim alike in the early eighteenth century, especially in the major cities of Western and Central Europe, see Shmuel Feiner, *The Origins of Jewish Secularization in Eighteenth-Century Europe*, trans. Chaya Naor (Philadelphia, 2010).

23. See Seymour Feldman, "Introduction" to Spinoza, *Theological-Political Treatise* (Gebhardt edition), 2nd edition, trans. Samuel Shirley (Indianapolis, 1998), xvii. The focus on Latin obscures the fact that several vernacular translations of the *Trea-*

tise appeared early on in the reception of the work, including in French (1678), English (1689), and Dutch (1693). On early translations of the *Treatise*, see Israel, *Radical Enlightenment*, 278–79.

24. Freudenthal, *Die Lebensgeschichte*, 24. For an English translation of one of the extant manuscripts of Lucas's biography, see *The Oldest Biography of Spinoza*, ed. Abraham Wolf (London, 1927), 75.

25. Paul Vernière, *Spinoza et la pensée française avant la Revolution*, vol. 1 (Paris, 1954), 27.

26. Freudenthal, 3; Wolf, 42. Unlike Spinoza's later biographers, Lucas never cited the sources of his information, and so the origin of this brazen untruth is not clear. From the rest of his account, it is hard to avoid Freudenthal's acid conclusion that "[t]he biographer describes Spinoza's origins as very lowly because they are Jewish." In fact, Spinoza's family was one of the most esteemed in the Jewish community, as evidenced by the various honorary offices to which both his father and grandfather were elected.

27. Freudenthal, 7; Wolf, 47.

28. Freudenthal, 8; Wolf, 50.

29. Freudenthal, 8–9; Wolf, 51. David Ives's recent play about the excommunication of Spinoza, *New Jerusalem* (2009), is only the latest work to draw heavily on this conceit of a standoff between a resolute Spinoza and a reluctant Mortera prior to the herem.

30. The work in question was *Triompho del Govierno Popular y de la antigüedad holandesa* (1683), a collection of opuscules on the history of Amsterdam Sephardic society. For the possible allusion to a conflict between Spinoza and Mortera, see Nadler, *Spinoza: A Life*, 90.

31. Prado, who was nearly two decades Spinoza's senior, arrived in Amsterdam in the middle of 1655 after escaping from Spain with his family in 1652 and reverting to Judaism during a stopover in Hamburg. The claim that Prado played a decisive part in spurring Spinoza to heresy was first ventured by the German Spinoza scholar Carl Gebhardt and then bolstered by the aforementioned Révah. In 1656 Prado managed to avoid sharing Spinoza's fate by publicly retracting his "evil beliefs" in a confession entered into the Amsterdam Sephardic community's Book of Ordinances (one page before Spinoza's writ of excommunication). Yet just two years later, the Talmud Torah officials found Prado guilty of "having returned to his evil and false beliefs against our Sacred Law and having corrupted through these beliefs young students," and on these grounds they ousted him for good. See Gebhardt, "Juan de Prado," in *Chronicon Spinozanum* III (1923) and Révah, *Des Marranes à Spinoza*, ed. Henry Méchoulan et al. (Paris, 1995).

32. Freudenthal, 20–21; Wolf, 69.

33. On these editions, see S. von Dunin-Borkowski, *Spinoza*, vol. 1 (Münster, 1933), 488–89.

34. This edition, which contained the false imprint of Hamburg, was in fact printed in Amsterdam in 1735.

35. Portions of Lucas's biography were spliced into an edition of Colerus's life of Spinoza that appeared in Lenglet-Dufresnoy's notorious compendium of Spinozist and anti-Spinozist literature *Réfutation des erreurs de Benoit de Spinosa* (1731).

36. Pierre Bayle, *Dictionaire historique et critique* (Rotterdam, 1697). For this and subsequent editions of Bayle's Enlightenment classic, see Fritz Bamberger, *Spinoza and Anti-Spinoza Literature: The Printed Literature of Spinozism* (Cincinnati, 2003), 77, 78, 86, 102, 162, 170, 173. For an English translation of Bayle's entry on Spinoza, see *Historical and Critcal Dictionary: Selections*, ed. and trans. Richard H. Popkin (Indianapolis, 1965), 288–338.

37. On the publication history of this book, see Freudenthal, *Die Lebensgeschichte*, 249–50; Bamberger, *Spinoza and Anti-Spinoza Literature*, 92–93, 150. Quotations in the text come from the English translation of 1706, *The Life of Benedict de Spinosa*, which was reprinted in Sir Frederick Pollock, *Spinoza: His Life and Philosophy* (London, 1899). This translation was based on the previous French translation and not on the original Dutch exemplar.

38. Freudenthal, 32; Popkin, 296.

39. Colerus, *The Life of Benedict de Spinosa*, 406.

40. Popkin, 299.

41. Ibid., 298. The sincerity of Bayle's objection to "Spinozism" has been a subject of heated debate from the appearance of the *Dictionaire* to the present. Most recently, Jonathan Israel has vigorously defended the view of Bayle as a disguised atheist and crypto-Spinozist whose skepticism was far more antitheological than fideistic in spirit. See Israel, *Enlightenment Contested*, 264–78. Without denying that Bayle left his readers with ample reason to doubt his professions of "orthodoxy," I nevertheless side with those who argue for the genuineness of Bayle's objection to Spinoza's metaphysical monism and, more broadly, to the whole premise of an all-encompassing philosophical system. See Adam Sutcliffe, "Spinoza, Bayle, and the Enlightenment Politics of Philosophical Certainty," in *History of European Ideas* 34 (2008): 66–76.

42. Freudenthal, 31; Popkin, 295.

43. Colerus, 395.

44. Ibid., 387.

45. Popkin, 288–93.

46. Colerus, 389–90.

47. Freudenthal, 29; Popkin, 290.

48. Colerus, 389.

49. This along with other works by Da Costa can be found in Carl Gebhardt, ed., *Die Schriften des Uriel da Costa* (Heidelberg, 1922).

50. Richard Popkin was one such skeptic. See R. H. Popkin, "Spinoza and La Peyrère," in *Southwestern Journal of Philosophy* 3 (1977), 177ff. Yosef Kaplan formerly believed this description was a forgery but has since changed his mind. See Kaplan, "The Social Functions of the Herem," in *An Alternative Path to Modernity*, 130–32.

51. Colerus, 391.

52. The text, labeled by Colerus "the form of the general excommunication used amongst the Jews," is omitted in the version of the biography that appears in Pollock. It can be found in *The Life of Benedict de Spinosa* (The Hague, 1906), 20–31, which is a reprint of the original 1706 copy.

53. Popkin, "Spinoza's Excommunication," in *Jewish Themes in Spinoza's Philosophy*, ed. Heidi M. Ravven and Lenn E. Goodman (Albany, 2002), 272.

54. Qtd. in Chimen Abramsky, "The Crisis of Authority Within European Jewry in the Eighteenth Century," in *Studies in Jewish Religious and Intellectual History: Presented to Alexander Altmann on the Occasion of His Seventieth Birthday*, ed. Siegfried Stein and Raphael Loewe (Tuscaloosa, AL, 1979).

55. J. G. Wachter, *Der Spinozismus im Jüdenthumb, oder, die von dem heutigen Jüdenthumb und dessen Geheimen Kabbala vergötterte Welt* (Amsterdam, 1699). There is now a reprint of Wachter's book. See Wachter, *Der Spinozismus im Jüdenthumb*, ed. Winfried Schröeder (Stuttgart-Bad Cannstatt, 1994).

56. On Rosenroth and his *Kabbalah denudata*, see Allison P. Coudert, "The Kabbalah Denudata: Converting Jews or Seducing Christians," in *Jewish Christians and Christian Jews: From the Renaissance to the Enlightenment*, ed. Richard H. Popkin and Gordon M. Weiner (Dordrecht, 1994), 73–96.

57. See Alexander Altmann, "Lurianic Kabbalah in a Platonic Key: Abraham Cohen Herrera's *Puerta de cielo*," in *Hebrew Union College Annual* 80 (1982): 1–38.

58. Perhaps the most noteworthy can be found in Genesis Rabbah 68:9, where it states that God is also known as *Makom* because "He is the place of the world [*mekomo shel 'olam*], the world is not his place."

59. Wachter, *Der Spinozismus im Jüdenthumb*, vol. 3, 77/399.

60. Ibid., vol. 3, 77.

61. *Spinoza: Complete Works*, ed. Michael L. Morgan, trans. Samuel Shirley (Indianapolis, 2002), 486.

62. Ibid., 942.

63. *The Collected Works of Spinoza*, 451.

64. Wachter, *Der Spinozismus im Jüdenthumb*, vol. 3, 60/382.

65. Gershom Scholem, "Die Wachtersche Kontroverse über den Spinozismus und ihre Folgen," in *Spinoza in der Frühzeit seiner religiöse Wirkung*, ed. Karlfried Gründer and Wilhelm Schmidt-Biggemann (Heidelberg, 1984), 15–25; Richard Popkin, "Spinoza, Neoplatonic Kabbalist?," in *Neoplatonism and Jewish Thought*, ed. L. E. Goodman (Albany, 1992), 387–409.

66. Jacques Basnage, *L'histoire et la religion des Juifs, depuis Jesus-Christ jusqu'à présent. Pour servir de supplement et de continuation à l'histoire de Joseph*, 5 vols. (Rotterdam, 1706–1707). For the second, augmented edition, see *Histoire des Juifs, depuis Jesus-Christ jusquà present* (La Haye, 1716).

67. This is taken from the English translation of 1708: Basnage, *The History of the Jews, from Jesus Christ to the Present Time: Containing Their Antiquities, Their Religion, Their Rites, the Dispersion of the Ten Tribes in the East, and the Persecutions This Nation Has Suffer'd in the West*, trans. Thomas Taylor (London, 1708), 294.

68. A. Foucher de Careil, ed., *Réfutation inédite de Spinoza par Leibniz* (Paris, 1854).

69. Schröder, "Introduction" to *Der Spinozismus im Jüdenthumb*, 23.

70. Wachter, 218.

71. J. G. Wachter, *Elucidarius Cabalisticus, sive reconditae Hebraeorum philosophiae brevis et succincta recensio*, ed. Winfried Schröeder (Stuttgart-Bad Canstatt, 1995 [1706]).

72. Wachter, *Der Spinozismus im Jüdenthumb*, 326.

Chapter 2: Refining Spinoza

1. The publisher of the 1742 *Guide* was Moses Wulff, and the translation was that of the medieval Provençal philosopher Samuel ben Judah Ibn Tibbon.

2. Isaac Euchel, *Toledot Rabenu Mosheh ben Menahem* (Berlin, 1788).

3. Alexander Altmann, *Moses Mendelssohn: A Biographical Study* (Philadelphia, 1973), 12.

4. For Joachim Lange's many publications against the rationalistic "Leibniz-Wolff school," see Bamberger, *Spinoza and Anti-Spinoza Literature*, 130, 133, 135, 137, 156. In one of his works, Lange claimed that Budde also took Wolff to be an atheistic Spinozist.

5. As part of his effort to situate Mendelssohn squarely in the "religious Enlightenment," which, unlike its radical and anticlerical counterpart, sought to use reason to revitalize faith and piety, David Sorkin downplays the boldness and significance of his pioneering rehabilitation of Spinoza. Regarding Spinoza, Sorkin writes only that "his position was so extreme that Mendelssohn could attempt to rehabilitate his thought." It is no doubt true that Mendelssohn's willingness to "rescue" Spinoza was in part a function of his confidence that the philosophical challenge of his Sephardic predecessor had been answered. But the implication that Mendelssohn did not have to worry about his own position being conflated with Spinoza's because they were so evidently far apart ignores a whole history of pietist attacks on the Leibniz-Wolff school for alleged Spinozism. Moreover, the way Mendelssohn uses Spinoza in this debut work to "de-Christianize" philosophy testifies, as will be shown later in this chapter, to an at least partial identification with the Amsterdam heretic. See David Sorkin, *Moses Mendelssohn and the Religious Enlightenment* (Berkeley, 1996), xxiv. For studies that ascribe greater weight to his vindication of Spinoza, philosophically and Jewishly, see Willi Goetschel, *Spinoza's Modernity: Mendelssohn, Lessing, and Heine* (Madison, WI, 2003), 92–93; and Dominique Bourel, *Moses Mendelssohn: La naissance du judaïsme moderne* (Paris, 2004), 98.

6. Moses Mendelssohn, "Dialogues," in *Philosophical Writings*, trans. Daniel Dahlstrom (Cambridge, UK, 1997), 104. This quotation is taken from the English translation to Mendelssohn's *Philosophische Schriften* of 1761, which contained a revised version of the *Philosophische Gespräche* of six years earlier. For the original, see Moses Mendelssohn, *Gesammelte Schriften. Jubiläumsausgabe* [henceforth *JubA*], vol. 1, ed. Alexander Altmann et al. (Stuttgart-Bad Cannstatt, 1971), 11–12.

7. On Mendelssohn's exaggeration of the proximity between Spinoza and Leibniz, see Alexander Altmann, "Moses Mendelssohn on Leibniz and Spinoza," in *Die trostvolle Aufklärung: Studien zur Metaphysik und politischen Theorie Moses Mendelssohns* (Stuttgart-Bad Canstatt, 1982), 28–49.

8. Mendelssohn, *Philosophical Writings*, 105–106; *JubA*, vol. 1, 13–14.

9. *Philosophical Writings*, 106; *JubA*, vol. 1, 14–15.

10. Three decades later Mendelssohn would suggest that Spinoza *had* in fact derived his monist metaphysics from the Jewish mystical tradition. By then, as we will see below, Mendelssohn's main concern was to prevent his rival F. H. Jacobi from branding all forms of Enlightenment rationalism—including the rational theism of

Leibniz and Wolff, to which Mendelssohn was heir—with the stigma of Spinozism. Linking Spinoza's pantheism to what Mendelssohn regarded as the irrationalism of Kabbalah was one of, though by no means his only strategy for parrying Jacobi's attack and distancing his own philosophy from that of the Amsterdam thinker. Still, it is, to my mind, significant that Mendelssohn ignored J. G. Wachter's well-known thesis with its "Judaizing" insinuations entirely in his early vindication of Spinoza. On Mendelssohn's later assertion of Spinoza's dependence on Kabbalah, see, most recently, the discussion in Michah Gottlieb, *Faith and Freedom: Moses Mendelssohn's Theological-Political Thought* (New York, 2011), 94–95.

11. "For one must not infer this philosopher's kind of mind from the intractable hardheadedness of the so-called 'free spirits.' He was led astray out of error and not out of the baseness of his heart": Mendelssohn, *Philosophical Writings*, 108; *JubA*, vol. 1, 16.

12. Qtd. in Mendes-Flohr and Reinharz, *The Jew in the Modern World*, 34.

13. Qtd. in Mendes-Flohr and Reinharz, 103.

14. As indicated above, among contemporary scholars, David Sorkin best represents the view of Mendelssohn as a staunch moderate in tune with the conservatism of the German Enlightenment. The opposite perception, of Mendelssohn as a more radical thinker than his rhetoric would indicate, and of *Jerusalem* as a rather wobbly attempt to reconcile liberalism and traditional Judaism, is associated with Allan Arkush. See Sorkin, *Moses Mendelssohn and the Religious Enlightenment*; Arkush, *Moses Mendelssohn and the Enlightenment* (Albany, NY, 1994).

15. The first thinker to juxtapose Spinoza and Mendelssohn on this basis was Saul Ascher in his early work of Reform theology, *Leviathan* (1792). On Ascher, see chap. 3 below. The twentieth-century historian of Jewish thought Julius Guttmann was the first to argue in detail the indebtedness of Mendelssohn's *Jerusalem* to Spinoza's *Treatise*. See Guttmann, "Mendelssohn's *Jerusalem* and Spinoza's *Theological-Political Treatise* [1931], in *Studies in Jewish Thought*, ed. and trans. Alfred Jospe (Detroit, 1981), 361–86.

16. Mendelssohn, *Jerusalem, or on Religious Power and Judaism*, trans. Allan Arkush (Hanover, NH: University Press of New England, 1987), 99.

17. The mention of Spinoza comes early in the book in the context of an analogy with Hobbes: "In matters of moral philosophy Hobbes has the same merit as Spinoza has in metaphysics. His ingenious errors have occasioned inquiry" (36).

18. See Friedrich Niewöhner, "'Es hat nicht jeder das Zeug zu einem Spinoza': Mendelssohn als Philosoph des Judentums," in *Moses Mendelssohn und die Kreise seiner Wirksamkeit*, ed. Michael Albrecht, Eva J. Engel, and Norbert Hinske (Tübingen, 1994), 291–313. Niewöhner dismisses outright the conventional wisdom that Mendelssohn had firsthand knowledge of Spinoza's *Treatise* and that *Jerusalem* was an implicit riposte. Michah Gottlieb takes a more nuanced approach: Though agnostic on the question of whether Mendelssohn had actually *read* the *Treatise*, he asserts that "[w]hether or not Mendelssohn knew the *TTP* directly, in *Jerusalem* he is clearly engaged with a Spinozistic analysis of Judaism, though he may have found the analysis in other sources." See Gottlieb, *Faith and Freedom*, 137f19.

19. Gérard Vallée, ed., *The Spinoza Conversations between Lessing and Jacobi: Texts with Excerpts from the Ensuing Controversy*, trans. G. Vallée, J. B. Lawson, and C. Chapple (Lanham, MD: University Press of America, 1988), 124. The translated

excerpts come from Heinrich Scholz, ed., *Die Hauptschriften zum Pantheismusstreit zwischen Jacobi und Mendelssohn* (Berlin, 1916).

20. This is the argument of Frederick Beiser, whose chapters on the "pantheism controversy" in *The Fate of Reason: German Philosophy from Kant to Fichte* (Cambridge, MA, 1987) remain the best introduction to this affair in English.

21. Vallée, *The Spinoza Conversations*, 134.

22. Altmann, *Moses Mendelssohn*, 37.

23. Ibid.

24. G. E. Lessing, *Sämtliche Schriften*, ed. Karl Lachmann and Franz Muncker, vol. 17 (Stuttgart, 1886–1924), 40, cited in Jonathan Skolnik, "Kaddish for Spinoza: Memory and Modernity in Celan and Heine," *New German Critique* 77 (1999): 170.

25. Vallée, *The Spinoza Conversations*, 95–96.

26. Mendelssohn, *Philosophical Writings*, 108–109; *GS*, 10.

27. Vallée, *The Spinoza Conversations*, 65.

28. Ibid., 77.

29. Ibid., 113.

30. Ibid., 121.

31. Ibid., 130.

32. This is apparently one of the first uses of the term *orthodox* to denote Jewish observance of Halakhah in modern times. See Christoph Schulte, "Saul Ascher's *Leviathan*, or the Invention of Jewish Orthodoxy in 1792," *Leo Baeck Institute Year Book* 45 (2000): 25–34.

Chapter 3: The First Modern Jew

1. See Christhard Hoffmann, "Constructing Jewish Modernity: Mendelssohn Jubilee Celebrations within German Jewry, 1829–1929," in *Towards Normality? Acculturation and Modern German Jewry*, ed. Rainer Liedtke and David Rechter (Tübingen, 2003), 27–52.

2. Leopold Zunz, *Rede gehalten bei der Feier von Moses Mendelssohns hundertjährigen Geburtstage* (Berlin, 1829), 7.

3. For studies on how Mendelssohn was fashioned into the "father of the Haskalah" and, next to Spinoza, the other major candidate for the title of "first modern Jew," see Shmuel Feiner; "Mendelssohn and Mendelssohn's Disciples: A Reexamination," in the *Leo Baeck Institute Yearbook* 40 (1995): 133–67; David Sorkin, "The Mendelssohn Myth and Its Method," in *New German Critique* 77 (Spring–Summer 1999): 7–28; and now, most exhaustively, in the first chapter ("Le legende de Mendelssohn") of Dominique Bourel's magisterial *Moses Mendelssohn: La legende du judaïsme moderne*, 21–43.

4. Ludwig Philippson, "Baruch Spinoza (Eine Skizze)," *Sulamit, eine Zeitschrift zur Beförderung der Kultur und Humanität der Israeliten* 7 (1832), 327–36. *Sulamith*, founded in 1806, was the first modern Jewish periodical in the German language.

5. Philippson, by then a rabbi in Magdeburg, founded the *Allgemeine Zeitung des Judentums* in 1837 and edited it until his death in 1889. The newspaper, which de-

spite its moderate liberal orientation was conceived as the organ of the German Jewish community as a whole and not of any religious denomination in particular, lasted until 1922. See Johanna Philippson, "Ludwig Philippson und die *Allgemeine Zeitung des Judentums,*" in *Das Judentum in der deutschen Umwelt,* ed. Hans Liebeschütz and Arnold Paucker (Tübingen, 1977).

6. Heinrich Heine, *Zur Geschichte der Religion und Philosophie in Deutschland* (Frankfurt a.M., 1966); Moses Hess, *Die heilige Geschichte der Menschheit, von einem Jünger Spinozas* (Stuttgart, 1837); *Rom und Jerusalem, die letzte Nationalitätsfrage* (Leipzig, 1862).

7. Benedictus de Spinoza, *B. v. Spinoza's sämmtliche Werke; aus dem lateinischen mit dem Leben Spinoza's, von Berthold Auerbach,* trans. Auerbach, 5 vols. (Stuttgart, 1841). The biography ("Das Leben Spinozas") served as the preface to the first of the five volumes, ix–cxxv. Auerbach's translation did not include works by Spinoza that were discovered only later in the nineteenth century, including the *Short Treatise* and a host of letters.

8. Auerbach, *Spinoza, ein historischer Roman* (Stuttgart, 1837). After he had already grown famous for his *Dorfgeschichten,* Auerbach came out with a revised edition of his Spinoza novel. See *Spinoza, ein Denkerleben* (Mannheim, 1854). The analysis in this chapter is for the most part limited to the first edition of the novel.

9. For excerpts of these biographies, see Jakob Freudenthal, *Die Lebensgeschichte Spinoza's in Quellenschriften, Urkunden und nichtamtlichen Nachrichten* (Leipzig, 1899). For my analysis of them, see chapter 1, above.

10. On the evolution of this legend, see George K. Anderson, *The Legend of the Wandering Jew* (Providence, RI, 1965).

11. Leo Strauss, "Preface to the English Translation" of his *Spinoza's Critique of Religion* (New York, 1982), 17.

12. Berthold Auerbach, *Das Judenthum und die neueste Literatur; kritischer Versuch* (Stuttgart, 1836).

13. The phrase "ruthless cosmopolitanism" comes from K. Anthony Appiah's *The Ethics of Identity* (Princeton, 2005), 220–23. Appiah's contrast between "rooted" and "ruthless" forms of cosmopolitanism bears a similarity to the tension in Auerbach's reception of Spinoza explored in this chapter.

14. Qtd. in Meyer Kayserling, *Ludwig Philippson: Eine Biographie* (Leipzig, 1898), 35–36. Italics mine.

15. Qtd. in Vallée, *The Spinoza Conversations,* 130.

16. On the pre-Haskalah roots of this drift away from Jewish tradition, see, most recently, Feiner, *The Origins of Jewish Secularization in Eighteenth-Century Europe.*

17. This was the view of the Pittsburgh Platform (1885), the crucial programmatic statement of nineteenth-century "classical Reform" theology that was largely authored by the Reform rabbi Kaufmann Kohler. Its fourth principle read: "We hold that all such Mosaic and Rabbinical laws as regulate diet, priestly purity and dress originated in ages and under the influence of ideas altogether foreign to our present mental and spiritual state. They fail to impress the modern Jew with a spirit of priestly holiness; their observance in our days is apt rather to obstruct than to further modern spiritual elevation." Qtd. in Mendes-Flohr and Reinharz, *The Jew in the Modern World,* 521.

18. Saul Ascher (1767–1822) was a Berlin-based bookseller and a prolific writer and public intellectual. Throughout the Romantic turn in late-eighteenth- and early-nineteenth-century Germany, he remained an Enlightenment stalwart.

19. Ascher, *Leviathan, oder über Religion in Rücksicht des Judenthums* (Berlin, 1792), 231. Trans. in Mendes-Flohr and Reinharz, 109.

20. "If we describe Judaism in this orthodox manner," Ascher writes on p. 157 of *Leviathan*, "it is only natural that we should come to the most severe conclusions."

21. Ascher, 149.

22. Beiser, *The Fate of Reason*, 44–45. The most complete study of German neo-Spinozism in the age of Goethe remains Hermann Timm, *Gott und die Freiheit: Studien zur Religionsphilosophie der Goethezeit. Band 1: Die Spinozarenaissance* (Frankfurt a.M., 1974).

23. Vallée, *The Spinoza Conversations*, 86.

24. G.W.F. Hegel, *Lectures in the History of Philosophy, vol. 3*, trans. Elizabeth S. Haldane and Frances H. Simson (London, 1896), 283.

25. Beiser, *The Fate of Reason*, 60.

26. J. W. von Goethe, *The Autobiography of J. W. von Goethe, vol. 2*, trans. John Oxenford (Chicago, 1974), 261.

27. Qtd. in Max Grunwald, *Spinoza in Deutschland* (Berlin, 1897), 119.

28. See Beiser, *The Fate of Reason*, 159.

29. Witness how Fränkel describes the Amsterdam philosopher as early as 1807, in the second volume of *Sulamith*: "Benedikt Spinoza was of the Jewish religion. Hounded by numerous zealots of his confession, he lived a very noble, virtuous life in Holland. . . . If his metaphysical principles are not all to be commended, as a person and philosopher he certainly deserves at the very least to become better known to, and more properly appreciated by, our fellow believers." See "Briefe an den Herausgeber der Sulamith. Fünfte Brief," in *Sulamith* 2 (1807): 118.

30. See Immanuel Wolf, "Ueber den Begriff einer Wissenschaft des Judentums," in *Zeitschrift für die Wissenschaft des Judenthums* 1 (1823): 1–24. Translated in Michael Meyer, *Ideas of Jewish History* (New York, 1974), 150.

31. Historians in recent decades have used archival data to quantify and qualify this tide of defections. Steven Lowenstein, who has studied these defections in more detail than anyone else, concludes that conversion was a significant problem that touched the lives of "a substantial proportion of Jewish families in early nineteenth century Berlin," even while falling short of epidemic proportions. See Lowenstein, *The Berlin Jewish Community: Enlightenment, Family, and Crisis, 1770–1830* (New York: Oxford Univ. Press, 1994), 120.

32. Ibid., 125.

33. Ibid., 247.

34. Berthold Auerbach, *Briefe an seinen Freund Jakob Auerbach: Ein biographisches Denkmal, vol. 1*, ed. Jakob Auerbach (Frankfurt a. M, 1884), 5. Jakob Auerbach was himself a well-known Jewish reform theologian and educator.

35. Most of this overview of Auerbach's early years here is based on Anton Bettelheim's *Berthold Auerbach: Der Mann, sein Werk—sein Nachlaß* (Stuttgart, 1907), still the only full-length biography of the German Jewish author to date. Bettelheim makes ample use of Auerbach's extensive archive at the Deutschesliteraturarchiv in Marbach, Germany.

36. See Jacob Katz, "Berthold Auerbach's Anticipation of the German-Jewish Tragedy," in *Hebrew Union College Annual* 53 (1982): 217.

37. On the nineteenth-century transformation of the rabbinate, especially in Germany, see Ismar Schorsch, "Emancipation and the Crisis of Religious Authority: The Emergence of the Modern Rabbinate," in Schorsch, *From Text to Context* (Hanover, NH, 1994), 9–50.

38. Bettelheim, 55.

39. *Briefe*, vol. 1, 9.

40. Bettelheim, 56–57.

41. On Strauss's years at Tübingen prior to the publication of his *Life of Jesus* in 1835, see Horton Harris, *David Friedrich Strauss and His Theology* (Cambridge, UK, 1973).

42. *Briefe*, vol. 1, 16.

43. Auerbach's involvement in one of the student fraternities was exceedingly rare for a Jew in this period. The fraternities had played a prominent role in the *völkisch* reaction against Jewish emancipation in the wake of the defeat of Napoleon. See Keith Pincus, *Constructing Modern Identities: Jewish University Students in Germany, 1815–1914* (Detroit, 1999).

44. Gutzkow, *Wally, die Zweiflerin* (Mannheim, 1835).

45. Menzel (1798–1873) was the nationalistic editor of the journal *Literaturblatt*. He turned against the Young Germans after the publication of Gutzkow's *Wally*.

46. *Das Judenthum*, 5.

47. Ironically, one of the main intellectual sources for Heine's "rehabilitation of the flesh" was the pantheism of Spinoza, though this goes completely unmentioned by Auerbach here.

48. *Das Judenthum*, 15.

49. Nancy A. Keiser, "The Dilemma of the Jewish Humanist from 'Vormärz' to Empire," *German Studies Review* 6 (1983), 399–419. The *Vormärz* (Pre-March) refers to the period between the 1815 Congress of Vienna and the March Revolution of 1848 in Germany.

50. *Das Judenthum*, 8.

51. There is a great deal of classic and contemporary scholarship on the largely negative image of Judaism in nineteenth-century German thought and on German Jewish rejoinders to this discourse. See Hans Liebeschütz, *Das Judentum im deutschen Geschichtsbild von Hegel bis Max Weber* (Tübingen, 1967), along with more recently Michael Mack, *German Idealism and the Jew: On the Inner Anti-Semitism of Philosophy and German Jewish Responses* (Chicago, 2003).

52. The main anthology of Geiger's writings translated into English remains *Abraham Geiger and Liberal Judaism: The Challenge of the Nineteenth Century*, ed. Max Wiener (Cincinnati, OH: Hebrew Union College Press, 1981). More recent biographies include Susannah Heschel, *Abraham Geiger and the Jewish Jesus* (Chicago, 1998); and Ken Koltun-Fromm, *Abraham Geiger's Liberal Judaism: Personal Meaning and Religious Authority* (Bloomington, IN, 2006).

53. On the Idealist tradition of German historiography, see George G. Iggers, *The German Idea of History: The National Tradition of Historical Thought from Herder to the Present* (Middletown, CT, 1968).

54. Qtd. in Wiener, 266.

55. *Das Judenthum*, 52.

56. Ibid., 38.

57. Ibid., 50.

58. Ibid.

59. *Briefe*, vol. 1, 31.

60. This is true only of the first edition of the novel from 1837 and not of the revised version of 1854. The attempt to marginalize the Jewish historical backdrop in the second edition is evident in the change in titles, from *Spinoza, a Historical Novel* to *Spinoza, a Thinker's Novel*.

61. Auerbach, "Das Ghetto," *Spinoza, ein historischer Roman*, vol. 1, iii.

62. Ibid.

63. It should be noted that the image of Spinoza as a prototype of the road "out of the ghetto" is a symbolic as opposed to historical construction, as there was no ghetto to which Jews were confined in seventeenth-century Amsterdam.

64. "Das Ghetto," *Spinoza, ein historischer Roman*, vol. 1, vii.

65. Relying on Johann Christoph Wolf's *Bibliotheca hebraea* (Hamburg, 1715–1733), Auerbach wrongly cites 1647 as the year of Da Costa's suicide, when in fact he is believed to have killed himself in 1640.

66. Auerbach's inclusion of bibliographic endnotes indicates his desire to link his novel to the historiographic project of Wissenschaft des Judentums. These endnotes were omitted in all subsequent editions.

67. Qtd. in Rudolf Vierhaus, "Bildung," in *Geschichtliche Grundbegriffe: Historisches Lexicon zur politisch-sozialen Sprache in Deutschland*, vol. 1., ed. Otto Brunner, Werner Conze, and Reinhart Koselleck (Stuttgart, 1972), 517.

68. *Spinoza*, vol. 2, 179. Ludwig (or Lodewijk) Meyer was a Dutch philosopher, rationalist biblical critic, and member of Spinoza's circle.

69. Ibid., 18.

70. Jacob Katz, "Spinoza und die Utopie einer Totalen Assimilation der Juden," in *Zur Assimilation und Emanzipation der Juden* (Darmstadt, 1982), 199–209.

71. Jonathan Skolnik, "Writing Jewish History between Gutzkow and Goethe: Auerbach's *Spinoza* and the Birth of Modern Jewish Historical Fiction," *Prooftexts* 19 (1999): 118.

72. Da Silva's *Tratado da immortalide da alma* [Treatise on the Immortality of the Soul] is printed in English translation in Acosta, *Examination of Pharisaic Traditions*, ed. and trans. H. P. Salomon & I.S.D. Sassoon (Leiden, 1993).

73. *Spinoza*, vol. 2, 242–43.

74. Ibid., 244.

75. *Das Judenthum*, 8.

76. On the probability that Spinoza "simply quit the community" and did not lodge any formal protest of the herem, see Nadler, *Spinoza: A Life*, 154.

77. *Spinoza*, vol. 2, 262.

78. This is how Skolnik interprets the claim that "[i]n our reason . . . here is Sinai." He cites this passage as evidence of how Auerbach connects Spinoza with the "revealed deism" attributed to Mendelssohn in *Das Judenthum*. For Skolnik, this serves as yet another indication of the continuity between the two works. Once again, I would contend that he overstates this continuity.

79. Holdheim became the principal advocate of radical reform starting in the 1840s. He demanded a total conformity of religion and modern rationalism and was less concerned than Geiger with organic continuity and historical consciousness in general. According to Michael Meyer, "Holdheim displays an interpretation of Judaism that has reached the furthest point of subjectivization: what is Jewish is what has passed into the religious consciousness of the individual Jew." This resonates with the outlook expressed by Auerbach's Spinoza in the excommunication scene. See Meyer, *Response to Modernity* (Detroit, 1988), 82.

80. *Spinoza*, vol. 2, 299–300.

81. Idem., "Berthold Auerbach's Anticipation of the German-Jewish Tragedy," 219.

82. Goethe conveyed this plan in the fourteenth book of his autobiography. The intertextual allusions of Auerbach's narrative are analyzed with great insight in Skolnik, "Writing Jewish History between Gutzkow and Goethe: Auerbach's *Spinoza* and the Birth of Modern Jewish Historical Fiction."

83. *Briefe*, vol. 1, 25.

84. His second novel was entitled *Dichter und Kaufmann: Ein Lebensgemälde aus der Zeit Moses Mendelssohn's* (Stuttgart, 1839). David Sorkin argues that Auerbach turned to German *Volksliteratur* deliberately after being unable to resolve the alienation of the individual from the community in his "Jewish novels." See "The Invisible Community: Emancipation, Secular Culture, and Jewish Identity in the Writings of Berthold Auerbach," *The Jewish Response to German Culture: From the Enlightenment to the Second World War* (Hanover, NH, 1985).

85. Qtd. in Geiger, *Abraham Geiger and Liberal Judaism*, 85.

86. Auerbach, *Spinoza. Ein Denkersleben. Neu durchgearb., stereotypirte Aufl.* (Mannheim, 1854), 250.

87. Mendelssohn, *Jerusalem*, trans. Arkush, 138.

88. Louis Seligman, *Allgemeine Zeitung des Judenthums* 2 (1838), No. 33 = (Literarisches und homiletisches Beiblatt, No. 7, 27–28).

89. Such thoughts were prompted by the immense controversy generated by Strauss's final work, *Die alte und die neue Glaube* [The Old Faith and the New], published in 1872 two years prior to his death. In it, Strauss called for a clean break from Christianity and theism in general in favor of a "new faith" grounded entirely in the secular values of universal reason and science, including the belief in Darwinian evolution. In Auerbach's letters to his cousin concerning this free-thinking confession, which he claimed had shaken him like no other work since his reading of Spinoza's *Treatise* as a student, we find the same ambivalence as in his Jewish writings of the 1830s: on the one hand, a powerful attraction to Strauss's undiluted embrace of the "naked truth" even at the expense of total rupture from the "old faith"; on the other hand, a recoiling from this example of "simple negation" and continued affirmation of the organic development of the historical religions. Of Strauss, he wrote in a letter of October 1872: "He has that same reclusiveness as Spinoza." See *Briefe*, vol. 2, 123–31.

90. David F. Strauss, *Charakteristiken und Kritiken. Eine sammlung zerstreuter Aufsätze aus den Gebieten der Theologie, Anthropologie, und Aesthetik* (Leipzig, 1844), 453. Strauss's review originally appeared in the *Jahrbücher für wissenschaftliche Kritik* 59 (1838), 470–72.

91. Berthold Auerbach, *Spinoza. Ein Denkersleben* (Mannheim, 1854).

92. See Jeffrey Sammons, "Observations on Berthold Auerbach's Jewish Novels," in *Orim: A Jewish Journal at Yale* 1 (1985): 61–74.

93. N. Fidel, "Borukh Shpinoza: A kurtse lebenshraybung," in *Yudishes Folksblat* 6 (October 1886), 683–87.

94. Sir Frederick Pollock, *Spinoza: His Life and Philosophy* (London, 1882), 372.

Chapter 4: A Rebel against the Past, A Revealer of Secrets

1. S. Rubin, *Moreh nevukhim he-hadash*, 2 vols. (Vienna, 1856–57).

2. A Hebrew poet, writer, translator, and editor, Letteris was one of the leading figures in the Galician Haskalah. For his biography, see Yosef Klausner, *Historyah shel ha-sifrut ha-'Ivrit ha-hadashah*, vol. 2 (Jerusalem, 1952), 360–400.

3. Letteris, "Toledot he-hakham ha-hoker Barukh di Shpinozah z'l," in *Bikure ha-'itim ha-hadashim* [The New First Fruits of the Times] 1 (1845): 27a–33b.

4. Reggio, known in Hebrew literature by the acronym YaShaR, was a biblical translator and commentator and a frequent contributor to the literary correspondence of the Hebrew Enlightenment. He was one of the founders of the Collegio Rabbinico in Padua, the first modern European rabbinical seminary. Luzzatto, or ShaDaL, an impassioned Hebraist and prolific scholar of biblical and medieval Jewish literature, was a key contributor to the nineteenth-century Hebrew Enlightenment—and at the same time one of the movement's strongest critics. See Morris B. Margolies, *Samuel David Luzzatto: Traditionalist Scholar* (New York, 1979).

5. Letteris, "Toledot," 31. Reggio specifically criticized Spinoza's claim in the opening chapters of the *Treatise* that biblical prophecy concerns the imagination alone and not the intellect—perhaps, not coincidentally, the point on which the gap between Spinoza and Maimonides is at its widest. Notably, Reggio restricted his censure of Spinoza to the *Treatise* and made no mention of the pantheism of the *Ethics*. And even his objection to Letteris's whitewashing of the *Treatise* did not keep him from publishing the biographical précis in his journal.

6. See the essays and letters reprinted in Luzzatto, *Mehkere ha-yahadut*, vol. 2 (Warsaw, 1912–13), 153–97.

7. From his introduction to *Ha-mishtadel* (Vienna, 1847), qtd. in "Neged Shpinozah," *Mehkere ha-yahadut*, vol. 2, 200.

8. See *Ha-tehiyah* 1 (1850): 33–35, 59–61. Sachs would expound further on the proximity between Spinozism and the immanentist character of Jewish Neoplatonism in *Kerem Hemed* 8 (1854): 22–34.

9. This appeared in the periodical *Otsar Nehmad* 2 (1856), qtd. in *Mehkere ha-yahadut*, 203–205.

10. Rubin, *Moreh nevukhim he-hadash*, vol. 1, 17.

11. See, in order of appearance, Luzzatto, *Otsar Nehmad* 2 (1856), qtd. in *Mehkere ha-yahadut*, 205–209; Rubin, *Moreh nevukhim he-hadash*, vol. 2; Luzzatto, *Ha-magid* 3 (1858–59), qtd. in *Mehkerei*, 209–212; Rubin, *Teshuvah nitsahat* (Lvov, 1859); Luzzatto, *Ha-magid* 3 (1859), qtd. in *Mehkere*, 212–17.

12. Though Rubin had intended to provide translations of the *Treatise* and the *Ethics* as part of his *New Guide to the Perplexed*, he later claimed to have been thrown off course by his controversy with Luzzatto. His translation of the *Ethics* would appear nearly thirty years after the project had been initially launched. See Baruch Spinoza, *Heker 'Elohah 'im torat ha-adam* [Ethics], trans. S. Rubin (Vienna, 1885). As for the *Treatise*, Rubin only published a translation of the first two chapters on prophecy. He incorporated them into the beginning of a work on prophecy titled *Ma'aseh merkavah* (Vienna, 1884). The *Treatise* would not be translated into Hebrew in its entirety until 1961. See *Ma'amar te'ologi-medini*, trans. Chaim Wirszubski (Jerusalem, 1961).

13. Spinoza, *Dikduk sefat 'ever* [Compendium of Hebrew Grammar], trans. S. Rubin (Krakow, 1905).

14. Rubin, *Spinoza und Maimonides: Ein psychologisch-philosophisches Antitheton* (Vienna, 1868).

15. Rubin, "Shitat Shpinozah be-filosofyah," *Ha-Shahar* 12 (1884); idem., *Hegyone Shpinozah* (Krakow, 1897); idem., *Barukh Shpinozah be-regesh 'ahavat 'Elohim* (Podgorze, 1910).

16. Israel, *Radical Enlightenment*, 11. Israel has further developed his case for the crucial importance of Spinoza and the Radical Enlightenment he spawned in the "making of modernity" in *Enlightenment Contested* (New York, 2006); and *A Revolution of the Mind: Radical Enlightenment and the Intellectual Origins of Modern Democracy* (Princeton, 2009).

17. Israel, *Radical Enlightenment*, vi. The importance of the reception of Spinoza in Enlightenment constructions of Jewishness is clearly borne out by Israel's student, Adam Sutcliffe, in his *Judaism and Enlightenment* (Cambridge, 2003).

18. Previous studies of the image of Spinoza in nineteenth-century Hebrew literature include Pinhas Lachower, "Shpinozah be-sifrut ha-haskalah ha-'ivrit," *'Al gevul ha-yashan veha-hadash* (Jerusalem, 1951), 109–22; Yosef Klausner, *Historyah shel ha-sifrut ha-'Ivrit ha-hadashah*, vol. 2 (Jerusalem, 1952), 102–107; Eliezer Schweid, *Toledot he-hagut ha-yehudit be-'et ha-hadashah: He-me'ah ha-tesha-'esreh* (Jerusalem, 1977), 338–55; Menahem Dorman, *Vikuhe Shpinozah be-aspaklaryah Yehudit* (Tel Aviv, 1990), 96–153; Shmuel Feiner, *Haskalah and History: The Emergence of a Modern Jewish Historical Consciousness*, trans. Chaya Naor and Sondra Silverston (Oxford, 2002), 146–50.

19. Feiner, *Haskalah and History*, 148.

20. The first generation comprised individuals born in the final decades of the eighteenth century or the first decade of the nineteenth who began contributing to Haskalah literature in the 1820s and 1830s. The second generation consisted of those who became active in the 1840s and 1850s.

21. On the origins of the Galician Haskalah, see Israel Bartal, "'The Heavenly City of Germany' and Absolutism à la Mode d'Autriche: The Rise of the Haskalah in Galicia," *Toward Modernity: The European Jewish Model*, ed. Jacob Katz (New Brunswick, NJ, 1987), 33–42; Nancy Sinkoff, *Out of the Shtetl: Making Jews Modern in the Polish Borderlands* (Providence, 2004).

22. *Moreh nevukhim he-hadash*, vol. 1, 10–11. Emphasis mine.

23. *Heker Elohah*, vii.

24. Though there was no united Germany until the last decade of Auerbach's life, his commitment to liberal German nationalism had originated long before.

25. On melitsah, see Moshe Pelli, "On the Role of *Melitzah* in the Literature of the Hebrew Enlightenment," *Hebrew in Ashkenaz*, ed. Lewis Glinert, 99–110; Jeremy Dauber, *Antonio's Devils: Writers of the Jewish Enlightenment and the Birth of Modern Hebrew and Yiddish Literature* (Palo Alto, CA, 2004).

26. Rubin, *Moreh nevukhim he-hadash*, vol. 1, 3. Emphasis mine.

27. For examples of the use of the phrase *Hokhmat Yisrael* to denote German Jewish Wissenschaft, see Gershom Scholem, "Mi-tokh hirhurim 'al Hokhmat Yisrael," *Devarim be-go* (Tel Aviv, 1975), 385–404; Paul Mendes-Flohr, *Hokhmat Yisrael: Hebetim historiyim u-filosofiyim* (Jerusalem, 1979). For a more nuanced distinction between Wissenschaft and Hokhmat Yisrael, see David N. Myers, *Re-inventing the Jewish Past: European Jewish Intellectuals and the Zionist Return to History* (New York, 1995), 25–29.

28. His models included the prototype of all medieval rabbinic dictionaries, the *Arukh* of the Italian rabbi Nathan ben Yehiel (ca. 1025–1106), as well as the Sephardic astronomer Abraham Zacuto's (ca. 1450–1510) chronicle *Sefer Yuhasin*, a work arranged in the form of a register. Rapoport's studies of the Gaonim and other early rabbinic sages, which began to appear in the Hebrew periodical *Bikkure ha-'itim* in the late 1820s, can be found in the collection *Toledot gedole yisrael* (Warsaw, 1913). See Gerson D. Cohen, "The Reconstruction of Gaonic History," *Studies in the Variety of Rabbinic Cultures* (Philadelphia, 1991), 99–103.

29. See Luzzatto, *Ha-mishtadel* (Vienna, 1847), introduction.

30. The original source is chapter 34 of *Sifre* to Deuteronomy, where the phrase appears in the midst of an exegesis of the command "and you shall recite them" (6:7). *Hokhmat Yisrael* is used here to signify specifically Jewish learning and is contrasted with *Hokhmat ha-'Umot*, i.e., the "wisdom of the nations" or "external knowledge." An etymological history of this term, which would trace its eventual application to modern Jewish scholarship, remains a desideratum.

31. Yosef Klausner, *Historyah shel ha-sifrut ha-'Ivrit ha-hadashah*, vol. 5 (Jerusalem, 1949), 305–18; Jakob Stern, *Dr. Salomon Rubin, sein Leben und seine Schriften* (Krakow, 1908). Rubin never wrote an autobiography, and neither of the two biographies reveals its sources, making it difficult to gauge their reliability.

32. On Schorr, see Ezra Spicehandler's introduction to Schorr, *Ma'amarim* (Jerusalem, 1972), 7–38; Schweid, *Toledot he-hagut ha-yehudit be-'et ha-hadashah*, 339–42.

33. Gutzkow, *Uriel Acosta*, trans. Shlomo Rubin (Vienna, 1856). The play *Uriel Acosta* debuted in December of 1846 and was published the following year in *Karl Gutzkow's dramatische Werke*, vol. 5 (Leipzig, 1847), 113–238.

34. The novella was entitled *Der Sadducaer von Amsterdam* and was first published in 1834.

35. Three German books appeared in 1847 that contained partial or complete translations of Acosta's Latin autobiography and identified the heretic with the spirit of revolution. One was by the Viennese left-wing journalist Hermann Jellinek, the brother of the scholar and liberal rabbi Adolph Jellinek. He penned an introduction to his translation of Acosta's autobiography lambasting Gutzkow for muting Acosta's

radicalism in his play. Hermann Jellinek would ultimately be executed for his part in the 1848 revolution in Vienna. See *Uriel Acostas Leben und Lehre. Ein Beitrag zur Kenntnis seiner Moral wie zur Berichtigung der Gutzkowschen Fictionen über Acosta, und zur Characteristik der damaligen Juden* (Vienna, 1847).

36. In addition to English, Dutch, Swedish, Polish, and Hungarian (among other languages), the play was eventually translated into Yiddish, and it became a staple of the Yiddish stage.

37. Witness the angry reaction to the play of the Russian maskil Judah Leib Gordon (1830–92), who went on to become one of the most famous poets of the Hebrew Enlightenment. Writing under the pseudonym Dan Gavriel, Gordon blasted Rubin for bringing "this Ammonite and Moabite into the congregation of Israel." See "Ha-tsofeh me-'erets Rusiyah," *Ha-magid* 2 (1858): 138. Ironically, it would be Gordon who, some two decades later, would compose arguably the most heretical poem in nineteenth-century Hebrew literature, "Tsidkiyahu be-bet ha-pekudot" [Zedekiah in Prison].

38. For a recent microhistorical study of the 1848 assassination of Rabbi Abraham Kohn by another Jew, see Michael Stanislawski, *A Murder in Lemberg: Politics, Religion, and Violence in Modern Jewish History* (Princeton, 2007).

39. Rubin, *Uriel Acosta*, 10. This appears to be the only source that sheds any light on Rubin's excommunication.url>

40. Ibid., 4–5.

41. Interestingly, Gutzkow did not include the character of Da Silva in his earlier novella about Acosta. Since his function in the play is similar to that of Auerbach's Da Silva, it might be that Gutzkow was motivated by the 1837 *Spinoza* novel to write this figure into his *Uriel Acosta*.

42. The renowned work of Jewish *Kalam* by Saadia (890–940), the prominent Babylonian Gaon, philosopher, and commentator.

43. The *Akedat Yitshak* was a philosophical and homiletical commentary on the Bible by Isaac Arama (1420–94), a Sephardic rabbi who went into exile in 1492 and died in Naples two years later.

44. The *Principles*, or *Ikkarim*, was a work of medieval rationalist dogmatics written by the Spanish theologican Joseph Albo (ca. 1380–1444).

45. By the Hebrew calendar, and equivalent to the year 1640 in the Gregorian calendar.

46. Isaiah 1:8, where this phrase connotes a flimsy structure susceptible to the elements.

47. *Uriel Acosta*, 5.

48. See Rubin, "Mikhtav," *Kokhave Yitshak* 25 (1858): 105–106, where the author protests Gordon's attack on Acosta by equating him to "one of the martyrs killed in sanctification of the faith in their hearts."

49. The work was edited by the German Jewish Wissenschaft scholar Leopold Zunz after Krochmal's death and first published in Lemberg (now Lviv) in 1851.

50. See David Sorkin, "The Early Haskalah," *New Perspectives on the Haskalah*, ed. Shmuel Feiner and Sorkin (London, 2001), 9–26.

51. On the image of Maimonides and its conflation with that of Mendelssohn in *Ha-me'asef*, see James H. Lehmann, "Maimonides, Mendelssohn and the Me'asfim:

Philosophy and the Biographical Imagination in the Early Haskalah," *Leo Baeck Institute Yearbook* 20 (1975): 87–108.

52. Isaac Euchel, *Toledot Rabenu Mosheh ben Menahem* (Berlin, 1788).

53. Salomon Maimon, *Salomon Maimon's Lebensgeschichte [1792]*, ed. K. P. Moritz and Zwi Batscha (Frankfurt a. M., 1984); *Givat ha-moreh* [The Hill of the Guide (1791)], ed. S. H. Bergmann and Nathan Rotenstreich (Jerusalem, 1965). Maimon's commentary was originally published as part of a 1791 Berlin reprint of the Hebrew translation of the *Guide to the Perplexed*. Two subsequent 1828 reprints of this edition, in Zolkiew and Vienna, also carried Maimon's *Givat ha-moreh*.

54. Feiner, *Haskalah and History*, 78.

55. The translator was Mendel Lefin (1749–1826), one of the oldest of the Galician maskilim. He rendered the *Guide* into the simple rabbinic Hebrew of the Mishnah. On Lefin, see Sinkoff, *Out of the Shtetl*. On the image of Maimonides in the work of early Galician maskilim such as Lefin, Rapoport, and Judah Leib Mieses, see Feiner, 96–115.

56. *Kerem Hemed* 1 (1833): 77.

57. See Amos Funkenstein, "Haskala, History, and the Medieval Tradition," *Perceptions of Jewish History* (Berkeley, 1993), 234–47.

58. Sinkoff, 128.

59. See Funkenstein, 241–43.

60. "I intend to explain this sacred book anew," Maimon writes in his introduction, "to expand on points that he, may his name be for a blessing, abbreviates, to provide proof for any law lacking thereof in this treatise, and to compare for the reader in all places the ideas of Aristotle and his followers with those of the best philosophers of our times." *Givat ha-moreh*, 4.

61. On Krochmal's biography, see Simon Rawidowicz's introduction to his now standard edition of Krochmal's writings: *Kitve Rabbi Nahman Krochmal*, ed. Rawidowicz, 2nd edition (Waltham: Ararat Press, 1961), 15–227; cf. Jay Harris, *Nachman Krochmal: Guiding the Perplexed of the Modern Age* (New York, 1995), 3–14.

62. From an 1836 letter sent by Krochmal to Luzzatto, qtd. in *Kitve Ranak*, 425.

63. Whether the goal of *The Guide to the Perplexed* was, in fact, to resolve the seeming friction between reason and revelation has long been a moot issue in Maimonidean studies. If most have understood Maimonides' motives as essentially harmonistic, others, most famously Leo Strauss and his disciples, have argued that he viewed the gap between religion and philosophy as ineradicable and believed the latter could be safeguarded only if shrouded in esotericism and thus concealed from the masses. Krochmal, however, clearly held the *Guide* to be a prototype of the reconciliation of philosophical and religious truth. As he wrote in 1839, "[t]he apparent *contradiction*, from a superficial point of view, between scriptural images and rational ideas in the philosophy of religion is the *perplexity* which the Rav, may his memory be for a blessing (i.e., Maimonides) was the first to grasp clearly in all its parts and extension." See *Kitve Ranak*, 436. On this controversy, see Eliezer Schweid, "Religion and Philosophy: The Scholarly-Theological Debate between Julius Guttmann and Leo Strauss," in *Maimonidean Studies* 1 (1990): 163–95.

64. See chapter (or "gate") 5 of Krochmal's *Guide*, in *Kitve Ranak*, 18–28.

65. Some question whether Maimonides's idea of God is in fact so radically transcendent to nature. See Moshe Idel, "*Deus sive Natura*—The Metamorphosis of a

Dictum from Maimonides to Spinoza," *Maimonides and the Sciences*, ed. R. S. Cohen and H. Levine (Boston: Kluwer, 2000), 87–110.

66. See Pinhas Lahower, "Nigleh ve-nistar be-kitve Ranak," *Knesset le-zekher Bialik* 3 (1941).

67. See the discussion of the first-generation Galician maskil Judah Leib Mieses's *Kinat ha-emet* in Feiner, 96–104.

68. For more detail see Harris, 61–70.

69. Qtd. in Harris, 71.

70. See *Kitve Rank*, 433.

71. On the centrality of this dichotomy in medieval Jewish exegesis, see Frank Talmage, "Apples of Gold: The Inner Meaning of Sacred Texts in Medieval Judaism," in *Apples of Gold in Settings of Silver: Studies in Medieval Jewish Exegesis and Polemics*, ed. Barry D. Walfish (Toronto, 1999), 108–150.

72. The phrase comes from Maimonides' introduction to the *Guide*.

73. "And this is in truth the glory of the Absolute Spirit that lives and dwells in our midst . . . namely, that He is always ascending from the sensual to the conceptual, from the image to the idea, *and from what is in some generations given to the soul from without . . . to what is an inner reality united with its essence for eternity*." See *Kitve Ranak*, 433. Emphasis mine. While some have argued for the existence of a notion of historical development in Maimonides' philosophy of religion, this is not subscribed to by most experts. See Funkenstein, *Perceptions of Jewish History*, 131–55; David Hartman, "Maimonides' Approach to Messianism and Its Contemporary Implications," *Da'at* 2–3 (1978–79): 5–33.

74. *Kitve Ranak*, 187. Emphasis mine. Translation based on Harris, 153, with some deviations.

75. See Simon Rawidowicz, "On Interpretation," *Proceedings of the American Academy of Jewish Research* 26 (1957): 83–126. Rawidowicz distinguishes between two modes of commentary in this essay—"*explicatio*," which aims to understand through formal and contextual analysis what a document means on its own terms, and "*interpretatio*," which seeks to penetrate to the "hidden layer" of the text and disclose "that which the document ought to have said" but "did not say," thus ensuring its continued vitality and relevance. Spinoza is a paradigm of "*explicatio*," Rawidowicz argues, whereas Maimonides is an exemplar of the opposing principle of "*interpretatio*." Krochmal perpetuates the latter tradition. For another interpretation of the *Guide to the Perplexed of the Time* that emphasizes its implicit criticism of Spinoza, see Harris, 18, 27–28, 44–45, 53, 79, 81–84.

76. Letteris, "Toledot ha-Rav he-hakham ha-hoker ha-mehulal Nahman ha-Kohen Krochmal," in *More neboche ha-seman* (Lemberg: Michael Wolf, 1863), 11–29. On Krochmal's desk, Letteris wrote, one could find

> the *Ethics* of Baruch de Spinoza lying on top of the *Yalkut Reuveni*, the *Me'or 'Enayim* of R' Azariah de Rossi and the *Sefer ha-Kanah* alongside the *Critique of Pure Reason* of the philosopher Kant, the commentary of Rabbi Moshe Alshikh, the Zohar, and the poems of Horace next to some tractates from the Babylonian and Jerusalem Talmud, and works of Lucian on top of them, and other books as ostensibly far from one another as east from west joined together in peace and tranquility, love and friendship (26).

77. Yosef Klausner, "Sheneur Sachs," *Historyah shel ha-sifrut ha-'ivrit ha-hadashah*, vol. 2 (Jerusalem, 1952), 128–47.

78. On A. Krochmal, see Klausner, *Historyah shel ha-sifrut ha-'ivrit ha-hadashah*, vol. 4 (Jerusalem, 1953), 78–104.

79. A. Krochmal, *Even ha-roshah* [Foundation Stone], introduced by Peretz Smolenskin (Vienna: Holzwarth, 1871); *Iyun tefilah* [A Study of Prayer] (Lvov, 1875).

80. The extent to which the views on Spinoza ascribed to the elder Krochmal in this work are indicative of his true feelings is unclear. Schweid claims that this dialogue "testifies" to the "close relationship between R' Nahman Krochmal (Ranak) and Spinoza," but this may be an overly naïve reading of the evidence. It is hard to imagine that Abraham Krochmal would have credited his father with sympathy for Spinoza if he knew this to be untrue. It is also hard to imagine that the younger Krochmal did not project some arguments onto Rabbi Nahman that were in fact his own. See Schweid, *Toledot he-hagut ha-yehudit be-'et ha-hadashah*, 428f16.

81. Émile Saisset (1814–1863) was a French philosopher associated with the Eclectic school of Victor Cousin. In 1842 he published a French translation of Spinoza's complete works in two volumes, the first of which he prefaced with a critical introduction to his philosophy. See *Oeuvres de Spinoza* (Paris: Charpentier, 1842).

82. Rubin, *Moreh nevukhim he-hadash*, vol. 1, 13.

83. See chapter 7 of the *Treatise* in *Spinoza: Collected Works*, 456–71.

84. Rubin, *Moreh*, vol. 1, 14.

85. Ibid., 16.

86. Auerbach, *Spinoza, ein Denkersleben* (Mannheim, 1854).

87. See Rubin, *Moreh*, vol. 2, 15–17, 19–21, 30–36.

88. Ibid., *Moreh*, vol. 2, 15–17. Rubin cites this excerpt at the very beginning of his Spinoza biography. Some thirty years later, he also placed it at the start of his introduction to his translation of the *Ethics*.

89. Auerbach, *Spinoza, ein Denkersleben*, 284; Rubin, *Moreh*, vol. 2, 17.

90. Jacob Katz, "Spinoza und die Utopie einer totalen Assimilation der Juden," in *Zur Assimilation und Emanzipation der Juden* (Darmstadt, 1982), 199–209.

91. Rubin, *Moreh*, vol. 1, 8.

92. Feiner, *Haskalah and History*, 148.

93. Rubin, *Moreh*, vol. 1, 21–22.

94. Ibid. The expression "through light clouds" (*be-arfilei tohar*) recalls a phrase used by Spinoza in suggesting that his doctrine of the identity of thought and extension might have Jewish antecedents: "Some of the Hebrews seem to have seen this, *as if through a cloud*, when they maintained that God, God's intellect, and the things understood by him are one and the same." Emphasis mine. See *The Collected Works of Spinoza*, vol. 1, 451.

95. Rubin, *Moreh*, vol. 1, 21–22. Emphasis mine.

96. Ibid. Not surprisingly, Rubin quotes the passage in Talmud Yebamot 15b that has traditionally served as a kind of *locus classicus* for Jewish panentheism. There, in an interpretation of the second half of the verse from Isaiah 6 that reads "His glory fills the entire earth," it is explained that "He (i.e., God) is the place of the world, but the world is not His place."

97. Ibid., 23. The numeric identity of the Hebrew terms for God (*Elohim*) and Nature (*ha-Teva*), both of which add up to eighty-six. In Hebrew, each of the twenty-

two letters possesses a numeric value. This gave rise to a particular form of mystical interpretation known in Aramaic as *gematria*, in which numeric equivalences of certain words (or combinations of words) are used to decode the "secrets of creation." On the history of this gematria of *Elohim* and *ha-Teva*, which might be considered the other *locus classicus* in Jewish religious literature for panentheism, see Idel, "*Deus Sive Natura*—the Metamorphosis of a Dictum from Maimonides to Spinoza."

98. Ibid., 22. Rubin cites the *Guide* 1:61, where Maimonides, in discussing the divine Tetragrammaton, claims that "[i]t is possible that in the Hebrew language, of which we now have but slight knowledge, the Tetragrammaton, in the way it was pronounced, conveyed the meaning of 'absolute existence.'"

99. Ibid., 23. Rubin quotes an unidentified passage from the *Zohar* that conveys the mystical concepts of continuous creation and of God as the *Weltseele*, claiming that were God to remove his breath of life, all of nature would be "like a body without a soul."

100. Ibid., 24. Rubin refers to an analogy in the *Sefer Yetsirah* that compares the relationship of nature to God with that of a flame to its source of light, without indicating the exact location of this statement.

101. The "poor man's wisdom" is the title of Krochmal's chapter on Ibn Ezra (chapter 17) in the *Guide to the Perplexed of the Time*.

102. Ibid., 22.

103. For Rubin's use of this phrase "purified faith" (*emunah tserufah*) with reference to Spinoza's idea of God, see *Moreh*, vol. 2, 4.

104. Heine, *Zur Geschichte der Religion und Philosophie in Deutschland* (Frankfurt a. M., 1966), 125.

105. Baruch Spinoza, *Heker 'Elohah 'im torat ha-'adam* [An Investigation of God with the Science of Man], trans. S. Rubin (Vienna, 1885). The German (though not the Hebrew) title page indicates that the translation, which included a preface of some sixty pages, was self-published. In the eleventh and twelfth volumes of Peretz Smolenskin's *Ha-shahar* [The Dawn], which previewed *Heker Elohah* with excerpts from the preface, we find several appeals by the editor not only for preorders of *Heker Elohah* (for the price of three Russian rubles, two German or Austrian florins, or two American dollars) but also for donations to help cover Rubin's expenses. See *Ha-shahar* 11 (1883): 597; *Ha-shahar* 12 (1884): 70, 252, 326.

106. See his *Ma'aseh bereshit* [The Mystery of Creation] (Vienna, 1872), a study of the cosmogony and theogony of the Phoenicians, which contained a long preface on the relationship of ancient mythology to the creation accounts of the Bible and the *Aggadah*.

107. In the words of the renowned Hebrew writer David Frischmann, on meeting Rubin "[i]t was clear at first glance: here was a "Spinozist" from head to toe. Do not laugh or cry; do not get angry or exuberant; do not become exercised or alarmed by the words and foolish deeds of mankind—only understand. . . . One could immediately see that this man did not merely read or translate Spinoza, but grasped and lived by him." See Frischmann, "Dr. Shlomo Rubin" (January 18, 1910), http://www.benyehuda.org/frischmann/rubin.html.

108. *Heker 'Elohah*, VII. The "stone of Spinoza" (*'even Shpinozah*) is perhaps an allusion to the biblical phrase "the stone that the builders rejected has become a

cornerstone" (Psalms 118:12), which, it may be recalled from earlier in the chapter, served as the background refrain to the opening of *The New Guide to the Perplexed*.

109. Ibid.

110. Ibid., L.

111. Ibid., IX.

112. Ibid., XLIV.

113. *Igrot David Ben-Gurion*, vol. 1, ed. Yehuda Erez (Tel Aviv, 1971), 4–5.

114. The term was coined by Hans Robert Jauss (1921–1997), a crucial figure in the development of the "Constance School" of reception theory in the 1960s and 1970s. See Jauss, *Toward an Aesthetic of Reception*, trans. Timothy Bahti (Minneapolis, MN, 1982).

115. Micah Josef bin Gorion [Berdichevksy], *Amal yom ve-haguto: pirke yoman*, ed. Emanuel bin Gorion, trans. [from German] Rachel bin Gorion (Tel Aviv, 1974), 109–111.

116. On Hirszenberg, see Richard I. Cohen, "Samuel Hirszenberg's Imagination: An Artist's Interpretation of the Jewish Dilemma at the Fin-de-Siècle," in *Texts and Contexts. Essays in Modern Jewish Historiography in Honor of Ismar Schorsch*, eds. Eli Lederhendler and Jack Wertheimer (New York, 2005), 219–55. I thank Prof. Cohen for allowing me to read in advance an article entitled "The Return of the Wandering Jew in Samuel Hirszenberg's Art," cowritten with Mirjam Rajner, that will appear in a forthcoming volume of *Ars Judaica*.

117. On Sokolow's early years as a Polish Jewish intellectual, before becoming a Zionist, see Ella Bauer, *Between Poles and Jews: The Development of Nahum Sokolow's Political Thought* (Jerusalem, 2005).

118. The review appeared in *He-'asif* 2/9 (1885–86), 39–41. Sokolow later included excerpts from this review in his *Barukh Shpinoza u-zemano* (Paris, 1928–29), 407–408. The quotations in the text are taken from this source.

Chapter 5: From the Heights of Mount Scopus

1. "Memorial for Spinoza at the Hebrew University" [Heb], *Davar*, February 22, 1927.

2. "Memorial for Spinoza at the University" [Heb], *Ha'aretz*, February 22, 1927.

3. Yosef Klausner, *Yeshu ha-Notsri: Zemano, hayav, ve-torato* (Jerusalem, 1922). The American Reform rabbi Stephen S. Wise gave a famous sermon in Carnegie Hall in December 1925, "A Jew's View of Jesus," which was essentially a favorable review of Klausner's book, which had recently been translated into English as *Jesus of Nazareth: His Life, Times, and Teaching*, trans. Herbert Danby (New York, 1925). The sermon provoked a firestorm among American Jewry. On this, see Stephen Prothero, *American Jesus: How the Son of God Became a National Icon* (New York, 2003), 231–37.

4. Klausner, "Shmuel David Luzzatto (le-mele'at me'ah shanah mi-yom holado)," *Ha-Shiloah* 7 (1901): 117–26, 213–25, 299–305; "Doktor Shlomo Rubin

(le-mele'at lo shemonim shanah be-yom aharon shel Pesah 5663), *Luah 'Ahi'asaf* 11 (1903): 285–300. Both of these profiles would be included with slight revisions in several future compilations of Klausner's essays.

5. It was first published in 1928 as "Ha-'ofi ha-yehudi shel torat Shpinozah," *Knesset* 1 (1928): 179–99. Later it was included in Klausner's compilation of essays on Jewish Platonic or Neoplatonic thinkers, *Filosofim ve-hoge de'ot*, vol. 1 (Jerusalem, 1934), 210–42. A German translation appeared in 1933 in a Festschrift marking the three-hundredth anniversary of Spinoza's birth: "Der jüdische Charakter der Lehre Spinozas," *Spinoza-Festschrift*, ed. S. Hessing and trans. Z. Ellner (Heidelberg, 1933), 114–45.

6. Klausner, *Filosofim ve-hoge de'ot*, vol. 1, 242.

7. See Scholem's letter to Siegfried Hessing of August 8, 1977, in Hessing, "Epilogue—Ban Invalid after Death," *Speculum Spinozanum 1677–1977*, ed. Hessing (London, 1977), 577.

8. See Bergmann's letter to Robert Weltsch of February 21, 1927, in Bergmann, *Tagebücher und Briefe*, ed. Miriam Sambursky, vol. 1 (Bonn, 1985), 215.

9. *Haaretz*, "Yesterday in Tel-Aviv—Impressions of the Moment—On Spinoza Street" [Heb], February 25, 1927. The name of the author is unclear. Spinoza Street in Tel Aviv—one of only two streets in Israel named after the philosopher (the other, the Spinoza Steps, is located in Haifa)—received its name in 1925. It is said that the impetus for naming a street after Spinoza came from the great physicist and Spinoza-admirer Albert Einstein. Visiting Tel Aviv in 1925, Einstein badgered the mayor of the city, Meir Dizengoff, about the fact there were no streets in the "first Hebrew city" named for Heinrich Heine and Spinoza. A Spinoza Street was created soon thereafter, although its present location, between Frischmann and Gordon Streets in the center of the city, dates only to the period after the 1948 war, when David Ben-Gurion (another avid Spinozist, as we will see) arranged to have a street named after Spinoza not far from his residence. Because of his apostasy, Heine had to wait much longer—until 1993, to be exact—for a street to be named after him in Tel Aviv. See Sraya Shapiro, "Twists and Turns in Street Naming," *Jerusalem Post*, October 17, 1993.

10. Bernard Heller, "Is Spinozism Compatible with Judaism," in *Central Conference of American Rabbis Yearbook* 37 (1927): 325.

11. "Ban Against Spinoza Revoked by Jews," *New York Times*, March 20, 1927. A little over three decades later, the subheading to the *Times'* obituary for Klausner read: "[Chaim] Weizmann's Rival for Israeli Presidency Is Dead—Ended Jewish Ban on Spinoza." See "Joseph Klausner, Hebrew Writer," October 28, 1958.

12. See Nahum Sokolow, *Baruch Shpinozah u-zemano: Midrash be-filosofyah u-ve-korot ha-'itim* (Paris, 1928–29), 267; I. Efroykin, "Ha-ta'un mishpat Shpinozah bedikah?," *Heshbon nefesh*, trans. from Yiddish Avraham Kariv (Tel Aviv, 1950), 251–65; Yehoshua Manoah, *Be-vikuah 'im David Ben-Gurion*, vol. 2 (Tel Aviv, 1953–56); Hessing, "Epilogue—Ban Invalid after Death"; Ze'ev Levy, *Baruch or Benedict: On Some Jewish Aspects of Spinoza's Philosophy* (New York, 1982), 201; Yirmiyahu Yovel, "Spinoza and His People: The First Secular Jew?," in *Spinoza and Other Heretics*, vol. 1, 197–202; Eliezer Schweid, "'In Amsterdam I Created the Idea of a Jewish State . . .': Spinoza and National Jewish Identity" [Heb], *Jewish Studies Political Review* 13 (Spring 2001): 1–20.

13. Klausner, review of Nahum Sokolow's *Shpinozah u-bene zemano* [Spinoza and His Time] in *Kirjath Sefer* 8 (1931): 332–36, 335. Klausner was answering an indirect slap that Sokolow had taken at him by claiming that "we do not cancel historical facts, but learn from them." See Sokolow, 367.

14. The phrase comes from Michael Meyer's apt characterization of Zionist identity in his *Jewish Identity in the Modern World* (Seattle, 1990).

15. The noted Zionist historian Yitzhak F. Baer would famously describe Spinoza in 1936 as "the first Jew to separate himself from his religion and his people without a formal religious conversion." See Baer, *Galut*, trans. R. Warshow (New York, 1947), 114.

16. The Zionist reception of Spinoza remains mostly understudied. For cursory overviews or studies of specific thinkers, see Paul Mendes-Flohr and Stephen L. Weinstein, "The Heretic as Hero," *Jerusalem Quarterly* 7 (1978): 57–63; Elhanan Yakira, "Spinoza et les sionistes," *Spinoza au XXème siècle* (Paris, 1993); Schweid, "In Amsterdam I Created the Idea of a Jewish State"; Yovel, "Spinoza and His People: The First Secular Jew; Dov Schwartz, *Faith at the Crossroads: A Theological Profile of Religious Zionism*, trans. Batya Stein (Leiden, 2002), 90–130; Gideon Katz, "In the Eye of the Translator: Spinoza in the Mirror of the *Ethics*' Hebrew Translations," *Journal of Jewish Thought and Philosophy* 15 (2007): 39–63; Jacob Adler, "The Zionists and Spinoza," *Israel Studies Forum* 24 (Summer, 2005): 25–38.

17. This was the focus of "Slavery within Freedom" (1891), Ahad Ha'am's landmark critique of Western Jewish assimilation. For an English translation of this essay, see Ahad Ha'am, *Selected Essays*, ed. and trans. Leon Simon (Cleveland, 1946), 171–94.

18. The most analytically rigorous attempt to elucidate the concept of "forerunners" remains the pathbreaking essay of Jacob Katz, "The Forerunners of Zionism," *Jerusalem Quarterly* 7 (Spring, 1978): 10–21. For a review of other historiographic approaches to the "precursor phenomenon," see Gideon Shimoni, *The Zionist Ideology* (Hanover, NH, 1995), 65–71. Studies of the formation of Zionist prototypes as part of the search for a "usable past" include Ezra Mendelsohn, *On Modern Jewish Politics* (Oxford, 1993) and Yael Zerubavel, *Recovered Roots: Collective Memory and the Making of Israeli National Tradition* (Chicago, 1995).

19. Spinoza, *The Complete Works*, trans. Shirley, ed. Morgan (Indianapolis, IN, 2002), 418.

20. Ibid., 425.

21. Ibid.

22. Spain never offered its converso population "full civic rights"; on the contrary, its "blood purity laws" discriminating against "New Christians" remained on the books into the eighteenth century. The reasons Spanish Marranism largely petered out in the century following the Spanish Expulsion while Portuguese crypto-Judaism flourished thus lie elsewhere. On this, see Yosef H. Yerushalmi, "Divre Shpinozah 'al kiyum ha-'am ha-yehudi," in *Divre ha-Akademyah ha-le'umit ha-yisre'elit le-mada'im* 6 (1982): 171–213.

23. Morris Raphael Cohen, an early twentieth-century Jewish American philosopher at City College who was a committed liberal integrationist on questions of the Jewish future, wrote in 1919, in an article sharply critical of Zionism, that "[t]he policy of assimilation was clearly expressed by Spinoza, who pointed out that

Jews like other groups are held together by a bond of common suffering; and that, as the nations become enlightened and removed their restrictions against the Jews, the latter would adopt the habits of Western civilization and the problem would be thus eliminated." See Cohen, "Zionism: Tribalism or Liberalism," *The New Republic* 18 (March 8, 1919): 182. Reprinted in Cohen, *The Faith of a Liberal* (New Brunswick, NJ, 1993), 329.

24. *The Complete Works*, 425. The Latin original for "were it not that the fundamental principles of their religion discourage manliness" reads "*nisi fundamenta suae religionis eorum animos effoeminarent*." A more apt translation might be "did not the principles of their religion make them effeminate." See Benedictus de Spinoza, *The Political Works*, ed. and trans. A. G. Wernham (Oxford, 1958), 63.

25. Jay Geller, "Spinoza's Election of the Jews: The Problem of Jewish Persistence," in *Jewish Social Studies* 12 (Fall 2005): 41.

26. There is a prolific literature on the subject of Zionism and masculinity. George Mosse, Michael Berkowitz, Daniel Boyarin, David Biale, Jay Geller, Sander Gilman, and Michael Stanislawski are only some of the main contributors to this area of inquiry. For a concise overview of the topic, see Tamar Mayer, "From Zero to Hero: Masculinity in Jewish Nationalism," in *Gender Ironies of Nationalism: Sexing the Nation*, ed. Tamar Mayer (London, 2000), 282–307.

27. On "feminizing" motifs in Jew-hatred dating to the Middle Ages—including the belief in male menstruation among Jews—see Joshua Trachtenberg, *The Devil and the Jews: The Medieval Conception of the Jew and Its Relation to Modern Anti-Semitism* (Philadlphia, 1983 [1943]), 50. For the modern period, see George Mosse, *The Idea of Man: The Creation of Modern Masculinity* (Oxford, 1996), 56–76. For a self-described "polemical essay" (indeed, more of a shooting spree) against Zionism and the "New Jewish Man" that asserts the immanence within rabbinic culture of a "feminized" ideal of the Jewish male (the "sissy") worthy of admiration and reclamation, see Boyarin, *Unheroic Conduct: The Rise of Heterosexuality and the Invention of the Jewish Man* (Berkeley, 1997).

28. On Nordau and the *Muskeljudentum* ideal, see Stanislawski, *Zionism and the Fin-de-Siècle: Cosmopolitanism and Nationalism from Nordau to Jabotinsky* (Berkeley, 2001), 74–97. As Stanislawski notes, in his eulogy for Theodor Herzl at the Seventh Zionist Congress in 1905, Nordau would laud Spinoza along with Judah the Maccabee, Bar Kokhba, Yehuda Ha-Levi, and Heine as Jewish historical heroes whom Herzl revered and who belonged in the Zionist pantheon. However, he does not appear ever to have invoked the passage from the *Treatise* where Spinoza criticizes Jewish effeminacy.

29. Nordau's essay "Muskeljudentum," which originally appeared in the journal *Jüdische Turnzeitung*, is translated in Mendes-Flohr and Reinharz, *The Jew in the Modern World*, 3rd ed., 616–17. Interestingly, Nordau criticizes the Jewish athletes and "circus fighters" in the ancient Hellenistic sports arenas for attempting "to conceal the sign of the Covenant [i.e., their circumcision] by means of a surgical operation," in contrast to "[o]ur new muscle-Jews," who "loudly and proudly affirm their national loyalty." Thus, circumcision—which in medieval Christian polemics was frequently associated with the castration and thus emasculation of the Jewish male—here functions as a sign of "manly" national pride and fidelity. Spinoza like-

wise appears to distinguish between the ritual of circumcision that has preserved the Jewish nation, and the effeminate foundations of Jewish religion. On the link between circumcision and effeminacy in medieval Christian texts, see Shaye Cohen, *Why Aren't Jewish Women Circumcised? Gender and Covenant in Judaism* (Berkeley, 2005), 153.

30. See Rina Peled, *"Ha-'adam he-hadash" shel ha-mahapekhah ha-tsiyonit: Ha-Shomer Ha-Tsa'ir ve-shorashav ha-'eropiyim* (Jerusalem, 2002); Oz Almog, *The Sabra: The Creation of the New Jew*, trans. Haim Watzman (Berkeley, 2000).

31. On the possibility that Spinoza was influenced by Machiavelli's use of the identical term, *effeminare*, in the *Discourses*, to criticize Christianity for its valorization of the monastic life over the this-worldly political orientation of the ancient Greeks, see Steven Smith, *Spinoza, Liberalism, and the Question of Jewish Identity* (New Haven, 1997), 101–102.

32. On Hess, see Ken Koltun-Fromm, *Moses Hess and Modern Jewish Identity* (Bloomington, IN, 2001).

33. His initial work, considered a pioneering text in the history of German socialist thought, was entitled *Die Heilige Geschichte der Menschheit, von einem Jünger Spinozas* (Stuttgart, 1837). It has recently been translated into English by Shlomo Avineri as *The Holy History of Mankind* (Cambridge, 2004).

34. Moses Hess, *Ausgewählte Schriften*, ed. Horst Lademacher (Cologne, 1962), 237.

35. See Katz, "The Forerunners of Zionism." Hess figured prominently in one of the first histories of Zionism, Adolf Boehm's *Die Zionistische Bewegung* (1920; Berlin reprint, 1934), where his *Rome and Jerusalem* is called "the first classic work of modern Zionism." Qtd. in Shimoni, *The Zionist Ideology*, 65.

36. For a list of reviews, see Edmund Silberner, *Moses Hess: Geschichte seines Lebens* (Leiden, 1966), 427–44.

37. The German Jewish author Ludwig Wihl, in a letter to Hess, wrote, "I cannot bring Spinoza into harmony with Judaism, though this does not keep me from considering him an important philosopher and great character"—a view that by 1862 probably represented the norm among most German Jews. See Hess, *Briefwechsel*, ed. E. Silberner (The Hague, 1959), 411. In the Orthodox-leaning *L'univers israélite*, after quoting an impassioned excerpt from *Rome and Jerusalem* in which Hess claims that, were he a paterfamilias, he would ensure that his family celebrated all the Jewish holidays, the editor S. Bloch noted that "[w]e will return to this curious expression of a man who calls himself a *spinozist*." It does not appear that he ever did so. See S. Bloch, *L'Univers israélite* 18 (October 1862), 53.

38. Pinsker, *"Autoemanzipation!": Mahnruf an seine Stammesgenossen von einem russischen Juden* (Berlin, 1932). For excerpts from Pinsker's *Autoemancipation* and other Zionist writings, see Arthur Hertzberg, *The Zionist Idea: A Historical Analysis and Reader* (Philadelphia, 1997).

39. Lovers of Zion (Hovevei Tsion) was a group founded in the wake of the 1881–82 pogroms. It consisted primarily of Russian Jewish nationalists committed to furthering Jewish settlement in Palestine.

40. Bilu, an acronym for the biblical verse from Isaiah 2:5 "Beit Yaakov lekhu ve-nelkhah" (House of Jacob, let us go up!), was another, smaller and younger group

of settlers founded in response to the 1881–82 pogroms and comprising primarily Russian Jewish university students. They placed greater emphasis on the political goal of achieving some kind of Jewish homeland.

41. Klausner, *Filosofim ve-hoge de'ot*, vol. 1, 217–18.

42. David Neumark, "Shpinozah 'al devar 'atidot Yisra'el," in *Ha-Shiloah* 2 (1897): 287–88.

43. Z., "Spinoza über den Zionismus," *Die Welt* (June 16, 1899): 5.

44. On other such "anthology projects," see Israel Bartal, *The Ingathering of Traditions: Zionism's Anthology Projects*, in *Prooftexts* 17 (1997): 77–93.

45. Dinur, "Mevasre ha-Tsiyonut," 89.

46. Ibid., 90.

47. Ibid., 169–71. On Dinur and his "inclusivist . . . view of Jewish culture in the diaspora"—as seen in his formation of a concept of a Zionist forerunner so capacious that it could embrace (among others) Spinoza, "[a] figure who just as easily could be remembered for his negative definition of Jewish identity"—see David Myers, *Re-inventing the Jewish Past* (Oxford, 1995), 148.

48. For a list of instances in which Ben-Gurion and others cast Spinoza as a herald of Zionism, see Simon Rawidowicz, *Bavel vi-Yerushalayim* (Waltham, MA, 1957), 521f14.

49. David Ben-Gurion, "Netaken ha-me'uvat," *Davar*, December 25, 1953. Reprinted in Yehoshua Manoah, *Be-vikuah 'im David Ben-Gurion*, vol. 2, 5–14. 13.

50. Saadia Gaon, *The Book of Beliefs and Opinions*, trans. from Arabic by Samuel Rosenblatt (New Haven, 1948), 158.

51. Qtd. in Shimoni, *The Zionist Ideology*, 53.

52. See Ahad Ha'am, "Yalkut katan—Tehiyah u-beri'ah" (1898), reprinted in *'Al parashat derakhim: Kovets ma'amarim*, vol. 3 (Berlin, 1921), 91–94. For a discussion of the Ahad Ha'amian notion of a "national pantheism," see Shmuel Almog, *Zionism and History: The Rise of a New Jewish National Consciousness*, trans. Ina Friedman (New York, 1987), 165–72.

53. Quoted in Shimoni, *The Zionist Ideology*, 122. Glickson was considered the leading theorist of "General Zionism," the stream within the movement that wished to avoid identifying Zionism with class-based ideologies on the Left and Right, less out of clear opposition than out of a fear that this would detract from the nationalist claim to representing *all* Jews.

54. Territorialism emerged as a result of the "Uganda controversy" of 1903, which brought a tension that had attended the national movement from the beginning— namely, did the proposed Jewish home have to be located in Palestine?—to the surface. Territorialists argued that this was not a prerequisite and that the possible British offer of a homeland in Uganda should be accepted. For Zeitlin, the demand that the Jewish homeland be in Palestine amounted to putting land above the needs of the *Volk*.

55. On Zeitlin, see the biography by Shraga Bar-Sela, *Ben sa'ar le-demamah* (Tel Aviv, 1999).

56. Hillel Zeitlin, *Baruch Shpinozah: Hayav, sefarav, ve-shitato ha-filosofit* (Warsaw, 1900), 152.

57. This outlook is further discussed below.

58. Jakob Klatzkin, *Baruch Shpinozah: Hayav, sefarav, shitato* (Leipzig, 1923); Spinoza, *Torat ha-midot*, trans. J. Klatzkin (Leipzig, 1923).

59. In the 1910s Klatzkin had studied philosophy at the University of Marburg under Hermann Cohen, the German Jewish Neo-Kantian philosopher and fiery critic of Spinoza. While Klatzkin would publicly break with Cohen's idealistic and integrationist view of Judaism, the sharp distinction he drew between monotheism and pantheism attested to the imprint made on him by his former teacher. See Klatzkin, *Hermann Cohen* (Berlin, 1919).

60. For instance, Klatzkin argued that the proposition that a true "idea" must agree with its object (or "ideatum") was more accurately translated into Hebrew than other languages. He based this on the fact that both Latin (*idea, ideatum*) and medieval philosophical Hebrew (*muskal, davar muskelet*) convey a relationship between these two entities, whereas other languages lack such a terminology. See the introduction to *Torat ha-midot*, xvii–xix.

61. Klatzkin, "Der Missverstandene" (1932), *Spinoza: Dreihundert Jahre Ewigkeit (Spinoza-Festschrift 1632–1932)*, ed. S. Hessing (The Hague, 1962), 101–108, 108.

62. For a recent scholarly biography of Sokolow that focuses on his early intellectual development before he embraced Zionism, see Ella Bauer, *Between Poles and Jews: The Development of Nahum Sokolow's Political Thought* (Jerusalem, 2005). There is, as yet, no satisfying account of his later period.

63. Sokolow, *Baruch Shpinozah u-zemano*, 6.

64. Ibid.

65. Ibid., 367.

66. The "Jewish Renaissance" and its implicit idea of a "new Jewish culture"—in its German Jewish and Russian Jewish incarnations, respectively—is the subject of two recent works of scholarship. See Asher Biemann, *Inventing New Beginnings: On the Concept of Renaissance in Modern Judaism* (Palo Alto, 2009); Kenneth B. Moss, *Jewish Renaissance in the Russian Revolution* (Cambridge, MA, 2009).

67. Ahad Ha'am, "Slavery in Freedom," in Ahad Ha'am, *Selected Essays*, ed. and intro. Leon Simon (Cleveland, 1946), 146.

68. Ibid., "Yalkut katan—Tehiya u-veri'ah," 93.

69. Ibid., "Yalkut katan—Shabbat ve-tsiyonut" [1898], in *'Al parashat derakhim*, 78–81, 79.

70. For a biography of Ahad Ha'am that places such discrepancies in his outlook at the center of its analysis, see Steven J. Zipperstein, *Elusive Prophet: Ahad Ha'am and the Origins of of Zionism* (Berkeley, 1993).

71. Qtd. in Hertzberg, *The Zionist Idea*, 294.

72. Ibid., 293. The most penetrating analysis of the conflict between Ahad Ha'am and Berdichevsky remains Arnold J. Band's classic essay, "The Ahad Ha-Am and Berdyczewski Polarity," in Jacques Kornberg, *At the Crossroads: Essays on Ahad Ha-Am* (Albany, NY, 1983), 49–59.

73. Berdichevsky, *Kol ma'amare Michah Yosef Berdichevsky* (Tel Aviv, 1952), 48.

74. See Shmuel Almog, "The Role of Religious Values in the Second Aliyah," *Zionism and Religion*, ed. S. Almog, Jehuda Reinharz, and Anita Shapira (Hanover, NH, 1998), 237–50.

75. Qtd. in Stanley Nash, *In Search of Hebraism: Shai Hurwitz and His Polemics in the Hebrew Press* (Leiden, 1980), 300.

76. Ish Ivri [Klausner], "Herut ve-Apikorsut," *Ha-Shiloah* 20 (1911): 88–91, 91.

77. An intellectual biography of Klausner remains a desideratum. The only study of Klausner in English is Simcha Kling's *Joseph Klausner* (New York, 1970), and its merits are few. Discussions of various aspects of Klausner's life and work can be found in Iris Parush, *Kanon sifruti ve-ideologyah le'umit* (Jerusalem, 1992); Myers, *Re-inventing the Jewish Past*; and Kenneth Moss, *Jewish Renaissance in the Russian Revolution*. For Klausner's autobiography, see *Darki li-krat ha-tehiyah veha-ge'ulah* (Tel Aviv, 1946).

78. Steven J. Zipperstein, *The Jews of Odessa: A Cultural History, 1794–1881* (Palo Alto, 1983).

79. Klausner coined this term in 1905 in reference to both the Territorialists and Yiddishists, whom he castigated for trying to form a modern Jewish culture that would be totally secular and cut off from the resources of the past. See "Ha-sakanah ha-kerovah," *Ha-Shiloah* 15 (1905): 419–31.

80. Klausner, *Filosofim ve-hoge de'ot*, vol. 1, 227.

81. Klausner, *The Messianic Idea in Israel*, trans. W. F. Stinespring (New York, 1955), 13.

82. Klausner, "Ha-sofistim ha-'atikim veha-hadashim" (1908), reprinted in *Filosofim ve-hoge de'ot*, vol. 1, 12–32.

83. On Klausner's reservations about the "New Yishuv" in Ottoman Palestine, see most recently Arieh Bruce Saposnik, *Becoming Hebrew: The Creation of a National Culture in Ottoman Palestine* (Oxford, 2009), 196–203.

84. "Ha-'ivri ha-tsa'ir," *Ha-Shiloah* 20 (1909): 405.

85. Ibid., 406.

86. Klausner, "Megamatenu (davar me'et ha-'orekh ha-hadash)," *Ha-Shiloah* 11 (1903): 1–10.

87. Klausner, *Yotsrim u-vonim*, vol. 3/2 (Jerusalem, 1930), 152–53.

88. Klausner, *Ha-Zeramim ha-hadashim shel ha-sifrut ha-'ivrit ha-tse'irah* (New York, 1907), 37.

89. Ibid., 40.

90. See Iris Parush, *Kanon sifruti ve-ideologyah le'umit*, 221.

91. Hermann Cohen, "Spinoza über Staat und Religion, Judentum und Christentum," in *Jahrbuch für die jüdische Geschichte und Literatur* 18 (1915): 56–150. Later reprinted in Cohen, *Jüdische Schriften*, vol. 3, ed. Bruno Strauss (Berlin, 1924), 290–372.

92. In fact, before his Kantian turn in the 1870s, Cohen had sounded a very different tune on the subject of pantheism. In an early essay, "Heinrich Heine und das Judentum" (1867), Cohen had argued for the compatibility of Jewish monotheism and pantheism in attempting to reclaim the German poet for Judaism. How Cohen came not only to repudiate this view, but to regard Spinoza with such deep contempt is a moot point among scholars. For two different approaches, one that emphasizes "extraphilosophical" factors and the other that sees Cohen's late-in-life polemic as fully consistent with his philosophical development, see, respectively, Ernst Simon, "Zu Hermann Cohens Spinoza-Auffassung" [1935], in *Brücken: Gesammelte Aufsätze* (Heidelberg, 1965), 205–14, and Franz Nauen, "Hermann Cohen's Percep-

tions of Spinoza: A Reappraisal," in *Association for Jewish Studies Review* 4 (1979): 111–24.

93. Cohen, "Spinoza über Staat und Religion, etc.," in *Jahrbuch für die jüdische Geschichte und Literatur* 18 (1915): 127.

94. Ibid., 124.

95. Qtd. in Carl Gebhardt, "Spinoza/Judentum und Barock. Rede bei der Feier des jüdischen Akademischen Philosophenvereins im kleinen Festsaal der Universität zu Wien am 12. März 1927," in *Spinoza; Vier Reden* (Heidelberg, 1927), 34.

96. Ibid.

97. For a list of the various commemorative works published in 1927, see Jean Préposiet, *Bibliographie Spinoziste* (Paris, 1973), 140–43.

98. Qtd. in Gebhardt, *op. cit.*, 33.

99. Societas Spinozana, 1932, Oko-Gebhardt Collection, Box 8, Columbia University.

100. Among the participants in this conference were Jakob Klatzkin, who was then engrossed in the project of editing the original German *Encyclopedia Judaica*, and Leon Roth, a British Jew who had written about Spinoza and Maimonides and would soon be appointed the first chair in philosophy at the Hebrew University.

101. Oko to William Leonard Benedict, 9 December 1926, Oko-Gebhardt Collection, Box 1.

102. Ibid.

103. Ibid., "Spinoza und der Platonismus," *Chronicon Spinozanum* 1 (1921): 181.

104. Gebhardt, "Spinoza und der Platonismus," 182.

105. Gebhardt, "*Spinoza. Rede bei der Feier der Societas Spinozana*," 12.

106. Gebhardt, "Spinoza/Judentum," 35.

107. Ibid., 36.

108. Ibid.

109. *The Collected Works of Spinoza*, ed. Curley, 462.

110. Gebhardt, "Spinoza. Rede bei der Feier der Societas Spinozana," 13.

111. On the politics surrounding the hiring of Klausner, see Myers, *Re-inventing the Jewish Past*, 53–54.

112. Isaiah Sonne, "'Yahaduto' shel Shpinozah," *Ha-Do'ar* 13 (1934): 7–8, 22–23, 56, 60, 70–71.

113. Klausner, "Rabbi Shlomo ibn Gabirol: Ha-adam, ha-meshorer, ha-filosof" (1926), reprinted in *Filosofim ve-hogei de'ot*, vol. 1, 92–171.

114. For the original title, see "Memorial for Spinoza at the Hebrew University" [Heb], *Davar* 2 (22 February 1927): 1.

115. Klausner, *Filosofim*, vol. 1, 219.

116. Ibid.

117. Cohen, "Spinoza über Staat und Religion, Judentum und Christentum."

118. Klausner, *Filosofim*, 220–21.

119. Leo Strauss, "Cohens Analyse der Bibelwissenschaft Spinozas," in *Der Jude* 8 (1924): 295–314. Klausner does not cite Strauss here.

120. Klausner, *Filosofim*, 220.

121. Ibid., 225.

122. Ibid., 227.

123. Ibid., 227–28.

124. Ibid., 230.

125. Ibid.

126. Ibid., 240.

127. Klausner would include a "biography" of Judah Maccabee in his collection of essays *Ke-she-'umah nilhemet 'al herutah* [When a Nation Fights for its Freedom], vol. 1 (Tel Aviv, 1935–36), 43–90.

128. Klausner, *Filosofim*, 241.

129. Immanuel of Rome (c. 1261–c. 1328) was a Hebrew poet who wrote poetry on love, friendship, wine, and other topics.

130. Klausner, "Tradition and Innovation in Hebrew Literature," *Filosofim ve-hoge de'ot*, vol. 1, 10.

131. Ibid.

132. Klausner, *Filosofim ve-hoge de'ot*, vol. 1 (Jerusalem, 1934), 242.

133. Klausner, "Shpinozah ve-torato," *Filosofim ve-hoge de'ot*, vol. 1, 209–18.

134. David Ben-Gurion, *Ben-Gurion Looks at the Bible*, trans. Jonathan Kolatch (New York: Jonathan David Publishers, 1972), 48.

135. Ibid., 52–54.

136. On Ben-Gurion's speech, see Aaron Zeitlin, "Shpinozah un a 'nevuah,'" *Der Tog*, September 7, 1951. For the "proto-Zionist" passage of the *Treatise* in Ben-Gurion's handwriting, see David Ben-Gurion diary, August 7, 1951, The Ben-Gurion Archives, Ben-Gurion University (Be'er Sheva, Israel).

137. Ben-Gurion, letter to G. H. Shikmoni, July 19, 1951, The Ben-Gurion Archives.

138. In what appears to be a memo about the Spinozaeum prepared for Ben-Gurion, dated September 26, 1951, Herz-Shikmoni is presented as someone "pleasant, a bit odd, unrealistic yet modest . . . an upstanding man but an 'amateur' and not of great caliber." The mission of the society is said to be "the cultivation of the 'Jewish-communist' idea, that is, a Judaism that transcends a national and religious Judaism."

139. The same memo of September 26, 1951, also lists some of the most prominent members of the Spinozaeum.

140. Leon Roth, the brother of Cecil Roth, taught at Hebrew University from 1928 to 1951, when, weary of what he saw as a growing parochialism in Zionism and Israeli culture, he returned to England. On Leon Roth, see Neve Gordon and Gabriel Motzkin, "Between Universalism and Particularism: The Origins of the Philosophy Department at Hebrew University and the Zionist Project," *Jewish Social Studies* 9, no. 2 (2003): 99–122.

141. Letter from Ben-Gurion to G. H. Shikmoni, July 19, 1951.

142. David Ben-Gurion diary, March 1, 1952, and November 30, 1952, The Ben-Gurion Archives.

143. In the November 30, 1952, diary entry, Ben-Gurion expresses a preference that the translator have a "Hebrew name" as well.

144. David Ben-Gurion, "Netaken ha-me'uvat," reprinted in *Be-vihuah 'im David Ben-Gurion*, vol. 2, ed. Yehoshua Manoah (Tel Aviv, 1956), 7.

145. Ibid., 14.

146. On the conversion of "countermemory" into "official" memory in the context of Zionism, see Yael Zerubavel, *Recovered Roots: Collective Memory and the Making of Israeli National Tradition* (Chicago, 1994).

147. Letter from Rabbi Isaac Halevi Herzog to G. Herz-Shikmoni, 6 Tishre 5714 (September 15, 1953), G. Herz-Shikmoni Papers, A2/32:2, Abba Hushi Archive, University of Haifa (Israel).

148. Qtd. in "Spinoza Project Stirs Amsterdam," *New York Times*, July 25, 1954.

149. These responses are culled from a two-page document titled "Baruch Shpinozah bi-shenat 5714" [Baruch Spinoza in the Year(s) 1953–54], The Ben-Gurion Archives.

150. Yehoshua Manoah, "Le-yeter hitbonenut," *Be-vikuah 'im Ben-Gurion*, 52.

Chapter 6: Farewell, Spinoza

1. David Biale, "Historical Heresies and Modern Jewish Identity," in *Jewish Social Studies* 8 (2002): 115.

2. In fairness, this is true only of I. B. Singer's published body of work. His private papers contain a few undated, handwritten Yiddish fragments of planned stories about Spinoza, including one entitled "The Last Years of Spinoza." See Isaac Bashevis Singer Papers, Box 38/4, 100/11, Harry Ransom Center, the University of Texas at Austin.

3. For all its prevalence, the image of Spinoza in Singer's work has received surprisingly little attention. Nearly all the scholarship on this topic pertains to "The Spinoza of Market Street." See Morris Golden, "Dr. Fischelson's Miracle: Duality and Vision in Singer's Fiction," *The Achievement of Isaac Bashevis Singer*, ed. Marcia Allentuck (Carbondale, IL, 1969), 26–43; Samuel I. Mintz, "Spinoza and Spinozism in Singer's Short Fiction," *Critical Views of Isaac Bashevis Singer*, ed. Irving Malin (New York, 1969), 207–17; Steven B. Smith, "A Fool for Love: Thoughts on I. B. Singer's Spinoza," in *Iyyun* 51 (2002): 41–50.

4. The questionable reliability of autobiography as a historical source is compounded in the case of I. B. Singer. The biographer not only has to contend with the sheer number of autobiographical texts produced by Singer over the course of his life, with their conflicting details and emphases. He or she is also confronted with the author's rather open transgression of the boundaries between fiction and autobiography. What is arguably Singer's most famous autobiographical work—*In My Father's Court*—is described by the writer as "an attempt to combine two styles—that of memoirs and that of belles-lettres"; at the same time, much of Singer's fiction is of an unmistakably autobiographical character. On this duality, see Chone Shmeruk, "Isaac Bashevis Singer—In Search of His Autobiography," in *Jewish Quarterly* 29 (Winter 1981/1982): 28–36. I have attempted to hedge against the reliability of any single autobiographical text by drawing on several, but this is by no means foolproof. There is simply no getting around the fact that the account given by Singer of his youthful wrestling with Spinoza may be a more accurate reflection of how the mature author remembered and chose to present this encounter than of the encounter itself.

5. I. B. Singer, "Isaac Bashevis Singer: An Interview," by Cyrena Pondrom, *Contemporary Literature* 10 (1969): 1–38. Reprinted in Grace Farrell (ed.), *Isaac Bashevis Singer: Conversations* (Jackson, MS, 1992), 92.

6. I. B. Singer, *In My Father's Court* (New York, 1966), 304. "Old Jewishness" and "The New Winds" are two of the chapter titles in this memoir. *In My Father's Court* was originally serialized in *Der Forverts* from February 18 to September 16, 1955 as *In mayn foters bezdn-shtub*. When first published in book form in 1956, it was titled *Mayn tatns bezdn-shtub*.

7. According to Ringelblum, Stupnicki poisoned himself at the *Umschlagplatz* of the Warsaw ghetto before being deported. See Ringelblum, *Notes from the Warsaw Ghetto: The Journal of Emmanuel Ringelblum*, ed. and trans. Jacob Sloan (New York, 1974).

8. Nahum Fiedel, "Borukh Shpinoza. A kurtse lebensbeshraybung [ferfertigt tsu zayn geburtstag. 12./24. November], in *Yudishes folks-blat* 43 (1886): 683–87; 44 (1886): 699–703; Berthold Auerbach, *Borukh Shpinoza: Dos leben un di ferfolgungen fun dem gresten idishen filozof, fervikelt in an antsienden roman*, trans. B. Gorin (New York, 1899); Phillip Krantz, *Borukh Spinoza, zayn leben un zayn filozofye* (New York, 1905). For bibliographies of Yiddish "Spinozana," see Y. Anilovitsh, "Spinoza bibliografye," in *Spinoza bukh, tsum drayhundertstn geboyrn-yor fun Benediktus Spinoza*, ed. Jacob Shatzky (New York, 1932), 175–83; Kay Schweigmann-Greve, "Spinoza in Jiddischer Sprache," in *Studia Spinozana* 13 (1997): 261–95; Brad Sabin Hill, *Spinoza in the Yiddish Mind: An Exhibition on the 350th Anniversary of the Excommunication of Benedictus de Spinoza, 1656–2006* (New York, 2006).

9. Shaul Stupnicki, *Borukh Shpinoza: zayn filozofye, bibel-kritik, shtatslere un zayn badaytung in der antviklung fun mentshlikhen denken* (Warsaw, 1917). From introduction, unpaginated.

10. *In My Father's Court*, 305.

11. I. B. Singer, *Love and Exile* (London, 1984), xix–xx.

12. *In My Father's Court*, 305. Isaac Bashevis does not present his father's condemnation of Spinoza in *In My Father's Court* as a rejoinder to Israel Joshua. He notes merely that after discovering Stupnicki's Spinoza, "I remembered how Father used to say that Spinoza's name should be blotted out." His brother's role in first exposing him to the Spinozan heresy is only mentioned in the preface to the English edition of *Love and Exile*, a compilation of three other memoirs by Bashevis Singer originally serialized in *Der Forverts*. Yet it makes sense that his pious father would only have castigated Spinoza by name in response to a specific provocation and not of his own initiative.

13. Ibid. The "Baal Shem" refers to Rabbi Israel ben Eliezer (1699–1760), often called the Baal Shem Tov or Besht, conventionally regarded as the spiritual founder of Hasidism. On the history of comparisons between Spinoza and the Baal Shem Tov in the Jewish reception of Spinoza, see Allan Nadler, "The Besht as Spinozist: Abraham Krochmal's Preface to Ha-Ketav ve-ha-Mikhtav," in *Rabbinic Culture and Its Critics: Jewish Authority, Dissent, and Heresy in Medieval and Early Modern Times*, eds. Daniel Frank and Matt Goldish (Detroit, 2008), 359–89.

14. *A Little Boy in Search of God* (New York, 1976)—a translation of the first part of the serialized autobioraphy *Gloybn un tsveyfl* (*Der Forverts*, 1974–78)—was later incorporated in *Love and Exile*. See *Love and Exile*, 16.

15. *Love and Exile*, 15. *The Pillar of Service* was a popularization of the cosmology of the sixteenth-century kabbalist R. Isaac Luria.

16. Salomon Maimon, *An Autobiography*, trans. J. Clark Murray (Champaign, IL, 2001 [1888]), 105.

17. Ibid., 219.

18. *Love and Exile*, 18.

19. Ibid., 32, emphasis mine.

20. Ibid., xxii.

21. Ibid., 23.

22. Spinoza, *The Collected Works*, 409.

23. For an overview of the different positions on this issue, see Steven Nadler, *Spinoza's Ethics: An Introduction* (Cambridge, UK, 2006), 68–69, 141–43.

24. Spinoza, of course, describes time as only a mode of thought existing within the imagination while ruling out of hand a God who plans and acts purposively. See *Ethics* I, D8, Appendix; II, D5.

25. *Love and Exile*, 34–35.

26. I. B. Singer, "Shpinoza un di Kabbalah," reprinted in *Mayn tatns bezdn-shtub [hemshekhim-zamlung]*, ed. Chone Shmeruk (Jerusalem, 1996), 298.

27. I. B. Singer, "Ikh fantazir vegn mayn manuskript—in 'Mizrahi,'" in *Mayn tatns bezdn-shtub [hemshekhim-zamlung]*, 301–306.

28. Singer published these pieces using the pseudonym Yitshok Varshavsky that he commonly used for newspaper articles. See Y. Varshavsky, "Di filozofye fun Borukh Shpinoza," *Forverts*, April 26, 1947, 2, 9; idem., "Shpinozas lere vegn der mentshlekher moral," *Forverts*, May 3, 1947, 2, 8.

29. Singer would eventually create a close fictional analogue to his autobiographical account of the "Spinoza and the Kabbalah" episode in his novel *The Certificate* (New York, 1992), originally serialized as *Der sertifikat* in *Forverts*, 1967.

30. I. B. Singer, "Isaac Bashevis Singer: An Interview," by Cyrena Pondrom, in Grace Farrell (ed.), *Isaac Bashevis Singer: Conversations* (Jackson, MS, 1992), 93. "Q" ("Question") signifies Pondrom, "A" ("Answer") Singer.

31. Borukh (Benedikt) Shpinoza, *Der teologish-politisher traktat*, trans. N. Perelman (New York, 1923). The first complete Hebrew translation of the *Treatise* by Chaim Wirszubski was first published in 1961.

32. Borukh Shpinoza, *Di etik [dervayzen oyf a geometrishen ufen]*, trans. W. Nathanson (Warsaw, 1923); idem., *Di etik [dervayzen, etc.]*, trans. W. Nathanson (Chicago, 1923). On Nathanson and other Yiddish Spinozists, see Shlomo Berger, "'Undzer Bruder Spinoza': Yiddish Authors and the Free Thinker," *Studia Rosenthaliana* 30 (1996): 255–68.

33. J. Shatzky, *Spinoza un zayn svivoh* (New York, 1927). For a list of reviews of Shatzky's book, see Schweigmann-Greve, "Spinoza in Jiddischer Sprache," 272–74.

34. See A. M. Deborin, *Shpinoza, der fargeyer [in likht fun Marxism]* (Warsaw, 1930); Jacob Milch, "Spinoza un Marx—a paralel," *Spinoza bukh* (New York, 1932), 54–93; Z. Rudi, "Spinoza un der materializm," *Spinoza bukh*, 137–57; Z. Neln, "Borukh Shpinoza un der dialektisher materializm," *Literarishe bleter*, September, 1932, 1–4.

35. Leo Finkelstein, "Di Spinoza-fayerungen in Hag," *Globus* 3 (1932): 74–83.

36. *Spinoza bukh*, ed. Jacob Shatzky (New York, 1932).

37. The sudden increase of Yiddish literature on Spinoza between the wars was a single, if notable illustration of the growth of Yiddish culture in the late nineteenth and early twentieth centuies. On this efflorescence, see, most recently, David E. Fishman, *The Rise of Modern Yiddish Culture* (Pittsburgh, 2005); Barry Trachtenberg, *The Revolutionary Roots of Modern Yiddish, 1903–1917* (Syracuse, NY, 2008); Kenneth Moss, *Jewish Renaissance in the Russian Revolution* (Cambridge, MA, 2009).

38. H. Leyvick, "Shpinoza," *Ale verk*, vol. 1 (New York, 1940 [1934]), 483–91; A. Sutzkever, "Shpinoze," *Poetishe verk*, vol. 1 (Tel Aviv, 1963 [1947]), 593–97.

39. M. Ravitch, *Poetisher priv in fir tsiklen. Der mentsh, dos verk, di shpin, ktoyres* (Vienna, 1919). Ravitch amended his Spinoza cycle for each printing. The excerpts cited in the text come from its final form, in Ravitch's anthology *Di lider fun mayne lider. A kinus—oyfgekliben fun draytsen zamlungen, 1909–1954* (Montreal, 1954), 51–74.

40. Ravitch led a famously peripatetic life. After leaving Warsaw in 1934 he lived in Melbourne, Buenos Aires, New York, Mexico City, and Montreal. He told his life story through 1934 in the three volumes of his autobiography, *Dos mayse-bukh fun mayn leben* (Buenos Aires, 1964). The account of his discovery of Spinoza can be found in volume 2, 335–39.

41. *Di lider fun mayne lider*, 63–64. The English translation is taken from Berger, "'Undzer Bruder Shpinoza," 259.

42. *Di lider fun mayne lider*, 72.

43. In 1956—while Ravitch was temporarily living in Israel with his son, the painter Yosl Bergner—he represented the Haifa-based *Bet Shpinozah* ("Spinoza House" or Spinozaeum) at a commemoration of the three-hundredth anniversary of Spinoza's excommunication held at the burial site of the philosopher in the churchyard of the Niewe Kerk in The Hague. To mark the occasion, the Spinozaeum donated a monument of black volcanic rock, hewn from the mountains of the Galilee, on which was inscribed a single Hebrew word: AMKHA (your people). At its unveiling in the Niewe Kerk that September, Ravitch stated, "It is true that the Jewish community was among the first to distance itself from this genius and his Torah—but on behalf of the *Bet Shpinozah* of Israel I hereby proclaim our reconciliation with him and admiration for him. The word AMKHA engraved on the stone cut from the mountains of Israel is a token of this." See Bet Shpinozah, '*Eser shanot Bet Shpinozah* (Haifa, 1961).

44. *Di lider fun mayne lider*, 52–53.

45. Ibid., 73.

46. On this journal and Yiddish modernism of 1920s Warsaw more broadly, see Seth Wolitz, "'Di Khalyastre,' the Yiddish Modernist Movement in Poland [after WWI]: An Overview," *Yiddish* 4, no. 3 (1981): 5–19.

47. The three founders of *Di Khalyastre* were divided by latent and later explicit ideological differences. The communist Markish returned to the Soviet Union in 1926 and was ultimately one of the fifteen Yiddish artists, writers, and poets murdered by Stalin in August 1952 in the "Night of the Murdered Poets." Greenberg immigrated to Palestine in 1923 and, after the 1929 riots, joined the radical Revisionist Right. Ravitch would reject both nationalism and communism in favor of a Spinoza-inflected secular humanism.

48. *Love and Exile*, 49.

49. Like Hillel and Aaron Zeitlin, whose hostility to the Yiddish Left he would come to share, I. B. Singer harbored a particular loathing for Peretz Markish, "who sang odes to Stalin until Stalin had him liquidated." *Love and Exile*, 50. In Singer's autobiographical novel *The Certificate*, the character Susskind Eikhl is an obvious (and withering) surrogate for Markish.

50. Ibid., 55.

51. For an extremely thorough description of the different cliques in Jewish literary Warsaw from the end of World War I through the great deportation from the Warsaw ghetto in the summer of 1942, see Natan Cohen, *Sefer, sofer, ve-'iton: Mercaz ha-tarbut ha-yehudit be-Varshah, 1918–1942* (Jerusalem, 2003).

52. I. B. Singer, "Concerning Yiddish Literature in Poland" (1943), *Prooftexts* 15, no. 2 (1995), 124.

53. On the surge of interest in parapsychology in the interwar period—an interest with roots in the fin-de-siècle—see Jay Winter, *Sites of Memory, Sites of Mourning: The Great War in European Cultural History* (Cambridge, UK, 1995), ch. 3.

54. *Love and Exile*, 57.

55. Singer would skewer this subordination of art to politics in an essay, published in an early issue of *Globus*, that has been called his "literary credo." See Yitshok Bashevis, "Tsu der frage fun dikhtung un politik," *Globus* 1, no. 3 (September 1932); Moshe Yungman, "Singer's Polish Period: 1924 to 1935," *Yiddish* 6, nos. 2–3 (Summer–Fall 1985): 34.

56. *Der sotn in Goray* would first be published as a stand-alone work in Warsaw 1935; then, after I. B. Singer had already immigrated to America, it will be published in New York as *Der sotn in Goray: A mayse fun fartsaytns un andere derstseylungen* [Satan in Goray: A Tale of Bygone Days, and Other Stories]. In 1955 it was translated into English as *Satan in Goray* by Jacob Sloan.

57. Aaron Zeitlin, "Perushim oyf toyres-Spinoza," *Globus* 8, no. 14 (September, 1933): 76–86; *Globus* 8, no. 15 (September 1933): 39–45.

58. "Perushim," *Globus* 8, no. 14, 86.

59. "Perushim," *Globus* 8, no. 15, 45. Zeitlin lost his whole family (including his father, wife, and children) in the Holocaust. He survived through a twist of fate: He happened to be in New York for the premiere of one of his plays when the Nazis invaded Poland in 1939, and he never returned. His animus toward Spinoza would surface again in his most famous post-Holocaust poem, which vindicates faith "in my living God of cataclysm / God of naked revenge and secret consolation" even while thundering against Him: "And who would rage / against a Spinozan god, / a nonbeing being?" See the excerpt of "I Believe" (1948), translated by Robert Friend, in Milton Teichman and Sharon Leder, eds., *Truth and Lamentation: Stories and Poems on the Holocaust* (Champaign, IL, 1994), 441.

60. "Perushim," *Globus* 8, no. 14, 82.

61. Ibid., 84.

62. *Love and Exile*, 87.

63. See *Der yid fun Bovl* [The Jew From Babylon], *Globus* 1, no. 2 (1932): 17–27; *Der sindikher Meshiekh* [The Sinning Messiah], serialized in *Forverts* in 1935–36; "Der hurbn fun Kreshev" [The Destruction of Kreshev], included along with other "demon" stories in the 1943 Yiddish reprinting of *Der Sotn in Goray: A mayse fun fartsaytns un andere dertseylungen* [Satan in Goray: A Tale of Bygone Days, and other

Stories] (New York, 1943). All of these works with the exception of *Der sindlikher Meshiekh* would eventually be translated into English.

64. See, among others, Ruth Wisse, "Singer's Paradoxical Progress," in *Commentary* 67, no. 2 (1979): 33–38; Edward Alexander, *Isaac Bashevis Singer: A Study of the Short Fiction* (Boston, 1990). Singer himself would indict the Yiddish literature inspired by the secular messianism of the 1920s and 1930s as an expression of "literary Sabbatianism." See I. B. Singer, "Concerning Yiddish Literature in Poland (1943), *Prooftexts* 15, no. 2 (1995).

65. Gershom Scholem, "Redemption through Sin," reprinted in *The Messianic Idea in Judaism and Other Essays on Jewish Spirituality* (New York, 1971 [1937, Heb.]), 78–141.

66. I. B. Singer, "The Destruction of Kreshev," trans. Elaine Gottlieb and June Ruth Flaum, in *The Collected Stories* (New York, 1983), 94. On Singer's "demon" stories, see David Roskies, "The Demon as Storyteller," *A Bridge of Longing: The Lost Art of Yiddish Storytelling* (Cambridge, MA, 1996), 266–306.

67. See Heinrich Graetz, *Geschichte der Juden*, 10:169–258 (Leipzig,1866). For later examples of this rhetorical linkage in the Jewish literary and theological imagination, see Israel Zangwill, *Dreamers of the Ghetto* (Philadelphia, 1898), 115–220; Felix Theilhaber, *Dein Reich komme! Ein chiliastischer Roman aus der Zeit Rembrandts und Spinozas* (Berlin, 1924); Jakob Wasserman, *Fränkische Erzälungen. Sabbatai Zewi, ein Vorspiel* (Frankfurt, 1925); Martin Buber, "Spinoza, Sabbatai Zvi, and the Baal-Shem" [1927], in idem., *The Origin and Meaning of Hasidism*, ed. and trans. Maurice Friedman (New York, 1961); and Josef Kastein, *Sabbatai Zewi, der Messias von Ismir* (Berlin, 1932). For more recent scholarly analysis of this pairing, see Michael Brennre, *The Renaissance of Jewish Culture in Weimar Germany* (New Haven, 1996), 148–50; David Biale, "Shabbtai Zvi and the Seductions of Jewish Orientalism," in *The Sabbatean Movement and Its Aftermath*, vol. II, ed. Rachel Elior (Jerusalem, 2001), 85–110; and Benjamin Lazier, *God Interrupted: Heresy and the European Imagination between the World Wars* (Princeton, 2009).

68. Max Scheler, *Person and Self-Value: Three Essays*, trans. Manfred Frings (Hingham, MA, 1987), 129–30.

69. This observation is made by Samuel I. Mintz in his "Spinoza and Spinozism in Singer's Shorter Fiction," *Studies in American Jewish Literature* 1 (1981): 207–208.

70. While Spinoza was certainly a bachelor, the image of him as a secular monk cloistered in his attic apartment has been convincingly shown to be more myth than fact. See Nadler, *Spinoza: A Life*, 289–90.

71. I. B. Singer, "The Spinoza of Market Street," trans. Martha Glicklich and Cecil Hemley, *The Collected Stories of Isaac Bashevis Singer* (New York, 1983), 79–80.

72. The saying comes from the Mishnah *Avot* (5:22).

73. *The Collected Stories*, 81.

74. Ibid., 79.

75. Colerus, *The Life of Benedict de Spinosa*, reprinted in Frederick Pollock, *Spinoza: His Life and Philosophy* (London: C. K. Paul, 1880), 421.

76. *Love and Exile*, xxi–xxii.

77. *The Collected Stories*, 82–83.

78. Indeed, if Fischelson had a true understanding of Spinoza's third and highest kind of knowledge, or intuition—which "proceeds from an adequate idea of certain

attributes of God to an adequate knowledge of things," and is the stepping stone to the "intellectual love of God"—then he would realize that his instinctual recoiling from the multitude represents yet another failure to live up to his Spinozan ideal. The right path would be to grasp how both the orderly "celestial bodies" *and* the apparent chaos of the "rabble" derive from the same rational necessity, which is equivalent to understanding them *sub specie aeternitatis* (under the aspect of eternity).

79. *The Collected Stories*, 83.

80. Intended or not, the "cracked eggs" bring to mind Freud's use of the egg as a metaphor for the fragility of the human psyche. To this point, Fischelson's mental breakdown seems largely a result of external stresses. The link between Black Dobbe and "cracked eggs" speaks to the pent-up eros in Fischelson, and foreshadows its eventual bursting out of his ego's overdelicate shell in the lovemaking at story's end. See Freud, *The Ego and the Id* (New York, 1923), 24. I thank my colleague Max Ticktin for this insight.

81. I. B. Singer, "The Destruction of Kreshev," in *The Collected Stories*, 94.

82. Morris Golden notes that "the wedding is the pervasive Singer symbol for the attempted miracle," the site of supernatural intervention that might lead either to good or to bad. See Golden, "Dr. Fischelson's Miracle: Duality and Vision in Singer's Fiction," 29.

83. *The Collected Stories*, 92–93. In the Yiddish original of the story, the unforgettable "Divine Spinoza" is simply "Borukh Shpinozah," which means, literally, "Blessed Spinoza," but is also, of course, Spinoza's name.

84. Steven B. Smith, *Spinoza's Book of Life: Freedom and Redemption in the Ethics* (New Haven, 2003), 166–67.

85. I. B. Singer, "Isaac Bashevis Singer: An Interview," by Cyrena Pondrom, 93.

86. Ibid., 69.

87. I. B. Singer published two articles about Spinoza and his philosophy in *Der Forverts* in the 1940s that coincided with the run of *The Family Moskat*. On these occasions, the reader would encounter the latest installment of the novel, under the name Isaac Bashevis, on the top half of the page, while the bottom half contained Singer's expository texts on the philosopher, under the pseudonym Isaac Varshavsky.

88. I. B. Singer, *The Family Moskat*, trans. A. H. Gross (New York, 1950), 20.

89. Ibid., 26–27.

90. On the habitual inertia and resignation to fate of male protagonists in Singer's fiction, see Dan Miron, "Passivity and Narration: The Spell of Bashevis Singer," *Critical Essays on Bashevis Singer*, ed. Grace Farrell (New York, 1996), 149–64.

91. Yitshok Bashevis, *Di familye Mushkat*, vol. 1 (New York, 1950), 83.

92. *The Family Moskat*, 237.

93. Ibid., 238.

94. Ibid., 262.

95. Ibid., 286–87.

96. Ibid., 259–60.

97. Ibid., 359.

98. Ibid., 398.

99. Ibid., 493–97.

100. Ibid., 237.

101. Ibid., 558.

102. Ibid., 559.

103. *Di familye Mushkat*, vol. 2, 759. The English translation is by Joseph C. Landis, in *Yiddish* 6, nos. 2–3 (Summer–Fall 1985): 105–16, 115.

104. *Di familye Muskhat*, vol. 2, 760; Landis, 116.

105. Thus argues Jospeh Landis in an editorial note to his own translation of the last chapter. See Landis, 105.

106. For this view, see Irving Saposnik, "Translating *The Family Moskat*: The Metamorphosis of a Novel," *Yiddish* 1, no. 2 (1973): 26–37.

107. *Di familye Mushkat*, 749–50; Landis, 105–106.

108. *Di familye Mushkat*, 757; Landis, 113.

109. *Di familye Mushkat*, 758; Landis, 114.

110. See, for example, the novels *Shosha* (New York, 1978), *The Certificate* (New York, 1992), *Meshugah* (New York, 1994), and *Shadows on the Hudson* (New York, 1998), as well as the short stories "Her Son," in *A Crown of Feathers and Other Stories* (New York, 1973), "A Tutor in the Village," in *Passions and Other Stories* (New York, 1975), and "The Impresario," in *The Death of Methuselah and Other Stories* (New York, 1988)

111. What part Singer himself had in the decision to delete chapter 65 from the English translation is unclear. On the one hand, Alfred Knopf conditioned his offer to publish *The Family Moskat* on Singer's making extensive cuts to the translated manuscript, and the letters between them indicate that Singer was initially resistant to Knopf's demands. On the other hand, Singer would become famous (some might say notorious) for the active role he took in tailoring the English translations of his work to the tastes of an American audience, and in an interview from 1963 he boasted of having "worked together with the translators of *The Family Moskat*." Saposnik, in any event, is inclined to believe that Singer agreed with the excision of the final chapter. See Paul Kresh, *Isaac Bashevis Singer: The Magician of West 86th Street* (New York, 1979), 182–84; Grace Farrell, ed., *Isaac Bashevis Singer: Conversations* (Jackson, MS, 1992), 16; Saposnik, "Translating *The Family Moskat*."

Epilogue: Spinoza *Redivivus* in the Twenty-First Century

1. Irving Howe, "The End of Jewish Secularism" (New York, 1995), 15. The master bibliographer Moritz Steinschneider (1816–1907) is said (perhaps aprocryphally) to have once quipped that "the task of Jewish studies is to provide the remnants of Judaism with a decent burial."

2. See Michael Stanislawski, "The Crisis of Jewish Secularism," in *Creating the Jewish Future*, eds. Michael Brown and Bernard Lightman (Walnut Creek, CA, 1999), 133.

3. This "tripartite description of Israel's culture conflict" is indebted to the work of the late Charles Liebman, one of the most astute observers of the complex and shifting relationship between the secular and the sacred in Zionism, the Yishuv, and the State of Israel. See his "Reconceptualizing the Culture Conflict among Israeli Jews," in *Israel Studies* 2, no. 2 (1997): 172–89.

4. Tom Segev, *Elvis in Jerusalem*, trans. Haim Watzman (New York, 2002).

5. Jonathan Sarna, "The Rise, Fall, and Rebirth of Secular Judaism," in *Contemplate* 4 (2007): 4–13.

6. The reference is to Egon Mayer and Barry Kosmin, *American Jewish Identity Survey: AJIS Report: An Exploration in the Demography and Outlook of a People* (New York, 2002).

7. On the controversy within the field of Jewish studies over the academic grants made by the Posen Foundation, see Eric Herschtal, "Jewish Studies Sans Religion?," in *Jewish Week*, February 22, 2011. For a list of current grantees and approved syllabi related to the study of secular Jewish culture, see http://www.posenfoundation.com /academicprograms/grantshighereducation.html.

8. See Lior Dattel, "Posen Foundation Hit by Madoff Fraud," *Haaretz*, January 8, 2009, http://www.haaretz.com/print-edition/business/posen-foundation-hit-by -madoff-fraud-1.267692.

9. Yirmiyahu Yovel and David Shaham, eds., *Zeman Yehudi hadash: Tarbut Yehudit be-'idan hiloni: mabat entsiklopedi*, 5 volumes (Jerusalem, 2007).

10. Yerushalmi, *Freud's Moses*, 10.

11. Yirmiyahu Yovel, *Shpinozah ve-kofrim 'aherim* (Tel Aviv, 1988).

12. Badly damaged by the Madoff fraud, the Jerusalem Spinoza Institute has survived, but only by being absorbed—at least for the present—by the Jerusalem Van Leer Foundation. It has continued to organize lectures and conferences on Spinoza's thought, however. My thanks to Professor Yovel for furnishing me with this information.

13. Leslie Susser, "Spinoza and the Religion of Reason," *Jerusalem Post*, March 9, 1989.

14. Daniel Williams, "Jewishness Debate: Once Again, Spinoza Stirs a Furor," *LA Times*, February 10, 1989.

15. Yovel, *Spinoza and Other Heretics, vol. 1: The Marrano of Reason*, ix.

16. Williams, "Jewishness Debate." The professor in question was Dr. Maurice Kriegel, then of the University of Haifa, who lit into Spinoza and the modern Jewish effort to reclaim him at one of the symposia held in the wake of Yovel's book. See Ya'acov Friedler, "Unexpected Attack on Spinoza at Symposium," *Jerusalem Post*, January 5, 1989.

17. Yovel used this phrase in Flora Lewis, "Foreign Affairs; Israel and Relevance," *New York Times*, December 27, 1989.

18. Yovel, *Spinoza and Other Heretics, vol. 1, The Marrano of Reason*, x.

19. Ibid., 174, 177.

20. Ibid., 201.

21. Ibid., 199.

22. Ibid., 190–93.

23. Steven B. Smith, *Spinoza, Liberalism, and the Question of Jewish Identity*, 200.

24. Ibid., 201.

25. See, for example, Heidi M. Ravven, "Spinoza's Rupture with Tradition— His Hints of a Jewish Modernity," in *Jewish Themes in Spinoza's Philosophy*, 187–223; Willi Goetschel, *Spinoza's Modernity*.

26. Rebecca Goldstein, *Betraying Spinoza*, 2006).

27. The two plays are Yehoshua Sobol, *Solo* (Tel Aviv, 1991) and David Ives, *New Jerusalem: The Interrogation of Baruch de Spinoza at Talmud Torah Congregation: Am-*

sterdam, July 27, 1656 (New York, 2009); the Israeli film is Igal Bursztyn, "*'Osher le-lo gevul, 'o hayav ve-harpatke'otav shel Baruch Shpinozah 'al pi divuhe ha-shekhenim* [Everlasting Joy: Or the Life and Adventures of Baruch Spinoza as Told by His Vigilant Neighbors] (1997).

28. Steven B. Smith, *Spinoza's Book of Life: Freedom and Redemption in the Ethics*; Benedictus de Spinoza, *Etikah*, trans. and ed. Yirmiyahu Yovel (Tel Aviv, 2003).

29. Yovel, "Hakdamah (Introduction)," in Spinoza, *Etikah*, 9. For a powerful critique of Yovel's "presentist" agenda in translating Spinoza into an accessible Hebrew—and its connection to his alleged attempt to appropriate the Amsterdam philosopher for secular Zionism more generally—see Oded Schechter, "Ha-kod ha-metafisi-ontologi: ha-muhlat shel Auschwitz ve-Shpinozah: masah filosofit," in *Mita'am* 1 (2005): 97–120.

30. Richard H. Popkin, "Notes from Underground," *The New Republic* 202, no. 21 (21 May 1990): 41.

31. Popkin, "Spinoza's Excommunication," in *Jewish Themes in Spinoza's Philosophy*, 275.

32. Steven Nadler, "Spinoza and the Origins of Jewish Secularism," in *Religion or Ethnicity? Jewish Identities in Evolution*, 62.

33. Allan Nadler, "Romancing Spinoza," *Commentary* 122, no. 5 (December 2006): 30.

34. Peter Novick, *That Noble Dream: The "Objectivity Question" and the American Historical Profession* (Cambridge, UK, 1988), 3.

35. Yerushalmi, *Freud's Moses*, 10.

36. Goldstein, *Betraying Spinoza*, 66.

Bibliography

I. Special Collections

Ben-Gurion Archive, Ben-Gurion University
G. Herz-Shikmoni Papers, Abba Khoushy Archive, University of Haifa
Isaac Bashevis Singer Papers, Harry Ransom Center, University of Texas at Austin
Oko-Gebhardt-Spinoza Collection, Columbia University
Yosef Klausner Papers, National Library of Israel

II. Printed Sources

Abramsky, Chimen. "The Crisis of Authority within European Jewry in the Eighteenth Century." In *Studies in Jewish Religious and Intellectual History. Presented to Alexander Altmann on the Occasion of His Seventieth Birthday.* Edited by Siegfried Stein and Raphael Loewe. Tuscaloosa: University of Alabama Press, 1979.

Acosta, Uriel. *Examination of Pharisaic Traditions.* Translated by H. P. Salomon. Leiden: Brill, 1993.

———. *Specimen of Human Life.* New York: Bargman, 1967.

———. *Die Schriften des Uriel da Costa.* Edited and translated by Carl Gebhardt. Amsterdam: M. Hertzberger, 1922.

Adler, Jacob. "The Zionists and Spinoza." In *Israel Studies Forum* 24 (2005): 25–38.

Alexander, Edward. *Isaac Bashevis Singer: A Study of the Short Fiction.* Boston: Twayne Publishers, 1990.

Almog, Oz. *The Sabra: The Creation of a New Jew.* Translated by Haim Watzman. Berkeley: University of California Press, 2000.

Almog, Shmuel. *Zionism and History: The Rise of a New Jewish National Consciousness.* Translated by Ina Friedman. New York: St. Martin's Press, 1987.

———. "The Role of Religious Values in the Second Aliyah." In *Zionism and Religion.* Edited by Shmuel Almog, Jehuda Reinharz, and Anita Shapira, 237–50. Hanover, NH: University Press of New England, 1998.

Altkirch, Ernst. *Spinoza im Porträt.* Jena: E. Diederichs, 1913.

———. *Maledictus und Benedictus; Spinoza im Urteil des Volkes und der geistigen bis auf Constantin Brunner.* Leipzig: F. Meiner, 1924.

Altmann, Alexander. *Moses Mendelssohn: A Biographical Study*. Birmingham: University of Alabama, 1973.

———. "Moses Mendelssohn on Leibniz and Spinoza." In *Die trostvolle Aufklärung: Studien zur Metaphysik und politischen Theorie Moses Mendelssohns*, 28–49. Stuttgart-Bad Canstatt: Frommann Holzboog, 1982.

———. "Lurianic Kabbalah in a Platonic Key: Abraham Cohen Herrera's *Puerta de cielo.*" In *Hebrew Union College Annual* 80 (1982): 1–38.

Anderson, George K. *The Legend of the Wandering Jew*. Providence: Brown University Press, 1965.

Anilovitsh. "Spinoza bibliografye." In *Spinoza-bukh, tsum drayhundertstn geboyrn-yor fun Benediktus Spinoza*. Edited by Jacob Shatzky. New York: Spinoza Institute of America, 1932.

Appiah, K. Anthony. *The Ethics of Identity*. Princeton: Princeton University Press 2005.

Arkush, Allan. *Moses Mendelssohn and the Enlightenment*. Albany: SUNY Press, 1994.

Ascher, Saul. *Leviathan, oder, über Religion in Rücksicht des Judenthums*. Berlin: Frankesche Buchhandlung, 1792.

Aschheim, Steven. *The Nietzsche Legacy in Germany, 1890–1990*. Berkeley: University of California Press, 1994.

Assmann, Jan. *Moses the Egyptian: The Memory of Egypt in Western Monotheism*. Cambridge, MA: Harvard University Press, 1997.

Auerbach, Berthold. *Das Judentum und die neueste Literatur; kritischer Versuch*. Stuttgart: Fr. Brodhag'sche Buchhandlung, 1836.

———. *Spinoza. Ein historischer Roman*. Stuttgart: Scheible, 1837.

———. "Das Leben Spinoza's." In *B. v. Spinoza's sämmtliche Werke*, vol. 1. Stuttgart: Scheible, 1841.

———. *Spinoza. Ein Denkerleben. Neu durchgearbeitete, stereotypirte Aufl*. Mannheim: Bassermann, 1854.

———. *Dichter und Kaufmann. Ein Lebensgemaelde aus der Zeit Moses Mendelssohn's. Neu durchgearbeitete, stereotypirte Aufl*. Mannheim: Bassermann, 1855.

———. *Briefe an seinen Freund Jakob Auerbach. Ein biographisches Denkmal*. 2 vols. Frankfurt a. M.: Rütten & Loening, 1884.

———. *Shpinozah*. Translated by T. P. Schapiro. Warsaw: Schuldberg & Co., 1898.

———. *Borukh Shpinoza: Dos leben un di ferfolgungen fun dem gresten idishen filozof, fervikelt in an antsienden roman*. Translated by B. Gorin. New York, 1899.

Baer, Yitzhak F. *Galut*. Translated by R. Warshow. New York: Schocken, 1947.

Bamberger, Fritz. *Spinoza and Anti-Spinoza Literature: The Printed Literature of Spinozism, 1665–1832*. Cincinnati: Hebrew Union College, 2003.

Band, Arnold J. "The Ahad Ha-Am and Berdyczewski Polarity." In *At the Crossroads: Essays on Ahad Ha-Am*, edited by Jacques Kornberg, 49–59. Albany: SUNY Press, 1983.

Bar-Sela, Shraga. *Ben sa'ar li-demamah: hayav u-mishnato shel Hillel Zeitlin*. Tel Aviv: Ha-kibbutz ha-me'uhad, 1999.

Bartal, Israel. "'The Heavenly City of Germany' and Absolutism à la Mode d'Autriche: The Rise of the Haskalah in Galicia." In *Toward Modernity: The European Jewish Model*, edited by Jacob Katz, 33–42. New Brunswick, NJ: Transaction Books, 1987.

———. "The Ingathering of Traditions: Zionism's Anthology Projects." In *Proof-texts* 17 (1997): 77–93.

Basnage, Jacques. *The History of the Jews, from Jesus Christ to the Present Time: Containing Their Antiquities, Their Religion, Their Rites, the Dispersion of the Ten Tribes in the East, and the Persecutions This Nation Has Sufferd in the West*. Translated by Thomas Taylor. London: J. Beaver & Co., 1708.

Bauer, Ela. *Between Poles and Jews: The Development of Nahum Sokolow's Political Thought*. Jerusalem: Hebrew University Magnes Press, 2005.

Bayle, Pierre. *Historical and Critical Dictionary: Selections*. Edited and translated by Richard H. Popkin. Indianapolis: Bobbs-Merrill, 1965.

Beiser, Frederick. *The Fate of Reason: German Philosophy from Kant to Fichte*. Cambridge, MA: Harvard University Press, 1987.

———. *The Romantic Imperative: The Concept of Early German Romanticism*. Cambridge, MA: Harvard University Press, 2005.

Ben-Gurion, David. "Netaken ha-me'uvat." *Davar*. December 25, 1953.

———. *Igrot David Ben-Gurion*, vol. 1. Edited by Yehuda Erez. Tel Aviv, 1971.

———. *Ben-Gurion Looks at the Bible*. Translated by Jonathan Kolatch. New York: Jonathan David Publishers, 1972.

Berdichevsky, Micha Y. *Kol ma'mare Micha Yosef Berdichevsky*. Tel Aviv: Am Oved, 1952.

———. *'Amal-yom ve-haguto: Pirke yoman*. Translated from German to Hebrew by Rahel bin-Gorion and edited by Immanuel bin-Gorion. Tel Aviv: Moreshet Mikhah Yosef, 1975.

Berger, Shlomo. "'Undzer Bruder Spinoza': Yiddish Authors and the Free Thinker." In *Studia Rosenthaliana* 30 (1996): 255–68.

Bergmann, S. Hugo. *Tagebücher und Briefe*, vol. 1. Edited by Miriam Sambursky. Bonn: Jüdischer Verlag, 1985.

Bet Shpinozah. *'Eser shenot Bet Shpinozah*. Haifa: Ha-bayit, 1961.

Bettelheim, Anton. *Berthold Auerbach: Der Mann, sein Werk—sein Nachlaß*. Stuttgart: J. G. Cotta, 1907.

Biale, David. "Shabbtai Zvi and the Seductions of Jewish Orientalism." In *The Sabbatean Movement and Its Aftermath*, vol. II. Edited by Rachel Elior. Jerusalem: Hebrew University Magnes Press, 2001.

———. "Historical Heresies and Modern Jewish Identity." In *Jewish Social Studies* 8 (2002): 112–32.

———. *Not in the Heavens: The Tradition of Secular Jewish Thought*. Princeton: Princeton University Press, 2010.

Biemann, Asher. *Inventing New Beginnings: On the Concept of Renaissance in Modern Judaism*. Palo Alto, CA: Stanford University Press, 2009.

Blumenberg, Hans. *The Legitimacy of the Modern Age*. Translated by Robert M. Wallace. Cambridge, MA: Harvard University Press, 1985.

Bourel, Dominique. *Moses Mendelssohn: La naissance du judaïsme moderne*. Paris: Gallimard, 2004.

Boyarin, Daniel. *Unheroic Conduct: The Rise of Heterosexuality and the Invention of the Jewish Man*. Berkeley: University of California Press, 1997.

Brenner, Michael. *The Renaissance of Jewish Culture in Weimar Germany*. New Haven: Yale University Press, 1996.

Buber, Martin. "Spinoza, Sabbatai Zvi, and the Baal-Shem" [1927]. In *The Origin and Meaning of Hasidism*. Edited and translated by Maurice Friedman. New York: Horizon Press, 1961.

Cohen, Gerson D. "The Reconstruction of Gaonic History." In *Studies in the Variety of Rabbinic Cultures*. Philadelphia: Jewish Publication Society, 1991.

Cohen, Hermann. "Spinoza über Staat und Religion, Judentum und Christentum." In *Jahrbuch für Geschichte und Literatur* 18 (1915): 57–150.

Cohen, Morris. "Zionism: Tribalism or Liberalism" [1919]. In *The Faith of a Liberal*, 326–33. New Brunswick, NJ: Transaction, 1993.

Cohen, Natan. *Sefer, sofer, ve-'iton: merkaz ha-tarbut ha-yehudit be-Varshah, 1918–1942*. Jerusalem: Hebrew University Magnes Press, 2003.

Cohen, Richard I. "Samuel Hirszenberg's Imagination: An Artist's Interpretation of the Jewish Dilemma at the Fin de Siècle." In *Text and Context: Essays in Modern Jewish History and Historiography in Honor of Ismar Schorsch*, 219–55. Edited by Eli Lederhendler and Jack Wertheimer. New York: Jewish Theological Seminary, 2005.

Cohen, Shaye. *Why Aren't Jewish Women Circumcised? Gender and Covenant in Judaism*. Berkeley: University of California Press, 2005.

Colerus, *The Life of Benedict de Spinosa*. Reprinted in Pollack, Frederick. *Spinoza: His Life and Philosophy*. London: Duckworth, 1899.

Coudert, Allison P. "The Kabbala Denudata: Converting Jews or Seducing Christians." In *Jewish Christians and Christian Jews: From the Renaissance to the Enlightenment*. Edited by Richard H. Popkin and Gordon M. Weiner, 73–96. Dordrecht: Kluwer, 1994.

Damasio, Antonio. *Looking for Spinoza: Joy, Sorrow, and the Feeling Brain*. Orlando: Harcourt, 2003.

Dauber, Jeremy. *Antonio's Devils: Writers of the Jewish Enlightenment and the Birth of Modern Hebrew and Yiddish Literature*. Palo Alto, CA: Stanford University Press, 2004.

Deborin, A. M. *Shpinoza, der fargeyer in likht fun materyalizm*. Warsaw: Bibliothek Mark Rakovski, 1930.

Deutscher, Isaac. *The Non-Jewish Jew and Other Essays*. London: Oxford University Press, 1968.

Dinaburg [Dinur], Ben-Zion. "Mevasre ha-tsiyonut." In *Sefer ha-Tsiyonut*. Vol. 1. Tel Aviv: Mosad Bialik, 1938.

Dorman, Menahem. *Vikuhe Shpinozah be-aspaklaryah yehudit: mi-David Niyeto 'ad David Ben-Gurion*. Tel Aviv: Ha-kibbutz ha-me'uhad, 1990.

Dubin, Lois. *The Port Jews of Trieste: Absolutist Politics and Enlightenment Culture*. Palo Alto, CA: Stanford University Press, 1999.

Dunin-Borkowski, S. v. *Spinoza nach dreihundert Jahren*. Berlin: Ferdinand Dümmler Verlag, 1932.

Efroykin, I. "Ha-ta'un mishpat Shpinozah bedikah?" In *Heshbon Nefesh*, translated by Avraham Kariv, 251–65. Tel Aviv: Hotsa'at Masadah, 1950.

Euchel, Isaac. *Toledot ha-rav he-hakham ha-hoker elohi Rabenu Moshe ben Menahem*. Berlin: Hevrat Hinukh ne'arim, 1788.

Farrell, Grace, ed. *Isaac Bashevis Singer: Conversations*. Jackson: University of Mississippi Press, 1992.

Feiner, Shmuel. "Mendelssohn and Mendelssohn's Disciples: A Re-examination." In *Leo Baech Institute Yearbook* 40 (1995): 133–67.

———. *Haskalah and History: The Emergence of a Modern Jewish Historical Consciousness.* Translated by Chaya Naor and Sondra Silverston. Portland, OR: Littman, 2002.

———. *The Origins of Jewish Secularization in Eighteenth-Century Europe.* Translated by Chaya Naor. Philadelphia: University of Pennsylvania Press, 2010.

Feldman, Seymour. "Ha-bikoret ha-yehudit ha-rishonah neged Shpinozah." In *Iyyun* 37 (1988): 222–37.

Fenelon, François. *Réfutation des erreurs de Benoit de Spinoza.* Brussels: F. Foppens, 1731.

Fidel, N. "Borukh Shpinoza: A kurtse lebenshraybung." In *Yudisches Folksblat* 6 (1886): 683–87.

Finkelstein, Leo. "Di Spinoza-fayerungen in Hag." In *Globus* 3 (1932): 74–83.

Fishman, David E. *The Rise of Modern Yiddish Culture.* Pittsburgh: University of Pittsburgh Press, 2005.

Fränkel, David. "Briefe an den Herausgeber der Sulamith. Fünfte Brief." In *Sulamith* 2 (1807).

Freud, Sigmund. *The Ego and the Id.* New York: W. W. Norton, 1923.

Freudenthal, Jacob. *Die Lebensgeschichte Spinoza's in Quellenschriften, Urkunden und nichtamtlichen Nachrichten; mit Unterstützung der Königl. Preussischen Akademie der Wissenschaften.* Leipzig: Veit, 1899.

———. *Spinoza, Leben und Lehre.* Ed. C. Gebhardt. Heidelberg: C. Winter, 1927.

Friedler, Ya'acov. "Unexpected Attack on Spinoza at Symposium." *Jerusalem Post.* January 5, 1989.

Funkenstein, Amos. *Perceptions of Jewish History.* Berkeley: University of California Press, 1993.

Gebhardt, Carl. "Spinoza und der Platonismus." In *Chronicon Spinozanum* 1 (1921): 178–234.

———. "Juan de Prado." In *Chronicon Spinozanum* 3 (1923): 269–91.

———. *Spinoza; vier Reden.* Heidelberg: C. Winter, 1927.

Geiger, Abraham. *Abraham Geiger and Liberal Judaism: The Challenge of the Nineteenth Century.* Edited by Max Wiener and translated by Ernst Schlochauer. Philadelphia: Jewish Publication Society, 1962.

Geller, Jay. "Spinoza's Election of the Jews: The Problem of Jewish Persistence." In *Jewish Social Studies* 12 (2005): 39–63.

Gillespie, Michael A. *The Theological Origins of Modernity.* Chicago: University of Chicago Press, 2008.

Goethe, J. W. von. *The Autobiography of J. W. von Goethe, vol. 2,* trans. John Oxenford. Chicago: University of Chicago Press, 1974.

Goetschel, Willi. *Spinoza's Modernity: Mendelssohn, Lessing, and Heine.* Madison: University of Wisconsin Press, 2003.

Golden, Morris. "Dr. Fischelson's Miracle: Duality and Vision in Singer's Fiction." In *The Achievement of Isaac Bashevis Singer.* Edited by Marcial Allentuck, 26–43. Carbondale: Southern Illinois Press, 1969.

Goldstein, Rebecca. *Betraying Spinoza: The Renegade Jew Who Gave Us Modernity.* New York: Nextbook and Schocken, 2006.

Gordon, Judah L. [Dan Gavriel]. "Ha-tsofeh me-'erets Rusiyah." In *Ha-magid* 2 (1858): 138.

Gordon, Judah L.. *Kol shire Yehuda Leib Gordon*, vol. 4, 112. St. Petersburg: G. F. Pines & Y. Tsederboim, 1884.

Gottlieb, Michah. *Faith and Freedom: Moses Mendelssohn's Theological-Political Thought*. New York: Oxford University Press, 2011.

Graetz, Heinrich. "Spinoza und Sabbatai Zvi." *Geschichte der Juden*, 10: 169–258. Leipzig: O. Leiner, 1866.

Grunwald, Max. *Spinoza in Deutschland: Gekrönte Preisschrift*. Berlin, 1897.

Guttmann, Julius. "Mendelssohn's *Jerusalem* and Spinoza's *Theological-Political Treatise* [1931]." In *Studies in Jewish Thought*, 361–86, ed. and trans. Alfred Jospe. Detroit: Wayne State Press, 1981.

Gutzkow, Karl. "Der Sadducäer von Amsterdam." In *Gesammelte Werke*, vol. 11, 99–170. Frankfurt a. M.: Literarische Anstalt, 1846.

———. *Uriel Acosta* [Heb]. Translated by S. Rubin. Vienna, 1856.

Ha'am, Ahad. "Yalkut katan—Shabbat ve-Tsionut" [1898]. In *'Al parashat derakhim: Kovets ma'amarim*, vol. 3, 78–81. Berlin: Jüdischer Verlag, 1921.

———. "Yalkut katan—Tehiyah u-beri'ah" [1898]. In *'Al parashat derakhim*, vol. 3, 91–94. Berlin: Jüdischer Verlag, 1921.

———. "Slavery within Freedom." 1891. In *Selected Essays*. Edited and translated by Leon Simon, 171–94. Philadelphia: Jewish Publication Society, 1912.

Halpern, Ben. "Secularism." In *Contemporary Jewish Religious Thought*. Edited by Arthur A. Cohen and Paul Mendes-Flohr, 863–66. New York: Free Press, 1987.

Hardt, Michael, and Antonio Negri. *Empire*. Cambridge, MA: Harvard University Press, 2000.

Harris, Horton. *David Friedrich Strauss and His Theology*. Cambridge, UK: Cambridge University Press, 1973.

Harris, Jay. *Nachman Krochmal: Guiding the Perplexed of the Modern Age*. New York: NYU Press, 1995.

Hartman, David. "Maimonides' Approach to Messianism and Its Contemporary Implications." In *Da'at* 2–3 (1978–79): 5–33.

Hegel, G.W.F. *Lectures in the History of Philosophy, vol. 3*, trans. Elisabeth S. Haldane and Frances H. Simson. London: Routledge & Kegan Paul, 1896.

Heine, Heinrich. *Zur Geschichte der Religion und Philosophie in Deutschland*. Frankfurt a. M.: Insel, 1966.

Heller, Bernard. "Is Spinozism Compatible with Judaism?" In *Central Conference of American Rabbis Yearbook* 37 (1927).

Herder, Johann Gottfried von. *God, Some Conversations* [1787]. Translated by Frederick H. Burkhardt. New York: Veritas Press, 1940.

Herschtal, Eric. "Jewish Studies Sans Religion?" *Jewish Week*. November 18, 2009.

Hertzberg, Arthur. *The Zionist Idea: A Historical Analysis and Reader*. Philadelphia: Jewish Publication Society, 1997.

Heschel, Susannah. *Abraham Geiger and the Jewish Jesus*. Chicago: University of Chicago Press, 1998.

Hess, Moses. *Die heilige Geschichte der Menschheit, von einem Jünger Spinozas*. Stuttgart: Hallberger, 1837.

———. *Rom und Jerusalem, die letzte Nationalitätsfrage*. Leipzig: Mengler, 1862.

———. *Jüdische Schriften*. Berlin: L. Lamm, 1905.

———. *Briefwechsel*. Edited by Edmund Silberner. 'S-Gravenhage: Mouton, 1959.

Hill, Brad Sabin. *Spinoza in the Yiddish Mind: An Exhibition on the 350th Anniversary of the Excommunication of Benedictus de Spinoza, 1656–2006*. New York: Yivo Institute for Jewish Research, 2006.

Hoffmann, Christhard. "Constructing Jewish Modernity: Mendelssohn Jubilee Celebrations within German Jewry, 1829–1929." In *Towards Normality? Acculturation and Modern German Jewry*, 27–52. Edited by Rainer Liedtke and David Rechter. Tübingen: Mohr Siebeck, 2003.

Howe, Irving. "The End of Jewish Secularism." New York: Hunter College of the City University of New York, 1995.

Idel, Moshe. "*Deus sive Natura*—The Metamorphosis of a Dictum from Maimonides to Spinoza." In *Maimonides and the Sciences*. Edited by R. S. Cohen and H. Levine, 87–110. Boston: Kluwer, 2000.

———. *Ascensions on High in Jewish Mysticism: Pillars, Lines, Ladders*. Budapest: Central European University Press, 2005.

Iggers, George G. *The German Idea of History: The National Tradition of Historical Thought from Herder to the Present*. Middletown, CT: Wesleyan University Press, 1968.

———. *Historiography in the Twentieth Century: From Scientific Objectivity to Postmodern Challenge*. Middletown, CT: Wesleyan University Press, 2005.

Israel, Jonathan I. *The Dutch Republic: Its Rise, Greatness, and Fall*. Oxford: Oxford University Press, 1995.

———. *Radical Enlightenment: Philosophy and the Making of Modernity, 1650–1750*. Oxford and New York: Oxford University Press, 2001.

———. *Enlightenment Contested: Philosophy Modernity, and the Emancipation of Man, 1670–1752*. Oxford: Oxford University Press, 2006.

———. "Philosophy, Deism, and the Early Sephardic Enlightenment." In *The Dutch Intersection: The Jews and the Netherlands in Modern History*. Edited by Yosef Kaplan, 173–201. Leiden: Brill, 2008.

———. *A Revolution of the Mind: Radical Enlightenment and the Intellectual Origins of Modern Democracy*. Princeton: Princeton University Press 2009.

Ives, David. "New Jerusalem: The Interrogation of Baruch de Spinoza at Talmud Torah Congregation: Amsterdam, July 27, 1656." New York: Dramatists Play Service Inc., 2009.

Jauss, Hans Robert. *Toward an Aesthetic of Reception*. Translated by Timothy Bahti. Minneapolis: University of Minneapolis Press, 1982.

Jellinek, Hermann. *Uriel Acosta's Leben und Lehre; ein Beitrag zur Kenntniss seiner Moral, wie zur Berichtigung der Gutzkow'schen Fiktionen über Acosta und zur Charakteristik der damaligen Juden*. Zerbst: Kummer'sche Buchhandlung, 1847.

Joël, Manuel. *Spinoza's Theologisch-politischer Traktat auf seine Quellen geprüft*. Breslau: H. Skutsch, 1870.

Jonge, Eccy de. *Spinoza and Deep Ecology: Challenging Traditional Approaches to Environmentalism*. Farnham, UK: Ashgate Publishing, 2004.

Kaiser, Nancy A. "The Dilemma of the Jewish Humanist from 'Vormärz' to Empire." In *German Studies Review* 6 (1983): 399–419.

Kaplan, Yosef. *From Christianity to Judaism: The Story of Isaac Orobio de Castro*. Translated by Raphael Loewe. Oxford and New York: Oxford University Press, 1989.

Kaplan, Yosef. "The Social Functions of the *Herem*." In *An Alternative Path to Modernity: The Sephardi Diaspora in Western Europe*, 108–42. Leiden: Brill, 2000.

———. "'Karaites' in the Early Eighteenth Century." In *An Alternative Path to Modernity: The Sephardi Diaspora in Western Europe*, 234–80. Leiden: Brill, 2000.

Kasher, Asa, and Shlomo Biderman. "Why Was Baruch Spinoza Excommunicated?" In *Sceptics, Millenarians, and Jews*. Edited by David S. Katz and Jonathan I. Israel, 98–141. Leiden: Brill, 1990.

Kastein, Josef. *Sabbatai Zwei, der Messias von Ismir*. Berlin: E. Rowohlt, 1930.

Katz, Gideon. "In the Eye of the Translator: Spinoza in the Mirror of the *Ethics*' Hebrew Translations." In *Journal of Jewish Thought and Philosophy* 15 (2007): 39–63.

Katz, Jacob. "The Forerunners of Zionism." In *Jerusalem Quarterly* 7 (1978): 10–21.

———. "Berthold Auerbach's Anticipation of the German-Jewish Tragedy." In *HUCA* 53 (1982): 215–40.

———. "Spinoza und die Utopie einer totalen Assimilation der Juden." In *Zur Assimilation und Emanzipation der Juden: Ausgewählte Schriften*. Darmstadt: Wissenschaftliche Buchgesellschaft, 1982.

Kayserling, Meyer. *Ludwig Philippson: Eine Biographie*. Leipzig: Hermann Mendelssohn, 1898.

Klatzkin, Jacob. *Barukh Shpinoza; hayav, sefarav, shitato*. Leipzig: B. G. Teubner, 1923.

———. "Der Missverstandene." In *Spinoza-Festschrift (1632–1932)*. Edited by Siegfried Hessing. Heidelberg: C. Winter, 1933.

Klausner, Joseph. "Megamatenu (Davar me'et ha-'orekh he-hadash)." In *Ha-Shiloah* 11 (1903): 1–10.

———. "Ha-sakanah ha-kerovah." In *Ha-Shiloah* 15 (1905): 419–31.

———. *Ha-Zeramim ha-hadashim shel ha-sifrut ha-'Ivrit ha-tse'irah*. New York, 1907.

———. "Ha-Sofistim ha-'atikim veha-hadashim" [1908]. In *Filosofim ve-hoge de'ot*, vol. 1, 12–32. Tel Aviv: Dvir, 1934.

———. "Ha-Ivri ha-tsa'ir." In *Ha-Shiloah* 20 (1909).

——— [Ish Ivri]. "Herut ve-Apikorsut." In *Ha-Shiloah* 20 (1911): 88–91.

———. *Yeshu ha-Notsri: Zemano, Hayav, ve-Torato*. Jerusalem: Shtibl, 1922.

———. *Jesus of Nazareth: His Life, Times, and Teaching*. Translated by Herbert Danby. New York: Macmillan, 1925.

———. "Ha-'ofi ha-yehudi shel torat Shpinozah." In *Knesset* 1 (1928): 179–99.

———. *Yotsrim u-vonim*. Vol. 3. Jerusalem, 1930.

———. "Der jüdische Charakter der Lehre Spinozas." In *Spinoza-Festschrift*, 114–45. Edited by S. Hessing and translated by Z. Ellner. Heidelberg: C. Winter, 1933.

———. "Baruch Shpinoza." In *Filosofim ve-hoge de'ot*, 209–42. Tel Aviv: Dvir, 1934.

———. *Historiyah shel ha-sifrut ha-'Ivrit ha-hadashah*. 6 vols. Jerusalem: Ahiasaf, 1952–60.

Koltun-Fromm, Ken. *Moses Hess and Modern Jewish Identity*. Bloomington: University of Indiana Press, 2001.

———. *Abraham Geiger's Liberal Judaism: Personal Meaning and Religious Authority*. Bloomington: University of Indiana Press, 2006.

Krantz, Phillip. *Borukh Shpinoza, zayn leben un zayn filozofye*. New York: International Library Publishing Company, 1905.

Krochmal, Abraham. "Even ha-roshah." With an introduction by Peretz Smolenskin. In *Ha-Shahar* 2 (1871).

Krochmal, Nahman. *Kitve Rabbi Nahman Krochmal*. Edited by Simon Rawidowicz. 2nd ed. London and Waltham, MA: Ararat, 1961.

Lahower, P. "Nigleh ve-nistar be-kitve Ranak." In *Knesset le-zekher Bialik* 3 (1941).

———. "Shpinozah be-sifrut ha-haskalah ha-'ivrit." In *'Al gevul ha-yashan ve-ha-hadash*, 109–122. Jersualem: Mossad Bialik, 1951.

Lazier, Benjamin. *God Interrupted: Heresy and the European Imagination between the Wars*. Princeton: Princeton University Press, 2009.

Lehmann, James H. "Maimonides, Mendelssohn and the Me'asfim: Philosophy and the Biographical Imagination in the Early Haskalah." In *Leo Baeck Institute Yearbook* 20 (1975): 87–108.

Letteris, Meir Halevi. "Toledot he-hakham ha-hoker Barukh di Shpinozah z'l." In *Bikkurei ha-'Itim ha-hadashim* 1 (1845): 27a–33b.

———. "Toledot ha-Rav he-hakham ha-hoker ha-mehulal Nahman ha-Kohen Krochmal." In *More neboche ha-seman*, 11–29. Lemberg: Michael Wolf, 1863.

Levy, Ze'ev. *Shpinozah u-musag ha-Yahadut: tefisah ve-gilguleha*. Tel Aviv: Sifriyat Po'alim, 1972.

———. *Baruch or Benedict: On Some Jewish Aspects of Spinoza's Philosophy*. New York: Peter Lang, 1989.

———. *Baruch Spinoza: seine Aufnahme durch die jüdische Denker in Deutschland*. Stuttgart: Kohlhammer, 2001.

Lewis, Flora. "Foreign Affairs; Israel and Relevance." *New York Times*. December 27, 1989.

Leyvick, H. "Shpinoza" [1934]. In *Ale verk*, vol. 1, 483–91. New York: H. Leyvick yubiley-komitet, 1940.

Liebeschütz, Hans. *Das Judentum im deutschen Geschichtsbild von Hegel bis Max Weber*. Tübingen: Mohr, 1967.

Liebman, Charles. "Reconceptualizing the Culture Conflict among Israeli Jews." In *Israel Studies* 2, no. 2 (1997): 172–89.

Lowenstein, Steven. *The Berlin Jewish Community: Enlightenment, Family, and Crisis, 1770–1830*. New York: Oxford University Press, 1994.

Löwith, Karl. *Meaning in History: The Theological Implications of the Philosophy of History*. Chicago: University of Chicago Press, 1957.

Lucas, Jean-Maximilien. *The Oldest Biography of Spinoza*. Edited and translated by Abraham Wolf. London: G. Allen & Unwin, 1927.

Lüsebrink, Hans-Joseph and Rolf Reichardt. *The Bastille: A History of a Symbol of Despotism and Freedom*. Translated by Norbert Schürer. Durham, NC: Duke University Press, 1997.

Luzzatto, Samuel D. *Ha-mishtadel*. Vienna: Francesca Nobile di Schmid, 1847.

———. "Neged Shpinoza." In *Mehkere ha-yahadut*, vol. 1, 198–222. Jerusalem: Makor, 1970.

Mack, Michael. *German Idealism and the Jew: On the Inner Anti-Semitism of Philosophy and German Jewish Responses*. Chicago: University of Chicago Press, 2003.

Maimon, Salomon. *Salomon Maimons Lebensgeschichte* [1792]. Edited by K. P. Moritz and Zwi Batscha. Frankfurt a. M.: Insel, 1984.

———. *An Autobiography* [1888]. Translated by J. Clark Murray. Champaign: University of Illinois Press, 2001.

Maimon, Salomon. *Givat ha-moreh* [1791]. Edited by S. H. Bergmann and Nathan Rotenstreich. Jerusalem: Ha-akademyah ha-le'umit ha-yisra'elit le-mada'im, 1965.

Manoah, Yehoshua. *Be-vikuah 'im David Ben-Gurion*. Vol. 2. Tel Aviv, 1953–56.

Margolies, Morris. *Samuel David Luzzatto: Traditionalist Scholar*. New York: Ktav, 1979.

Mayer, Egon, and Barry Kosmin. *American Jewish Identity Survey: AJIS Report: An Exploration in the Demography and Outlook of a People*. New York: The Graduate Center of the City University of New York, 2002.

Mayer, Tamar. "From Zero to Hero: Masculinity in Jewish Nationalism." *Gender Ironies of Nationalism: Sexing the Nation*. Edited by Tamar Mayer. London: Routledge, 1999.

Meinsma, K. O. *Spinoza und sein Kreis; historisch-kritische Studien über holländische Freigeister*. Translated from the Dutch by Lina Schneider. Berlin: K. Schnabel, 1909.

Mendelsohn, Ezra. *On Modern Jewish Politics*. New York: Oxford University Press, 1993.

Mendelssohn, Moses. *Moses Mendelssohn. Gesammelte Schriften. Jubiläumsausgabe*. Edited by Alexander Altmann et al. Stuttgart-Bad Canstatt: F. Frommann, 1971.

———. *Jerusalem, or, On Religious Power and Judaism*. Translated by Allan Arkush. Hanover, NH: University Press of New England, 1983.

———. *Philosophical Writings*. Cambridge, England, and New York: Cambridge University Press, 1997.

Mendes-Flohr, Paul. *Hokhmat Yisrael: hebetim historiyim u-filosofiyim*. Jerusalem: Merkaz Zalman Shazar, 1979.

Mendes-Flohr, Paul, and Jehuda Reinharz, eds. *The Jew in the Modern World: A Documentary History*. 3rd ed. New York: Oxford University Press, 2011.

Mendes-Flohr, Paul, and Stephen L. Weinstein. "The Heretic as Hero." In *Jerusalem Quarterly* 7 (1978): 57–63.

Meyer, Michael. "Abraham Geiger's Historical Judaism." In *New Perspectives on Abraham Geiger*. Edited by Jakob J. Petuchowski. Cincinnati: Hebrew Union College-Jewish Institute of Religion, 1975.

———. *Response to Modernity: A History of the Reform Movement in Judaism*. Detroit: Wayne State University Press, 1988.

———. *Jewish Identity in the Modern World*. Seattle: University of Washington Press, 1990.

Milch, Jacob. "Spinoza un Marx—A Paralel." In *Spinoza bukh*. Edited by Jacob Shatzky. New York: Spinoza Institute of America, 1932.

Mintz, Samuel I. "Spinoza and Spinozism in Singer's Short Fiction." In *Critical Views of Isaac Bashevis Singer*. Edited by Irving Malin, 207–17. New York: New York University Press, 1969.

Miron, Dan. "Passivity and Narration: The Spell of Bashevis Singer." In *Critical Essays on Bashevis Singer*. Edited by Grace Farrell, 149–64. New York: G. K. Hall, 1996.

Moss, Kenneth B. *Jewish Renaissance in the Russian Revolution*. Cambridge, MA: Harvard University Press, 2009.

Mosse, George. *The Idea of Man: The Creation of Modern Masculinity*. Oxford: Oxford University Press, 1996.

Myers, David N. *Re-inventing the Jewish Past: European Jewish Intellectuals and the Zionist Return to History*. New York: Oxford University Press, 1995.

Nadler, Allan. "Romancing Spinoza." In *Commentary* 122, no. 5 (December, 2006).

———. "The Besht as Spinozist: Abraham Krochmal's Preface to *Ha-Ketav ve-ha-Mikhtav*." In *Rabbinic Culture and Its Critics*. Edited by Daniel Frank and Matt Goldish, 359–89. Detroit: Wayne State University Press, 2008.

Nadler, Steven M. *Spinoza: A Life*. New York: Oxford University Press, 1999.

———. *Spinoza's Heresy: Immortality and the Jewish Mind*. New York: Oxford University Press, 2001.

———. *Spinoza's Ethics: An Introduction*. Cambridge, UK: Cambridge University Press, 2006.

———. "Spinoza and the Origins of Jewish Secularism." In *Religion and Ethnicity? Jewish Identities in Evolution*. Edited by Zvi Gitelman, 59–68. New Brunswick, NJ: Rutgers University Press, 2009.

———. "The Jewish Spinoza." In *Journal of the History of Ideas* 70, no. 3 (2009): 491–510.

Nash, Stanley. *In Search of Hebraism: Shai Hurwitz and His Polemics in the Hebrew Press*. Leiden: Brill, 1980.

Nauen, Franz. "Hermann Cohen's Perceptions of Spinoza: A Reappraisal." In *Association for Jewish Studies Review* 4 (1979): 111–24.

Neln, Z. "Borukh Shpinoza un der dialektisher materialzm." In *Literarishe bleter* (September, 1932): 1–4.

Neumark, David. "Shpinoza 'al do'ar 'atidot yisroel." In *Ha-shiloah* 2 (1897).

Niewöhner, Friedrich. "'Es hat nicht jeder das Zeug zu einem Spinoza': Mendelssohn als Philosoph des Judentums." In *Moses Mendelssohn und die Kreise seiner Wirksamkeit*. Edited by Michael Albrecht, Eva J. Engel, and Norbert Hinske, 291–313. Tübingen: Niemeyer, 1994.

Novick, Peter. *That Noble Dream: The "Objectivity Question" and the American Historical Profession*. Cambridge, UK: Cambridge University Press, 1988.

Oko, Adolph S. *The Spinoza Bibliography*. Boston: G. K. Hall, 1964.

Parush, Iris. *Kanon sifruti ve-ideologyah le'umit: bikoret ha-sifrut shel Frishman be-hashva'ah le-vikoret ha-sifrut shel Klozner u-Vrener*. Jerusalem: Mossad Bialik, 1992.

Peled, Rina. *'Ha-'adam he-hadash' shel ha-mahapekhah ha-tsiyonit: Ha-Shomer Ha-Tsa'ir ve-shorashav ha-'eropiyim*. Jerusalem, 2002.

Pelli, Moshe. "On the Role of *Melitzah* in the Literature of the Hebrew Enlightenment." In *Hebrew in Ashkenaz: A Language in Exile*, 99–110. Edited by Lewis Glinert. New York: Oxford University Press, 1993.

Philippson, Johanna. "Ludwig Philippson und die *Allgemeine Zeitung des Judentums*." In *Das Judentum in der deutschen Umwelt*. Edited by Hans Liebeschütz and Arnold Paucker. Tübingen: Mohr Siebeck, 1977.

Philippson, Ludwig. "Baruch Spinoza (eine Skizze)." In *Sulamith, eine Zeitschrift zur Beförderung der Kultur und Humanität unter den Israeliten* 17 (1832): 327–36.

Pincus, Keith. *Constructing Modern Identities: Jewish University Students in Germany, 1815–1914*. Detroit: Wayne State University Press, 1999.

Pollock, Frederick. *Spinoza: His Life and Philosophy.* London: Duckworth, 1899.

Popkin, Richard. "Notes from Underground." Review of *Spinoza and Other Heretics, vol. 1: The Marrano of Reason,* by Yirmiyahu Yovel, and *From Christianity to Judaism,* by Yosef Kaplan. *The New Republic* 202, no. 21 (May 21, 1990).

———. "Spinoza, Neoplatonic Kabbalist?" In *Neoplatonism and Jewish Thought.* Edited by Lenn E. Goodman, 387–409. Albany: SUNY Press, 1992.

———. "Spinoza's Excommunication." In *Jewish Themes in Spinoza's Philosophy.* Edited by Heidi M. Ravven and Lenn E. Goodman, 263–79. Albany: SUNY Press, 2002.

Préposiet, Jean. *Bibliographie spinoziste.* Paris: Les Belle Lettres, 1973.

Prothero, Stephen. *American Jesus: How the Son of God Became a National Icon.* New York: Farrar, Straus, and Giroux, 2003.

Ravitch, Melech. *Shpinozah: poetisher priv in fir tsiklen. Der mentsh, dos verk, di shpin, ktoyres.* Vienna, 1919.

———. *Di lider fun mayne lider. A kinus—oyfgekliben fun draytsen zamlungen, 1909–1954.* Montreal, 1954.

———. *Dos mayse-bukh fun mayn leben.* 3 vols. Buenos Aires, 1964.

Ravven, Heidi M. "Spinoza's Rupture with Tradition—His Hints of a Jewish Modernity." In *Jewish Themes in Spinoza's Philosophy.* Edited by Ravven and Lenn E. Goodman, 187–223. Albany, NY: SUNY Press, 2002.

Rawidowicz, Simon. "On Interpretation." In *Proceedings of the American Academy for Jewish Research* 26 (1957): 83–126.

———. *Bavel vi-Yerushalayim.* Waltham, MA: Ararat, 1957.

Renan, Ernst. *Spinoza; conférence tenue à la Haye, le 12 février 1877, deux-centième anniversaire de la mort de Spinoza.* Paris: Ancienne maison M. Lévy frères, 1877.

Révah, I. S. *Des Marranes à Spinoza.* Edited by Henry Méchoulan and Pierre-François Moreau. Paris: J. Vrin, 1995.

Ringelblum, Emmanuel. *Notes from the Warsaw Ghetto: The Journal of Emmanuel Ringelblum.* Translated and edited by Jacob Sloan. New York: Schocken, 1974.

Roskies, David. "The Demon as Storyteller." In *A Bridge of Longing: The Lost Art of Yiddish Storytelling,* 266–306. Cambridge, MA: Harvard University Press, 1996.

Rubin, S. *Moreh nevukhim he-hadash.* 2 vols. Vienna: J. Holzwarth, 1856–57.

———. *Teshuvah nitsahat.* Lvov: Stauropigianische Instituts-Druckerei, 1859.

———. *Spinoza und Maimonides; ein psychologisch-philosophisches Antitheton.* Vienna: Herzfeld & Bauer, 1868.

———. *Hegyone Shpinoza.* Krakow: A. Faust, 1897.

———. *Barukh Shpinoza be-regesh 'ahavat 'Elohim.* Podgorze, 1910.

Rudi, Z. "Spinoza un der materialism." In *Spinoza bukh.* Edited by Jacob Shatzky. New York: Spinoza Institute of America, 1932.

Sachs, Senior. *Ha-tehiyah* 1 (1850).

———. "Kol kore." In *Kerem hemed* 8 (1854): 213–20.

Sammons, Jeffrey. "Observations on Berthold Auerbach's Jewish Novels." In *Orim: A Jewish Journal at Yale* 1 (1985): 61–74.

Saposnik, Arieh Bruce. *Becoming Hebrew: The Creation of a National Culture in Ottoman Palestine.* Oxford: Oxford University Press, 2009.

Saposnik, Irving. "Translating *The Family Moskat*: The Metamorphosis of a Novel." In *Yiddish* 1, no. 2 (1973): 26–37.

Sarna, Jonathan. "The Rise, Fall, and Rebirth of Secular Judaism." In *Contemplate* 4 (2007): 4–13.

Schapkow, Carsten. *"Die Freiheit zu philosophieren": Jüdische Identität im Spiegel der Rezeption Baruch de Spinozas in der deutschsprachigen Literatur*. Bielefeld: Aisthesis Verlag, 2001.

Schechter, Oded. "Ha-kod ha-metafisi-ontologi: ha-muhlat shel Auschwitz ve-Shpinozah: masah filosofit." In *Mi-ta'am* 1 (2005): 97–120.

Scheler, Max. *Person and Self-Value: Three Essays*. Translated by Manfred Frings. Hingham, MA: Kluwer Academic Publishers, 1987.

Schmitt Carl. *Political Theology: Four Chapters on the Concept of Sovereignty*. Translated by George Schward. Chicago: University of Chicago Press, 2006.

Scholem, Gershom. "Redemption through Sin" [1937, Heb]. Reprinted in *The Messianic Idea in Judaism and Other Essays on Jewish Spirituality*, 78–141. New York: Schocken, 1971.

———. "Mi-tokh hirhurim 'al Hokhmat Yisrael." In *Devarim be-go: Pirke morashah u-tehiyah*, 385–404. Tel Aviv: 'Am 'Oved, 1975.

———. "Die Wachtersche Kontroverse über den Spinozismus und ihre Folgen." In *Spinoza in der Frühzeit seiner religiösen Wirkung*, 15–25. Edited by Karlfried Gründer and Wilhelm Schmidt-Biggemann. Heidelberg: L. Schneider, 1984.

Scholz, Heinrich, ed. *Die Hauptschriften zum Pantheismusstreit zwischen Jacobi und Mendelssohn*. Berlin: Reuther & Reichard, 1916.

Schorr, Osias [Joshua Heschel]. *Ma'amarim*. Edited by Ezra Spicehandler. Jerusalem: Mossad Bialik, 1972.

Schorsch, Ismar. "Emancipation and the Crisis of Religious Authority: The Emergence of the Modern Rabbinate." In *From Text to Context: The Turn to History in Modern Judaism*, 9–50. Hanover, NH: University Press of New England, 1994.

———. "Breakthrough into the Past: the *Verein für Cultur und Wissenschaft der Juden*," In *From Text to Context: The Turn to History in Modern Judaism*, 205–32. Hanover, NH: University Press of New England, 1994.

Schulte, Christoph. "Saul Ascher's *Leviathan*, or the Invention of Jewish Orthodoxy in 1792." In *Leo Baeck Institute Year Book* 45 (2000): 25–34.

Schwartz, Dov. *Faith at the Crossroads: A Theological Profile of Religious Zionism*. Translated by Batya Stein. Leiden: Brill, 2002.

Schweid, Eliezer. *Ha-yehudi ha-boded veha-yahadut*. Tel Aviv: Am Oved, 1974.

———. *Toldot he-hagut ha-Yehudit ba-'et ha-hadashah: Ha-me'ah ha-tesha' 'esreh*. Jerusalem: Ha-kibbutz ha-me'uchad, 1977.

———. "Religion and Philosophy: The Scholarly-Theological Debate between Julius Guttmann and Leo Strauss." In *Maimonidean Studies* 1 (1990): 163–95.

———. *Toledot filosofiyat ha-dat ha-Yehudit bi-zeman he-hadash*. Tel Aviv: Am Oved, 2001.

———. "'In Amsterdam I Created the Idea of a Jewish State . . .': Spinoza and National Jewish Identity" [Heb]. In *Jewish Studies Political Review* 13 (Spring 2001): 1–20.

Schweigmann-Greve, Kay. "Spinoza in Jiddischer Sprache." In *Studia Spinozana* 13 (1997): 261–95.

Segev, Tom. *Elvis in Jerusalem*. Translated by Haim Watzman. New York: Metropolitan Books, 2002.

Shapiro, Sraya. "Twists and Turns in Street Naming." *Jerusalem Post*. October 17, 1993.

Shatzky, Jacob. *Spinoza un zayn svivoh*. New York: privately printed, 1927.

———, ed. *Spinoza bukh*. New York: Spinoza Institute of America, 1932.

Shimoni, Gideon. *The Zionist Ideology*. Hanover, NH: University Press of New England, 1995.

Shmeruk, Chone. "Isaac Bashevis Singer—In Search of His Autobiography." In *Jewish Quarterly* 29 (Winter 1981/1982): 28–36.

Silberner, Edmund. *Moses Hess. Geschichte seines Lebens*. Leiden: E. J. Brill, 1966.

Simon, Ernst. "Zu Hermann Cohens Spinoza-Auffassung." 1935. In *Brücken: Gesammelte Aufsätze*, 205–14. Heidelberg: Verlag Lambert Schneider, 1965.

Singer, Isaac Bashevis. "Tsu der frage fun dikhtung un poliitk." In *Globus* 1, no. 3 (September, 1932).

———. *Di familye Mushkat*. 2 vols. New York: M. Sh. Sklarski, 1950.

———. *The Family Moskat*. Translated by A. H. Gross. New York: Farrar, Straus, & Giroux, 1950.

———. *In My Father's Court*. New York: Farrar, Straus, and Giroux, 1966.

———. "Isaac Bashevis Singer: An Interview." By Cyrena Pondrom. *Contemporary Literature* 10 (1969) 1–38. Reprinted in Farell, Grace, ed. *Isaac Bashevis Singer: Conversations*.

———. "The Destruction of Kreshev." Translated by Elaine Gottlieb and June Ruth Flaum. In *The Collected Stories*. New York: Farrar, Straus, and Giroux, 1983.

———. "The Spinoza of Market Street." Translated by Martha Glicklich and Cecil Hemley. In *The Collected Stories of Isaac Bashevis Singer*. New York: Farrar, Straus, and Giroux, 1983.

———. *Love and Exile*. Garden City, NY: Doubleday, 1984.

———. "The Family Moskat: Chapter 65." Translated by Joseph C. Landis. In *Yiddish* 6, nos. 2–3 (Summer-Fall 1985): 105–16.

———. *The Certificate*. Translated by Leonard Wolf. New York: Farrar, Straus, and Giroux, 1992.

———. "Concerning Yiddish Literature in Poland." [1943]. In *Prooftexts* 15, no. 2 (1995).

———. "Shpinoza un di Kabbalah." In *Mayn tatns bezdn-shtub [hemshekhim-zamlung]*. Edited by Chone Shmeruk, 296–301. Jerusalem: Hebrew University Magnes Press, 1996.

———. "Ikh fantazir vegn mayn manuscript—in 'Mizrahi.'" In *Mayn tatns bezdn-shtub [hemshekhim-zamlung]*. Edited by Chone Shmeruk, 301–306. Jerusalem: Hebrew University Magnes Press, 1996.

Sinkoff, Nancy. *Out of the Shtetl: Making Jews Modern in the Polish Borderlands*. Providence: Brown University Press, 2004.

Skolnik, Jonathan. "Writing Jewish History between Gutzkow and Goethe: Auerbach's *Spinoza* and the Birth of Modern Jewish Historical Fiction." In *Prooftexts* 19 (1999): 101–25.

———. "Kaddish for Spinoza: Memory and Modernity in Celan and Heine." In *New German Critique* 77 (1999): 169–86.

Smith, Steven B. *Spinoza, Liberalism, and the Question of Jewish Identity*. New Haven: Yale University Press, 1997.

————. "A Fool for Love: Thoughts on I. B. Singer's Spinoza." In *Iyyun* 51 (2002): 41–50.

————. *Spinoza's Book of Life: Freedom and Redemption in the Ethics*. New Haven: Yale University Press, 2003.

Sobol, Yehoshua. *Solo*. Tel Aviv: Or-Am, 1991.

Sokolow, Nahum. *Barukh Shpinozah u-zemano: Midrash be-filosofiyah u-bekorot ha-'itim*. Paris, 1928–29.

Sonne, Isaiah. "'Yahaduto' shel Shpinozah." In *Ha-Do'ar* 13 (1934): 7–8, 22–23, 56, 60, 70–71.

Sorkin, David. "The Invisible Community: Emancipation, Secular Culture, and Jewish Identity in the Writings of Berthold Auerbach." In *The Jewish Response to German Culture: From the Enlightenment to the Second World War*. Edited by Jehuda Reinharz and Walter Schatzberg. Hanover, NH: University Press of New England, 1985.

————. *Moses Mendelssohn and the Religious Enlightenment*. Berkeley: University of California Press, 1996.

————. "The Mendelssohn Myth and Its Method." In *New German Critique* 77 (1999): 7–28.

————. "The Early Haskalah." In *New Perspectives on the Haskalah*, 9–26. Edited by Sorkin and Shmuel Feiner. London: Littman Library of Jewish Civilization, 2001.

————. *The Religious Enlightenment: Protestants, Jews, and Catholics from London to Vienna*. Princeton: Princeton University Press, 2008.

Spinoza, B. d. *Heker elohah 'im torat ha-'adam* [Ethics]. Translated by S. Rubin. Vienna, 1885.

————. *Der teologish-politisher traktat*. Translated by N. Perelman. New York, 1923.

————. *Di etik [dervayzen oyf a geometrishen ufen]*. Translated by W. Nathanson. Warsaw: Kulturlige, 1923.

————. *Di etik [dervayzen, etc.]*. Translated by W. Nathanson. Chicago: Naye gezelshaft, 1923.

————. *Torat ha-midot me'et Barukh Spinoza* [Ethics]. Translated by Jacob Klatzkin. Leipzig: A. Y. Shtibl, 1923.

————. *Ma'amar teologi-politi* [Heb]. Translated by Chaim Wirszubski. Jerusalem: Magnes Press, 1961.

————. *Igrot* [Letters]. Translated by Efraim Shmueli. Jerusalem: Mossad Bialik, 1963.

————. *The Collected Works of Spinoza*. Vol. 1. Translated by Edward Curley. Princeton: Princeton University Press, 1985.

————. *Complete Works*. Edited by Michael L. Morgan and translated by Samuel Shirley. Indianapolis: Hackett, 2002.

————. *Etikah*. Translated and edited by Yirmiyahu Yovel. Tel Aviv: Ha-kibbutz ha-me'uhad, 2003.

Spinoza-Festschrift; hrsg. von Siegfried Hessing, zum 300. Geburtstage Benedict Spinozas (1632–1932). Heidelberg: C. Winter, 1933.

Stanislawski, Michael F. "The Crisis of Jewish Secularism." In *Creating the Jewish Future*. Edited by Michael Brown and Bernard Lightman. Walnut Creek, CA: AltaMira Press, 1999.

Stanislawski, Michael F. *Zionism and the Fin-de-siècle: Cosmopolitanism and Nationalism from Nordau to Jabotinsky*. Berkeley: University of California Press, 2001.

———. *A Murder in Lemberg: Politics, Religion, and Violence in Modern Jewish History*. Princeton: Princeton University Press, 2007.

Stern, Jakob. *Dr. Salomon Rubin, sein Leben und seine Schriften*. Krakow: F. H. Wetstein, 1908.

Strauss, David F. *Charakteristiken und Kritiken. Eine Sammlung zerstreuter Aufsätze aus den Gebieten der Theologie, Anthropologie, und Aesthetik*. Leipzig: O. Wigand, 1844.

Strauss, Leo. "Cohens Analyse der Bibelwissenschaft Spinozas." In *Der Jude* 8 (1924): 295–314.

———. "Preface to the English Translation" [1962]. In *Spinoza's Critique of Religion*. Translated by E. M. Sinclair. Chicago: University of Chicago Press, 1997.

Stupnitski, Shaul. *Borukh Shpinoza: zayn filozofye, bibel-kritik, shtatslere un zayn badaytung in der antviklung fun mentshlikhen denken*. Warsaw: Farlag Yidish, 1917.

Susser, Leslie. "Spinoza and the Religion of Reason." *Jerusalem Post*. March 9, 1989.

Sutcliffe, Adam. *Judaism and Enlightenment*. Cambridge: Cambridge University Press, 2003.

———. "Spinoza, Bayle, and the Enlightenment Politics of Philosophical Certainty." In *History of European Ideas* 34 (2008): 66–76.

Sutzkever, A. "Shpinoze" [1947]. In *Poetishe verk*, vol. 1, 593–97. Tel-Aviv: Yoyvel Komitet, 1963.

Talmage, Frank. "Apples of Gold: The Inner Meaning of Sacred Texts in Medieval Judaism." In *Apples of Gold in Settings of Silver: Studies in Medieval Jewish Exegesis and Polemics*. Edited by Barry D. Walfish, 108–50. Toronto: Pontifical Institute of Medieval Studies, 1999.

Taylor, Charles. *A Secular Age*. Cambridge, MA: Harvard University Press, 2007.

Theilhaber, Felix. *Dein Reich komme! Ein chiliastischer Roman aus der Zeit Rembrandts und Spinozas*. Berlin: C. A. Schwetschke & Sohn, 1924.

Timm, Hermann. *Gott und die Freiheit: Studien zur Religionsphilosophie der Goethezeit*. Frankfurt a. M.: Vittorio Klostermann, 1974.

Trachtenberg, Barry. *The Revolutionary Roots of Modern Yiddish, 1903–1917*. Syracuse, NY: Syracuse University Press, 2008.

Vallée, Gérard, ed. *The Spinoza Conversations between Lessing and Jacobi: Texts with Excerpts from the Ensuing Controversy*. Translated by G. Vallée, J. B. Lawson, and C. Chapple. Lanham, MD: University Press of America, 1988.

Vernière, Paul. *Spinoza et la pensée française avant la Revolution*. Vol. 1. Paris: Presse Universitaire de France, 1954.

Vierhaus, Rudolf. "Bildung." In *Geschichtliche Grundbegriffe: Historisches Lexicon zur politisch-sozialen Sprache in Deutschland*. Edited by Otto Brunner, Werne Conze, and Reinhart Koselleck, vol. 1. Stuttgart: E. Klett, 1972.

Vlessing, Odette. "The Excommunication of Spinoza: A Conflict between Jewish and Dutch Law," *Studia Spinozana* 13 (2003): 15–47.

Wachter, Johann G. *Der Spinozismus im Jüdenthumb, oder, die von dem heutigen Jüdenthumb und dessen Geheimen Kabbala vergötterte Welt* (1699). Edited by Winfried Schröder. Stuttgart-Bad Canstatt: Frommann-Holzboog, 1994.

———. *Elucidarius Cabalisticus* [1706]. Edited by Winfried Schröder. Stuttgart-Bad Canstatt: Frommann-Holzboog, 1995.

Walther, Manfred. "Spinoza und das Problem einer jüdischen Philosophie." In *Die philosophische Aktualität der jüdischen Tradition*, 281–330. Edited by Werner Stegmaier. Frankfurt a. M.: Suhrkamp, 2000.

Wassermann, Jakob. *Fränkische Erzählungen. Sabbatai Zewi, ein Vorspiel.* Frankfurt: S. Fischer, 1925.

Wellhausen, Julius. *Prologomena to the History of Israel; With a Reprint of the Article "Israel" in the Encyclopedia Britannica.* Translated by J. Sutherland Black and Allan Menzies. Edinburgh: Black, 1885.

Williams, Daniel. "Jewishness Debate: Once Again, Spinoza Stirs a Furor." *Los Angeles Times.* Feburary 10, 1989.

Winter, Jay. *Sites of Memory, Sites of Mourning: The Great War in European Cultural History.* Cambridge, UK: Cambridge University Press, 1995.

Wisse, Ruth. "Singer's Paradoxical Progress." In *Commentary* 67, no. 2 (1979): 33–38.

Wolf, Immanuel. "On the Concept of a Science of Judaism." In *Ideas of Jewish History*, 143–55. Edited by Michael Meyer. New York: Behrman House, 1974.

Wolfson, Harry A. *The Philosophy of Spinoza.* 2 volumes. Cambridge: Harvard University Press, 1934.

Wolitz, Seth. "'Di Khalyastre,' the Yiddish Modernist Movement in Poland [after WWI]: An Overview." In *Yiddish* 4, no. 3 (1981): 5–19.

Yakira, Elhanan. "Spinoza et les sionistes." In *Spinoza au XXème siècle.* Paris: Presses universitaires de France, 1993.

Yerushalmi, Yosef H. "Divre Shpinozah 'al kiyum 'am ha-yehudi." In *Divrey ha-Akademiah ha-le'umit ha-yisra'elit le-mada'im* 6 (1982): 171–213.

———. *Freud's Moses: Judaism Terminable and Interminable.* New Haven: Yale University Press, 1993.

Yovel, Yirmiyahu. *Shpinozah ve-kofrim 'aherim.* Tel Aviv: Sifriyat Po'alim, 1988.

———. *Spinoza and Other Heretics.* Vol. 1, *The Marrano of Reason.* Princeton: Princeton University Press, 1989.

———. *Spinoza and Other Heretics.* Vol. 2, *The Adventures of Immanence.* Princeton: Princeton University Press, 1992.

Yovel, Yirmiyahu, and David Shaham, eds. *Zeman Yehudi hadash: tarbut Yehudit be-'idan hiloni: Mabat entsiklopedi.* 5 vols. Jerusalem: Posen Foundation, 2007.

Yungman, Moshe. "Singer's Polish Period: 1924 to 1935." In *Yiddish* 6, nos. 2–3 (Summer–Fall 1985).

Zangwill, Israel. "The Maker of Lenses." In *Dreamers of the Ghetto*, 186–220. Philadelphia: Jewish Publication Society, 1898.

Zeitlin, Aaron. "Perushim oyf toyres-Spinoza." In *Globus* 8, no. 14 (September, 1933): 76–86; *Globus* 8, no. 15 (September1933): 39–45.

———. "I Believe" [1948]. Translated by Robert Friend. In *Truth and Lamentation: Stories and Poems on the Holocaust.* Edited by Milton Teichman and Sharon Leder, 441. Champaign, IL: University of Illinois Press, 1994.

Zeitlin, Hillel. *Barukh Shpinoza; hayav, sefarav, ve-shitato.* Warsaw: Hotsa'at Tushiyah, 1900.

Zerubavel, Yael. *Recovered Roots: Collective Memory and the Making of Israeli National Tradition*. Chicago: University of Chicago Press, 1994.

Zipperstein, Steven J. *The Jews of Odessa: A Cultural History, 1794–1881*. Palo Alto, CA: Stanford University Press, 1983.

———. *Elusive Prophet: Ahad Ha'am and the Origins of Zionism*. Berkeley: University of California Press, 1993.

Zunz, Leopold. *Rede gehalten bei der Feier von Moses Mendelssohns hundertjährigen Geburtstage*. Berlin, 1829.

Index